International Practices of Criminal Justice

International Practices of Criminal Justice: Social and Legal Perspectives examines the practitioners, practices, and institutions that are transforming the relationship between criminal justice and international governance. The book links two dimensions of international criminal justice by analyzing the fields of international criminal law and international police cooperation. Although often thought of separately, each of these fields presents criminal justice as a governance method for resolving international challenges and crises. By focusing on examples from international criminal tribunals, transitional justice, transnational crime, and transnational policing and prosecution, the contributors to this collection examine how criminal justice is unmoored from the state, while also attending to the struggles and challenges that emerge when criminal justice is used as a form of international action. *International Practices of Criminal Justice: Social and Legal Perspectives* breaks new ground in criminology, international legal studies and the sociology of law, and will be of interest to students, scholars, and practitioners across a wide array of fields in criminal justice, international law, and international governance.

Mikkel Jarle Christensen is Associate Professor at the Danish National Research Foundation's Centre of Excellence for International Courts (iCourts), Faculty of Law, University of Copenhagen.

Ron Levi is the George Ignatieff Chair of Peace and Conflict Studies, Deputy Director of the Munk School of Global Affairs, and Associate Professor of Global Affairs and Sociology at the University of Toronto. He is also cross-appointed in the Faculty of Law, the Department of Political Science, and the Centre for Criminology & Sociolegal Studies.

International Practices of Criminal Justice

Social and legal perspectives

Edited by
Mikkel Jarle Christensen
and Ron Levi

Routledge
Taylor & Francis Group
LONDON AND NEW YORK

First published 2018
by Routledge

2 Park Square, Milton Park, Abingdon, Oxfordshire OX14 4RN
52 Vanderbilt Avenue, New York, NY 10017

Routledge is an imprint of the Taylor & Francis Group, an informa business

First issued in paperback 2019

British Library Cataloguing-in-Publication Data
A catalogue record for this book is available from the British Library

Library of Congress Cataloging-in-Publication Data
Names: Christensen, Mikkel Jarle, author. | Levi, Ron, author.
Title: International practices of criminal justice: social and legal perspectives / Mikkel Jarle Christensen and Ron Levi.
Description: Abingdon, Oxon [UK]; New York: Routledge, 2017. | Includes bibliographical references and index.
Identifiers: LCCN 2017024420| ISBN 9781138688377 (hardback) | ISBN 9781351384636 (adobe reader) | ISBN 9781351384629 (epub) | ISBN 9781351384612 (mobipocket)
Subjects: LCSH: Criminal justice, Administration of. | International criminal law.
Classification: LCC K5001.C49 2017 | DDC 345—dc23
LC record available at https://lccn. loc.gov/2017024420

ISBN: 978-1-138-68837-7 (hbk)
ISBN: 978-0-367-23240-5 (pbk)

Typeset in Galliard
by Keystroke, Neville Lodge, Tettenhall, Wolverhampton

Contents

Contributors

Michael Amiraslani has a BA in Political Science with High Distinction from the University of Toronto, where he is completing a Master of Global Affairs and a Master of Business Administration. He is currently an Investment Analyst with the Ontario Teachers' Pension Plan's Global Strategic Relationships group.

Kirsten Campbell is a Reader in Sociology at Goldsmiths College, University of London. She is currently the principal investigator of the European Research Council funded project, 'The Gender of Justice'. This four-year study analyses the prosecution of sexual violence in armed conflict through a case study of the International Criminal Tribunal for the former Yugoslavia and the Bosnian courts. Campbell has published extensively in the areas of gender, conflict-related sexual violence, international criminal law, and transitional justice.

Kerstin Bree Carlson is an Assistant Professor at Syddansk Universitet (University of Southern Denmark) and the American University of Paris. She received her law degree and PhD in Jurisprudence & Social Policy from the University of California, Berkeley, and her BA from the Johns Hopkins University. Carlson's research considers structural challenges inherent in international criminal justice practice as a means of considering the potential social impact of international criminal law. In addition to her work in the former Yugoslavia, Kerstin's research projects include the impact of the trial of Hissène Habré on international criminal law jurisprudence and domestic institutions and ideologies, and mapping the criminology of international criminal law.

Mikkel Jarle Christensen is Associate Professor of the Sociology of Law at the Faculty of Law, University of Copenhagen, where he is part of the Danish National Research Foundation's Centre of Excellence for International Courts (iCourts). iCourts is funded by grant no. DNRF105. His work has been published in a number of international peer-reviewed journals, including *Law & Social Inquiry*, *The Leiden Journal of International Law*, *Current Sociology* and *International Criminal Law Review*. Christensen's current research investigates both foundational and recent developments in the field of international criminal justice as well as border regions between international core crimes and transnational crimes.

Sara Dezalay is a Lecturer in International Law and International Relations at the Cardiff School of Law and Politics, in Wales. She is also a Visiting Fellow at King's College London, a Senior Research Fellow at the Munk School of Global Affairs in Toronto, and an Affiliate Researcher at the Cluster of Excellence, 'The formation of normative orders', at the Goethe Universität in Frankfurt. Her work has been published in a number of international peer-reviewed journals in English and French, including *International Criminal Law Review*, *International Journal of the Legal Profession*, *Comparativ: Journal for Global History and Comparative Social Science*, *Law and Contemporary Problems*, *Actes de la recherche en sciences sociales*, *Politique africaine*, *Gouvernement & Action Publique*, and *Critique Internationale*. Anchored in structural sociology, Dr Dezalay's current research investigates the roles played by lawyers in state trajectories across the African continent and as intermediaries of globalization. She is the editor of a volume on point published by *Politique africaine*.

Mark A. Drumbl is the Class of 1975 Alumni Professor at Washington and Lee University, School of Law, where he also serves as Director of the University's Transnational Law Institute. He has held visiting appointments and has taught intensive courses at law schools worldwide, including Oxford University (University College), Université de Paris II (Panthéon-Assas), Free University of Amsterdam, University of Ottawa, Masaryk University, Trinity College Dublin, University of Melbourne, Monash University, Vanderbilt University, and University of Sydney. His research and teaching interests include public international law, global environmental governance, international criminal law, post-conflict justice, and transnational legal process. His work has been relied upon by the Supreme Court of Canada, the United Kingdom High Court, United States Federal Court, and the Supreme Court of New York in recent decisions. As well as many articles, Drumbl has authored two books: *Reimagining Child Soldiers in International Law and Policy* (Oxford University Press, 2012) and *Atrocity, Punishment and International Law* (Cambridge University Press, 2007), both of which have been widely reviewed and have received critical acclaim.

Sigall Horovitz is a Crime Prevention and Criminal Justice Officer at the Corruption and Economic Crime Branch of the United Nations Office on Drugs and Crime (UNODC), where she works on education and private sector initiatives. Horovitz previously served as a Legal Officer at the United Nations International Criminal Tribunal for Rwanda (ICTR) and the UN-backed Special Court for Sierra Leone, and headed the Department of Human Rights Education at the International Nuremberg Principles Academy in Germany. She also held academic positions at the Hebrew University of Jerusalem, Tel Aviv University and other academic institutions. Her areas of interest include international law, transitional justice, and justice education. Horovitz holds a Master of Laws (LLM) from Columbia University, and a Doctor of Laws (LLD) from the Hebrew University. She is a member of the New York and Israeli Bar Associations, and a founding member of ALMA – the Association for the Promotion of International Humanitarian Law.

Mark Kersten is a Research Fellow based at the Munk School of Global Affairs, University of Toronto, and the Director of Research of the Wayamo Foundation. His research focuses on the effects of judicial interventions by the International Criminal Court (ICC) on conflict, peace, and justice processes, the politics of international criminal law, and the nexus between social media and mass atrocity prevention. In 2011, Kersten founded the blog 'Justice in Conflict', which regularly publishes articles on the challenges of pursuing transitional justice in the context of ongoing violent political conflicts. He has taught courses on genocide studies, the politics of international law, diplomacy, and conflict and peace studies at the London School of Economics and SOAS. In 2016, Oxford University Press published his book, *Justice in Conflict – The Effects of the International Criminal Court's Interventions on Ending Wars and Building Peace*. Kersten has previously been a Research Associate at the Refugee Law Project in Uganda and researcher at Justice Africa in London.

Nicola Langille is a Staff Lawyer with the Legal Aid Commission of the Northwest Territories, practising in criminal law. She holds a BCL, LLB from McGill University, Faculty of Law, and a BA (Honours with High Distinction) from the University of Toronto. In 2014–2015, she served as Law Clerk to the Honourable Justice Clément Gascon of the Supreme Court of Canada.

Ron Levi holds the George Ignatieff Chair of Peace and Conflict Studies and is Associate Professor of Global Affairs and Sociology at the University of Toronto, where he serves as Deputy Director for the Munk School of Global Affairs. He directs the Global Justice Lab at the University of Toronto, which focuses on justice systems under stress and strain worldwide, whether that pressure comes from social change, crime and violence, political demands, or organizational dilemmas. Levi's research focuses on how we respond to crime and violence from a global perspective, including responses to mass violence and atrocities. His work on these issues has been published in a range of venues such as *Law & Contemporary Problems*, *Journal of International Law & Politics*, *Law & Social Inquiry*, *Social Forces*, and *Actes de la recherche en sciences sociales*.

Michiel Luchtman is Professor of Transnational Law Enforcement and Fundamental Rights at the Willem Pompe Institute for Criminal Law & Criminology. He studied law at Utrecht University and received his doctor's degree cum laude from that university in 2007. He received the Siracusa Prize in 2009 from the International Association of Penal Law and the International Institute of Higher Studies in Criminal Sciences (ISISC) for his book *European Cooperation Between*

Financial Supervisory Authorities, Tax Authorities and Judicial Authorities. His research and teaching focus on the consequences of Europeanization for criminal justice and law enforcement in general; on criminal law and fundamental rights; on economic criminal law, as well as criminal tax law. Luchtman is a member of the management team of the Utrecht Centre of Regulation and Enforcement in Europe/Renforce. He is also a member of the Standing Committee of Experts on International Immigration, Refugee and Criminal Law (Meijers Committee), rechter-plaatsvervanger (honorary judge) at the District Court of Amsterdam and a member of the European Commission's Expert Group on Criminal Policy.

Antoine Mégie is Lecturer in Politics at the University of Rouen. He is editor of the *Review Politique Européenne* and a member of the editorial team of *Cultures et Conflits*. He is an associate researcher at the University of Montréal (International Centre for Comparative Criminology). His research focused on the international transformation of law and authority towards networked expertise specifically in criminal matters and counterterrorism (Program Polilexes from University Paris 1, La Sorbonne and Program EUROPOLIX from Sciences Po Paris). His current publications concern the practices of the judiciary counterterrorism authorities at the European and national levels. Since 2015, he has been studying terrorism criminal trials during an ethnographical study in France.

Frédéric Mégret is an Associate Professor and Dawson scholar at the Centre for Human Rights and Legal Pluralism, Faculty of Law, McGill University. He holds an LLB from King's College London, a DEA from the Université de Paris I, and a PhD from the Graduate Institute of International Studies (Geneva), as well as a diploma from Sciences Po Paris. He publishes on international law, international human rights law, international criminal justice and the laws of war.

Valsamis Mitsilegas is Professor of European Criminal Law, Dean for Research (Humanities and Social Sciences) and, since 2012, Head of the Department of Law at Queen Mary University of London (QMUL). He has been the Director of the Queen Mary Criminal Justice Centre since 2011. From 2001 to 2005 he served as legal adviser to the House of Lords European Union Committee. His research interests and expertise lie in the fields of European criminal law; migration, asylum and borders; security and human rights, including the impact of mass surveillance on privacy; and legal responses to transnational crime, including organized crime and money laundering. He is the author of six monographs and over 100 articles and chapters in academic volumes. His latest books are *The Criminalisation of Migration in Europe* (Springer, 2015) and *EU Criminal Law After Lisbon* (Hart, 2016). He is a regular adviser to parliaments, governments and EU institutions, including the European Commission, the European Parliament and the EU Fundamental Rights

Agency. He has been appointed for a second term to the European Commission's Expert Group on Criminal Policy.

Victor Peskin is an Associate Professor in the School of Politics and Global Studies at Arizona State University and a Senior Research Fellow at the UC Berkeley Human Rights Center. Peskin is a co-author of *Hiding in Plain Sight: The Pursuit of War Criminals from Nuremberg to the War on Terror* (University of California Press, 2016). He is also the author of *International Justice in Rwanda and the Balkans: Virtual Trials and the Struggle for State Cooperation* (Cambridge University Press, 2008), which was named a *Choice* magazine Outstanding Academic Title. Peskin's current work focuses on the politics of accountability in Kosovo and the role of the International Criminal Court in Africa and in the context of the Israeli-Palestinian conflict. Peskin received his doctorate in Political Science from the University of California, Berkeley.

Jamie Rowen is Assistant Professor of Legal Studies and Political Science at the University of Massachusetts, Amherst. Dr Rowen received a JD from Berkeley School of Law in 2009, a PhD from the Jurisprudence and Social Policy Program at Berkeley School of Law in 2012, and was a doctoral fellow at the American Bar Foundation in 2012–2013. Prior to her current position in legal studies at UMass, Dr Rowen taught in the Centre for Criminology and Sociolegal Studies at the University of Toronto. Dr Rowen's new book, *Searching for Truth in the Transitional Justice Movement*, was published by Cambridge University Press and focuses on efforts to found truth commissions in the Balkans, Colombia and the United States. Her work has been published in *Law and Social Inquiry*, *International Journal of Transitional Justice*, *Human Rights Quarterly*, *Journal of International Law and International Relations*, *Encyclopedia of Law and Behavioral Science*, among other outlets. Dr Rowen's current research examines the confluence of domestic immigration and international criminal law within the Department of Homeland Security, as well as the experience of US veterans in the criminal justice system.

John Vervaele is full-time Professor of Economic and European Criminal Law at Utrecht Law School (the Netherlands) and Professor of European Criminal Law at the College of Europe in Bruges (Belgium). Since September 2014 he has been President of the oldest world organization for criminal justice (AIDP). Vervaele is co-director of the Utrecht Centre of Regulation and Enforcement in Europe/Renforce at Utrecht Law School. His scholarly work deals with white-collar crime and fraud and European criminal law and procedure. The main topics of his research are: enforcement of Union law; criminal law and procedure and regional integration; criminal procedure and procedural safeguards. Vervaele has conducted research for both Dutch Departments and European Institutions and also worked as a consultant for them. He regularly teaches as visiting professor in foreign universities, in Europe, the

US, Latin America and China. He has published widely on OLAF, European enforcement agencies and the European Public Prosecutor's Office. He has been involved as an expert in the procedural preparation of the EPPO-file (Green Paper) and in the impact assessment of the PIF Directive.

Introduction

An internationalized criminal justice: paths of law and paths of police

Mikkel Jarle Christensen and Ron Levi

> *Besides its immediate victim, the crime attacks the sovereign: it attacks him personally, since the law represents the will of the sovereign; it attacks him physically, since the force of law is the force of the prince.*
>
> (Foucault 1979: 47)

> *'Nuremberg' is booming ... Since the end of the Cold War such a law appears more attractive than ever before ... Almost every day there are media reports of new attempts at and demands for the confrontation of historical injustice by legal means.*
>
> (Frei 2003: 333)

> *The growth of international crime control is evident in the proliferation of new criminal laws and an aggressive push for cross-national homogenization of such laws; expansion of agency budgets, responsibilities, and enforcement powers; efforts by more proactive states to extend their claims to extraterritorial jurisdiction; deployment of more sophisticated global surveillance and tracking technologies; heightened police cooperation and communication through an increasingly dense set of transgovernmental networks and international institutions at the regional and global levels ...*
>
> (Andreas and Nadelmann 2006: 16)

Something peculiar is happening in the field of criminal justice. For hundreds of years representing the state's sovereign power as evidenced with the above epigraph from Foucault – appears as if it is being unmoored from the state itself. This is an effect of two parallel changes. On the one hand, there is the growth, particularly since the 1990s, of a field of international criminal law, along with the creation of new legal doctrines and new institutions such as the International Criminal Court (ICC). On the other hand, there is also ever-growing coordination of criminal investigation and prosecution across countries, and the creation of new professional relationships and institutions for responding to transnational crime. There is the prosecution of war crimes, genocide, and crimes against humanity on one side, working often at the level of diplomacy and connected to human rights movements; and on the other side there is the investigation of crime across borders, working often at the level of bureaucracy, and connected with law enforcement and regulatory bodies.

These two paths of internationalized criminal justice are usually thought of as distinct. After all, they rely on different legal doctrines, they stem from different political imperatives, and they draw on different social and professional networks active in building these fields and their institutions. They rely on different intellectual histories and speak to different audiences, with one connected to social movements of international human rights and the other to transnational enforcement. These two paths of criminal justice are also split between a 'high politics' and a 'low politics'. Due to its structure and subject matter, international criminal law frequently encounters international diplomacy, while transnational policing is often in closed networks operating under the political radar while officially representing the state and being tied to its bureaucracy (Christensen 2016). While both paths connect with diplomacy and politics, one presents itself through a vision of pure law that connects the legal cultures of 'criminal law' and 'international law' (Bassiouni 1974; Wedgwood 1995), and one through a vision of police that connects law enforcement with good governance, security, state administration and the 'smooth running of society' (Levi and Hagan 2006: 210).

Yet we argue that there is much to be gained by considering both of these paths of internationalized criminal justice together. Collectively, the changes and transformations that are occurring along these paths have substantial impact on criminal law and how legal tools are imagined, used and promoted by politicians, legal professionals, NGO advocates and academics. This book highlights how the internationalization of criminal justice is occurring along both of these dimensions at once – a fact that is often ignored by scholars and practitioners who are invested professionally and intellectually in one side or another of this split.

From our perspective, this split is itself one of the stakes of how both of these fields are built in distinction to one another: the one focusing on claims to universals and a global discourse on human rights, legalism, and international law, and the other focusing instead on claims to enforcement, state security, and policing. The demarcation between these two fields – with an emphasis on 'pure law' on the one hand, and 'police' on the other – has long been central to international justice. A core point of this book is that the division between international criminal law and transnational crime enforcements serves a crucial ideological and functional role in the constitution and maintenance of these fields. Keeping these two domains separate manages expectations of international justice: for example, the inability of international criminal law to arrest suspects and enforce its indictments can be chalked up to its lack of police force and its need to rely on state cooperation, while international policing can proceed along administrative and enforcement paths to pursue security, maintaining some distance from the stric-tures of legal theories of the international sphere.

When taken as two sides of the same coin, it becomes ever more striking that both fields have experienced striking growth – at times parallel, at times in competition, and at times intertwined – over the twentieth and twenty-first centuries.

A surge of activity occurred during the interwar years and the immediate post-World War II era, which included the creation of Interpol, the International Military Tribunals at Nuremberg and for the Far East, and the negotiation of the Genocide Convention (Mettraux 2008; Wilt 2012); the Cold War era saw a reluctance to try war crimes internationally, but left them open to be prosecuted within domestic jurisdictions, along with treaties negotiated through the UN and the Council of Europe on law enforcement cooperation that aimed to harmonize and coordinate the policing of transnational crimes such as drug trafficking, unlawful seizures of aircraft, hostage taking, piracy and mercenaries (Alter 2014: 142–60; Clarke and Goodale 2010: 1–2); and the fall of the Berlin Wall saw a dramatic parallel investment in new institutions of international criminal law, including the creation of international criminal tribunals in the wake of atrocities in the former Yugoslavia and in Rwanda, and the formation of the ICC and ever greater integration of police intelligence across Europe (Bigo and Tsoukala 2008; Bigo 2016; Christensen 2015; Hagan 2003; Hagan and Levi 2005).

While these fields have often developed in parallel, the post-9/11 era, on the other hand, demonstrates how a focus on internationalized criminal law can shift in relative emphasis and priority. There have been marked successes for both fields during this time: this includes ever greater coordination of criminal law enforcement on issues of counter-terrorism, money-laundering, and human trafficking, and the permanent International Criminal Court made historic strides with its first indictments, trials, and convictions. Yet there has also been a realignment of priorities, prestige, and political emphasis. In recent years, heightened concerns over terrorism and national security have led to waning enthusiasm for the project of international criminal law. This has exacerbated other concerns, including the continued refusal of the US, China and Russia to sign or ratify the Rome Statute, atrocities in Syria that make headlines worldwide yet are not referred by the Security Council to the Court, questions regarding the Court's efficacy, and political concerns in Africa over the Court's caseload and emphasis on African-based atrocities (Clarke 2016). Precisely because they are in an emerging space that potentially challenges the legal prerogatives of the state, the field of international criminal law is heteronomous, often subject to the demands of powerful states and of diplomats (Hagan et al. 2006). As a result, international criminal courts are best understood as fragile institutions and must be analyzed in relation to their overall place in a larger system of criminal justice power (Mégret 2016). In contrast, counter-terrorism, money-laundering, and human trafficking concerns have drawn ever greater resources and political attention during this time, magnified by migrant crises that have intensified demands for security and international police cooperation.

Taken together, it can safely be said that despite its successes, international criminal law has been buffeted by counter-currents – and that these same counter-currents have, on the other hand, propelled forward other forms of international criminal justice. In our analysis, both the fields of international criminal law and of transnational police experience boom and bust cycles related to international politics that give priority to specific ideas, technologies and practitioners at the expense of others.

From our perspective, this is the point that is often missed by practitioners and researchers alike. However the allocation is made in any given era, criminal justice has continued to internationalize in rapid ways over the course of the last century. Sometimes the investments and prestige are on the side of international criminal law and legal doctrines for responding to atrocities in war (Dezalay and Garth 2006), and sometimes they are on the side of police cooperation, investigation, and law enforcement (Andreas and Nadelmann 2006; Christensen 2016; Deflem 2004; Sheptycki 2000). Yet in both incarnations, the internationalizing of criminal justice provides new frameworks for making claims – always rooted in expertise and a vocabulary of crime, punishment, and justice – to respond to crises and to advance new frameworks for building international institutions and networks. In turn, these frameworks are the subject of substantial professional, legal and political controversy (Christensen 2017).

In our account, the division between theorized legal arguments and high politics on the one hand, and administrative capacities of enforcement on the other, is what paradoxically allows both fields to thrive by allowing practitioners to develop practices and strategies that respond to political demands of the day (Hagan et al. 2006). This is visible, for instance, in the fact that avant-garde claims can gain prominence precisely when they suggest *crossing* this boundary: as an example, Luis Moreno Ocampo, after his term as Prosecutor of the International Criminal Court, garnered international attention by arguing that the so-called Islamic State ought to be prosecuted at the ICC, moving terrorism away from military action and into the orbit of international criminal law. Moreno Ocampo here explicitly sought to move the field of international criminal law closer to its police-focused counterpart, asking rhetorically, 'How do you deal with criminals in Paris? Carefully, you don't bomb them' (Kassel 2016). Another example is the call for an International Anti-Corruption Court promoted by, among others, American senior judge Mark L. Wolf (Christensen 2017).

Rather than maintain this division, this volume focuses on the actors, institutions, and practices that are central to the internationalization of criminal justice and criminal law. To us this is the key to understanding how criminal justice appears increasingly unmoored from the state, and how it gains ever greater attention as a method for resolving international crises by playing up either police or legal technologies, and in some cases fusing the two. Who is doing the work of internationalized criminal justice, what tools are they using, and where are they practicing this new form of the criminal law? Has this internationalization indeed pushed the criminal law outside of the immediate purview of the state, or do these new actors and the practices they deploy continue to be tied to the national approaches from which they have been trained? Have new forms of legal practice, legal doctrine, and law enforcement been created as a result?

To investigate these questions, the chapters in this book focus on emblematic moments and institutions that have emerged since the fall of the Berlin Wall, all part of this broader unhinging of criminal justice from the state – but of course never completely relegating the state to irrelevance. These contributions illustrate how, by tracing the crossroads of the criminal and the international, we see a dramatic pace of change. In so doing, these contributions attend to legal developments all placed within their social and political contexts; they include attention to everyday legal and police practices, and to the networks of professionals and institutions they engage; and they attend to different sites of internationalization, whether these involve international courts or transnational practices that are more firmly embedded in national jurisdictions. Taken together, the chapters in this book demonstrate how, across sites, the internationalization of criminal justice has been driven by competing political stakes, legal doctrines, networks, and the quotidian practices of professionals.

The book is divided into three main sections. Part I focuses on the *practitioners* actively involved in pulling criminal justice onto an international scene of governance where it competes with other technologies and approaches. The strategies and innovations crafted by these practitioners had significant impact for the internationalization of criminal justice as they set in motion new institutional, professional and normative developments. Part II focuses on how new *practices* of criminal law have been developed beyond the state. Here the focal point is how practices – shaped by geopolitical, structural and institutional contexts – have had the effect of unhinging criminal justice from the state. Part III focuses on the *institutions* that play a central role in the internationalization of criminal justice. Here it becomes apparent that the state has never in fact disappeared from the story. The construction of effective criminal justice beyond the state is a major challenge and these institutions face a range of struggles that lead to institutional fragility, failures, and mutations. While more of the contributions in this volume focus on the field of international criminal law than that of international policing, both forms of criminal justice are highlighted in each Part of the book. We thus learn how criminal justice practitioners, practices, and institutions are promoted as mechanisms for international governance – and how these activities are often framed as belonging to distinct fields of international criminal justice.

Part I begins with the people and groups who promote or administer internationalized criminal justice in specific contexts. As such the chapters in this section are inspired broadly by a sociological turn in international law scholarship, building among other work on the structural sociology of Pierre Bourdieu (Bourdieu and Wacquant 1992). This range of approaches emphasizes the importance of agents (Dezalay and Garth 1996, 2002), elites (Hagan and Levi 2005; Kauppi and Madsen 2013) and networks (Glasius 2006; Keck and Sikkink 1999; Sikkink 2011) as key to understanding both change and continuity, and the ways in which international legal struggles partly mirror and partly rebalance power relations. These practitioners, always embedded within their own professional trajectories, social relations and national contexts, are active forces in conceptualizing and building new technologies and normative frameworks that promote criminal law as an internationalized governance tool.

We begin this Part with a chapter by Mikkel Jarle Christensen. He investigates how legal and political elite agents involved in the reunification of Germany and reconstruction of the European project were also involved in unhinging criminal justice from direct state control. Situated at a point in history at which Europe was being reimagined as a social, legal and political entity, the promotion of criminal law as a form of governance was both forward- and backwards-looking. Building on the conceptual schemes developed by legal professionals during the Cold War, criminal law was imagined as a tool for healing European wounds as well as for strengthening Europe's political role in a new global setting. This vision was crystallized in the proposal of the German and French ministers of foreign affairs, both of whom were trained lawyers, to create the International Criminal Tribunal for the former Yugoslavia (ICTY). This emblematic proposal spurred on the wider impetus for unhinging criminal law from traditional state practices by creating new international institutions, and more broadly worked to reconfigure European criminal justice in terms of police cooperation. Christensen builds here on sociological field approaches to international criminal law to explain how internal developments in the field are tied to power politics beyond the social spaces in which new approaches to internationalized criminal law and police were developed.

Investigating a later period in the Europeanization of criminal law, Antoine Mégie investigates how professional elites helped create new forms of criminal justice cooperation that transformed the state of law within Europe. Chapter 2 sets out to explain how justice became spatially removed from the state. By focusing on the creation of the European Arrest Warrant and Eurojust, Mégie analyzes how specific individuals helped create a new legal technology that would influence criminal justice within Europe. This highly specialized group of legal professionals did so by building a shared culture and perception of criminal justice that tied it to wider processes of coordination and harmonization within Europe. Given their position at the center of the European institutional game, these agents managed the policy-building agenda while promoting specific solutions, in writings and policy-building, that centered on the role of criminal law. In trying to create a new understanding of criminal justice at the European level, the push for an unhinged criminal law in this context was structured by interactions with national judges whose support or opposition was crucial for the success of these newly crafted legal approaches. In other words, these agents worked incrementally to build European tools of criminal justice that could successfully coexist with others' policy preferences and professional values. This chapter provides further evidence that the internationalization of criminal law within the EU was a technocratic endeavor partly defined by transnational networks of experts – or elites – that used the wider context of harmonization and securitization to create space for new forms of criminal justice (Bigo 2013).

Moving away from the European context of regional cooperation, in Chapter 3 Jamie Rowen identifies how specific actors drove the ways in which transitional justice was marshalled to describe post-conflict situations, and how transitional justice was then deployed to prescribe solutions for affected countries. Rowen is acutely aware of the nexus between law and politics, and she analyzes how different actors, including policy makers and advocates, shape the transformation of legal ideas and the promotion of solutions in countries marked by conflict. She then zooms in on how the language of transitional justice is now increasingly used in countries not undergoing regime change – and is thus disjointed from its original meaning – and highlights how political tensions are exacerbated by actors who use the language of transitional justice for their own professional ends. In so doing, Rowen shows how the unhinging of justice models can create new professional opportunities and conflicts over the goals of legal models. What counts here are the investments of actors whose careers and professional practices become closely associated with specific normative perspectives on how justice should be done.

Valsamis Mitsilegas then turns to a global space of criminal law, to point to a 'justice deficit' that occurs when individual experts work to drive normative innovations behind closed doors. In so doing, he provides a typology of norm-making in the field of transnational criminal law, and points to the shift from traditional treaty-based forums to more informal approaches in which specific states, professionals, and elites dominate. Responses to transnational crimes, such as terrorism and money-laundering, are thus developed within a new paradigm of global multi-level governance – but one which raises concerns about transparency and democratic legitimacy. As Mitsilegas shows, the unhinging of criminal justice can create a vacuum in which transnational professional networks gain ever greater influence over the norm-making process. Police power thus becomes concentrated among a small group of professionals whose practices are not tied down by the national bureaucracy and are not situated squarely in a national system of checks and balances.

Part II focuses on the international practices of criminal justice, and the consequences these practices have for how the law and lawyers operate. This builds on several strands of research in international law, political science, and sociology, that seek to draw out the legal, bureaucratic, and diplomatic practices required for justice mechanisms to function internationally (Adler and Pouliot 2011; Brunnée and Toope 2010; Wendt 1999). Much of this research emphasizes the work of international criminal courts, whether to document these courts' operations in challenging political contexts (Campbell 2013, 2014; Meierhenrich 2013a, 2013b), or to investigate how experts come to testify on technical issues (Anders 2014; Eltringham 2013). This has parallels in research on transnational law enforcement, with research investigating how new criminal law practices emerge to respond to crimes such as corruption (Nuijten and Anders 2007) or environmental crimes (Lynch 2014). Similarly, researchers in Europe have turned their attention to the practices of technical experts, who must reconcile data collection approaches on crime patterns across an array of national approaches (Aebi et al. 2015; Body-Gendrot 2014).

Part II begins with a chapter by Ron Levi, Sara Dezalay and Michael Amiraslani, who investigate the practices of prosecutors in international criminal courts. They demonstrate that the opening statements of prosecutors reflect how these courts negotiate and maneuver the wider geopolitical context in which they are embedded. Levi, Dezalay and Amiraslani identify an important transformation in the symbolism on which international criminal law prosecution builds: the broad claims of justice formulated by the prosecutors at the Nuremberg Trial have been supplanted by a narrower set of claims around effectiveness and efficiency in the opening statements of ICC prosecutors. By showing how this development is related to the geopolitical context within which the prosecutors find themselves, the chapter points to an important feature of the decoupling of criminal law from the state. Internationalized practices of criminal justice enjoy relatively weak authority compared to traditional forms of criminal law, and these courts thus continually work to reflect and recast geopolitical constraints. They are thus prone to reflect and adapt to the ebbs and tides of international diplomacy.

Chapter 6 on practices is written by Nicola Langille and Frédéric Mégret, focusing on a specific legal technology developed by Interpol. Analyzing the development and increased use of 'Red Notices' as a specific tool that exists in a legal 'grey zone', Langille and Mégret point to the existence of a set of transnational policing practices that have developed beyond the control of the state and that play an important but in many ways hidden role in international criminal law enforcement. Their emphasis on legal and political grey zones is crucial for understanding that the unmooring of criminal law practices is not necessarily tied to visible efforts of promotion or institutional innovations. Rather, it is by being hidden from traditional political and legal lines of influence that some practices can become influential for the work of police forces worldwide. Their analysis then underlines how the existence of this system, unhinged from some legal constraints, comes into conflict with pre-established judicial balances and human rights norms.

This attention to informality is extended by Kerstin Bree Carlson's analysis of plea bargaining in the ICTY. Carlson traces the development and circulation of plea bargaining as a specific legal practice, imported from the United States, and analyzes the impact of this practice in the ICTY. With the practice of plea bargaining travelling to the international stage without its broader context, Carlson shows that central elements of traditional plea bargaining were 'lost in translation' to the potential detriment of the rights of the defendants. Without the system of legal support and recognition of plea bargaining that structures its use in the US, the process became opaque and thus difficult for defendants to foresee the implications of 'striking a deal'. As the chapter shows, the results of unhinging national practices and importing them to the institutions of international criminal law can be difficult to predict – and may result in practices that are very different from those suggested by the adopted legal terminology.

Kirsten Campbell analyzes how perceptions of gender shape legal practices. Building on the sociological approaches of both Pierre Bourdieu and Bruno Latour, Campbell shows how the field of international criminal law is structured by specific practices and perceptions of what is considered legal and non-legal. Dependent on what forms of law enjoy priority in this specific field, not all claims can be made with the same force, and gendered perspectives on sexual violence have often been pushed to the periphery. The practices of international criminal law, in other words, lead to significant blind spots. As such this chapter demonstrates that the internationalization of criminal law is shaped by contested perspectives on what this new form of law ought to do. In this larger competitive space, to gain legal and political salience, the success of gendered perspectives depends on whether they succeed in crafting new legal practices that reimagine international criminal law as a whole – and thus mobilize the legal practices necessary to target sexual violence.

Mark Drumbl provides an analysis that unpacks the jurisprudential footprint of international criminal justice in the US. His chapter is also about the circulation of legal ideas and practices, but whereas Carlson follows plea bargaining as it moves from national to international contexts, Drumbl follows the return of international ideas to domestic settings. By contributing the first mapping of how the US Alien Tort Statute has been used to try cases involving international crimes, Drumbl reveals an unexpected 'extracurricular legacy' of international criminal justice, as the Statute has been used to try cases concerning aiding and abetting, genocide and crimes against humanity, and corporate criminal liability. By analyzing the jurisprudential imprint of international criminal law in domestic civil litigation, Drumbl highlights how this form of law circulates into new domestic contexts where it takes on alternative forms that, potentially, generate new legal and social impacts. In other words, new practices of internationalized criminal law can take on a life of their own as they return to national jurisdictions from which criminal law was first unhinged.

After surveying practitioners and practices, Part III of this volume then turns to the international institutions of criminal justice.

A central concern of scholarship on internationalized criminal law has been the creation of new institutions and the power they exert in a larger legal and political space. This is not surprising: after all, institution-building, especially in the form of new international courts, was the most visible and striking evidence of the internationalization of criminal law. Since the mid-1990s several international and hybrid criminal courts proliferated after the creation of the International Criminal Tribunals for Rwanda (ICTR) and the former Yugoslavia (ICTY), a process that also led to the creation of the permanent ICC, also located in The Hague. Outside of this field of international criminal justice focused on the so-called 'core crimes' of genocide, crimes against aggression, war crimes (and potentially aggression), a number of other institutions have emerged at the regional level dealing also with other forms of crime. In the EU the effort to harmonize approaches to criminal law and develop new tools for cooperation was supplemented by the creation of new institutions, initially under the third pillar as initiatives that built on collaboration between national units. With the implementation of the Lisbon Treaty the institutions of Europol and Eurojust, the EU units responsible for police and prosecutorial cooperation, will become full EU institutions that will coexist, potentially, with the European Public Prosecutor's Office (EPPO) outlined in article 86 of the treaty. These institutions supplement and occasionally conflict with older institutions that have taken on new roles in the new space of internationalized criminal law. For instance, Interpol – probably the best known international police organization – has gone through several transformations since its initial creation in 1923, finally readjusting to the current landscape of institutions dealing with criminal law beyond the state. The boom years of the 1990s thus coexisted with other, more incremental, trends of internationalization in which institutions reinvented themselves within global criminal law enforcement.

While international and transnational institutions are central to this unhinging and internationalization of criminal law, the work of these institutions makes it clear that the state has never left the scene. This is evident in the chapter by Michiel Luchtman and John Vervaele. In their analysis of the proposed EPPO, they point to the difficulty in stitching together international institutions in an atmosphere characterized by competing state interests and increased skepticism towards European integration. Still under negotiation, the EPPO would represent a striking innovation as the first supranational prosecution service in the world holding investigative and prosecutorial powers in the single legal area of the EU. By contributing a legal analysis of the applicable law of the EPPO as it is currently envisaged, the authors demonstrate some of the challenges to internationalized criminal law as it comes into conflict with other forms of legal safeguards and judicial review, in particular human rights regimes. As the chapter points out, trying to piece together an international institution of criminal law is a complex and high-stakes game. Such challenges to previously established legal and political balances can face strenuous opposition.

Victor Peskin's chapter investigates how the two foundational international criminal tribunals of the 1990s – the ICTR and the ICTY – worked with states to secure diplomatic as well as practical support. Peskin demonstrates how the ICC continues this legacy by similarly depending on the power of states to investigate and prosecute individuals. This chapter shows that these 'virtual trials' of international criminal law have substantial impact on courts' legal authority and ability to impact their surroundings. Unhinged from the 'right hand of the state' and without their own policing apparatus, international criminal courts are fragile and depend on the support of the states that formed them, but whose leaders they are mandated to investigate and, potentially, prosecute. The paradox is that the ICC – an international institution designed to take criminal law beyond the state – remains attached to traditional state-based forms of authority and power. Rather than decoupling criminal law from national contexts, this chapter shows that at an institutional level the state remains a core partner for this internationalized criminal justice.

Yet if the state remains central to international criminal justice, the chapter by Sigall Horovitz demonstrates how institutions that work with internationalized criminal justice can fail to benefit the national communities they were designed to assist. In her chapter, she investigates the role of criminal justice in the wider framework of national reconciliation in Rwanda. Through an analysis of the

Kabgayi Trial and her own fieldwork in Rwanda, Horovitz assesses the impact of the ICTR on national reconciliation. She identifies a schism between what international criminal courts produce, and their effects on delivering some sort of justice to national communities. She finds that in practice, the ability of these international justice institutions to promote reconciliation is predicated on how their legal ideas are received locally. As the initiatives of the ICTR were exported into the Rwandan context they were influenced and reinterpreted by local elites. Given the political, legal, and professional distance of international tribunals from conflict areas, Horovitz demonstrates how local agents and networks can influence, and trump, the intended effects of these courts for local communities.

The final chapter of the book points to the future and thus provides a fitting end to this collective volume. Mark Kersten analyzes one potential and emergent answer to the difficulty of crafting international criminal law institutions and securing state support for them in a space characterized by boom and bust cycles of investments into international law and policing practices. This chapter investigates the unlikely return of hybrid criminal courts, a form of internationalized criminal justice institution that – rather than unhinging – mixes international and national elements. While this form of institution was initially believed to become obsolete with the creation of the permanent ICC, different hybrid formats continue to emerge. By positioning the resurgence of these institutions within a wider historical and political context, Kersten shows how the limitations of the ICC and waning support for this institution coexists with specific political and legal advantages of hybrid courts, precisely because they build on both international engagement and national state support. The chapter thus demonstrates how international practices of criminal law are constantly being reconceived and reworked to adapt to changing political climates.

Seen from our perspective, these boom and bust cycles of international criminal justice have led the fields of law and police to evolve together. Depending on external opportunities, the practitioners, practices, and institutions of criminal law and of police have become more or less unhinged from national contexts. Internationalization has thereby created new opportunities as well as new challenges within the fields of law and police. By drawing both fields together in this volume, just how rapid the internationalization of criminal justice has been – precisely because it has proceeded along two fronts, with legal responses to war crimes in some cases and by investing in transnational policing networks in responding to other crimes. Yet as the chapters in this book demonstrate, the unhinging that we see in both fields is also always contested: as political logics change, the international practices of criminal justice are reconfigured to support new institutions, demands for justice, and police action. In this way, the professional fields of international criminal justice refract external political demands and investments. The pace of change, the degree of unhinging, and the relative power of these fields are thereby dependent on the refraction of political demands, professional ambitions, innovative practices and adaptive ways of working, and the impact of institutional constraints.

References

Adler, Emanuel and Pouliot, Vincent (2011), 'International Practices', *International Theory,* 3 (1), 1–36.

Aebi, Marcelo F., Linde, Antonia, and Van Dijk, Jan (2015), 'The Case for Survey-Based Comparative Measures of Crime', *European Journal of Criminology*, 12 (4), 437–56.

Alter, Karen J. (2014), *The New Terrain of International Law: Courts, Politics, Rights* (Princeton: Princeton University Press).

Anders, Gerhard (2014), 'Contesting Expertise: Anthropologists at the Special Court for Sierra Leone', *Journal of the Royal Anthropological Institute*, 20 (3), 426–44.

Andreas, Peter and Nadelmann, Ethan Avram (2006), *Policing the Globe: Criminalization and Crime Control in International Relations* (Oxford; New York: Oxford University Press).

Bassiouni, Cherif (1974), 'An Appraisal of the Growth and Developing Trends of International Criminal Law', *Revue internationale de droit pénal*, 45, 405–33.

Bigo, Didier (2013), 'The Transnational Field of Computerised Exchange of Information in Police Matters and its European Guilds', in Niilo Kauppi and Mikael Rask Madsen (eds), *Transnational Power Elites: The New Professionals of Governance, Law and Security* (London: Routledge), 155–82.

— (2016), 'Sociology of Transnational Guilds', *International Political Sociology*, 10 (4), 398–416.

Bigo, Didier and Tsoukala, Anastassia (2008), *Terror, Insecurity and Liberty: Illiberal Practices of Liberal Regimes After 9/11* (London; New York: Routledge).

Body-Gendrot, Sophie (2014), *The Routledge Handbook of European Criminology*, 1st edn (New York: Routledge).

Bourdieu, Pierre and Wacquant, Loic (1992), *An Invitation to Reflexive Sociology* (Chicago: University of Chicago Press).

Brunnée, Jutta and Toope, Stephen J. (2010), *Legitimacy and Legality in International Law: An Interactional Account* (Cambridge: Cambridge University Press).

Campbell, Kirsten (2013), 'The Making of Global Legal Culture and International Criminal Law', *Leiden Journal of International Law*, 26 (1), 155–72.

— (2014), 'Reassembling International Justice: The Making of "the Social" in International Criminal Law and Transitional Justice', *International Journal of Transitional Justice*, 8 (1), 53–74.

Christensen, Mikkel Jarle (2015), 'From Symbolic Surge to Closing Courts: The Transformation of International Criminal Justice and its Professional Practices', *International Journal of Law, Crime and Justice*, 34 (4), 609–25.

— (2016), 'International Prosecution and National Bureaucracy: The Contest to Define International Practices within the Danish Prosecution Service', *Law & Social Inquiry*, DOI: 10.1111/lsi.12254.

— (2017), 'Crafting and Promoting International Crimes: A Controversy between Legal Professionals of Core Crimes and Anti-Corruption', *Leiden Journal of International Law*, 30, 501–21.

Clarke, Kamari Maxine (2016), *Africa and the ICC, Perceptions of Justice* (Cambridge: Cambridge University Press).

Clarke, Kamari Maxine and Goodale, Mark (2010), *Mirrors of Justice: Law and Power in the Post-Cold War Era* (Cambridge; New York: Cambridge University Press).

Deflem, Mathieu (2004), *Policing World Society, Historical Foundations of International Police Cooperation* (Oxford: Oxford University Press).
Dezalay, Yves and Garth, Bryant G. (1996), *Dealing in Virtue, International Commercial Arbitration and the Construction of a Transnational Legal Order* (Chicago; London: University of Chicago Press).
— (2002), *The Internationalization of Palace Wars, Lawyers, Economists, and the Contest to Transform Latin American States* (Chicago: University of Chicago Press).
— (2006), 'From the Cold War to Kosovo: The Rise and Renewal of the Field of International Human Rights', *Annu. Rev. Law. Soc. Sci.*, 2, 231–55.
Eltringham, Nigel (2013), '"Illuminating the Broader Context": Anthropological and Historical Knowledge at the International Criminal Tribunal for Rwanda', *Journal of the Royal Anthropological Institute*, 19 (2), 338–55.
Foucault, Michel (1979), *Discipline and Punish* (New York: Vintage).
Frei, Norbert (2003), 'Before and after Nuremberg' (Book Review), *Journal of Contemporary History*, 38 (2), 333–43.
Glasius, Marlies (2006), *The International Criminal Court: A Global Civil Society Achievement* (New York: Routledge).
Hagan, John (2003), *Justice in the Balkans: Prosecuting War Crimes in the Hague Tribunal* (Chicago: University of Chicago Press).
Hagan, John and Levi, Ron (2005), 'Crimes of War and the Force of Law', *Social Forces*, 83 (4), 1499–534.
Hagan, John, Levi, Ron, and Ferrales, Gabrielle (2006), 'Swaying the Hand of Justice: The Internal and External Dynamics of Regime Change at the International Criminal Tribunal for the Former Yugoslavia', *Law & Social Inquiry*, 31 (3), 585–616.
Kassel, Whitney (2016), 'Mr Baghdadi, You're Under Arrest: Could the International Criminal Court Really Play a Role in Ending the Conflict in Syria?', *Foreign Policy* http://foreignpolicy.com/2016/01/07/mr-baghdadi-youre-under-arrest-islamic-state-syria-icc/.
Kauppi, Niilo and Madsen, Mikael Rask (eds) (2013), *Transnational Power Elites: The New Professionals of Governance, Law and Security* (London: Routledge).
Keck, Margaret and Sikkink, Kathryn (1999), 'Transnational Advocacy Networks in International and Regional Politics', *International Social Science Journal*, 51 (1), 89–101.
Levi, Ron and Hagan, John (2006), 'International Police', in Markus D. Dubber and Mariana Valverde (eds), *The New Police Science: The Police Power in Domestic and International Govenance* (Stanford: Stanford University Press), 207–47.
Lynch, Michael J. (2014), *Exploring Green Criminology, Toward a Green Criminological Revolution* (Farnham, UK; Burlington, Vermont: Ashgate).
Mégret, Frédéric (2016), 'International Criminal Justice as a Juridical Field', *Champ pénal/Penal field*, 13, DOI: 10.4000/champpenal.9284.
Meierhenrich, Jens (2013a), 'Foreword to Special Edition: The Practices of the International Criminal Court', *Law and Contemporary Problems*, 76 (3–4), i–x.
— (2013b), 'The Practice Of International Law: A Theoretical Analysis', *Law and Contemporary Problems*, 76 (3–4), 1–84.
Mettraux, Guénaël (2008), *Perspectives on the Nuremberg Trial* (Oxford: Oxford University Press).

Nuijten, Monique and Anders, Gerhard (eds) (2007), *Corruption and the Secret of Law: A Legal Anthropological Perspective* (Farnham: Ashgate).

Sheptycki, J.W.E. (ed.) (2000), *Issues in Transnational Policing* (London: Routledge).

Sikkink, Kathryn (2011), *The Justice Cascade: How Human Rights Prosecutions are Changing World Politics* (New York: W.W. Norton).

Wedgwood, Ruth (1995), 'Prosecuting War Crimes', *Mil. L. Rev.*, 149, 217.

Wendt, Alexander (1999), *Social Theory of International Politics* (Cambridge: Cambridge University Press).

Wilt, Harmen van der (2012), *The Genocide Convention: The Legacy of 60 Years* (Leiden: Nijhoff).

Part I

Chapter 1

Reunited Europe and the internationalization of criminal law

The creation and circulation of criminal law as an international governance tool

Mikkel Jarle Christensen

Introduction

Taking stock of how criminal law has been internationalized over the course of the past three decades reveals an impressive number of relatively young institutions, legal instruments and professional networks. At an international level, the emergence of international criminal courts tasked with adjudicating criminal responsibility for what became known as core crimes coexisted with the crafting of conventions aimed at combating a wide range of different crimes. In Europe, and particularly within the European Union (EU), institution-building was supplemented with the creation of new professional networks involved in designing and executing transnational practices of criminal law. While the developments in and around the international criminal courts and on the European continent were perhaps the most striking in the wider internationalization of criminal law, they are usually seen as distinct. The important convergences of social, legal and political preferences that shaped their parallel expansion in the post-Cold War era are largely forgotten.

This chapter investigates the legal, political and professional practices that helped define and transform the spaces of European and international criminal law. Focusing on elements of the conjoint genesis of these two spaces of law, the chapter is composed of four analytical parts. The first lays out the theoretical framework of the chapter and presents its empirical material. The second investigates one of the Cold War laboratories of internationalized criminal law thinking as scholars and practitioners built the conceptual frameworks that would diffuse into the political mainstream from the mid-1990s. The third section analyzes how criminal law moved onto the political agenda in Europe, particularly in the closely linked context of German reunification and EU federalism as promoted by specific Member States. It was in this atmosphere that the German and French Foreign Ministers jointly suggested the creation of what became the

International Criminal Tribunal for the former Yugoslavia (ICTY) that would reinvent international criminal law (ICL). The fourth section demonstrates how two new markets were created around regional and international innovations and how the professionals engaged in these markets became drivers in the expansion of criminal law to new social and political contexts. The conclusion will specify the findings of the chapter and relate it to the more general internationalization of criminal law practices.

A sociological approach to the internationalization of criminal law

Within most scholarship, European and international criminal law have been seen as separate spheres of law. Legal scholarship has generally taken the formal legal boundaries of these forms of law at face value and has systematized and analyzed their internal developments. Within international criminal law (ICL), legal scholars have helped conceptualize the general traits of this new system through large treatises and introductory volumes (Ambos 2013; Cassese 2008; Schabas 2013). While some forms of legal scholarship of ICL have been very closely associated with the practical innovations of this field in which many academics have also worked as practitioners (Stahn 2012), in recent years critical legal scholars have also contributed important analyses of the political and social forces that drive this space (Schwöbel 2014). The European space of criminal law has also, by and large, been seen by legal scholars as a fixed and insulated area (Delmas-Marty et al. 1996; Husabø 2005; Klip 2012; Ligeti 2012; Mitsilegas 2009). Much as within the scholarship of ICL (Christensen 2016a), the legal academics engaged with European criminal law are divided along two opposing poles: The society pole that draws scholars close to practice through the demand for and professional advantages of producing practically relevant research, and the scientific pole whose gravitational pull is linked to norms of disinterestedness and autonomy.

International Relations (IR) scholars and political scientists have largely reproduced the focus on what is seen as two separate forms of law. In the field of international criminal justice, they have targeted their inquiries towards the political processes that shaped the international criminal tribunals (Bosco 2014; Roach 2009) and how politics formats the politics around these institutions and their interventions into concrete conflict areas (Branch 2007; Peskin 2008). In European criminal law, IR scholars and political scientists have focused mainly on the politics of cooperation between different countries and how criminal law has been impacted by changing security situations in Europe (Guild et al. 2010) as well as by the external relations of the union (Balzacq 2009; Walker 2004). Adding to the contributions of political scientists, but often choosing different research objects that allow them to follow concrete legal professionals, networks or elites, sociologists have also contributed scholarship of ICL. An emerging sociology of this field (Christensen 2015a) has situated the international criminal courts in a larger legal, political and social setting in which concrete agents work as translators between internal dynamics and external pressures (Hagan 2003; Hagan et al. 2006) in a larger internationalized field of practice (Christensen 2015b; Dixon and Tenove 2013). This new space of law is fenced off by national bureaucracies that remain skeptical towards international practices and are often reluctant to engage with the institutions that drive them. With regard to European practices of criminal law, sociologists have investigated how the space of EU internal security was reconstructed after the end of the Cold War (Bigo 2007, 2010) and reimagined specific institutions such as Europol (Bigo 2013) and Eurojust (Mégie 2007; Mégie 2014). Despite the innovative and sometimes groundbreaking scholarship on ICL and European criminal justice performed by legal scholars, IR experts and sociologists, very few contributions have investigated the linkages between what is most often considered by academics as well as by practitioners as separate spaces of law, whether they be international and regional forms of criminal law or the forms law developed to deal with particular crimes such as the so-called core crimes of ICL and what are now widely known as transnational crimes, such as corruption (Christensen forthcoming). As a result of naturalizing what is perceived as the boundaries between these spaces, the political and professional overlaps that helped energize the early developments of international criminal law and European criminal justice have largely been ignored.

To investigate precisely the social and political dynamics that were driving factors in the emergence of both of these two spaces of internationalized criminal law, the chapter is inspired by the sociological tools of Pierre Bourdieu (Bourdieu and Wacquant 1992). In the context of investigating the emergence of the French state, Bourdieu crafted what he called a genetic history (Bourdieu 2012: 150–54) aimed at laying bare the DNA of this particular social space in which the legal profession developed in parallel to the new *État* that it helped construct and legitimize. In a space of internationalized law, the study of the political and social circumstances in which new legal mechanisms and institutions evolved is influenced by a myriad factors not present in the national field. Due to this complexity, the chapter does not pretend to contribute a comprehensive investigation into the genesis of European and international criminal law: It investigates a particular drive for internationalizing criminal law tools and ideas pushed onto the scene by converging legal and political elites. These agents saw criminal law as adept for crafting a united and strong Europe not only outside the shadow of the defunct USSR but also establishing its own authority by distancing itself from the dominance of the US. Empirically informing the chapter are almost 120 interviews and more than 500 publically available CVs. The analysis will zoom in on a particular group of legal professionals and politicians located at the crossroads between European reunification and criminal law, who promoted this form of law as a regional and international governance tool. This analysis shows how ideals of internationalized criminal law, produced and championed by specific professionals, moved onto the political scene in Europe in a very particular context, where it was used to signal a distance from past regimes and a new form of national German and regional European unity that could also be invested internationally. While this narrative does not necessarily contradict the thesis of how a justice cascade originating in many different sites helped establish a new set of ideals around human rights prosecutions (Sikkink 2011), it does show the importance of understanding the particular political and professional dynamics that led to the rise of this form of law. As the analysis will show, the process of promoting a specific set of legal norms organized around criminal law as a governance tool was closely linked with efforts of crafting a new political unity in Europe and with the endeavor of creating a new professional market for criminal law expertise.

Towards new European practices of internationalized criminal law

The idea of catapulting criminal law onto the international scene as a governance technology goes back at least to the interwar period (Lewis 2014), when it was formed at the crossroads between international diplomacy and scholarly investments as characterized, for instance, by the activities of the International Association of Penal Law (AIDP) (M. Cherif Bassiouni 1989). While the idea of creating an international criminal court was raised after the First World War (WWI) and built on a protracted process of law-making aimed at codifying the rules of war, exemplified by the 1864 Geneva Conventions that recognized the role of International Committee of the Red Cross (ICRC), it was not until after the Second World War (WWII) that such a court materialized at Nuremberg. While the building of more courts did not characterize the Cold War period, many of the conceptual schemas and concrete projects defined in the interwar period, including that of an international criminal court, were reproduced at the crossroads between scholarship, practice and diplomacy. In terms of new legal instruments, this is evidenced in the range of international Conventions and UN resolutions passed during the Cold War including, to name only a few, on narcotic drugs (1961), racial discrimination (1963), unlawful seizure of aircraft (1970), protection of diplomats (1973), against taking hostages (1979), piracy (1982), unlawful acts against the safety of maritime navigation (1988) and against piracy (1989). The Council of Europe (CoE) also aimed at facilitating cooperation in criminal justice matters and passed Conventions on the transfer of sentences (1983) on the search, seizure and confiscation of the proceeds from crime (1990).

Outside of these legal and diplomatic innovations, the AIDP was a central reproducer of the ideals defined in the interwar period and incubator of new initiatives. The association was reformed from an earlier organization in 1924 and has since organized a number of academics, legal diplomats and practitioners who worked to propose practical solutions to criminal problems that transcended borders. As such the initiatives of the AIDP had a distinctly normative and prescriptive character not unlike that found in other forms of legal scholarship (Christensen 2016a; Kahn 1999). Core efforts were aimed at harmonizing criminal law and crafting new forms of international cooperation and institutions. These ambitions are visible in the *Revue Internationale de Droit Pénal* published by the

AIDP that took on different criminal problems of international concern such as the drafting of an international criminal code (1981), international and regional cooperation in criminal matters (1983), the death penalty (1987) and criminal law and biomedicine (1988).

During the Cold War, the meetings of the AIDP were attended by scholars and practitioners as well as stakeholders from the international NGOs who were slowly expanding their international influence in the same period (Clark 2001): The May 1979 meeting, for instance, was attended by Maureen Berman of the International League of Human Rights, Nigel Rodley from Amnesty International (AI) in London and Yves Sandoz from the ICRC. In addition to these profiles, the Council of Europe was also represented at some meetings, for instance through Aglaia Tsitsoura who served as council's Head of the Division of Crime Problems in the 1980s before going into academia at the Panteion University in Athens, Greece. Collectively these profiles embodied the focus of the association: the creation, adoption and promotion of prescriptions or models aimed at resolving concrete problems. This mission was also written into the very statute of the AIDP, article 2(1) of the current by-laws stipulating that the association 'aims to promote the development of legislation and institutions with a view towards improving a more humane and efficient administration of justice'. This article mirrors what was article 1(3) in the original statute that targeted the theoretical and practical development of criminal law with the goal of conceiving a universal criminal code.

In terms of scholarly engagement in the AIDP, Cherif Bassiouni was perhaps the most prominent and served as Secretary General of the AIDP from 1974–89 and as president from 1989–2004, a period in which he also published seminal texts on international criminal law and courts (M. Cherif Bassiouni 1989; M. Cherif Bassiouni 2015; de la Cuesta and Ottenhof 2015). As evidenced in the AIDP statute, the effort to create an international criminal code was not an individual quest but was debated continuously in the association. Building on preliminary reports in the *Revue* in 1964 and 1974, a full draft code for an international criminal court was published by the AIDP in 1981 and was supported by the majority of its members, remaining, however, controversial also internally (Bouzat 1981: 10). The drafting of this code had direct professional links to Nuremberg: it was introduced in the *Revue* by French law professor Pierre Bouzat, who had served as the secretary to a French judge at the International Military Tribunal (IMT), Donnedieu de Vabres, also a member of the AIDP, and who had helped coordinate post-war interactions between the tribunal and the association of penalists. In an atmosphere characterized by the UN General Assembly that settled the controversial question of defining aggression with 1974 Resolution 3314 (XXIX), the AIDP report promoted a double vision of international criminal jurisdiction: It was conceived as a practical tool able to cope with specific problems of global crime and more normatively as a new form of international cooperation built around common values of 'world community' (M. Cherif Bassiouni 1981a: 41–42). To create an effective mechanism, the AIDP advocated the creation of a court with a broad mandate that covered 20 different crimes including what would later become known as 'international core crimes', such as aggression, war crimes, genocide, crimes against humanity, as well as a range of other crimes such as piracy, illegal uses of post services, drug-related crimes, counterfeiting, corruption of foreign officials and trafficking of obscene material (M. Cherif Bassiouni 1981b: 90).

The production of the draft code was part of a wider project to promote criminal law as a viable supplement to politics on the international stage that was also being championed by international NGOs and institutions such as the CoE. This collective endeavor was supported by the accumulated expertise of a group of professionals who focused on promoting criminal law as a technology. In this context the AIDP was also used as a forum for reflecting on the possibilities of creating an international police force, an international criminal register and an international criminal court (Koering-Joulin 1984: 23–24). At the basis of the conceptual work of the AIDP was the positing of a universality principle seen as 'an expression of the solidarity of the civilized world against crime' (Vogler 1984: 40). Investing their considerable expertise towards elevating criminal law as an international tool of law that could structure politics, AIDP members worked not only to promote a certain form of law as governance but also to construct a market for their knowledge and services, an effort that was reflected in their career trajectories at the international and regional level. European scholars in the AIDP were active as practitioners both in the domain of core crimes – names like Otto Trifterer and later judge at the ICC Christine van der Wyngaert and A.M.M. Orie of the ICTY contributing to the 1989 *Revue* volume on international crimes or to other publications – and at the level of regional cooperation, through professionals who worked closely with European institutions, such as professor Pierre-Henri Bolle, Swiss representative to the European Committee on Crime Problems under the auspices of the CoE from 1974–1988, French professor Marc Ancel who chaired a 1962 CoE committee on criminal problems in Europe, and was involved in particular with the question of the death penalty (Ancel 1962), and professor at the University of Freiburg, Klaus Tiedemann, a specialist on corporate criminal law (Tiedemann 2002) and long-time supporter of European competences in this space of law.

As these profiles demonstrate, the push for Europeanization and internationalization of criminal law was fought in scientifically oriented policy development as well as in print through scholarly publications. Perhaps the most prolific example of how scholarship and academic capital was used to promote a common regional and specifically European space of criminal affairs was Mireille Delmas-Marty, professor at the Collège de France, who not only spearheaded a French commission on the interplay between criminal law and internationally embedded human rights norms, but also headed the Corpus Iuris study that crafted a set of rules for a future EU public prosecutor (Delmas-Marty and Vervaele 2000), an expert group in which Klaus Tiedemann and current AIDP president John Vervaele also served. Closely related to these policy-building initiatives, her academic publications set out to investigate the contours of a future common European criminal law (Delmas-Marty 1994; Delmas-Marty et al. 1996) as well as more global problems of terrorism and the role of legal pluralism in a transformed world (Delmas-Marty and Norberg 2003, 2009; Delmas-Marty et al. 2010). Through profiles such as that exemplified by Delmas-Marty, the independent professional role of academics was a fundamental factor in crafting new ideals for internationalized criminal law that could be imported into specific political contexts in which scholars used their expertise and the symbolic capital associated with professorships to raise new debates and reproduce the idea of creating new international institutions capable of producing a joint approach to criminal justice. Crucially, this production of new ideas was finely attuned to political realities and aimed not only to theorize for the sake of theory, but also to prescribe legal solutions to real problems in concert with AIDP practitioners and in the process to promote criminal law as a viable governance technology also beyond the state.

Within the context of Europe, AIDP members were active nationally and regionally in the attempt to translate their own version of world solidarity in the fight against crime into political policy. In this effort they were joined by European institutions and politicians working for similar ends. Here the CoE as well as the EC was active, for instance, in relation to the problem of terrorism. Within the EC the Trevi group was set up in 1975 between the 12 states of the Community to counter terrorism and coordinate policing (Anderson et al. 1995; Bunyan 1993). Trevi had two active working groups, of which one had an operational role and the other concerned police cooperation and the exchange of information and would lay the ground for what became Europol after the Maastricht Treaty. In addition to this initiative, the CoE passed the European Convention on the Repression of Terrorism in 1977 coordinated by the European Committee on Crime Problems in which AIDP members also worked. As a result of these concomitant and interrelated investments into European criminal law an intellectual and practical infrastructure was created around ideals of coordination, harmonization and supra-nationality that had been reproduced since the interwar period.

Reunification of Europe and a new criminal law

With the fall of the Berlin Wall in November 1989, the idea of a united Europe was reconceived and the political and legal frameworks of the continent reconstructed. It was in this context that criminal law came into political vogue as a new governance mechanism able to support the recreation of Europe and the construction of a new form of international law. On the background of strong economic (Keohane and Hoffmann 1994) and systemic (Mutimer 1989) dynamics at play in the transformation of Europe, there was a significant political pressure to rethink the EC and its role in a larger global context (Baun 1995). While the process of rethinking Europe was also characterized by competition between, in particular, the German and French Governments, the latter potentially losing international influence with a reunited Germany and President François Mitterrand initially trying to stall reunification, by late 1990 the Franco-German axis seemed to be restored and to be working towards a monetary as well as political union. In this wider context, influential politicians aimed to accelerate economic and political integration with the twin purpose of tying Germany to Europe and crafting a union not dependent on the United States. In the words of French president François Mitterrand: 'There is no longer an imposed order. Europe is now master of its choices, or it can be' (quoted in Cogan 2001: 7). One key political and legal outcome of this line of thinking was the Maastricht Treaty of 1993 that established a common currency as set out in the 1989 Delors report and established the European Union (EU), a legal and political entity that built on a tighter regional cooperation embedded in three pillars: the European communities, the Common Foreign and Security Policy, and Justice and Home Affairs. While only the first pillar built on increased community integration, the intergovernmental dynamics of the second and third pillar would also give rise to new institution- and policy-building.

After the end of Cold War, European integration was reimagined around a Franco-German alliance. It was in this context that criminal law moved onto the political scene in Europe and this platform also served as one of the venues from which criminal law was pushed onto the international level. Under the third pillar, collaboration between European police forces and judiciaries slowly increased momentum: The Europol Convention was negotiated from the mid-1990s and took effect just before the millennium, and Eurojust was established as an outcome of the 1999 European Council meeting at Tampere, Finland, in an effort to curb serious organized crime by creating a cooperation unit for prosecutors to mirror that of the police. The Tampere meeting and the Treaty of Amsterdam also established a new portfolio of the Directorate General (DG) of Justice, Freedom and Security, originally formed in 1995, that would become central for planning what could be called a true area of European criminal law (interview with EU official 17 October 2013). These institutions sprung from the previous emergence of groups and networks of professionals that worked together beyond boundaries with regard to practical questions of law enforcement as well as, frequently overlapping, groups of professionals involved in policy-building at the regional level, for instance through the CoE or at the level of EU cooperation. Some of these professionals had been intimately involved in the AIDP and were now able to barter criminal law knowledge and experience at the national level and in the context of a reunited and increasingly integrated Europe in which ideas of independent regional prosecutors also emerged as driven and promoted by Delmas-Marty and others. Others took a more national route to these forms of cooperation, having worked in domestic systems either with complex crimes with frequent transnational links or close to policy-building circles that recalibrated their strategies to fit new international currents of thinking.

Within the EU itself, the Maastrich Treaty accelerated cooperation in criminal matters and activated some of the ideas of harmonization and cooperation previously promoted by the AIDP. This also led to increased network-building within the union and intensified cooperation among practitioners who worked, for instance, with terrorism, drug trafficking and organized crime, and who focused primarily on policing, while judicial cooperation was less impactful. This development coexisted with the practices of the Council of Europe that had worked on cooperation on criminal matters for decades, often in close contact with AIDP members in the European Committee on Crime Problems set up in 1958, and its subordinate bodies the Committee of Experts on the Operation of European Conventions on Co-Operation in Criminal Matters (PC-OC) created in 1981 and the Council for penological co-operation (PC-CP) established in 1985. But the council networks and activities became more active in the new political setting organizing rule of law support to formerly communist countries in relation to their criminal justice system. Also, with the enlargement process where new countries, especially in Central and Eastern Europe, would be admitted in accordance with the Copenhagen Criteria defined in 1993, all union countries would be part of the European Judicial Network (EJN) formed in 1998 to establish contact points for judicial cooperation in each of the Member States. Collectively the networks and institutions formed around the new Europe were driven by practitioners and policy-makers for whom the new political order was seen as a chance to embed criminal law in the workings of the EU and CoE. To create coherent and well-functioning regional forms of cooperation, criminal law was seen as an important technology, a role that was accentuated by the Schengen Convention that entered into force in March 1995 and effectively ended border control in the parts of the union that signed the treaty. In this new space, policing was the driving force, and Europol rather than Eurojust set the pace for EU cooperation (Bigo 2007).

The usages of criminal law as a tool of integration to safeguard cooperation and the interests of the union extended beyond the professional interests and intergovernmental dynamics of the third pillar. The schemes of thought that had been crafted and reproduced at the crossroads between academia and policy-building circulated into EU foreign relations in an attempt to distance Europe from the US, treading a careful line between insisting on continued American influence in post-Cold War Europe and outlining a situation where a reunited continent would change the state of play. One of the first signs of the use of criminal law by European politicians as a symbolic tool in international politics was tied to the first Gulf War, where western leaders had floated the idea of holding Saddam Hussein criminally liable for crimes committed during his reign. This idea was championed by German foreign minister Hans-Dietrich Genscher and backed by the 12 EC countries. Genscher, a trained lawyer, had played a large role in shaping Willy Brandt's *Ostpolitik* that was predicated on unilateral normalization of relations with Eastern Europe and the USSR (a policy that often greatly annoyed the US) and was deeply involved in the transformation of Europe after the fall of the Berlin Wall. The proposal to prosecute Hussein turned out to be too controversial, as it would mean the trial of a formerly US and

Western-backed ruler. None the less, the idea of using criminal law as a tool in foreign policy development would resurface during the conflict in the former Yugoslavia. Besides playing a crucial role in the reunification of Germany and the peaceful transition to a post-communist Europe, Genscher also pushed for German recognition of Croatia's independence and later that of Slovenia, hoping that quick EU recognition would halt hostilities.

From reunited Europe to ICL

While the creation of the International Criminal Tribunal for the former Yugoslavia (ICTY) and the wider diffusion of international criminal courts can hardly be credited to one source, European engagement with criminal law as a form of regional and international governance was crucial for its genesis. Criminal law practitioners, professors and European politicians, often trained in law themselves, helped create a market for this form of law by building on expertise and thinking patterns reproduced since Nuremberg but that were now adapted to new conditions. Through these profiles, the idea of criminal law as a governance tool for Europe and its reimagined position in the world circulated into policy-building that would affect EU mechanisms as well as help spur innovations in the field of international criminal law organized around core crimes. Repeating an idea raised by a Yugoslav journalist in the spring of 1992, criminal lawyer, professor and former French minister of foreign affairs Robert Badinter, who also served as head of the Commission of Arbitrage for the former Yugoslavia from 1991 (Hazan 2004: 15) and eventually as honorary vice-president of the AIDP, repeated the proposal to form an international criminal court to adjudicate criminal responsibility for the conflict. The call for what became the ICTY was closely linked to the perceptive schemas of criminal law deeply embedded in the reunification process of Germany and in the integrative rethinking of Europe. In this context the integration of Europe aimed to give the EU a new role and enable it to speak with one voice on the international scene (Kinkel 1996: 511).

Criminal law as a governance tool in Europe and beyond was embedded in the very profiles of the two foreign ministers who proposed the tribunal: Roland Dumas, born in 1922, educated in law and economics, was a member of the French socialist party and became Minister of European Affairs in 1984 only to move into the chair of minister of foreign affairs a few months later and remain until 1986, returning after Mitterrand's re-election in 1988. Having been part of French resistance to German occupation during WWII, his tenure in French government coincided with the fall of communism and the reorientation of socialist policies towards European integration rather than national protectionism (Haywood 1993). He negotiated the Maastricht Treaty, supported the federalist-leaning European policies of Mitterrand (Dumas 1985) and argued for increased international solidarity and burden-sharing between the US and a more integrated and stronger EC (Dumas 1992) based on the rule of law. His German counterpart, Klaus Kinkel, was also trained in law and held a doctorate from the University of

Cologne (Kinkel 1964). Employed in the foreign ministry in 1968, he served as personal assistant to Hans-Dietrich Genscher from 1970–1974, following him after Genscher was appointed Minister of Foreign Affairs in 1974. Kinkel then served as head of the Federal Intelligence Service (BND) from 1979–1982 and as Secretary of State in the Ministry of Foreign Affairs from 1982–1991, before becoming briefly Federal Minister of Justice. In this position he publicly called for the return to Germany of former General Secretary of the Communist Party in the German Democratic Republic (DDR), Erich Honecker, to face legal proceedings. In 1992 Kinkel was appointed Minister of Foreign Affairs, in which capacity he served as an avid supporter of European integration and enlargement, and was personally involved in negotiations of the Maastricht Treaty. Taking over after Genscher, Kinkel called for a cease of especially Serbian aggression in the former Yugoslavia and was one of the earliest promoters of establishing a tribunal to adjudicate criminal responsibility for the conflict. He also spearheaded changes in the German constitution that allowed military deployments to peacekeeping missions and actively advocated the use of criminal law as a governance tool in the reunited Germany and sought to expand this form of legally driven control to international relations referring to the Nuremberg trials, a court case against Saddam Hussein and the potentially preventative impact of international tribunals (Kinkel 1992: 487).

As evidenced in the trajectories of Kinkel and Dumas, the emergence of criminal law as a governance tool was closely related to the transformation of Europe towards a more integrated union that was searching for a new role at the international level. Criminal law was activated as a potential European and international governance technology in an atmosphere characterized by social and political restructuring. The concepts and ideals reproduced and reconfigured in the AIDP and elsewhere were imported into politics through legal professionals active in both contexts as well as through politicians trained in law who were balancing a new role for the EU and Europe and in this process constructing new forms of regional and international institutions. Through policy-building around the new union, European politicians turned to criminal law as a technology that could support the unification of Europe and be used also as a foreign policy tool. This circulation of conceptual schemes of criminal law that served specific purposes within Europe was an active element in setting the agenda for the ICTY.

However, despite the European investments into criminal law and the fact that the tribunal initially received support from the union, no joint EU policy was identifiable after the ICTY was formed and national governments were less than enthusiastic about supporting this new international criminal tribunal. EU nations such as France and the UK were heavily involved in the former Yugoslavia and while the German and French foreign ministers had supported the building of the tribunal, there was push-back from military commanders in charge of peacekeeping operations that also influenced political policies as well as concrete cooperation with the newly formed tribunal that initially struggled with forces on the ground being unwilling to execute warrants and arrest suspects (Hagan 2003:

102–9). Where the idea of criminal law as a governance tool was embedded in legal professionals that were mirrored by political profiles, the preference for peace guaranteed by military and diplomatic means rather than legal processes was deeply instilled in other parts of the state's system of power. In other words, the schism between peace and justice so frequently mentioned in the scholarship on international criminal law was embodied in different professionals active in the state apparatus and its response to atrocities. In addition, the creation of the International Criminal Tribunal for Rwanda (ICTR) in 1994 activated foreign policies attuned to former colonies that continued to influence the relationship between France and Rwanda. As Europe was focused on reimagining its role and international criminal law stimulated push-back from the military as well as foreign ministries, the US invested heavily in the tribunal and the ICTY soon became dominated by Anglo-Americans as the US saw the tribunal as a way to exert symbolic influence. This development was also influenced by a change in government. Bill Clinton was sworn in as president in January 1993 after having repeatedly called for the prosecution of war criminals, although he quickly recanted on previous plans to send troops to the Balkans (Bass 2000: 213–14). Instead, the new administration, particularly through the very vocal support of Secretary of State Madeleine Albright, whose office was staffed with supporters of genocide trials and international criminal justice, supported the creation of the ICTY that was passed by the unanimous Security Council Resolution 808 in February 1993. When the tribunal was staffed and financed, the US dominated the ICTY through human and financial resources (Hazan 2004: 38) and as the tribunal became operational, the US seconded vital staff especially to the Office of the Prosecutor (OTP) (Hagan 2003: 63–68).

While European countries also seconded personnel to the tribunals, it was not until negotiations around the Rome Statute that the EU would be able to organize a concerted effort and a fairly unified position. The EU is now the largest donor of the International Criminal Court (ICC) (Groenleer and Van Schaik 2007; Ingadottir 2010; Wierda and Triolo 2012: 137), something that marked a wider shift in the funding of international criminal law that exemplifies the move from American dominance to European investment (Ford 2011). As a result the ICC has been drawn in an image that is more European than the ad hocs, and European investment in international criminal law solidified with the EU common position on the International Criminal Court (ICC) (2001/443/CFSP) from 2001 and the establishment of the Genocide Network as part of Eurojust in 2002 (Council Decision 2002/494/JHA), initiatives that also have the solid backing of the European Parliament which was an early supporter of the court and adopted a resolution on EU support for the ICC in 2011 (P7_TA-PROV(2011)0507). In parallel to EU engagement, permanent Security Council members who had voted in favor of the ICTY remained outside of the ICC – China did not sign the Rome Statute, the US signed only to withdraw from ratifying, Russia withdrew its signature in 2016. As a result, the early staff of the court was dominated by Europeans who made a conscious effort of Europeanizing in particular the procedural rules of the permanent court (interview with senior ICC official 4 September 2014). In building the foreign policy of the EU, support for the ICC has been written into several trade and association agreement with third parties, for instance the Cotonou Agreement with the African, Caribbean and Pacific Group of States of 2003, as well as with single countries such as the Association Agreement with the Ukraine signed in 2014. The use of criminal law as a form of governance, first tested in the AIDP whose members helped carry it into Europe and construct conceptual schemes available for other stakeholders, often with legal backgrounds, is now an integral part of the external relations policy of the EU aimed at creating a new form of global authority in which European countries play a significant role.

New institutions and new careers

The conceptual formation of criminal law activated as a form of authority was deeply rooted in professional networks within and beyond Europe. Beyond its role in reconfiguring EU foreign policies in specific areas, the circulation of criminal law onto the regional European and global scene of politics also had striking consequences for the professionals who helped formulate the ideals on which this expansion built and for the legal space in which new international practices of criminal law were developed. Having worked for decades to promote criminal law and to construct a new market for their ideas and practices, the integrative dynamics of the EU and the emergence of new international criminal courts offered new opportunities for AIDP members. In the context of Europe, Delmas-Marty remained a prominent proponent of a supranational EU prosecutor's office (EPPO) and current president John Vervaele and vice president Katalin Ligeti have both published extensively on this proposed institution and on EU criminal harmonization more generally (Ligeti and Simonato 2013; Vervaele 1992), besides working as experts for the European Commission, European Parliament, the OECD and some of the international criminal courts. In these institutions, European scholars and practitioners have also been crucial, Baroness van der Wyngaert serving as one of the most visible judges at the ICC alongside her French colleague, Marc Perrin de Brichambaut, who served as chief-of-staff for Roland Dumas while he was minister of foreign affairs and German judge Bertram Schmitt who was previously ad hoc judge in the European Court of Human Rights before becoming German national member of the Joint Supervisory Body of Eurojust. In this European cooperation unit for prosecutors many national members have extensive experience from the CoE and decades of international cooperation.

While these two legal spaces have increasingly been specialized and some newer career trajectories are often tied primarily to one of them, the trajectory of many core professionals still alternates between them and underlines the interrelatedness of international and European criminal law as professional and intellectual phenomena. The agents active in European and international criminal law are very often the usual suspects, which points not only to a transnationalization of criminal law activities but also to the formation of a distinct professional ecology beyond the state that has specific professional dynamics (Christensen 2015b). The professionals active in these ecologies that allow for a certain movement between them are essentially working in spaces envisaged by legal scholars, practitioners and diplomats of the AIDP. As they invest their professional expertise in these fields, and consequently tie their career closer to their ideals of a global or regional rule of criminal law, an investment that has a clear temporal dimension as continued engagement can also decrease professional value on national markets (Christensen 2016b), they become the main bearers of specific conceptions of criminal law and work to promote them from their specific position in an international institution. The success of this promotional activity, of course, depends on the currents of international politics, the opportunities for legally trained professionals in rising to the top of national diplomacies and the market they can find for specific criminal law solutions.

Across these two spaces of criminal law, professionals have built careers at the borders between international and national markets. Leaving the context in which they were originally trained, they become part of a new group of agents characterized by a close connection between career trajectories and the development of new forms of law and cooperation. As international criminal law professionals, many become repeat players in the different institutions and networks formed since the end of the Cold War. Serge Brammertz, for instance, the current prosecutor for the Mechanism for International Criminal Tribunals (MICT), which took over operations for the ICTY and the Rwanda Tribunal (ICTR), worked as an expert for the Council of Europe and served on the EU Justice and Home Affairs Committee before moving into ICL. Similar trajectories characterize professionals currently working to strengthen European and international criminal law. They have typically worked with complex forms of law in a national setting before moving into international settings that were created through the promotion of criminal law as a governance mechanism. In contrast to the Cold War era, two separate spaces of criminal law now exist. In formal legal terms they are distinct and their current social dynamics are also characterized by specific professional investments that frequently target one of them, although some agents move between them. While they operate independently and are governed by separate legal ideas and technologies, European and international criminal law both remain committed to furthering a specific form of technology embedded in the professional culture of criminal law agents. This commitment is embodied in the professionals who occupy this space and continuously compete to interpret and market the idea of criminal law as a global or regional governance tool.

Concluding remarks

The ideal of criminal law as a global form of governance was formed at the border between law and politics, and, at a deeper social level, was driven by the professional practices and conceptual patterns mobilized by specific agents who promoted the internationalization of this form of law. The converging investments of criminal law professionals organized for instance in the AIDP or active as practitioners involved with transnational cooperation and European politicians was crucial in formatting the space in which new forms of criminal law were constructed. While two distinct fields developed, international criminal law and European criminal justice share part of their genesis in the reimagining of Europe after reunification. One sphere evolved quietly under the radar of politics and focused on police and judicial cooperation, while the other built on highly publicized innovations such as the ad hoc tribunals and the ICC. That these spheres were never completely separated is also evidenced in the trajectories of scholars, practitioners and politicians. Criminal law was internationalized and Europeanized as part of a historical boom in which political investments coexisted with the efforts to open a new market for criminal law professionals built around norms with roots as far back as the interwar period, but modernized in a range of sites, including the AIDP, that met with new political priorities of a transformed Europe. These specific political circumstances allowed for specific forms of governance mechanism to become politically viable and for different forms of criminal law to become internationalized.

Analyzing the social DNA from which European engagement with criminal law grew effectively debunks any singularly normative narrative of how international criminal courts were created around the specific goal of ending impunity. While these narratives certainly exist and played a crucial role in legitimizing different promotional activities around internationalized forms of law (Christensen 2017), they must be analyzed as an element in the wider contest to define the organizational formats that operate at the international level. When criminal law was pushed onto the international scene, European priorities became part of a much more complex and contentious space where diplomatic preferences were often entangled with different legal ideas and technologies. To flesh out the tacit dynamics that characterized the internationalization of criminal law requires a scholarship that builds on theoretical and methodological insights that allow for a disinterested study of norms, practices and their connection as specific professionals formed practices that promoted new forms of law at the regional and international level.

Beyond contributing a historical investigation into the deeper social constitution that characterized the surge of internationalized criminal law in the 1990s, analyzing the social and intellectual DNA active in this process also provides an empirically embedded starting point for further investigation into the contemporary structure of ICL and European criminal justice. While they are often considered distinct social and legal spaces, they share parts of their genesis. This shared provenance points to important dynamics. While developing into two seemingly distinct fields, ICL focusing on law and institution-building and European criminal justice on more tacit forms of police cooperation, this distinction was not self-evident in their genesis. Understanding the structural dynamics that pushed one field towards policing and the other towards law is not trivial and may yield new knowledge about the political, social and legal battles and compromises that formed what we now perceive to be two distinct forms of law.

References

AIDP, International Association of Penal Law (2016), 'By-laws of the International Association of Penal Law', accessed 5 June 2017 at www.penal.org/sites/default/files/New%20Statuts%20en.pdf.

Ambos, Kai (2013), *Treatise on International Criminal Law*, 1st edn (Oxford: Oxford University Press) 3 vols.

Ancel, Marc (1962), *European Committee on Crime Problems, the Death Penalty in European Countries* (Strasbourg: Council of Europe).

Anderson, Malcolm, et al. (1995), *Policing the European Union* (Oxford: Clarendon).

Balzacq, Thierry (2009), *The External Dimension of EU Justice and Home Affairs, Governance, Neighbours, Security* (Basingstoke: Palgrave Macmillan).

Bass, Gary Jonathan (2000), *Stay the Hand of Vengeance: The Politics of War Crimes Tribunals* (Princeton: Princeton University Press).

Bassiouni, M. Cherif (1981a), 'Le droit pénal international: Son histoire, son objet, son contenu', in M. Cherif Bassiouni (ed.), *Revue international de droit international: Projet de code international pénal*, 52 (Toulouse: Editions Erès), 41–71.

— (1981b), 'Introduction a la structure et a l'emploi fonctionel du project de code pénal international', in M. Cherif Bassiouni (ed.), *Revue internationale de droit pénal*, 52 (Toulouse: Editions Erès).

— (1989), 'AIDP: International Association of Penal Law: Over a Century of Dedication to Criminal Justice and Human Rights', *DePaul Law Revue*, 38.

— (2015), 'AIDP: Over a Century of Dedication to Criminal Justice and Human Rights', *Revue internationale de droit pénal*, 86 (3), 1095–120.

Baun, Michael J. (1995), 'The Maastricht Treaty as High Politics: Germany, France, and European Integration', *Political Science Quarterly*, 110 (4), 605–24.

Bigo, Didier (2007), *Mapping the Field of EU Internal Security Agencies* (Paris: L'Harmattan).

— (2010), *Europe's 21st Century Challenge: Delivering Liberty* (Farnham, UK; Burlington, VT: Ashgate).

— (2013), 'The Transnational Field of Computerised Exchange of Information in Police Matters and its European Guilds', in Niilo Kauppi and Mikael Rask Madsen (eds), *Transnational Power Elites: The New Professionals of Governance, Law and Security* (London: Routledge), 155–82.

Bosco, David L. (2014), *Rough Justice: The International Criminal Court in a World of Power Politics* (Oxford: Oxford University Press).

Bourdieu, Pierre (2012), *Sur l'État: Cours au Collège de France 1989–1992* (Paris: Seuil).

Bourdieu, Pierre and Wacquant, Loic (1992), *An Invitation to Reflexive Sociology* (Chicago: University of Chicago Press).

Bouzat, Pierre (1981), 'Introduction', in M. Cherif Bassiouni (ed.), *Revue internationale de droit pénal: Projec de code pénal international*, 52 (Toulouse: Edition Erès), 7–12.

Branch, Adam (2007), 'Uganda's Civil War and the Politics of ICC Intervention', *Ethics & International Affairs*, 21 (2), 179–98.

Bunyan, Tony (1993), 'Trevi, Europol and the European state', in Tony Bunyan (ed.), *Statewatching the New Europe* (London: Statewatch), 1–15.

Cassese, Antonio (2008), *International Criminal Law*, 2nd edn (Oxford; New York: Oxford University Press).

Christensen, Mikkel Jarle (2015a), 'The Emerging Sociology of International Criminal Courts: Between Global Restructurings and Scientific Innovations', *Current Sociology*, 63 (6), 825–49.

— (2015b), 'From Symbolic Surge to Closing Courts: The Transformation of International Criminal Justice and its Professional Practices', *International Journal of Law, Crime and Justice*, 34 (4), 609–25.

— (2016a), 'Preaching, Practicing and Publishing International Criminal Justice: Academic Expertise and the Development of an International Field of Law', *International Criminal Law Review*, 17 (2), 239–58.

— (2016b), 'International Prosecution and National Bureaucracy: The Contest to Define International Practices within the Danish Prosecution Service', *Law & Social Inquiry*, DOI: 10.1111/lsi.12254.

— (2017), 'Crafting and Promoting International Crimes: A Controversy between Legal Professionals of Core Crimes and Anti-Corruption', *Leiden Journal of International Law*, 30 (2), 501–21.

Clark, Ann Marie (2001), *Diplomacy of Conscience, Amnesty International and Changing Human Rights Norms* (Princeton, NJ: Princeton University Press).

Cogan, Charles (2001), *The Third Option, the Emancipation of European Defense, 1989–2000* (Westport, CT: Praeger).

de la Cuesta, Jose Luis and Ottenhof, Reynald (2015), 'The Association Internationale de Droit Pénal and the Establishment of the International Criminal Court', *Revue internationale de droit pénal*, 86 (3), 1237–50.

Delmas-Marty, Mireille (1994), *Pour un droit commun* (La Librairie du XXe siècle; Paris: Editions du Seuil) 305.

Delmas-Marty, Mireille and Norberg, Naomi (2003), *Global Law: A Triple Challenge* (Ardsley, NY: Transnational Publishers).

— (2009), *Ordering Pluralism: A Conceptual Framework for Understanding the Transnational Legal World* (Portland, OR: Hart).

Delmas-Marty, Mireille, Laurens, Henry, and Collège de France (2010), 'Institut du monde contemporain', *Terrorismes: histoire et droit* (Paris: CNRS).

Delmas-Marty, Mireille, et al. (1996), *What Kind of Criminal Policy for Europe?* (The Hague; Boston: Kluwer).

Delmas-Marty, Mireille and Vervaele, John (eds) (2000), *The Implementation of the Corpus Juris in the Member States: Penal Provisions for the Protection of European Finances* (Antwerp: Intersentia) 4 vols.

Dixon, Peter and Tenove, Chris (2013), 'International Criminal Justice as a Transnational Field: Rules, Authority and Victims', *International Journal of Transitional Justice*, 7 (3), 393–41.

Dumas, Roland (1985), 'Pour en finir avec l'europessimisme', *Politique Étrangère*, 50 (2), 309.

— (1992), 'Time to Share the Burden?: Adjusting US Attitudes to a Multi-polar World', *Harvard International Review*, 14 (4), 18–20.

Ford, Stuart (2011), 'How Leadership in International Criminal Law is Shifting from the United States to Europe and Asia: An Analysis of Spending on and Contributions to International Criminal Couts', *Saint Louis University Law Journal*, 55 (3), 853–999.

Groenleer, Martijn L.P. and Van Schaik, Louise G. (2007), 'United We Stand? The European Union's International Actorness in the Cases of the International Criminal Court and the Kyoto Protocol', *JCMS: Journal of Common Market Studies*, 45 (5), 969–98.

Guild, Elspeth, Carrera, Sergio, and Balzacq, Thierry (2010), 'The Changing Dynamics of Security in an Enlarged European Union', in Didier Bigo, et al. (eds), *Europe's 21st Century Challenge: Delivering Liberty* (Farnham, UK: Ashgate), 31–48.

Hagan, John (2003), *Justice in the Balkans: Prosecuting War Crimes in the Hague Tribunal* (Chicago: University of Chicago Press).

Hagan, John, Levi, Ron, and Ferrales, Gabrielle (2006), 'Swaying the Hand of Justice: The Internal and External Dynamics of Regime Change at the International Criminal Tribunal for the Former Yugoslavia', *Law & Social Inquiry*, 31 (3), 585–616.

Haywood, Elizabeth (1993), 'The European Policy of Francois Mitterrand', *Journal of Common Market Studies*, 31 (2), 269–82.

Hazan, Pierre (2004), *Justice in a Time of War: The True Story Behind the International Criminal Tribunal for the former Yugoslavia*, 1st edn (College Station: Texas A & M University Press).

Husabø, Erling Johannes (2005), *Harmonization of Criminal Law in Europe* (Antwerp: Intersentia).

Ingadottir, Thordis (2010), *The Financing of Internationalized Criminal Courts and Tribunals* (Oxford University Press online).

Kahn, Paul W. (1999), *The Cultural Study of Law, Reconstructing Legal Scholarship* (Chicago: University of Chicago Press).

Keohane, Robert O. and Hoffmann, Stanley (1994), 'Institutional Change in Europe in the 1980s', in Brent Nelsen and Alexander Stubb (eds), *The European Union* (London: Palgrave), 237–55.

Kinkel, Klaus (1964), 'Die Lehre von Popitz für die Gestaltung des gemeindlichen Finanzausgleichs und ihr Verhältnis zum gegenwärtigen Rechtszustand in der Bundesrepublik' (Rechtswissenschaftliche Fakultät der Universität).

— (1992), 'Wiedervereinigung und Strafrecht', *JuristenZeitung*, 47 (10), 485–9.

— (1996), 'L'agenda européen à l'horizon 2000', *Politique Étrangère*, 61 (3), 507–11.

Klip, André (2012), *European Criminal Law, an Integrative Approach* (Cambridge: Intersentia).

Koering-Joulin, Renée (1984), 'Commentaire de la question IV: "Structures et méthodes de la coopération internationale et régionale en materière pénale"', *Revue internationale de droit pénal*, 55 (Toulouse: Editions Evrès), 15–52.

Lewis, Mark (2014), *The Birth of the New Justice: The Internationalization of Crime and Punishment, 1919–1950* (Oxford: Oxford University Press).

Ligeti, Katalin (ed.) (2012), *Toward a Prosecutor for the European Union Volume 1: A Comparative Analysis* (Modern Studies in European Law; Oxford: Hart).

Ligeti, Katalin and Simonato, M. (2013), 'The European Public Prosecutor's Office: Towards a Truly European Prosecution Service?', *New Journal of European Criminal Law*, 4 (1), 7–22.

Megie, Antoine (2007), 'Mapping the Actors of European Judicial Coorporation', in Didier Bigo (ed.), *The Field of the EU Internal Security Agencies* (Centre d'Etudes sur les Conflits; Paris: L'Harmattan), 67–96.

Mégie, Antoine (2014), 'The Origin of EU Authority in Criminal Matters: A Sociology of Legal Experts in European Policy-Making', *Journal of European Public Policy*, 21 (2), 230–47.

Mitsilegas, Valsamis (2009), *EU Criminal Law* (Modern Studies in European Law; Oxford: Hart).

Mutimer, David (1989), '1992 and the Political Integration of Europe: Neofunctionalism reconsidered', *Journal of European Integration*, 13 (1), 75–101.

Peskin, Victor (2008), *International Justice in Rwanda and the Balkans: Virtual Trials and the Struggle for State Cooperation* (Cambridge: Cambridge University Press).

Roach, Steven C. (2009), *Governance, Order, and the International Criminal Court, Between Realpolitik and a Cosmopolitan Court* (Oxford: Oxford University Press).

Schabas, William (2013), *The Ashgate Research Companion to International Criminal Law, Critical Perspectives* (Farnham, UK; Burlington, VT: Ashgate).

Schwöbel, Christine (ed.) (2014), *Critical Approaches to International Criminal Law: An Introduction* (London: Routledge).

Sikkink, Kathryn (2011), *The Justice Cascade: How Human Rights Prosecutions are Changing World Politics* (New York: W.W. Norton & Co).

Stahn, Carsten (2012), 'EDITORIAL: Between "Faith" and "Facts": By What Standards Should We Assess International Criminal Justice?', *Leiden Journal of International Law*, 25 (2), 251–82.

Tiedemann, Klaus (ed.) (2002), *Wirtschafstrafrecht in der Europäischen Union, Rechtsdogmatik-Rechtsvergleich-Rechtspolitik* (Köln: Carl Heymanns Verlag).

Vervaele, John A.E. (1992), *Fraud Against the Community, the Need for European Fraud Legislation* (Deventer: Kluwer).

Vogler, Théo (1984), *Rapport Général* (Revue internationale de droit pénal, 55; Toulouse: Editions Erès) 33–52.

Walker, Neil (2004), *Europe's Area of Freedom, Security, and Justice* (Oxford: Oxford University Press).

Wierda, Marieke and Triolo, Anthony (2012), 'Ressources', in Luc Reydams, Jan Wouters, and Cedric Ryngaert (eds.), *International Prosecutors* (Oxford: Oxford University Press), 113–70.

Chapter 2

Displacing and replacing the criminal law within the European space

Antoine Mégie

Introduction

Understanding the dynamics of transnational crimininal law enables us to explain how justice is removed in its spatial dimension and in its relationship to the law. Through the implementation of the field of European criminal law cooperation and particular through the Eurojust units[1] and the European Arrest Warrant,[2] we observe a redefinition of the territories of legal action. During the Europeanisation of Criminal Law, various concepts of 'a European space' emerged to legitimise the adoption of new cooperation mechanisms. The mobilisations and projects in favour of strengthened judicial cooperation introduce variable-geometry approaches within a European criminal law space. This definition is at the heart of the struggle between the projects in favour of an intergovernmental approach and those in favour of a community approach (Den Boer 2002; Bigo et al. 2007).

According to the promoters of the intergovernmental method, it is necessary to build a 'European judicial space' defined through the 25 territories in a logic of 'strengthened' transnational cooperation. In contrast to this approach, the basic idea of the promoters of the second perspective is the concept of a 'European judicial space' through a logic of harmonisation that leads to uniform national systems and the creation of a European legal territoriality. The adoption of the Eurojust project in 1999 and the rejection of *corpus juris* in favour of a European Prosecutor suggest that the logic of convergence is usually preferred over that of harmonisation (Mégie 2006).

1 Eurojust, the first European unit devoted exclusively to judicial cooperation, was a multilateral office with a prosecutor from the legal system of each EU Member State. Council of the European Union, Decision 187/JAI setting up Eurojust to reinforce the fight against serious organised crime, OJEC C 063, 6 March 2002.

2 The European Arrest Warrant (EAW) is a specific procedure for extradition between EU Member States. The EAW marked the implementation of the European principle of mutual recognition of legal decisions in a new field of law. Council of the European Union, 'Framework decision of the European Council 13 June 2002 on the European arrest warrant and the surrender procedures between member states', OJEC L 190, 18 July 2002.

Nevertheless, the creation of the Eurojust unit and the European Arrest Warrant (EAW) represents a transnational extension of national judicial powers. The participation of the French judges from Eurojust in criminal affairs concerning one or several other states illustrates the transnationalisation of national judicial power, which remains entirely limited to the decision of foreign national judges. More precisely, this dynamic concerns the recognition of foreign judicial decisions, through an acceleration of the procedures concerning the exchange of information and people. In the case of the EAW, this transformation is translated by the introduction of the principle of mutual recognition (Mitsilegas 2006). For example, in a Belgian extradition procedure, a judicial decision taken by an Italian court takes on an equivalent legal authority to a decision taken by a Belgian judge. The implementation of new transnational judicial mechanisms signifies a deep transformation of the traditional territories of justice.

To explain how the justice is removed in its spatial dimension and in its relationship to the state, Jacques Commaille shapes the concept of *Detraditionnalisation* to qualify the judicial space's transformations and the relationship between justice and law (Commaille and Kaluszynski 2007). In this perspective, the Europeanisation of criminal law involves a transformation of the relationship between justice and law as a reference element and an instrument of action. The adoption of judicial mechanisms is the outcome of a process of negotiation that is characterised by an operational approach in which the rules of organisation are usually preferred over normative content. At the heart of the mechanisms for making policy changes (Schmidt and Radaelli 2004), the discursive representations and norms promoted by 'policy entrepreneurs' took on a life of their own and became the dominant representations because their promoters had succeeded in acquiring the status of 'European experts' (Madsen 2014; Mégie 2013). To understand this process, we must undertake a specific analysis of the 'policy entrepreneurs' and their ability, as European sector actors, to determine which representations and solutions would define the content of the cooperation instruments (see Part I below).

In this new judicial territory, it will be essential to focus on the practical dimension. The national judges also appear in the European judicial field as holders of 'material power'. Research carried out in the sociology of law sheds light on the importance of judges in the construction and development of 'the legal' at the European level (Schepel 2005; Vauchez 2008). It is usually assumed that the symbolic use of 'the legal' is still the prerogative of governments and legislators. However, judges are pivotal to a large extent to its technical dimension as operators. This aspect can be seen in cooperation mechanisms such as the Eurojust unit. Eurojust's representatives have admitted that their institutions can endure and produce tangible outcomes only if national judges resort to it. Beyond such legal mechanisms, the most important issue remains the level of mutual confidence between the national judicial authorities (see Part II below).

I. Transnational circulation of actors and expertise in criminal law

To understand the movement of displacing and replacing the criminal law within the European space, it is essential first to analyse the process of policy-making and its actors. Although the national framework had a significant influence in shaping their course of action, a certain degree of social unity existed among the actors within the European criminal law sector, which led them to produce and share a set of beliefs, practices and know-how regarding judicial cooperation. This cognitive approach dominated in the problem stream owing to the position of the actors as legitimate 'policy entrepreneurs' (Becker 1985). Later on, it was because these same actors also played a central role in the policy stream that their solutions prevailed during intergovernmental negotiations (Trauner and Servent 2015). In other words, the actors' ability to shape the negotiation agenda and take advantage of policy windows had a tangible effect on the content of the decisions on which Eurojust and the EAW were based. The strength of policy entrepreneurs lay, as one might expect, in their ability to take advantage of various 'policy windows'. Indeed, they seized these 'windows of opportunity' to put instruments of judicial cooperation on the European decision-making agenda, at a time when the projects were still in progress and/or held up for legal and political reasons.

The specialisation of transnational criminal law 'entrepreneurs'

The institutionalisation of the European area of criminal law during the 1990s resulted in a sharp increase in the number of posts in charge of these issues at the national and European levels. The aim of this section is to understand the trajectories and resources used by national entrepreneurs on criminal matters to build up transnational policy capital and thereby develop their knowledge and win recognition as European policy-makers. From this point of view, the ability of certain actors to circulate between the various national and European judicial and political areas proved to be a path of specialisation, socialisation, and above all, indispensable legitimation (Dezalay and Garth 2012; Vauchez and De Witte 2013).

When we compare the career paths of the various interviewees, there appears to have been two main avenues to becoming a specialist in European criminal matters and later on to being appointed to a post of responsibility in the field.[3]

3 We interviewed these actors, some of them several times, between March 2001 and early 2012. While most of the actors were magistrates, the specificity of each national institution in charge of legal questions implies the presence of different types of actors as senior civil servants. In this way, we propose to round out the study of the members of the General Secretariat of the Council of the European Union (GSCEU) and the legal experts who took part in institutionalising European judicial cooperation. By including the representatives of the GSCEU in our analysis, we will also be looking at other jurists working at the national or European level.

Jurists entered the area of judicial cooperation either by occupying a post in an institution with national jurisdiction over these issues or through experience in the field. Typical trajectories took shape, leading civil servants and magistrates to invest in European criminal matters.

In the case of specialisation via the institutional route, the actors began building their expertise within various central political institutions with jurisdiction over criminal matters by helping to formulate criminal justice rules for transnational cooperation and ensuring their legal implementation. In some Member States, these legal experts were not necessarily magistrates. One example was the person in charge of judicial cooperation issues at the Belgian Ministry of Justice, who played an active role in formulating the Eurojust project and the framework decision that created the EAW. The work of these actors in chancelleries or ministries in charge of European issues focused primarily on the technical and diplomatic dimensions of mutual assistance.

The other main avenue to specialisation, which could be described as access via the uses of criminal matters, also deserves some discussion. Indeed, many judges in Member States had no exposure to the area of European judicial cooperation, despite the growing number of offences qualifying as transnational. In practice, these cases represented a minority of the caseload handled by national judicial authorities. The possibility of specialising in the area of mutual assistance in criminal matters depended on the judges' ability to acquire further experience in this type of litigation and build a track record in the field based on the number of cases they handled. Experience in combating 'transnational organized crime' (TOC) phenomena was one of the main common denominators of a large percentage of magistrates who became involved in European cases during the 1990s. The fact that judicial cooperation was defined as a European political challenge through the fight against TOC (Mitsilegas 2001) is certainly linked to this process of redeployment. Finally, the institutionalisation of systems of cooperation such as the Schengen magistrates or the European Judicial Network (EJN) in the early 1990s meant that certain magistrates were constantly working on European mutual assistance procedures.

Certain types of experience enabled these actors to stake out positions for themselves in European law and turn the field into a fully-fledged specialty, but not all of them participated to the same extent in developing systems of cooperation. Their diverse national origins and career paths made them a heterogeneous group. Understanding this dimension brings us directly back to the problem of legitimacy and the reasons why some of them succeeded in establishing their authority as 'policy entrepreneurs' in a rapidly evolving area of European policy. The organisational changes that took place in national and European administrations beginning in the mid-1990s enhanced the institutional and symbolic value of a European specialisation in the area of criminal justice (Roussel 2003). To assert their authority on European issues, experts in judicial cooperation had to marshal certain resources specific to this area that would give weight later on to their proposals during negotiations. The variety of these resources, owing to their individual career paths and the national frameworks in which they developed, appears to have been an important factor (Mégie 2013).

In the case of a group as disparate and heterogeneous as the one being discussed, it is difficult to establish a coherent typology of the attributes these individuals acquired in order to be appointed and speak with an authoritative voice in the field of European judicial cooperation. It is therefore relevant to look more specifically at the question of resources by examining why certain actors succeeded in the task of formulating and implementing European criminal policies.

In addition to their personal investment in European legal affairs, the actors needed to develop further professional expertise and significantly transform the know-how they had previously acquired. The jurists who were most successful in making these adjustments were those who had accumulated the widest range of resources to become multi-positioned actors. The hypothesis of multiple positioning, which places these individuals at the intersection of the various fields of national authority through their involvement in different networks, is particularly instructive (Georgakakis and Weisbein 2010). In an area at the crossroads of politics, law and academia, the actors' ability to move easily among various circles allowed them to establish themselves as experts and above all ensure their long-term involvement in the European security field.

Most of the professionals who became key experts on European judicial cooperation in the mid-1990s found ways of combining institutional posts with publishing and/or teaching activities, as well as trade union or political party involvement at the European or national level. This created a closed circle, limiting even further the number of specialists assigned important roles during the process of adopting and implementing the policies behind Eurojust and the EAW. Those who failed to position themselves as multiple actors were eliminated from the game and kept from formulating the rules of cooperation over the long term.

There were pronounced cleavages along national lines. Belonging to a Common Law system was often considered a 'deviation' from the idea of European integration in legal matters. The national dimension no doubt represented the primary dividing line between members of the group. The actors' legal training and culture affected the way they defined themselves. Another distinction was also promoted by the actors to confirm their own legitimacy. Initial learning experiences influenced the way these professionals defined themselves and validated their approach to judicial cooperation by determining the resources they could engage and, later on, some of their empirical training. Being able to highlight institutional or operational knowledge lent legitimacy to the actions and position of the individuals we encountered.

Legal professionals who began their specialisation by handling Europe-wide judicial cases claimed their knowledge of the field as a fundamental component of their expertise. From this perspective, they defined their added value as the ability to combine practical experience with technical knowledge. In seeking legitimacy, the actors therefore called attention to their 'practical' and/or 'policy' skills, depending on their position and work.

Thus, the community of legal professionals involved in European judicial cooperation starting in the mid-1990s defined and positioned themselves on the basis of numerous dividing lines concerning nationality, socio-professional position, path to specialisation and level of intervention in public action. At the same time, despite their heterogeneity, the group was shaped by a certain number of shared representations and perceptions, particularly with regard to the issue of the legal and political form of European criminal law cooperation. The social dynamics that traditionally irrigate the European process (Favell and Guiraudon 2011) help to explain the homogeneity of their categories of perceptions and representations, despite numerous divisions and the singularity of their personal trajectories.

Defining and sharing an operational expertise on criminal law cooperation

The first type of shared representation was the jointly held conviction that European cooperation is a political and institutional solution essential to European integration (Scherrer 2009). All the actors we interviewed expressed a variation of this idea, including the belief that cooperation among Member States is the most effective way to combat transnational organised crime. Social representations identifying organised crime and terrorism as transnational threats lie at the core of their discursive logic (Den Boer 2002). Thus, the actors played an essential role in disseminating genuine public policy discourse presenting European judicial cooperation as a fully-fledged political and judicial solution to the problem of transnational organised crime (Beare 2003; Edwards and Gill 2003).

These perceptions and beliefs embodied the dominant, legitimate representations to such an extent that they achieved a sort of autonomy and gained a solid foothold at the centre of the problem and policy streams. The principle of transgovernmental cooperation did not gain general acceptance in the security field until the early 1980s, notably as a result of the first institutional experiments in police cooperation (Bigo 1996). The European criminal law enforcement area was thus developed through a discourse of legitimation that, from 2001, made the prevention of 'transnational organized crime' and of 'international terrorism' the principal political and judicial challenge of the EU. Imposing this narrative of public policy fundamentally altered the configuration and balance of the European penal system (Guild and Geyer 2008). Intergovernmental negotiations were henceforth oriented towards introducing systems that emphasised arrest and punishment, at the expense of the legal aspects of stable criminal procedures. At the same time, the actors we are studying also view stronger judicial cooperation as vital to the legitimacy of the European security sector and to supervise police force action.

In another register, these legal professionals all have what they describe as shared experience. Seeing themselves as 'inventors' of European cooperation in the 1990s is essential to the way the magistrates and senior civil servants define their approach to European cooperation, both individually and collectively. In their view, they built up a set of specific skills at the European level by learning different rules from the ones inculcated during their initial training. They all claimed to value 'interpersonal skills', 'diplomatic imperatives' and the ability to 'go beyond national practices'. In their opinion, this shared 'technocratic mentality' (Radaelli and O'Connor 2009) enabled them to stand out clearly from the actors who remained at the national level.

Finally, the members of this group define themselves collectively as intermediaries, at the intersection of national legal interaction and transnational processes. Closely linked to this common definition of their role, the magistrates and senior civil servants share and advocate a method that they themselves describe as 'pragmatic'. This approach, which they present as the 'European method', nevertheless differs from a European Union method because it does not require prior integration of judicial authorities at the EU level. In this type of configuration, national authorities remain the principal decision-makers. As a result, diplomatic and political experience is viewed as a fundamental asset. The example of Schengen is regularly invoked as a reference to support this view. It is therefore no coincidence that some of the senior civil servants and magistrates who contributed to the Schengen accords also intervened in the cognitive and legal construction of instruments of judicial cooperation such as Eurojust and the EAW. Thus, the social dynamics underlying the Schengen accords, analysed by Virginie Guiraudon (2003), also influenced the way the European judicial system was set up. The rejection of recommendations in favour of a European prosecutor formulated by the Corpus Juris movement and the Geneva Appeal reflects the same thinking.

This tendency to encourage an operational view of judicial cooperation was at the heart of European policy-making. It had a concrete effect on how the two main instruments of mutual assistance – Eurojust and the EAW – were formulated.

II. The pratices of the European criminal law: the Eurojust unit

The real mechanisms of cooperation as the recognition of foreign judicial decisions, the implementation of the Joint Investigations Team, or the procedures to accelerate the exchange of informations, introduce new practices for the European and also national criminal law authorities. By placing the tangible circumstances of the day-to-day cooperation at the core of our analysis, we can examine the consequences of this transnational extension of national criminal law. In this new legal territory, how do the national judges consider these new instruments to investigate at the transnational level? What sort of resistance and constraints do their dissemination efforts encounter from a legal and social standpoint. For this perspective, we focus our discussion on the Eurojust case. Eurojust, set up in 2002, is the first European agency devoted exclusively to judicial cooperation. It is a multilateral organisation with a Prosecutor-Magistrate appointed from the legal system of each EU Member State; together, they are charged with promoting cooperation among the national jurisdictions of the European Union. From an institutional point of view, the main purpose of the agency is to cement its position as an essential actor in European cooperation between national as well as supranational bodies.

How Eurojust judges cope with national judicial cultures

National judicial authorities are the only ones that can refer cases and trigger transnational criminal investigations in a binding way. As a result, the European unit Eurojust appears above all as a 'service provider'[4] for the national authorities. Relations with national jurisdictions therefore have a direct impact on the number of cases handled by Eurojust and on the likelihood of seeing the agency become established as an essential link in judicial cooperation. Eurojust members are the first to admit that the unit cannot become sustainable and produce results unless national judges refer cases and appeal to it. Yet, despite a steady increase in the volume of cases handled since 2002,[5] the attitude of the unit itself is relatively pessimistic: 'Some Member States send us fewer cases than we might expect and even in jurisdictions that regularly appeal to Eurojust, many cases have been handled without its cooperation, even though it would, without a shadow of a doubt, contribute added value' (Eurojust Report 2005: 68). Outside the official discourse, considerable uncertainty seems to predominate in relations between Eurojust and the national authorities, due in particular to resistance on the part of national judges. In interviews with French, Belgian, Dutch and Italian judges exercising their judicial power at the national level,[6] we learned that a majority consider themselves 'far removed' from European criminal issues because none of the cases they are given has a European dimension. Realistically, transnational cases are relatively rare. Along with this primary explanation related to the nature of the offences, other factors account for the resistance encountered at the national level.

Undoubtedly, the primary factor lies in the national judges' knowledge of the other European judicial systems. The difficulty arises from the point of view of judicial technique as well as linguistic competence. These knowledge-related issues are not specific to the Eurojust unit but concern the entire area of European cooperation in security matters. We shall see how these questions concretely influence the everyday work of Eurojust when we examine the technical tools of cooperation produced by the unit.

The second type of determining factor is of a structural nature. National judges frequently consider European procedures complex and time-consuming. In the

4 Interview with a Eurojust prosecutor-magistrate, June 2005.

5 In 2011, Eurojust recorded 1,441 cases.

6 The aim of such interviews is to see how the Eurojust unit is perceived by the judges at the national level who are specialised in this type of litigation.

case of France, for example, judges often hesitate to mobilise instruments of cooperation such as Eurojust, because, in their view, they do not always meet the efficiency requirements imposed by the national system that is increasingly focused on streamlined productivity. The need to hear and try cases as quickly as possible often prompts them to avoid taking the Eurojust framework into consideration. Another judge summed up the increasingly prevalent trend in national judicial cabinets: 'Taking the European dimension into account requires competence and time. It demands an investment that is not always feasible given the number of cases we have to handle and the means available to us.'[7] Some refusals may also stem from judicial practices and customs: 'Judges still feel strongly about their independence. Most of us are used to handling our cases on our own.'[8] Sharing a judicial investigation with another judge – and what is more a foreigner – is often perceived as a loss of power and authority over how the procedure is conducted.

Faced with these multiple constraints, Eurojust focuses much of its action on national judicial authorities. This approach, in line with its strategy of legitimation, has represented an essential part of the activity of unit members since 2002. The aim is to raise awareness among national judges about the advantages of the unit, which forces Eurojust members to emphasise their successes. The points of resistance we mentioned earlier emerge front and centre in the discourse of Eurojust members: 'We have to explain all the advantages and say we can help them if they are not very familiar with the law of the other country or if they don't speak the language. We also have to tell them we can facilitate their work and therefore save them time, etc.'[9] Even now, one of primary purposes of taking part in national professional training and conferences, as well as drafting informative reports, is to broaden awareness of the benefits of working with Eurojust.

While resistance to cooperation is found mainly on the side of the national authorities, it should be noted that Eurojust members show little inclination to engage in autonomous action without the consent of the national level. The fact that Articles 6 and 7 of the framework decision of 2002 are almost never invoked demonstrates their reluctance. These articles authorise Eurojust to make an official request for case submission when the national authorities are unwilling to do so. Only two such referral requests have ever been issued. The College's official position on this point is revealing: 'The national members are reluctant to act against the will of the national authorities. They view having to present an official request in accordance with Articles 6 and 7 as a loss of prestige [...]. Furthermore, to a certain extent, the national members feel and act more like ambassadors of their national authorities than partisans of the idea of cross-border cooperation in criminal cases' (Eurojust Report 2005: 111). In fact, despite the non-binding character of referral requests, national members seem hesitant to use

7 Interview with a Dutch judge, February 2003.
8 Interview with a member of Eurojust, February 2004.
9 Interview with a member of Eurojust, February 2003.

such a procedure for fear of generating conflict with the national authorities of their own countries, which might view it as a violation of their independence. In other words, for the members of Eurojust, constantly using such prerogatives could become an obstacle to awareness-raising actions targeted at colleagues at the national level. In such situations, they show a clear preference for an informal, personal approach to establish a relationship of trust.

Finally, in some cases, even when cooperation exists between Eurojust and national judges, there is still uncertainty as to the balance of legal power between them. Due to its prerogatives, the European unit may intervene in certain procedures to settle conflicts of jurisdiction between national authorities. In such cases, the agency tends to focus on achieving maximum efficiency in order to consolidate its own position. Indeed, these cases are of crucial importance for Eurojust to demonstrate its 'usefulness' and hence its legitimacy in handling issues such as terrorism or compensation for the Erika oil spill. In areas as sensitive as terrorism, euthanasia, drug trafficking and racism, the failure to harmonise the designation of offences and penalties at the European level can result in disagreements over the proper course of legal action and problems adapting national judicial frameworks to each other and determining how they should be used. Given the diversity of European criminal law systems, the choice of the jurisdiction, and hence of the Member State, could seriously affect the way an offence is defined and the type of legal proceedings and sentencing of the person involved.

Thus, a considerable amount of uncertainty from an operational and legal standpoint weighs on the relationship between Eurojust and national jurisdictions. The search for legitimacy in the eyes of national judges has consequently become the core issue for Eurojust members. In view of their limited judicial powers, Eurojust members have turned to other resources to gain recognition as 'credible' and 'indispensible' partners. Instead of a common judicial culture, they have sought to disseminate technical tools of cooperation to facilitate the work of their national counterparts. This strategic choice, sometimes presented as a default option, brings us back to issues of operational cooperation, which can be quite complex.

Managing operational cooperation in criminal matters

The question of arriving at a common set of European judicial principles takes very concrete form in the handling of procedures, for example letters of request, or extradition requests using an EAW (Mégie 2010). Many national and Eurojust judges emphasise the importance of practical experience: 'The field is where we learn the rules and how to use them effectively'.[10]

Judges acquire field knowledge through hands-on experience with cooperation and its techniques. Differences between national procedures and judicial traditions

10 Interview with a French judge working in the area of judicial cooperation, 2013.

sometimes complicate this learning process. To avoid having their requests rejected, judges have to obtain exact information on the many particular features of the national judicial systems. The knowledge required to issue a request for mutual assistance appears to be highly specific. A request for cooperation can be seriously complicated and the likelihood of its validation compromised by ignorance of prescribed time limits, a problem with the translation of the offence or failure to observe due process.

Eurojust members regularly mention extradition and search procedures in this regard. In the case of the EAW, certain requests have been refused – or more exactly dismissed – for failing to meet formal requirements. Depending on the type of mistake, some forms have nevertheless been validated, causing problems later on in the case of an appeal before a legal authority. Even though they were duly recorded, certain requests for extradition were subsequently threatened with possible annulment due to non-compliance with formal rules. For this reason, a tool known as 'Spanish datasheets' was introduced in Eurojust. The so-called Spanish datasheets outline the organisation and procedures of the main national legal systems, which may be idiosyncratic in relation to the national cultures of the other European judges. The datasheets, distributed by Eurojust, reflect the unit's desire to demonstrate its operational virtues. Through these technical tools, Eurojust aims to make knowledge of the many judicial cultures of the Member States readily available. Yet such aids alone cannot ensure harmonised application of principles and procedures in criminal matters. Some principles mean quite different things according to the national culture and judicial system. The examples most frequently mentioned by the judges we interviewed include presumption of innocence, the right to a fair hearing, wiretapping procedures and the rules governing delivery of a search warrant. A search warrant request drafted by French authorities may be refused by British or Spanish authorities if the judicial qualification of the French authorities fails to take into account differences between the legal systems regarding motivation and interpretation. The judges also mentioned differences in the use of undercover agents or in DNA sample procedures.

The diplomatic and judicial relations between Member States can also help to explain how judicial authorities manage extradition requests in practice. Distant diplomatic relations between certain Member States may adversely affect cooperation between their judicial authorities in extradition matters, particularly in areas or cases considered especially sensitive, such as terrorism.

This type of operational deadlock offers Eurojust an opportunity to enhance its role. The agency seeks to provide technical solutions to national authorities faced with legal disparities, which can have very real repercussions on the day-to-day management of criminal cases. Nevertheless, the national authorities must first refer the matter to Eurojust, whereupon it will organise and fund coordination meetings. In these instances, the unit aims to provide concrete coordination of cooperation procedures and assignments. This is precisely what happened at several meetings organised by Eurojust to facilitate the transmission of evidence between European authorities. In one case, mentioned in the 2014 Eurojust report, evidence obtained from wiretapping had been classified as confidential due to poor translation and the laws of one of the Member States involved, making it impossible to transmit the evidence. Under such circumstances, the Eurojust judges look for another way to describe the surveillance so that it can be legally transmitted. The unit widely highlights this type of intervention to demonstrate its relevance.

Eurojust is therefore viewed as a resource by certain national authorities. For example, due to the laws governing wiretapping in the United Kingdom, the British authorities regularly call upon Eurojust to ask their European counterparts to conduct surveillance. The objective here is to be able to gather information by taking advantage of differences in telephone interception procedures. Using Eurojust as a resource can also benefit national authorities from a financial standpoint, particularly via the system of joint investigation teams and coordination meetings organised at Eurojust headquarters.

Conclusion

The adoption of an operational view of European judicial cooperation must therefore be understood partly as the product of the European specialisation of certain legal professionals who became acknowledged policy experts through the circulation between multiple institutional positions. Their shared culture of compromise oriented towards an operational approach of criminal law explains how and why, in a context dominated by security issues, European policy-making in judicial matters adhered to a vision focused exclusively, at the beginning, on procedural cooperation rather than on harmonising criminal law at the European level. These policy experts played an important role at the heart of the European institutional game, managing the policy agenda as well as writing about and promoting solutions for public action. Their impact symbolises, moreover, at this period of Europeanisation, the centrality of executive authorities in producing European criminal standards as opposed to legislative and judicial authorities.

Concerning more precisely the criminal law practices in this new judicial territory, the institutional and practical relations between Eurojust and national judges are essentials. The national judges also appear in the European judicial field as holders of 'material power'. Research carried out in sociology of law sheds light on the importance of judges in the construction and the development of 'the legal' at the European level. We have shown this dimension throughout the case of the Eurojust unit and its operational practices. It has been admitted by Eurojust's representatives that their institution can only become perennial and produce tangible outcomes provided national judges resort to it. Hence the standpoints of the national professionals vary between learning and resisting. Along with the obstacles related to cognitive issues (language, knowledge of foreign legal systems, etc.), structural factors also seem to be crucial in the analysis of the logics of resistance within this new spatial territory of criminal law.

References

Beare, Margaret E., *Critical Reflections on Transnational Organized Crime, Money Laundering and Corruption* (Toronto: University of Toronto Press, 2003).

Becker, Howard, *Outsiders* (Paris: éditions Métailié, 1985).

Bigo, Didier, *Polices en Réseaux: L'expérience Européenne* (Paris: Presses de la Fondation Nationale des Sciences Politiques, 1996).

Bigo, Didier, Philippe Bonditti, Laurent Bonelli, Dario Chi, Antoine Mégie, and Christian Olsso, *The Field of the EU Internal Security Agencies* (Paris: L'Harmattan, 2007).

Commaille, Jacques, and Martine Kaluszynski (eds.), *La Fonction Politique de la Justice* (Paris: La Découverte, 2007).

Den Boer, Monica, *Organised Crime: A Catalyst in the Europeanisation of National Police and Prosecution Agencies?* (Maastricht: European Institute of Public Administration, 2002).

Dezalay, Yves, and Bryant Garth (eds.), *Lawyers and the Construction of Transnational Justice* (Abingdon: Routledge, 2013).

Edwards, Adam, and Peter Gill (eds.), *Transnational Organised Crime: Perspectives on Global Security* (London: Routledge, 2004).

Eurojust Report, 'Criminal Justice Across Borders', Annual Report, 2005.

Favell, Adrian, and Virginie Guiraudon (eds.), *Sociology of the European Union* (London: Palgrave Macmillan, 2011).

Georgakakis, Didier, and Julien Weisbein, 'From Above and From Below: A Political Sociology of European Actors' *Comparative European Politics* 8 (1) (2010): 93–109.

Guild, Elspeth, and Florian Geyer, *Liberty vs Security? Police and Judicial Cooperation in the European Union* (Farnham: Asghate, 2008).

Guiraudon, Virginie, 'The Constitution of a European Immigration Policy Domain: A Political Sociology Approach' *Journal of European Public Policy* 10 (2) (2003): 263–282.

Madsen, Mikael R., 'The International Judiciary as Transnational Power Elite' *International Political Sociology* 8 (3) (2014): 332–334.

Mégie, Antoine, 'Behind the Development of European Union Authority in Criminal Matters: A Sociology of Legal Experts in EU Policymaking' *Journal of European Public Policy* 21 (2) (2013): 230–247.

Mégie, Antoine, 'L'adoption du mandat d'arrêt Européen: D'une instrumentalisation de l'agenda politique à une expertise operationnelle de l'entraide pénale' *Cahiers Européens de Sciences Po* 5 (2010): 1–36.

Mégie, Antoine, 'Arrêter et Juger en Europe: Genèse, Luttes et Enjeux de la Coopération Pénale' *Cultures et Conflits* 62 (2006): 11–41.

Mitsilegas, Valsamis, 'Defining Organised Crime in the EU' *European Law Review* 26 (2001): 565–581.

Mitsilegas, Valsamis, 'The Constitutional Implications of Mutual Recognition in Criminal Matters in the EU' *Common Market Law Review* 43 (2006): 1277–1311.

Radaelli, Claudio M., and Karl O'Connor, 'How Bureaucratic Elites Imagine Europe: Towards Convergence of Governance Beliefs?' *Journal of European Public Policy* 16 (7) (2009): 971–989.

Roussel, Violaine, 'Les Magistrats Français, des Cause Lawyers Malgré Eux?' *Politix* 16 (62) (2003): 93–113.

Schepel, Harm, 'Professorenrecht?' *Critique Internationale* 1 (2005): 147–158.

Scherrer, Amandine, *G8 Against Transnational Organized Crime* (Farnham: Ashgate, 2009).

Schmidt, Vivien A., and Claudio M. Radaelli, 'Policy Change and Discourse in Europe: Conceptual and Methodological Issues' *West European Politics* 27 (2) (2004): 183–210.

Trauner, Florian, and Ariadna Ripoll Servent, *Policy Change in the Area of Freedom, Security* (London and New York: Routledge, 2015).

Vauchez, Antoine, 'The Force of a Weak Field: Law and Lawyers in the Government of the European Union (for a renewed research agenda)' *International Political Sociology* 2 (2) (2008): 128–144.

Vauchez, Antoine, and Bruno De Witte (eds.), *Lawyering Europe. European Law as a Transnational Social Field* (Oxford: Hart, 2013).

Chapter 3

The transformation of legal ideas

The globalization and politicization of transitional justice in the Middle East

Jamie Rowen

I. Introduction

Over the past two decades, transitional justice has become ubiquitous in scholarly, policy-making and advocacy circles. The term 'transitional justice' originated as a way to describe the political compromises forged in the South American and Eastern European political transitions, where authoritarian regimes fell and new democratic leaders sought to consolidate their power. The idea is an outgrowth of the effort to promote international criminal law but it is distinct in that transitional justice is part discourse, identifiable with phrases such as truth and reconciliation, part prescriptive, with goals that extend beyond retributive justice, and part descriptive, referring to a range of interventions that transitional justice proponents hope will ensure accountability, improve survivor well-being, and prevent future violence (Subotić 2009).

Scholars now suggest that transitional justice has 'globalized' as policy-makers around the world create tribunals, truth commissions, reparations programs, and other interventions associated with the idea (Teitel 2014). Importantly, whereas 'transitional justice' was coined to describe countries that were emerging from authoritarian regimes or brutal violence, scholars, policy-makers and advocates now use it to prescribe solutions for countries that are not transitioning to democracy, are not undergoing an identifiable regime change, and are not free from destabilizing violence (Kritz 1995; Teitel 2008).

For those interested in establishing and legitimatizing transitional justice as a field, discipline, or even as a theoretical and practical idea for advocacy, the expansion of transitional justice discourse into countries that are in the midst of conflict should give pause. The globalization of transitional justice, particularly into countries with destabilizing violence, may undermine the goals of those who draw on the idea in order to stop, prevent, or redress mass violence.

To explain why it is important to be wary of drawing on transitional justice to prescribe solutions for countries in the midst of conflict, this chapter first outlines the transformations in transitional justice as an idea that scholars first drew upon to describe democratic transitions. This section points to early discussions of the 'irreconcilable goals' of transitional justice scholarship, which describe the contradictory goals, values and memories inherent in political transitions (Leebaw 2008). Drawing on transitional justice to describe and prescribe solutions in countries that are not undergoing regime change means that these irreconcilable goals have become even harder to address.

The next sections describe the circulation of transitional justice discourse to the Middle East. The analysis focuses on how different actors, including scholars, policy-makers, and advocates have drawn on the idea to explain both the need for interventions, and interventions that have already been created, in Afghanistan and Iraq. The fourth section focuses on Syria, where there is ongoing, destabilizing violence. This case reveals that promoting the idea of transitional justice to countries in ongoing conflict assumes that there is a transition towards democratic rule, whereby legal institutions will function to punish past abuses. Simply put, describing countries as places in need of transitional justice can misrepresent the nature of the conflict and its resolution. Without paying attention to the growing number of irreconcilable goals of promoting transitional justice when used to describe countries in the midst of destabilizing violence, those who promote the idea and its associated interventions may find themselves contributing to conflict dynamics rather than contributing their resolution.

The concluding section of the chapter points to future directions for research on the so-called globalization of transitional justice. It suggests that, rather than study transitional justice as a given, meaning as an idea that has a shared meaning, scholars would do better to analyze how different actors understand and utilize the idea, and the political and social effects of these usages. A bottom-up analysis would reveal that the globalization of transitional justice may simply reflect how the idea has become a tool of legal politics rather than an idea that can actually meet the needs of individuals in countries that are experiencing destabilizing violence (Massoud 2013).

II. The many meanings of transitional justice

Scholarship on transitional justice ranges from purely normative to purely descriptive, which often masks its political uses. Those who focus on its normative properties refer to it as a theory, discipline, or field (Gready and Robins 2014; De Greiff 2012). Forsythe (2011), for example, suggests that transitional justice reflects the academic effort to create a 'principled approach' to justice during political transition (85). Normatively-minded scholars debate what these principles are, and often focus on the importance of retributive justice, creating an accurate record of violence, compensating victims, and other policy goals. Scholars, policy-makers, and advocates often characterize transitional justice as 'victim-centered', in order to contrast transitional justice with international criminal justice, which focuses on perpetrators (Sriram 2013). At the same time, the difference between transitional justice and international criminal justice is not clear, as transitional justice advocacy has professionalized in a way that leads to increasing the creation of templates of 'best practices' that often emphasize the creation of criminal tribunals (Subotić 2012).

As transitional justice circulates, understandings of the idea have shifted. Teitel, who claims to have coined the idea in the 1990s, argues that the ongoing circulation of transitional justice reveals that the idea has 'globalized' because of its utility in helping address pressing legal and political issues in political transition (Teitel 2014). However, the assertion that transitional justice has globalized masks the fact that this globalization is uneven, both in theory and in practice. Understandings of transitional justice in Colombia, where there is an ongoing armed conflict, are distinct from understandings of transitional justice in Canada, where there is a democratic regime. In both places, scholars, policy-makers, and advocates have drawn on the idea to explain the utility of particular interventions, namely truth commissions. Pursuing transitional justice in Colombia, for obvious reasons, is very different from pursuing transitional justice in Canada.

Because the idea is often used descriptively, studies of transitional justice have broadened understandings of the idea away from its origins in democratic transitions in order to apply the idea to countries that have created interventions such as truth commissions, regardless of the political contexts. In writing about the application of transitional justice in settler societies such as Australia and New Zealand, Winter (2013) has suggested that transitional justice is better understood as a way to describe 'radical changes to legitimating regime' (224). By engaging with scholarship on post-colonialism, conflict resolution and peacebuilding, other studies on transitional justice try to bridge the divides between broader ideas about conflict resolution and scholarship that focuses on law as a tool for social and political change (Balint et al. 2014; Gready and Robins 2014; Laplante 2008). This new line of scholarship tries to explain how a truth commission or tribunal might redress historic injustices, further expanding the notion of transition in the study of transitional justice.

While useful as a way to think about the various meanings of justice, scholars who analyze countries that are not in transition as cases of transitional justice often enter a circular argument. First, they argue that policy-makers should create, implement or apply legal interventions to deal with the conflict. Alternatively, they argue that the presence of one of these interventions reveals that a political transition is underway. Moreover, in uncritically broadening understandings of transitional justice, scholars overlook how both the idea and the associated interventions become part of domestic legal and political bargains, whether or not the country is willing or even capable of ensuring democratic social and political change (Rowen 2017). The idea of transitional justice, and the mechanisms it describes, can reinforce a problematic, liberal assumption of individual agency and a linear narrative of progressive social and political change (Bueno-Hansen 2010; Koskenniemi 2011). In other words, the 'principled justice' underlying transitional justice scholarship is predicated on western, liberal models of democratic social and political policies, which is a very specific notion of justice, useful in very specific contexts.

Leebaw (2008), for one, suggests that these dilemmas reflect the 'irreconcilable goals' of transitional justice. Her descriptions of these irreconcilable goals reflect political challenges in the 1990s and early 2000s, where debates about the trade-offs between truth-seeking, judicial accountability, and other justice-related goals remained at the forefront of scholarly discussions (Zalaquett 1994; De Brito et al. 2001; Roht-Arriaza 2006). Leebaw notes that this assumption of a linear, progressive path helps 'reinforce approval of political negotiations and, perhaps, reinforce faith in state law' (2008, 117). Her main worry is that the apolitical discourse of transitional justice can conceal the nature of political negotiations (Leebaw 2008, 95). Legal interventions such as tribunals and truth commissions can empower victims, but they can also cover up the nature of violence, particularly state-sponsored violence (Leebaw 2008, 97). Simply put, political transitions reflect political disputes, not legal disputes, and legalistic discourse related to justice can mask the goals, values, and practices will have to take precedence in order to ensure a resolution (Leebaw 2008, 117).

These irreconcilable goals have taken on new dimensions as the idea gets applied to new settings, and new types of political conflict. By looking at transitional justice 'in practice', or how it is promoted and appropriated in places that are not only politically unstable but where there is ongoing violence, one can see that the globalization of transitional justice presents a moral quandary. In such fraught contexts, drawing on the idea of transitional justice is, at best, a misnomer and, at worst, can be appropriated in ways that mask the political trade-offs that are necessary to ensure accountability, improve survivor well-being, and prevent future violence.

III. The politics of transitional justice in unstable transitions

Afghanistan

Few scholars examine transitional justice in Afghanistan because, despite the efforts of policy-makers and advocates, there have not been any international tribunals, national tribunals, truth commissions or other national-scale interventions to redress the violence. At the same time, the idea circulated among scholars, policy-makers, and advocates in the wake of the 2002 overthrow of the Taliban. The appropriation and promotion of transitional justice in Afghanistan reflects how the globalization of the idea has created a situation in which political actors feel they need to draw on transitional justice, and promote its associated interventions, even when their utility is questionable.

Soon after the Taliban fell, the new government began discussing the idea of transitional justice and which interventions might be useful in the country. A UN official who participated in the 2001 Bonn agreement, which established the interim government, wrote about the furor that arose over negotiations about an amnesty clause and how to address the violence perpetrated by all groups throughout the years of armed struggle (Rubin 2003). The leaders who took over after the Taliban's fall had to weigh the fact that the US was implicated in many of the past and ongoing abuses. Some feared that transitional justice interventions would destabilize the government, stabilize the government as an unjust order, and return Afghanistan to a more 'unjust disorder' (Rubin 2003).

Despite these concerns, these leaders agreed to the creation of a Human Rights Commission with an understanding that there would be no amnesties for war crimes or crimes against humanity. Transitional justice, for them, meant that there had to be some form of judicial accountability. This decree sparked conflict among participants, as they had different perspectives on the utility of criminal accountability for the conflict's violence. Some participants, especially those who had taken part in direct hostilities, worried that they would ultimately be targeted by criminal justice policies.

While the threat of criminal accountability would raise alarm bells for any new regime, the concerns about transitional justice had as much to do with questions over how the interventions would represent the war's violence as it did with who should be punished. At the opposite end of the legal spectrum, memorialization became a contentious issue. President Karzai could not even agree to create a museum on the mujahideen, as there were many other groups that fought for the country's independence.

Despite these competing needs, the new government was keen on showing the UN, its US allies, and other interested parties that it was concerned with transitional justice. Alex Boraine, then president of the International Center for Transitional Justice (ICTJ), a transnational organization that consults with governments around the world (at the time, it boasted consultations with over 30 countries) about how to implement criminal justice measures, truth-seeking mechanisms, reparations, institutional reforms and memorials, was contracted to help with the Human Rights Commission. His consultation helped the government publish its 'Action Plan for Justice, Reconciliation and Peace in Afghanistan' in 2005. The Action Plan included provisions on symbolic measures, institutional reform, truth-seeking and documentation, as well as reconciliation and strategies for criminal justice, which are all categories for interventions that the ICTJ promoted under its broad banner of transitional justice.

The Action Plan did not go very far. Despite the comprehensive nature of the plan, many Afghans, at least those engaged in national politics, viewed transitional justice as an idea that undermined criminal justice. According to Nadery's (2007) analysis of transitional justice in Afghanistan, one of the few studies on this case, political elites drew on transitional justice with an emphasis on forgiveness and reconciliation, while most Afghans wanted judicial accountability for the violence. When an amnesty bill was passed in 2007, the promise of judicial accountability for war crimes vanished, as did any movement on the Action Plan. A new coalition, called the Afghanistan Transitional Justice Coordination Group, was active in 2010 and 2011, and tried to revive this Action Plan and promote transitional justice interventions. However, its activities were limited by the challenge of organizing with domestic and international NGOs.

With ongoing threats of a Taliban return, there is little to no political will or even capacity to prosecute even a fraction of the massive abuses that have occurred in the past four decades. In addition to the problems with creating a tribunal, a truth commission for Afghanistan would present additional challenges. Within the country, there is no clarity on who started the violence. There are a number of different narratives related to the past 30 years of war, and an 'official' narrative produced by a court or truth commission will likely be unable to change these different perspectives. The mujahideen, who overthrew the Russians, view themselves as freedom fighters, while the Taliban, who came to power in 1994, see themselves as defenders of Islam who toppled a corrupt and violent regime. Moreover, with little communication between the different communities, most people have little idea about what was and is going on in the rest of the country. The country remains divided along ethnic as well as regional lines, and efforts to promote transitional justice before there is any clarity on what the long-term possibilities are for peace and stability in the country could entrench, not bridge, divisions between individuals and groups that need to work alongside one another.

Iraq

Iraq, unlike Afghanistan, actually created a tribunal in order to try leaders of the former regime, specifically Saddam Hussein after he was overthrown in 2003. While the case of Afghanistan highlights the coordination challenges involved in creating transitional justice interventions and the potential problems of doing so, lessons from the Iraq tribunal highlight the dilemmas that can occur when an intervention, particularly a tribunal, is actually implemented.

Over a year before the US invaded Iraq, the Department of State created a Future of Iraq Project with a working group on transitional justice. This group included Iraqis familiar with the context, and worked on how to promote the rule of law in Iraq, and how to initiate judicial reform with the training of judges and lawyers. Ironically, one of its participants, an Iraqi ex-pat living in the United States, suggested that concerns that Iraq would fall into chaos after an invasion were unfounded.[1]

After the invasion, in another example of the lack of foresight within the Bush regime about helping reconstruct post-invasion Iraq, the group's report was never circulated (Bassiouni 2007, 26). After the fall of Iraq, the Transitional Authority considered whether to create an international tribunal based on the United Nations ad hoc tribunals, a hybrid tribunal, as was used in East Timor, or an Iraqi tribunal based on domestic law and run by local actors. The Transitional Authority chose a domestic model, the goal was to allow the Iraqi people more sovereignty

1 Iraq Watch, Working Group on 'Transitional Justice' Meets in Washington, 12 July 2002, accessed 28 May 2016 at http://www.iraqwatch.org/government/US/State/state-workinggroup-071202.htm.

over the course of events and allow for the possibility of a death penalty for Saddam Hussein (Afrin 2008). One of their considerations was that the death penalty would be difficult to enforce for an international tribunal, and the regime's opponents wanted to ensure that a death penalty would be handed down and enforced.

The Iraqi High Tribunal (IHT), originally known as the Iraqi Special Tribunal (IST) was established on 10 December 2003. The IST statute, approved by the Coalition Provisional Authority (CPA), stated that the tribunal would 'try Iraqi nationals or residents of Iraq accused of genocide, crimes against humanity, war crimes or violations of certain Iraqi law'. All members of the IHT including the judges, prosecutors, and lawyers were required to be Iraqi nationals. Non-Iraqi lawyers could only serve as advisors. The IHT had to decide among the multitude of crimes committed by the Hussein regime, which was responsible for an estimated 500,000 deaths between 1968 and 2005. Shia and Kurds were the most victimized, though anyone who was deemed a threat to the regime was also targeted. In addition to those directly victimized, over one million Iraqis lost their lives in the Iran and Kuwait wars (Bassiouni 2005).

The first case facing the tribunal was the Dujali case, in which Saddam and his government were accused of the murder of 148 Shia Muslims in Dujali in 1982. In describing the trial's opening statements, one of the leading proponents of using criminal law to redress mass violence, M. Cherif Bassiouni (2007), explained that the courtroom drama resembled something from a US television show, and was 'wholly alien' to Iraqi society (22). Bassiouni argued that the underlying principle of prosecuting Hussein and his collaborators for their violence was good, but the trials themselves undermined legitimacy, credibility or a legacy that would be beneficial for the Iraq population (Bassiouni 2007, 25) He suggested that a strict adherence to the rule of law would have helped avoid the tribunal's shortcomings. These included egregious violations of Western-style due process, such as Saddam Hussein being denied a defense attorney for the first year of the trial.

Critics of the tribunal suggest that it had to have greater independence from the occupying forces. However, given that Iraq was under occupation when the tribunal was created, calls for greater independence seem far more idealistic than realistic. In writing about this tribunal, Stover et al. (2005) point out how difficult it would be to foster any sense of justice in light of the levels of violence, the multi-ethnic nature of Iraqi identity, the US occupation, questions about who holds political power and who will hold political power, and the fact that security concerns trump all others. During the trial, a British newspaper leaked the names of the judges, and one was killed. There were security threats to Iraqi journalists covering the tribunals as well as Iraqis who wanted to participate in them. Given the problems with due process at the tribunal, the process came to look disturbingly like victor's justice, or vengeance masked in a show trial.

From Bassiouni's perspective, the poor planning and implementation undermined the opportunity for Iraqis to have a sense of justice, feel closure, or believe in rule of law (Bassiouni 2007, 27). Bassiouni's goals may seem far-fetched, as it is unclear how a trial could ever bring closure to a country with such a legacy of violence, or belief in the rule of law when all that Iraqis had known since 1958 was the Hussein regime. However, the globalization of transitional justice contributes to the belief that transitional justice interventions, even tribunals, can and should be implemented in a variety of contexts, including contexts as politically unstable as post-invasion Iraq.

IV. Transitional justice in destabilizing violence

The attempt to implement transitional justice, and the failed experiment in Iraq, provide important insights into the dilemma of promoting transitional justice in Syria, which is arguably more problematic than Iraq because of the geopolitics involving Russia and the US. In fact, looking at the promotion of transitional justice in Syria reveals that there is a new, deeply problematic set of irreconcilable goals in transitional justice advocacy. Promoting the idea can misrepresent the nature of the conflict and its possible solutions. While no one is going to be confused about whether or not a country is experiencing destabilizing violence, promoting transitional justice too soon can divert attention from more pressing concerns, such as stopping the violence.

Beginning in 2011, Syria transitioned from an oppressive yet stable government to a country enmeshed in a full-blown brutal civil war, with massive human rights violations and international crimes. Estimates now put the death toll at half a million individuals; thousands have been detained or disappeared, over 5 million people have fled the country, and millions more are internally displaced. Reports of rape, torture and other violations come from the few journalists who remain in the country. The civil war is ongoing, very few are able to imagine when or how it will end.

In the midst of the ongoing bloodshed, which became more barbaric over time, scholars, policy-makers and advocates became interested in how the idea of transitional justice might help ensure accountability, improve survivor well-being and prevent ongoing and future violence in the country. Early on in the Syrian conflict, these different actors were quick to spread their message about the importance of thinking about what a future government might do in order to redress the violence of the past regime. However, all of these initiatives made a major assumption: Assad would be overthrown or would step down, and they would be able to implement interventions in a post-Assad Syria.

In 2011, advocacy organizations were ambitious, referring to the full package that 'transitional justice' would entail, particularly the prospect of trials against perpetrators of abuse within the Assad regime. In 2012, the United States Institute of Peace formed a project with opposition parties called 'The Day After' to discuss how transitional justice principles might inform the inevitable political transition. The group was explicit about its political affiliation and goal of a post-Assad Syria:

> The Day After project was established to contribute to a successful transition in a post-Assad Syria. We are a group of approximately forty-five Syrians who

> represent the diversity of the opposition and who are leading an independent transition-planning project with the facilitation of USIP, in partnership with the German Institute for International and Security Affairs (SWP).[2]

The group, with the backing of foreign donors, put together a Coordinating Group of Transitional Justice in Syria to discuss the kind of interventions they would implement in post-Assad Syria.[3] In 2014, the Group stated its plans to establish itself as the Syrian Coalition of Transitional Justice.

Others drew on the idea of transitional justice with less explicit policy goals, but still under the assumption of a post-Assad Syria. In 2013, the Syria Justice and Accountability Center contracted a research group to produce a qualitative study of 45 individuals who the researchers claim are representative of different ethnic and religious groups.[4] Predictably, the researchers found that the majority of respondents want both judicial accountability and truth commissions, even though they were unfamiliar with what truth commissions are. They also wanted compensation and above all else, an end to the violence (Charney and Quirk 2013).[5] Of course, one dilemma with such studies is that the ideal of judicial accountability, an accurate historical record, financial and other goals associated with transitional justice are universally appealing. This is why the idea has globalized. However, trade-offs are necessary to ensure these goals, which is why the idea is more idealistic than realistic.

Similarly, the Syrian Center for Political and Strategic Studies (SCPSS) formed a transitional justice working group in 2013 to articulate opportunities for accountability and a clarification of the historical record after Assad steps down. The president of this Center was part of the National Council, an opposition group, and tried to build bridges with the opposition military leaders. In a 2014 meeting between this organization and the head of the Free Syrian army, the military leader emphasized the need for more support, particularly financial, administrative and military, in order to continue to fight not only the Assad regime but the growing Islamic State threat in the north of the country (Ghadban 2014). Ironically, by 2014, the Free Syrian Army no longer existed as a cohesive and effective coalition.

2 The Day After, 'The Day After Project: Supporting a Democratic Transition in Syria Executive Summary' *The Day After*, August 2012, accessed 5 June 2017 at http://thedayafter-sy.org/excutive-summary-2.

3 The Day After Association, 'Statement: Coordinating Group of Transitional Justice Established' *The Syrian Observer*, 28 February 2014, accessed 5 June 2017 at www.ictj.org/news/statement-coordinating-group-transitional-justice-syria-established.

4 The limitation of this study largely has to do with the sampling, which they call a modified snowball sample. This is a convenience sample that cannot be extrapolated to the broader population.

5 Interestingly, this organization utilized the idea of transitional justice in a way that harks back to the early days of transitional justice research and advocacy, referring to transitional justice 'alternatives' to criminal trials.

Until the Islamic State threat became impossible to ignore, Western liberal governments supported opposition forces and hoped they would overcome Assad's forces. At the first Geneva talks, in 2012, various parties believed that there would be a transitional government for Syria. Quickly, however, discussions shifted as the opposition became fragmented and reports of abuses perpetrated by all sides surfaced. At the Geneva II talks, held at the beginning of 2014, divisions remained. Questions about the transition from the Assad regime were central to the negotiations, but the transition no longer seemed inevitable. Iran refused to join the new round because they were predicated on the 2012 Geneva talks, which were predicated on a post-Assad transition. The United States, represented by John Kerry, took a firm stance that a transition is necessary and cannot include Assad (Pearson et al. 2014). Along with opposition forces, representatives from the US put pressure on the UN to exclude Iran from the talks. Without Iran, there could be no agreement.

Even as Islamic State (Daesh) began taking territorial control in Syria, and the conflict took a new turn, elites were still meeting to discuss transitional justice. In March 2014, The Hague Institute for Global Justice worked with Impunity Watch, PAX and HIVOS to bring 30 scholars, advocates, and policy-makers to discuss transitional justice in Syria. They noted, 'The situation in Syria is more intricate than previous conflicts and periods of mass atrocities'.[6] In addition to the complicated nature of the violence, the country has long struggled to manage its diverse citizenry.[7] As the situation deteriorated, scholars, policy-makers, and advocates focused less on specific mechanisms and more on documentation of abuses.

Still, most advocates who talk about transitional justice are assuming that there will be a post-Assad regime, which denies the very clear reality that pro-regime forces are strong, and the inevitable outcome in Syria will be a negotiated settlement. There has never been a discussion of transitional justice from the Assad side of the table, as such language was inherently threatening to his regime. In 2014, Syrian officials refused to participate in any further talks predicated on a transition (Dagher 2014). The Syrian government, pro-government Syrians, and their international backers created a narrative that is focused on fighting terrorism, and emphasized that foreigners are meddling in the internal affairs of Syria. In February 2014, opposition leaders from the National Coalition, the group that helped create the working group on transitional justice, were put on the state's list of

6 See Charlotte Divin, 'Challenges to Transitional Justice in Syria. The Hague Institute Roundtable Series. Facing the Geopolitical Context' *The Hague Institute for Global Justice*, 12 March 2014, accessed 5 June 2017 at www.thehagueinstituteforglobaljustice.org/events/challenge-to-transitional-justice-in-syria-facing-the-geopolitical-context/.

7 Syrian society contains different sects and religions, whereby Sunnis roughly constitute 74 per cent of the population, Alawites make up 12 per cent, Christians 10 per cent and Druze 3 per cent. The rest are Ismailis, Yazidis and a small number of Jewish families.

terrorists and their assets were seized. When asked why the government would put members of the opposition Nation Coalition umbrella group on its terrorism list and freeze their bank accounts, a government delegate said: 'You are trying to terrorize me and you won't succeed … This has nothing to do with the Geneva conference. Whoever refuses to fight terrorism is part of terrorism' (Oweis 2014).

Focusing on transitional justice options may have seemed important at the start of the conflict, when there were high hopes for a quick resolution. However, promoting future tribunals or truth commissions may be more politically palatable than addressing the rapidly growing needs of survivors and other necessary, but more challenging, political interventions (Massoud 2011). Syria provides a striking example of how the globalization of transitional justice may obfuscate political realities and divert attention from the most important goal: to stop the conflict.

V. Legal ideas in practice: rethinking the globalization of transitional justice

The globalization of transitional justice reflects a widely shared hope that, if scholars, policy-makers, and advocates think creatively about what justice entails, they can develop similar solutions for any number of conflicts. However, as this chapter emphasizes, there are problems when actors try to utilize the idea too broadly. Much like promoting human rights in settings where the governments are not responsive to rights-based claim-making, promoting transitional justice can create the false hope that both a transition and justice are possible in countries where there is active, destabilizing violence (Massoud 2011).

Although there are important theoretical gains to be made from conceptualizing the meaning of justice as separate from political contexts, context matters. The problem of promoting law-related ideas such as transitional justice, much like promoting Western models of criminal law in countries without a Western legal tradition, is that these efforts try to separate law and politics. Qualifying the idea of justice with the word 'transitional' simply reinforces this problem because it flattens the distinctions between the types of transitions that governments undergo. While the idea, as currently conceptualized, may be useful in countries that are transitioning towards democratic regimes, the idea seems useless when the transition is towards more violence and political instability.

Through a deeper understanding of the ongoing circulation of transitional justice where there is ongoing conflict, we begin to recognize some of the challenges that face future scholarship, advocacy, and policy-making around the idea. Here, I outline three of these challenges in order to propose a shift in the scholarship on transitional justice towards clarifying how calling the circulation of transitional justice 'globalization' can mask the instrumentalization, and even the politicization, of the idea.

First, if we are to accept that transitional justice has globalized, it is essential to understand what exactly about transitional justice has globalized? Is it simply that the term has replaced the idea of human rights and other, related legal ideas that justify and legitimate Western liberal law and democratic institutions? Is it the increasing prevalence of tribunals, truth commissions and other interventions that scholars describe with the idea of transitional justice? Or, is it simply that professionalized organizations that identify with transitional justice have created a market for themselves by consulting with policy-makers and advocates to promote new interventions?

Second, and related, what exactly is a 'principled approach' to justice in the wake of ongoing, destabilizing violence? The Iraq High Tribunal was certainly not a principled approach to justice. A 'principled approach to justice' may focus on court-based strategies to legitimate state law. However, the 'irreconcilable' goals of transitional justice, which involve the simultaneous critique and reification of state law, are all the more problematic where there is destabilizing violence (Leebaw 2008). In particular, the discourse associated with transitional justice, specifically with words like truth, reconciliation and reparation, have a distinctly undemocratic subtext. This discourse can reinforce pacification and hierarchy (Nader and Grande 2002; Wilson 2001). Actors may appropriate transitional justice discourse in order to gain legitimacy with international elites even if they have no real interest in promoting democratic values.

Third, it remains critical to continue to focus on who promotes transitional justice in different places and, more importantly, how and why they do so (Rowen 2017). In this chapter I suggest that the globalization of transitional justice might better be understood as yet another example of humanitarian politics, whereby actors draw on the idea and promote its associated interventions as a complement to, or even a substitute for, humanitarian relief in places where conflict is ongoing. The dilemma with these usages is that, as Massoud (2013, 209) suggests, the positive effects of promoting legal ideas comes from fulfilling material and symbolic needs. Promoting transitional justice in the absence of a transition, and where it is unlikely that an intervention will provide material and symbolic needs for survivors, may simply serve elites looking for ways to explain and legitimate their work.

Building from this theoretical approach, Winter (2013) suggests that the idea of transition justice, truth commissions, reparations programs, memorials and other approaches should be understood as part of 'transitional politics' in which new governments try to increase their legitimacy. This idea of transitional politics, like humanitarian politics, is useful to examine how governments may utilize the idea in order to redress certain types of violence while leaving other types of violence for the criminal justice system or off the political radar altogether. It is also crucial to continue to examine the international and domestic advocates who promote transitional justice, and how this advocacy is affecting countries dealing with past and ongoing violence. Without looking at who appropriates and adopts the idea, and for what ends, scholars simply reinforce the uncritical assertion that transitional justice has globalized because governments actually want to redress atrocities.

In conclusion, looking at the appropriation of transitional justice in countries where there is destabilizing violence reveals a concurrent globalization, instrumentalization, and even politicization of transitional justice. Legal ideas such as transitional justice are a tool that a variety of actors, including policy-makers, advocates, and even rebels, can use to ensure their goals and strategies. The idea allows different actors to tell themselves and others a story they want to tell about their own motivations.

Moreover, it is important to continue to interrogate what the future of transitional justice will be if actors continue to promote and appropriate it in countries that are enmeshed in violent conflict. The new applications highlight that a linear, progressive notion of transition was never accurate. The core of transitional justice involves policy decisions, not legal decisions, that involve trade-offs between different goals, values and memories. As actors appropriate it and apply it to places where the underlying assumptions about democratic regime change, notably a functioning government, are absent, transitional justice may even become ineffective as a tool of legal politics.

References

Afrin, Zakia (2008) 'Post Conflict Justice in Iraq' *Annual Survey of International & Comparative Law* 14(1): 23–37.

Balint, Jennifer, Julie Evans, and Nesam McMillan (2014) 'Rethinking Transitional Justice, Redressing Indigenous Harm: A New Conceptual Approach' *International Journal of Transitional Justice* 8(2): 194–216.

Bassiouni, M. Cherif (2005) 'Post-Conflict Justice in Iraq: An Appraisal of the Iraq Special Tribunal' *Cornell International Law Journal* 38(2): 328–334.

Bassiouni, M. Cherif and Michael Wahid Hanna (2007) 'Ceding the High Ground: The Iraqi High Criminal Court Statute and the Trial of Saddam Hussein' *Case Western Journal of International Law* 39(1): 21–27.

Baxter, Victoria, Audrey R. Chapman, and Huga Van der Merwe (2009) *Assessing the Impact of Transitional Justice: Challenges for Empirical Research* (Washington: United States Institute of Peace).

Bueno-Hansen, Pascha (2010) 'Engendering Transitional Justice: Reflections on the Case of Peru' *Journal of Peacebuilding & Development* 5(3): 61–74.

Chapman, Audrey R., and Hugo van der Merwe (2008) *Truth and Reconciliation in South Africa: Did the TRC Deliver?* (Philadelphia: University of Pennsylvania Press).

Charney, Craig, and Christine Quirk (2014) 'Introduction – He Who Did Wrong Should Be Accountable: Syrian Perspectives on Transitional Justice' *Syrian Justice and Accountability Centre*, Dec., accessed 5 June 2017 at http://syrianperspectives 2013.pressbooks.com/front-matter/intro/.

Chulov, Martin (2014) 'Syrian rebels begin Homs evacuation' *The Guardian*, 7 May, accessed 5 June 2017 at www.theguardian.com/world/2014/may/07/syrian-rebels-homs-evacuation.

Clarke, Kamari Maxine, and Mark Goodale (2009) *Mirrors of Justice: Law and Power in the Post-Cold War Era* (New York: Cambridge University Press).

Dagher, Sam (2014) 'Syrian Official Casts Doubts on Geneva Talks, Says Assad Won't Go' *Wall Street Journal*, 18 March, accessed 5 June 2017 at http://online.wsj.com/articles/SB10001424052702303287804579447490076879988.

Daly, Erin (2008) 'Truth Skepticism: An Inquiry into the Value of Truth in Times of Transition' *The International Journal of Transitional Justice* 2(1): 23–41.

De Brito, Alexandra Barahona, Carmen Gonzalez Enriquez, and Paloma Aguilar (2001) *The Politics of Memory: Transitional Justice in Democratizing Societies* (Oxford: Oxford University Press).

De Greiff, Pablo (2012) 'Theorizing Transitional Justice' in *Transitional Justice: Nomos Li*, ed., Melissa Williams, Rosemary Nagy, and Jon Elster (New York: NYU Press).

Dudai, Ron, and Hillel Cohen (2010) 'Dealing with the Past When the Truth is Still Present: Civil Society Truth-Seeking Initiatives in the Israeli-Palestinian Conflict' in *Localizing Transitional Justice: Interventions and Priorities after Mass Violence*, ed. Rosalind Shaw and Lars Waldorf (Stanford: Stanford University Press).

Forsythe, David P. (2011) 'Human Rights and Mass Atrocities: Revisiting Transitional Justice' *International Studies Review* 13(1): 85–95.

Gardner, James A. (1980) *Legal Imperialism: American Lawyers and Foreign Aid in Latin America* (Madison: University of Wisconsin Press).

Ghadban, Mojahed (2014) 'Dr. Radwan Ziadeh meets with Head of Supreme Military Council of Free Syrian Army' *Syrian Center for Political and Strategic Studies*, August, accessed 5 June 2017 at scpss.org/en/wpcontent/uploads/2014/09/SCPSS_SEH_Supreme_Military_Council_En.pdf.

Goodale, Mark, and Sally Engle Merry (2007) *The Practice of Human Rights: Tracking Law Between the Global and the Local* (Cambridge: Cambridge University Press).

Gready, Paul, and Simon Robins (2014) 'From Transitional to Transformative Justice: A New Agenda for Practice' *International Journal of Transitional Justice* 8: 339–361.

Hazan, Pierre (2006) *Morocco: Betting on a Truth Commission* (Washington: United States Institute of Peace).

Koskenniemi, Martti (2011) *The Politics of International Law* (Oxford; Portland: Hart).

LaPlante, Lisa J. (2008) 'Transitional Justice and Peace Building: Diagnosing and Addressing the Socioeconomic Roots of Violence through a Human Rights Framework' *The International Journal of Transitional Justice* 2(3): 331–355.

LaPlante, Lisa J., and Kimberley Theidon (2006) 'Transitional Justice in Times of Conflict: Colombia's Ley de Justicia y Paz' *Michigan Journal of International Law* 28(1): 49–107.

Leebaw, Bronwyn Anne (2008) 'The Irreconcilable Goals of Transitional Justice' *Human Rights Quarterly* 30(1): 95–118.

Levitt, Peggy, and Sally Merry (2009) 'Vernacularization on the Ground: Local Uses of Global Women's Rights in Peru, China, India and the United States' *Global Networks* 9(4): 441–461.

Lynch, Dennis O. (1983) 'Hundred Months of Solitude: Myth or Reality in Law and Development?' *Law Social Inquiry* 8(1): 223–239.

Madlingozi, Tshepo (2010) 'On Transitional Justice Entrepreneurs and the Production of Victims' *Journal of Human Rights Practice* 2(2): 208–228.

Massoud, Mark Fathi (2011) 'Do Victims of War Need International Law? Human Rights Education Programs in Authoritarian Sudan' *Law & Society Review* 45(1): 1–32.

— (2013) *Law's Fragile State: Colonial, Authoritiarian, and Humanitarian Legacies in Sudan* (Cambridge: Cambridge University Press).

McCann, Michael (1994) *Rights at Work: Pay Equity Reform and the Politics of Legal Mobilization* (Chicago: University of Chicago).

Miller, Zinaida (2008) 'Effects of Invisibility: In Search of the "Economic" in Transitional Justice' *The International Journal of Transitional Justice* 2(3): 266–291.

Nader, Laura, and Elisabetta Grande (2002) 'Current Illusions and Delusions about Conflict Management – In Africa and Elsewhere' *Law and Social Inquiry* 27(3): 573–591.

Nadery, Ahmad Nader (2007) 'Peace or Justice? Transitional Justice in Afghanistan' *The International Journal of Transitional Justice* 1(1): 173–179.

Nagy, Rosemary L. (2013) 'The Scope and Bounds of Transitional Justice and the Canadian Truth and Reconciliation Commission' *International Journal of Transitional Justice* 7(1): 52–74.

Olsen, Tricia D., Leigh A. Payne, Andrew G. Reiter, and Eric Wiebelhaus-Brahm (2010) 'When Truth Commissions Improve Human Rights' *International Journal of Transitional Justice* 4(3): 457–476.

Oweis, Khaled Yacoub (2014) 'Syria adds opposition peace talks delegates to "terrorist list"' *Reuters*, 15 February, accessed 5 June 2017 at www.reuters.com/article/2014/02/15/us-syria-crisis-blacklist-idUSBREA1E0QI20140215.

Pearson, Michael, Elise Labott, and Saad Abedine (2014) 'Syria defiant at conference; Kerry rules out al-Assad' *CNN*, 22 January, accessed 5 June 2017 at www.cnn.com/2014/01/22/world/europe/syria-geneva-talks/index..

Robins, Simon (2012) 'Transitional Justice as an Elite Discourse: Human Rights Practice Where the Global Meets the Local in Post-Conflict Nepal' *Critical Asian Studies* 44: 3–26.

Roht-Arriaza, Naomi (2006) 'The New Landscape of Transitional Justice' in *Transitional Justice in the Twenty-First Century: Beyond Truth Versus Justice*, ed. Naoemi Roht-Arriaza and Javier Mariezcurrena (Cambridge; New York: Cambridge University Press).

Roman, David, and Susanne Choi Yuk-ping (2005) 'Victims on Transitional Justice: Lessons from the Reparation of Human Rights Abuses in the Czech Republic' *Human Rights Quarterly* 27(2): 392–435.

Rowen, Jamie (2017) *Searching for Truth in the Transitional Justice Movement* (New York: Cambridge University Press).

Rubin, Barnett R. (2003) 'Transitional Justice and Human Rights in Afghanistan' *International Affairs* 79(3): 567–581.

Sriram, Chandra Lekha (2013) *Transitional Justice and Peacebuilding on the Ground: Victims and Ex-combatants* (Abingdon; New York: Routledge).

Stover, Eric, Hanny Megally, and Hania Mufti (2005) 'Bremer's "Gordian Knot": Transitional Justice and the US Occupation of Iraq' *Human Rights Quarterly* 27: 830–857.

Subotić, Jelena (2012) 'The Transformation of International Transitional Justice Advocacy' *International Journal of Transitional Justice* 6(1): 106–125.

Teitel, Ruti (2008) 'Editorial Note-Transitional Justice Globalized' *The International Journal of Transitional Justice* 2(1): 1–4.

— (2014) *Globalizing Transitional Justice: Contemporary Essays* (New York: Oxford University Press).

— (2011) *Humanity's Law* (New York: Oxford University Press).

Theidon, Kimberly (2009) 'Editorial Note' *International Journal of Transitional Justice* 3(3): 295–300.

Trubek, David M., and Marc Galanter (1974) 'Scholars in Self-Estrangement: Some Reflections on the Crisis in Law and Development Studies in the United States' *Wisconsin Law Review* 1(4): 1062–1103.

Valji, Nahla (2007) *Gender Justice and Reconciliation* (Berlin: Friedrich-Ebert-Stiftung).

Van Antwerpen, Jonathan (2008) 'Moral Globalization and Discursive Struggle: Reconciliation, Transitional Justice, and Cosmopolitan Discourse' in *Globalization, Philanthropy, and Civil Society: Projecting Institutional Logics Abroad*, ed. David C. Hammack and Steven Heydemann (Bloomington, IN: Indiana University Press) 95–135.

Wilson, Richard (2001) *The Politics of Truth and Reconciliation in South Africa* (Cambridge; New York: Cambridge University Press).

Winter, Stephen (2013) 'Towards a Unified Theory of Transitional Justice' *International Journal of Transitional Justice* 7(2): 224–244.

Zalaquett, José (1994) 'Balancing Ethical Imperatives and Political Constraints: The Dilemmas of New Democracies Facing Past Human Rights Violations' *Hastings Law Journal* 43(6): 1425–1438.

Chapter 4

The global governance of transnational crime

Implications for justice and the rule of law

Valsamis Mitsilegas

I. Introduction

The past three decades have witnessed the adoption at the global and regional level of a plethora of regulatory and legislative measures aimed at countering transnational crime. Rather than forming a homogeneous body of norms, these measures have been adopted in a variety of forms and fora. The aim of this chapter is to provide a comprehensive typology of norm-making in transnational criminal law, by focusing on both the adoption of norms at the global level and on issues of implementation and compliance. Transnational criminal law is to be distinguished from international criminal law in this context in involving the production of norms which must be implemented by – and be enforced in – *domestic* criminal justice systems, being transformed in this process largely into domestic criminal law rules. When implemented in domestic systems, transnational criminal law norms have thus a significant impact on the relationship between the individual and the state and the protection of human rights at the domestic level. The chapter will look in particular at how the making of transnational criminal law has shifted from traditional forms of international law-making – namely multilateral international treaties – to other forms of governance including regionalism, 'soft' or 'informal' law and 'global administrative law'. The next sections will thus examine the global governance of transnational crime under these headings. The interaction and interrelationship between these forms of governance in the development of a multi-level paradigm of global governance of transnational crime will be highlighted and the implications of this paradigm on justice and the rule of law will be explored. Questions on justice will focus on issues of interstate justice but also the impact of transnational criminal law on domestic criminal justice systems. Questions on the rule of law will focus primarily on the process of global norm-making, and in particular democracy, transparency and accountability, but will also explore questions of rule of law such as judicial review, in addressing the changing paradigm of international law having a direct impact on individuals. A number of parallel and innovative processes of internationalisation and globalisation will be highlighted in this context and their impact on law-making in a complex global arena will be explored.

II. Legislating by multilateral Conventions: the case of United Nations treaties on transnational crime

The classic example of global law-making, including in the field of transnational crime, is the multilateral Convention and the key actor in this context has been the United Nations. United Nations (UN) intervention in this context can be seen as traditional in that it attempts to promote global standards while rooted firmly within state sovereignty and equality.[1] The emergence of multilateral Conventions in the field of transnational crime is inextricably linked with changes in the post-Cold War security landscape. The end of the Cold War has had broader implications for the reconfiguration of the global security agenda. The shift from the emphasis on military threats to the securitisation of broader phenomena has been well documented.[2] A key element of this securitisation shift has been the elevation of forms of criminality as security threats which require urgent and concerted response by governments.[3] In this securitisation process, perceived security threats have proliferated and assumed a chameleon nature over the years – from drug trafficking in the '80s to organised crime in the '90s and terrorism in the '00s.[4] This evolving securitisation agenda has led to the production of what Nadelmann has termed 'global prohibition regimes', which involve the introduction of security standards by dominant societies and states – in particular the United States – and their internationalisation and internalisation by the rest of

1 See in this context also Walker, who notes that 'the UN system links law to a claimed monopoly of the means of legitimate violence in a manner that stands both as a powerful (if fitful) reminder of conventional understandings of the paradigm of state-centred legal authority and as a direct challenge to the dominance of that paradigm': N. Walker, *Intimations of Global Law* (Cambridge: Cambridge University Press, 2015), 63.

2 See in particular B. Buzan, *People, States and Fear. An Agenda for International Security Studies in the Post-Cold War Era* (Brighton: Harvester Wheatsheaf, 1991); B. Buzan, 'New Patterns of Global Security in the Twenty-First Century' *International Affairs*, (1999) 67 (3), 431–451. In the context of securitisation and crime, see D. Bigo, *Polices en Réseaux. L'Experiénce Européenne* (Paris: Presses de Sciences Po, 1996).

3 On the securitisation process, see B. Buzan, O. Waever and J. de Wilde, *Security. A New Framework for Analysis* (Boulder; London: Lynne Rienner, 1998); and O. Waever, 'Securitization and De-securitization' in R.D. Lipschutz (ed.), *On Security* (New York: Columbia University Press, 1995), 46–86.

4 On this changing focus in the context of the development of money-laundering counter-measures, see V. Mitsilegas, 'Countering the Chameleon Threat of Dirty Money: "Hard" and "Soft" Law in the Emergence of a Global Regime against Money Laundering and Terrorist Finance' in A. Edwards and P. Gill (eds.), *Transnational Organised Crime: Perspectives on Global Security* (Abingdon: Routledge, 2003), 195–211.

the world.[5] The globalisation of this securitisation agenda has been reflected in the intervention by the UN via the adoption of multilateral Conventions in the field of transnational crime. A major step towards the globalisation of criminal law in this context was undertaken by the UN in the 1980s in the form of the conclusion of the 1988 Vienna Convention against Illicit Trafficking in Narcotic Drugs and Psychotropic Substances. To a great extent prompted by the so-called US 'war on drugs', the Convention introduced a number of detailed provisions on drug trafficking, as well as – for the first time – the criminalisation of money laundering at the global level.[6] The Vienna Convention was followed in ensuing decades by two further major UN Conventions in the field: the UN Convention on Transnational Organised Crime (UNTOC), and the UN Convention Against Corruption (UNCAC). UNTOC constitutes perhaps the most impressive contribution of a UN multilateral treaty towards the globalisation of criminal law. It was negotiated throughout the 1990s and signed symbolically in Palermo in 2000. Reflecting the growing securitisation of organised crime at the time, the Convention is an ambitious and comprehensive multilateral instrument aiming at combating and preventing organised crime. It contains provisions ranging from the criminalisation of participation in an organised crime group, money laundering and corruption, to provisions on judicial cooperation with regard to organised crime, police cooperation and the law of criminal procedure. The Convention is complemented by three Protocols, on human trafficking, human smuggling, and the illicit manufacturing of and trafficking in firearms.[7] UNTOC was followed by the adoption of the 2003 UNCAC. UNCAC aims to establish a comprehensive anticorruption framework, by focusing on both prevention and control.[8]

5 E.A. Nadelmann, 'Global Prohibition Regimes: the Evolution of Norms in International Society' *International Organization*, (1990) 44 (4), 479–526. On the dominance of the United States in this context see also P. Andreas and E. Nadelmann, *Policing the Globe. Criminalization and Crime Control in International Relations* (Oxford: OUP, 2008); and on the role of powerful players such as the US more broadly see G. Shaffer, 'The Dimensions and Determinants of State Change' in G. Shaffer (ed.), *Transnational Legal Ordering and State Change* (Cambridge: CUP, 2013), 23–49.

6 For an analysis of the Vienna Convention, see W.C. Gilmore, *Dirty Money. The Evolution of International Measures to Counter Money Laundering and the Financing of Terrorism*, 3rd edn (Strasbourg, Council of Europe Press, 2004), ch.3; see also D.P. Stewart, 'Internationalizing the War on Drugs: the UN Convention Against Illicit Traffic in Narcotic Drugs and Psychotropic Substances' *Denver Journal of International Law and Policy*, (1990) 18, 387.

7 See D. McClean, *Transnational Organized Crime. A Commentary on the UN Convention and its Protocols* (Oxford: Oxford University Press, 2007). For an overview of the background to, and negotiating history of, the Convention, see also D. Vlassis, 'Drafting the United Nations Convention against Transnational Organized Crime', in P. Williams and D. Vlassis (eds), *Combating Transnational Crime. Concepts, Activities and Responses* (London and Portland, Ore.: Frank Cass, 2001), 356.

8 For an overview, see P. Webb, 'The United Nations Convention against Corruption. Global Achievement or Missed Opportunity?' *Journal of International Economic Law*, (2005) 8, 191.

The adoption by the UN of multilateral Conventions on transnational crime with a global reach poses significant challenges of implementation and compliance by States Parties. More recent Conventions have tried to address these challenges by the introduction of specific mechanisms of monitoring and review. Leading these mechanisms are the so-called 'Conferences of the Parties'.[9] The establishment of Conferences of the Parties has been justified by the need to create strong regimes, as decision-making by a treaty body can be more efficient than the traditional consent-based treaty-making process.[10] In this context, Conferences of the Parties are viewed as autonomous institutional arrangements introducing a model of interstate collaboration which is more informal and more flexible, and often innovative in relation to norm creation and compliance.[11] Questions of compliance are multilateral in character and promote resolution in a cooperative rather than an adversarial manner.[12] Both the UNTOC and the UNCAC contain provisions on Conferences on the Parties. Article 32 UNTOC entrusts the Conference of the Parties to the Convention with the objectives of improving the capacity of States Parties to combat transnational organised crime and to promote and review the implementation of the Convention (Article 32(1)). According to Article 32(3), the Conference of the Parties will agree upon mechanisms for achieving these objectives inter alia by reviewing periodically the implementation of this Convention and making recommendations to improve this Convention and its implementation (Article 32(3)(d) and (e)). For these purposes, the Conference of the Parties must acquire the necessary knowledge of the measures taken by States Parties in implementing this Convention through information provided by them and through such supplemental review mechanisms as may be established by the Conference of the Parties (Article 32(4)). A similar clause has been included in UNCAC (see Article 63(1), 63(4)(e) and (f) and 63(5) respectively).

At the time of writing, it is under the UNCAC that review mechanisms have been mostly developed. Resolution 3/1 of the Conference of the States Parties adopted Terms of Reference of the Mechanism for the Review of Implementation of UNCAC. The guiding principles include commitments that the review mechanism must not produce any form of ranking (point 3(b)), must be non-adversarial and non-punitive (point 3(f)), must be an intergovernmental process

9 For a background and discussion of the legal nature of Conferences of the Parties see M. Fitzmaurice, 'Law-Making and International Environmental Law: The Legal Character of Decisions of Conferences of the Parties' in R. Liivoja and J. Petman (eds.), *International Law-Making. Essays in Honour of Jan Klabbers* (Abingdon: Routledge, 2014), 190–210.

10 D. Costelloe and M. Fitzmaurice, 'Lawmaking by Treaty: conclusion of a treaty and the evolution of a treaty regime in practice' in K. Brölmann and Radi (eds.), *Research Handbook on the Theory and Practice of International Lawmaking* (Cheltenham UK: Edward Elgar, 2016).

11 R. Churchill and G. Ulfstein, 'Autonomous Institutional Arrangements in Multilateral Environmental Agreements: A Little-Noticed Phenomenon in International Law' *American Journal of International Law*, (2000) 94 623–659, 625.

12 Ibid., 645.

(point 4), must not serve as an instrument for interfering in the domestic affairs of States Parties but must respect the principles of equality and sovereignty of States Parties, and the review process must be conducted in a non-political and non-selective manner (point 5) and must take into account the levels of development of States Parties, as well as the diversity of judicial, legal, political, economic and social systems and differences in legal traditions (point 8). A system of peer review between states has been established (point 18). The review will be primarily a desk exercise based on the responses to states' self-assessment and will be complemented by further means of direct dialogue such as country visits only if agreed by the State Party under review (points 27 and 29). The country review reports will remain confidential although States Parties are encouraged – under their sovereign rights – to give some publicity (points 37 and 38). It can thus be seen that the monitoring mechanisms established by the UNCAC Conference of the Parties are firmly anchored within the principles of equality between states, state sovereignty and national diversity. The emphasis on these principles may be explained by the criticism levelled at existing attempts towards the introduction of global anti-corruption rankings, which have been seen as reflecting the interests of particular countries and parts of the world.[13] There are also limits to transparency with evaluation reports remaining in principle confidential. A similar model is envisaged in the development of concrete monitoring mechanisms for UNTOC, which are currently being developed.[14]

The above analysis has demonstrated the progress but also the limits in terms of norm-making and compliance by means of multilateral treaties with a global reach. In terms of norm-making, the international community has indeed legislated in major areas of transnational crime, including drug trafficking, money laundering, organised crime and corruption. However, there are aspects of these phenomena which have not been regulated by the UN Conventions analysed above. Moreover, the absence of similar multilateral treaties addressing other serious security threats, including terrorism and cyber-crime, is also striking. The limits to international norm-making in the files can be explained by the difficulties in reaching a global consensus on how to respond to such threats. This difficulty has led to what Krisch has termed 'the decay of consent' in international law.[15] Krisch notes that consent-based structure presents a structural bias against effective action on global public goods, especially given the large number of sovereign

13 See M. Bukovansky, 'Corruption Rankings: Constructing and Contesting the Global Anti-Corruption Agenda' in A. Cooley and J. Snyder (eds.), *Ranking the World. Grading States as a Tool of Global Governance* (Cambridge: CUP, 2015), 60–84.

14 On the terms of reference of the UNTOC review mechanism, see annex 1 to Conference of the Parties Resolution 5/5. On recent impetus towards the establishment of such a mechanism see Resolution 7/1 and the Progress Report submitted to the Conference of the Parties meeting in Vienna, 21–26 October 2016, CTOC/COP/2016/13, 29 July 2016.

15 N. Krisch, 'The Decay of Consent: International Law in an Age of Global Public Goods' *American Journal of International Law*, (2014) 108, 1–40.

states today increasingly favouring more effective problem-solving mechanisms.[16] This trend towards moving away from an exclusive focus on global multilateral Conventions can be clearly discerned in the field of security and transnational criminal law. Legal responses to the emerging global securitisation landscape take many different, overlapping and interrelated forms. The following sections will look at each of these in detail: from the turn to regional multilateralism (and focusing here on the activities of the Council of Europe), to the production of norms on transnational crime via 'informal' 'soft' or 'global administrative law' (with the examples of the Financial Action Task Force against Money Laundering and Terrorist Finance and the United Nations Security Council emerging prominent in the field). The emergence of these new regulatory avenues is significant not only in terms of norm-making, but also in terms of compliance and effective implementation – with the circumvention of the traditional multilateral UN route being explained or justified by the necessity not only to respond swiftly to perceived security threats, but also to achieve effective compliance in order to create a true global level playing field in the fight against transnational crime.

III. From regionalisation to globalisation: the case of the Council of Europe

The Council of Europe (CoE) has been a major driver of regional standard setting in the field of serious and transnational crime, having emerged as a significant norm entrepreneur in the field.[17] The first wave of CoE measures in the field adopted in the early years of the organisation consisted of a number of traditional Conventions on judicial cooperation in criminal matters including Conventions on extradition[18] and mutual legal assistance in criminal matters.[19] In the absence of express criminal law competence of what was then the European Community, these Conventions constituted the cornerstone of intergovernmental judicial cooperation between Western European countries, including European Union Member States. The post-Cold War security landscape renewed legislative ambition in the field of transnational criminality by the CoE, via the adoption since the 1990s of a series of comprehensive, avant-garde multilateral Conventions covering both substantive and procedural criminal law in areas such as money laundering[20]

16 Ibid., 4.

17 On the CoE as norm entrepreneur more generally, see G. Sasse, 'The Council of Europe as a Norm Enterpreneur: The Political Strengths of a Weak International Institution' in N. Walker and Jo Shaw (eds), *Europe's Constitutional Mosaic* (Oxford: Hart, 2011), 171–204.

18 European Convention on Extradition, Paris, 13.12.1957, ETS no.024.

19 European Convention on Mutual Legal Assistance in Criminal Matters, Strasbourg, 20.4.1959, ETS no.030.

20 Convention on Laundering, Search, Seizure and Confiscation of the Proceeds of Crime, Strasbourg, 8.11.1990, ETS no.141.

(followed by a Convention on money laundering and terrorist finance),[21] corruption,[22] the suppression[23] and prevention[24] of terrorism and cyber-crime.[25] The CoE has thus produced a series of detailed and sophisticated legal standards to counter transnational criminality.[26] At the same time, it has acted as a catalyst for the strengthening of the legal framework in the field at both the EU and the global level. At the EU level, membership of the CoE and compliance with CoE standards has acted as a laboratory for membership of the European Union in the context of EU enlargement, with CoE Conventions forming benchmarks with which compliance is required as a criterion of membership of the EU. Such compliance is also a benchmark in the development of relations between the Union and its neighbours in the context of the European Neighbourhood Policy.[27] Council of Europe measures also serve as EU benchmarks in areas where the EU is itself reluctant to legislate, such as anti-corruption law.[28]

At the global level, the CoE has advanced and strengthened international norms against transnational crime via the adoption of comprehensive and pioneering Conventions.[29] Importantly, this has occurred in areas such as terrorism and cyber-crime, where CoE Conventions have been developing in the absence of a global consensus. Law-making by the CoE acts as a laboratory for globalisation in this context. A number of CoE Conventions in the field of transnational crime have been open for participation to non-European states. A prime example in this context is the Convention on cyber-crime, where the participation of the United States signals the evolution of a transatlantic enforcement regime where a global consensus in favour of this particular form of legislative intervention may be

21 Council of Europe Convention on Laundering, Search, Seizure and Confiscation of the Proceeds from Crime and on the Financing of Terrorism, Warsaw, 16.5.2005, ETS no.198.

22 Criminal Law Convention on Corruption, Strasbourg, 27.1.1999, ETS no.173. The Convention is complemented by a Civil Law Convention on Corruption, Strasbourg, 4.11.1999, ETS no.174.

23 European Convention on the Suppression of Terrorism, Strasbourg, 27.1.1977, ETS no.090.

24 Council of Europe Convention on the Prevention of Terrorism, Warsaw, 16.5.2005, ETS no.196.

25 Convention on Cybercrime, Budapest, 23.11.2001, ETS no.185.

26 For an overview of the evolution of the activities of the Council of Europe in criminal matters, see P. Csonka, 'Organised and Economic Crime (an overview of the Relevant Council of Europe Activities)', in P.J. Cullen and W.C. Gilmore, *Crime sans Frontières: International and European Legal Approaches* (Edinburgh University Press, 1998), 93–99.

27 V. Mitsilegas, 'The EU and the Implementation of International Norms in Criminal Matters' in M. Cremona, J. Monar and S. Poli (eds.), *The External Dimension of the Area of Freedom, Security and Justice* (Peter Lang, 2011) (College of Europe Studies No. 13), 239–272.

28 V. Mitsilegas, 'The Aims and Limits of EU Anti-Corruption Law' in J. Horder and P. Alldridge (eds.), *Modern Bribery Law: Comparative Perspectives* (Cambridge: Cambridge University Press, 2013), 160–195.

29 See Gilmore, *Dirty Money*, fn.6 above. See also as regards one of the first Conventions in this context H. Nilsson, 'The Council of Europe Laundering Convention: A Recent Example of a Developing International Criminal Law' *Criminal Law Forum*, (1991) 2, 419–441.

lacking.[30] This development poses a number of rule of law challenges. From the perspective of the CoE legal order, participation in its regional Conventions is allowed by states which are not its members and thus not bound by the entirety of its standards (including the European Convention on Human Rights). From the perspective of globalisation of criminal law, standards which have been developed and agreed at a specific regional context may de facto become global standards via the opening of participation to Conventions by third states and in particular in areas of law which involve extraterritoriality (such is the case with elements of the cyber-crime Convention). In a system of multi-level security governance, CoE intervention may act as a legitimising factor for a number of initiatives which have not originated via traditional public international law means. A key example is recent legislation on the criminalisation and prevention of terrorism, notably via targeting the phenomenon of 'foreign fighters'. In this field, standards were first put forward by the UN Security Council in another example of the application of 'global administrative law'.[31] The key provisions in UN Security Council Resolution 2178 have been introduced in the CoE legal order by the Additional Protocol to the Council of Europe Convention on the Prevention of Terrorism adopted by the CoE.[32] The CoE has thus legitimised sweeping and controversial changes in the criminal law of terrorism: in addition to widening the categories of preparatory offences[33] the Protocol introduces a series of provisions expressly criminalising mobility and travel. These changes in turn are in the process of being legitimised further by the EU, whose institutions are currently negotiating a revision of its counter-terrorism law to introduce the CoE standards in the EU legal order.

The Council of Europe has not only been innovative in producing transnational criminal law norms. Its normative efforts have been coupled with strong efforts to secure compliance with these standards. In this context, a number of innovative compliance and implementation monitoring procedures have been put forward by the CoE. These mechanisms go beyond the set up envisaged by the Conferences of the Parties in UN Conventions, whose provisions seem rather timid in comparison to the CoE monitoring frameworks. Rather, the Council of Europe mechanisms are closer to invasive monitoring mechanisms introduced by bodies such as the Financial Action Task Force (FATF)[34] and there is a high degree of interconnection between the CoE and bodies and organisations such as the FATF and the EU in terms of the development of multi-layered evaluation processes on

30 J. Clough, 'The Council of Europe Convention on Cybercrime: defining "crime" in a digital world' *Criminal Law Forum*, (2012) 23 (4), 363–391.

31 On the UN Security Council and global administrative law see Part V below.

32 For a background to the Protocol see N. Piacente, 'The Contribution of the Council of Europe to the Fight against Foreign Terrorist Fighters' *Eucrim*, (2015) 1, 12–15.

33 See the provisions on criminalising the participation in an association or group for the purpose of terrorism (Article 2) and receiving training for terrorism (Article 3).

34 See Part IV below.

the basis of a plethora of EU, regional and global standards. The first example of innovative compliance mechanisms relates to the mechanisms established within the framework of the Group of States Against Corruption (GRECO). Legal bases for GRECO can be found in the CoE Civil and Criminal Law Conventions on Corruption.[35] According to the Conventions, GRECO will monitor their implementation. Ratification of or accession to the Conventions will entail automatic membership to GRECO for non-Member States.[36] GRECO's objective is to improve the capacity of its members to fight corruption by monitoring their compliance with CoE anti-corruption standards through a process of mutual evaluation and peer pressure. All members participate in, and submit themselves without restriction to, the mutual evaluation and compliance procedures, which include on-site visits and evaluations on the ground.[37]

A rigorous monitoring mechanism is thus introduced, which places emphasis on evaluation of law in action and on the achievement of compliance of members with CoE anti-corruption standards. The potential of the regional evaluation mechanism set out by GRECO to promote anti-corruption standards more broadly is significant. It is noteworthy that membership of GRECO includes the United States, and that regional organisations such as the Organization of American States have observer status.[38] Moreover, the GRECO system is envisaged to be both mirrored and internalised at EU level as regards the evaluation of anti-corruption law: in its Communication on EU anti-corruption policy, the European Commission committed to setting up a new mechanism, the *EU Anti-Corruption Report*, to monitor and assess Member States' efforts against corruption. Alongside this mechanism, the EU should participate in the CoE GRECO.[39] In addition to the efforts of the GRECO, another innovative evaluation mechanism based upon peer review has been set up within the framework of the CoE in order to ensure compliance with CoE standards against transnational crime: the MONEYVAL system aims at ensuring compliance with CoE anti-money laundering standards and beyond.[40] MONEYVAL was established to address in particular

35 'The Group of States against Corruption (GRECO) shall monitor the implementation of this Convention by the Parties': Criminal Law Convention on Corruption, Article 24; Civil Law Convention on Corruption, Article 14.

36 Articles 32 and 33 of the Criminal Law Convention; Articles 15 and 16 of the Civil Law Convention.

37 Council of Europe, *How Does Greco Work?*, accessed 5 June 2017 at www.coe.int/t/dghl/monitoring/greco/general/4.%20How%20does%20GRECO%20work_en.asp.

38 Council of Europe, *GRECO, Members and Observers*, accessed 5 June 2017 at www.coe.int/t/dghl/monitoring/greco/general/members_en.asp.

39 COM (2011) 308 final, p.2.

40 Council of Europe, *Committee of Experts on the Evaluation of Anti-Mondey Laundering Measures and the Financing of Terrorism (MONEYVAL)*, accessed 6 June 2017 at www.coe.int/moneyval/. For an overview, see W. Rau and J. Ringguth, 'Evaluation in the framework of the Council of Europe', in A. Weyembergh and S. de Biolley (eds), *Comment Évaluer le Droit Pénal Européen?* (Bruxelles: Editions de l'Université de Bruxelles, 2006), 33–44.

the fact that not all CoE members are also members of the FATF on money laundering, which, as will be seen below, is the main international body leading with regard to developing and ensuring compliance with detailed standards in the field.[41] MONEYVAL membership consists primarily of countries from Central and Eastern Europe, both EU and non-EU Members. The establishment of a specific peer review mechanism for these states serves to ensure that the FATF peer review was complemented for non-Members in Europe, but also serves to ensure compliance of these states with EU standards in the field – as MONEYVAL benchmarks are not limited to CoE standards but also include FATF, UN and EU anti-money laundering standards.[42] Both GRECO and MONEYVAL constitute attempts to legitimise further the production of norms not only by the CoE, but also by other international fora, by focusing on their implementation based in a system of expert evaluation.

IV. From 'soft' to 'informal' law: the case of the FATF

The establishment and operation of the Financial Action Task Force (FATF) represents perhaps the most prominent departure from the traditional paradigm of multilateral 'hard' law-making in the field of transnational criminal law. The FATF is an ad hoc body, established by the G7 in 1989 within the auspices of the OECD.[43] Its main normative output has been a series of Recommendations, evolving over time and covering a wide range of aspects of the fight against money laundering. The 40 FATF Recommendations produced in 1990 were revised in 1996, 2003 and 2012, with money laundering counter-measures being deemed necessary to counter a series of emerging and new threats, from drug trafficking to organised crime to terrorism.[44] The revisions of the FATF Recommendations have gone hand in hand with the renewal and gradual expansion of the FATF mandate to now include action against money laundering, the financing of terrorism and now proliferation.[45] The rapid evolution and expansion in the FATF mandate, standards and membership can be attributed to its informal nature[46] and network structure

41 Gilmore, *Dirty Money*, fn.6 above, 206.

42 See the MONEYVAL terms of reference at Council Of Europe, *MONEYVAL Terms of Reference*, accessed 6 June 2017 at www.coe.int/t/dghl/monitoring/moneyval/About/MONEYVALTERMS.pdf.

43 For a detailed analysis of the role and work of the FATF, see Gilmore, *Dirty Money*, fn.6 above, ch s 4–6.

44 See V. Mitsilegas, 'Countering the Chameleon Threat of Dirty Money: "Hard" and "Soft" Law in the Emergence of a Global Regime against Money Laundering and Terrorist Finance' in A. Edwards and P. Gill (eds), *Transnational Organised Crime: Perspectives on Global Security* (Abingdon: Routledge, 2003), 195–211.

45 *Financial Action Task Force Mandate (2012–2020)*, Washington DC, 20 April 2012.

46 On the concept of informal international law-making see J. Pauwelyn, R. Wessel and J. Wouters (eds), *Informal International Lawmaking* (Oxford: Oxford University Press 2012);

which aims at flexibility and adaptability.[47] Although membership of the FATF is limited and its output takes the form of Recommendations which could be characterised as 'soft law',[48] informal law,[49] or global administrative law,[50] in juxtaposition to standards adopted in the form of multilateral international treaties, their impact on global law reform in the field has been immense.[51] Such impact has been achieved in two ways: by the constant willingness of major international players, such as the EU (some of whose Member States and the European Commission have played a part in shaping the FATF standards in the first place) to legitimise the FATF standards by implementing them with legislation in their internal legal orders;[52] and by accompanying the adoption of FATF Recommendations by a system of rigorous evaluation of their implementation and compliance by the FATF members and non-members alike, which takes the form of mutual evaluation and peer review.[53] Over time, the FATF has developed detailed evaluation methodologies and guidelines.[54] These evaluation mechanisms have ensured that FATF is

Informal law-making is defined as dispensing with certain formalities traditionally linked to international law having to do with output, process, or the actors involved: J. Pauwelyn, 'Informal International Lawmaking: Framing the Concept and Research Questions', in J. Pauwelyn, R. Wessel and J. Wouters (eds), *Informal International Lawmaking* (Oxford: OUP, 2012), 13–34 at 15.

47 On the network nature of the FATF see A-M Slaughter, *A New World Order* (Princeton University Press, 2004). Slaughter highlights the advantages of what she calls 'government networks', marrying hard and soft power and using information, persuasion and socialisation: see 168 *et seq.*

48 In the context of the FATF, it can be argued that the regular revision of both mandate and standards has been easier compared to a more formal international organisation – see in this context A. Boyle, 'Some Reflections on the Relationship of Treaties and Soft Law' *International and Comparative Law Quarterly* (1999) 48, 901, 903, noting that soft law instruments are easier to amend or replace than treaties.

49 See Pauwelyn, Wessel and Wouters, fn.46 above.

50 On the concept of global administrative law see Part V below.

51 For further discussion see Valsamis Mitsilegas, 'The European Union and the Globalisation of Criminal Law' *Cambridge Yearbook of European Legal Studies* (2010) 12, 337–407.

52 All four EU money laundering Directives have been justified on the basis of the need to adjust the EU legal framework to the FATF requirements: on the interrelationship between EU and FATF law over time see V. Mitsilegas, *Money Laundering Counter-Measures in the European Union: A New Paradigm of Security Governance versus Fundamental Legal Principles* (The Hague: Kluwer, 2003), V. Mitsilegas and B. Gilmore, 'The EU legislative framework against money laundering and terrorist finance: A critical analysis in the light of evolving global standards' *International and Comparative Law Quarterly* (2007) 56, 119–141; and V. Mitsilegas and N. Vavoula, 'The Evolving EU Anti-Money Laundering Regime. Challenges for Fundamental Rights and the Rule of Law' *Maastricht Journal of European and Comparative Law* (2016) 23, 261–293.

53 M. Levi and W. Gilmore, 'Terrorist Finance, Money Laundering and the Rise and Rise of Mutual Evaluation: A New Paradigm for Crime Control?' *European Journal of Law Reform* (2002) 4, 337–363.

54 FATF, *Methodology for Assessing Technical Compliance with the FATF Recommendations and the Effectiveness of AML/CFT Systems*, 2016.

a body with selective membership but global reach. The emphasis on the regional dimension has been key in ensuring the achievement of global compliance with FATF standards. There have been three ways in which the incorporation of a regional dimension has contributed to global compliance with FATF standards: the expansion of FATF membership to include non-Western countries from key, strategically important regions; the expansion of the FATF system and methodology via the establishment of a series of FATF regional-style bodies; and the inclusion of regional elements in assessing compliance with FATF standards, most notably when extending such assessment beyond FATF members.

The growing importance of the regional dimension is reflected in the evolution of the membership of the FATF – which, being initially essentially a G7 initiative, consisted primarily of G7 and related Western countries as well as the European Commission.[55] Since its establishment, FATF membership has expanded significantly to include regional powers such as Russia, China, India, Mexico, Argentina and Brazil.[56] This move reflects the strategic importance of these countries in an era of financial globalisation and the changing balance of power in the global financial and political system. It has been seen as increasing the efficiency and legitimacy of the FATF[57] – with the expansion of FATF membership in these terms ensuring the representation of broader national and regional interests beyond a narrow Western perspective. This is particularly relevant as regards the development and adoption of FATF standards. The importance of the regional dimension in the work of the FATF is also evident in the organisation's criteria for membership. A fundamental criterion for FATF membership is the strategic importance of the jurisdiction, one of the indicators in this context being its regional prominence in efforts against money laundering and financing of terrorism. Membership should also lead to the enhancement of the geographical balance of the FATF. Additional technical membership criteria include (in addition to adhering to the FATF standards and evaluation process) full and active membership of a relevant FATF-style regional body.[58] This 'club' drives not only the development of the FATF Recommendations, but also their implementation by FATF members and beyond. A major weapon in this context is a 'naming and shaming' process consisting of identifying and engaging with jurisdictions

55 In addition to the participants in the G7 summit establishing the FATF (Canada, France, Germany, Italy, Japan, United Kingdom, United States and the Commission) eight other states (Australia, Austria, Belgium, Luxembourg, Netherlands, Spain, Sweden and Switzerland) were invited to take part: Gilmore, *Dirty Money*, fn.6 above, 89.

56 See Gilmore, *Dirty Money*, fn.6 above. For a more specific regional dimension, see M.R. Machado, 'Similar in their Differences: Transnational Legal Processes Addressing Money Laundering in Brazil and Argentina', in G. Shaffer (ed.), *Transnational Legal Ordering and State Change* (Cambridge: CUP, 2014), 50–88.

57 R. Hülsse and D. Kerwer, 'Global Standards in Action: Insights from Anti-Money Laundering Regulation' *Organization* (2007) 14, 625–642.

58 See www.fatf-gafi.org/pages/aboutus/membersandobservers/fatfmembershippolicy.html, accessed 6 June 2017.

that have strategic deficiencies and is carried out by the FATF's International Co-operation Review Group (ICRG), which reviews and monitors a large number of potentially high-risk and non-cooperative jurisdictions around the world. Initial referral to the ICRG is based on information on threats, vulnerabilities or particular risks emanating from a specific jurisdiction that comes to the ICRG's attention. Such information includes, but is not exclusively based on, the results of mutual evaluation reports (MERs); or the lack of a clear commitment to implementing the FATF standards through non-participation in any of the FATF-style regional bodies. Jurisdictions identified as having serious AML/CFT threats and vulnerabilities or posing significant risks are referred to the ICRG for a preliminary or prima facie review conducted by one of the four regional review groups, covering, respectively: the Africa/Middle East, the Americas, the Asia/Pacific, and the Europe/Eurasia regions. Based upon reports from these groups, the FATF decides whether it should conduct a more in-depth, targeted review of the relevant jurisdiction's strategic AML/CFT deficiencies. The FATF specifically requests high-level political commitment to implement these action plans.

On the basis of the results of the ICRG review, jurisdictions may be publicly identified in the FATF Public Statement. The Public Statement identifies two groups of countries, namely jurisdictions for which the FATF calls on its members and non-members to apply counter-measures, and jurisdictions for which the FATF calls only on its members to consider the risks arising from the deficiencies associated with the countries. This second category includes jurisdictions that have not made sufficient progress in addressing the deficiencies or have not committed to an action plan developed with the FATF to address the deficiencies.[59] Since 2008, the FATF has issued public statements, three times a year, expressing concerns and calling for particular actions from FATF members and other jurisdictions. The classification of states in this context has evolved over time. The most recent FATF statement at the time of writing called on its members and other jurisdictions to apply counter-measures in the case of the Democratic Republic of Korea;[60] called for the application of enhanced due diligence measures in the case of Iran;[61] identified eight jurisdictions with strategic deficiencies;[62] and one jurisdiction (Guyana) which has been 'de-listed', i.e. no longer subject to the FATF on-going compliance process.[63] The recent documents confirm a process of on-going monitoring and assessment on a global scale.

59 FATF Annual Report 11–12.

60 FATF Public Statement, 21 October 2016, accessed 6 June 2017 at www.fatf-gafi.org/publications/high-riskandnon-cooperativejurisdictions/documents/public-statement-october-2016.html.

61 Ibid.

62 FATF, Improving Global AML/CFT Compliance: on-going process 21 October 2016, accessed 6 June 2017 at www.fatf-gafi.org/publications/high-riskandnon-cooperativejurisdictions/documents/fatf-compliance-october-2016.html.

63 Ibid.

The above analysis demonstrates that the FATF Recommendations are 'soft' law with hard teeth, with the FATF creating a global normative orthodoxy in the field of money laundering and terrorist finance. However, the evolution of the FATF continues to pose fundamental rule of law challenges. A primary challenge lies at the level of production of anti-money laundering norms. As mentioned above, the FATF is a single-agenda body with a renewable mandate, informal structures and selective membership, which give it flexibility in adopting and revising its standards. A number of authors have stressed the advantages of informality, with Pollack and Shaffer noting that formal legal instruments such as treaties are particularly problematic 'where it presupposes a fixed condition when situations of uncertainty demand constant experimentation and adjustment, where it requires uniformity when a tolerance of national diversity is needed, and where it is difficult to change when frequent change may be essential'.[64] The flexibility of 'soft' or 'informal' law is a particular asset coupled with the ensuing strong compliance mechanisms. As Boister notes, 'while treaty provisions are coupled with only very weak powers for enforcement of implementation, soft law is faster and cheaper to make than treaty law and is thus more adaptive, and can be combined with fairly coercive name and shame tools to ensure implementation'.[65] However, the production of norms by the FATF raises significant challenges of democratic participation, transparency and accountability. Particular challenges arise in this context by the fact that norms are produced by a club with selective membership and then imposed by a sophisticated and invasive system of multi-level implementation monitoring across the globe; and by the fact that norms are produced behind closed doors, mainly by experts representing national executives. The uncritical emphasis and reliance on expertise serves to depoliticise the issues and shield them from political debate.[66] The FATF has responded to these criticisms by introducing public consultations regarding the revision of its Recommendations.[67] However, the the FATF norm-making process leaves much to be desired in terms of participatory and transparent debate. A particular challenge in this context is

64 M.A. Pollack and G.C. Shaffer, 'The Interaction of Formal and Informal International Lawmaking', in G. Shaffer (ed.), *Transnational Legal Ordering and State Change* (Cambridge: Cambridge University Press, 2014), 241–270, 246.

65 N. Boister, 'Further Reflections on the Concept of Transnational Criminal Law' *Transnational Legal Theory*, (2015) 6(1), 9–30, 23.

66 On various aspects of such 'depoliticisation', see: A. Somek, *Administration without Sovereignty* (University of Iowa Legal Studies Research Paper 09-04, January 2009); J. Klabbers, 'Institutional Ambivalence by Design: Soft Organizations in International Law' *Nordic Journal of International Law*, (2001) 70, 403; and D. Kennedy, 'Challenging Expert Rule: The Politics of Global Governance' *Sydney Law Review*, (2005) 27, 5 (talking inter alia about 'the expert consensus'). For a more positive view, emphasising the benefits of professional socialisation, see A.-M. Slaughter, *A New World Order* (Princeton: Princeton University Press, 2004).

67 For a recent example, see Public Consultation on the Revision of Recommendation 8 (Non-profit organisations), accessed 6 June 2017 at www.fatf-gafi.org/publications/fatfrecommendations/documents/public-consultation-npo-r8.html.

that the FATF is a single-agenda body which has to justify its existence in order for its mandate to be renewed. This does not allow for a more rounded debate on the necessity and content of further anti-money laundering standards, or the balancing of enforcement or efficiency considerations with broader fundamental rights or rule of law imperatives.

V. The emergence of 'global administrative law': the role of the UN Security Council

Calls for global, emergency counter-terrorism action post-9/11 have not resulted in the adoption of measures in the form of the traditional multilateral 'hard law' Conventions at the level of the United Nations. Rather, global standards have been adopted and promoted principally under the format of what legal scholars have labelled as 'global administrative law'.[68] It has been noted that 'underlying the emergence of global administrative law is the vast increase in the reach and forms of transgovernmental regulation and administration designed to address the consequences of globalized interdependence in such fields as security', and that 'much in the detail and implementation of such regulation is determined by transnational administrative bodies – including international organizations and informal groups of officials – that perform administrative functions but are not directly subject to control by national governments or domestic legal systems or, in the case of treaty-based regimes, the states parties to the treaty'.[69]

It is contested whether all or some of the norms included under the rubric of 'global administrative law' can really be classified as 'law'.[70] However, the term is a useful analytical tool in focusing on the *process* of the adoption of norms and in this context highlighting key differences between the development of global norms and the traditional adoption of multilateral legally binding treaties. The production of normative standards at the level of 'global administrative law' or 'government networks' differs from the adoption of multilateral, expressly legally binding standards at the multilateral level in four main respects: standards are put forward by a limited number of states without the need for a global consensus; standards are adopted with a minimum of transparency; standards are adopted speedily (a factor which may explain the appeal of this form of normative production in times of perceived emergency); and standards are not explicitly legally binding rules of general application, but in reality have far-reaching consequences for law reform around the world.

68 B. Kingsbury, N. Krisch and R.B. Stewart, 'The Emergence of Global Administrative Law' *Law and Contemporary Problems*, (2004–05) 68, 15.

69 Ibid., 16.

70 See in this context B. Kingsbury, 'The Concept of "Law" in Global Administrative Law' *European Journal of International Law*, (2009) 20, 23; and A. Somek, 'The Concept of "Law" in Global Adminstrative Law: A Reply to Benedict Kingsbury' *European Journal of International Law*, (2009) 20, 985.

The adoption by the UN Security Council of preventative counter-terrorism sanctions constitutes a prime example of global administrative law in this context. The production by the UN Security Council of normative standards in criminal matters has been linked to global counter-terrorism efforts as part of a two-fold strategy. The first element of this strategy has been the adoption, beginning pre-9/11, of a set of Resolutions targeting specifically the Taliban, Osama bin Laden, Al-Qaida and those associated with them. The first step in this direction has been Resolution 1267 (1999), which imposed a series of restrictive measures against the Taliban, including an arms embargo, banning travel and the freezing of funds. Resolution 1333 (2000) extended the freezing regime expressly to individuals in the Al-Qaida organisation and requested the Sanctions Committee to maintain an updated list of the individuals and entities designated as being associated with bin Laden, including those in Al-Qaida.[71] The next substantive amendment to the sanctions regime came about after 9/11, with Resolution 1390 (2002). The latter adjusted the content of Resolution 1267 to take into account political developments since its adoption but continued and consolidated the freezing regime established in paragraph 4(b) thereof. The emphasis on the adoption of legislative measures is even more prominent in the second element of the Security Council counter-terrorism strategy. Resolution 1373 (2001), adopted less than three weeks after the 9/11 attacks, called upon all states in particular to prevent and suppress the financing of terrorist acts; criminalise terrorism finance; and extend the freezing regime to cover in general persons who commit or attempt to commit terrorist acts or participate in or facilitate the commission of such acts, entities owned or controlled directly or indirectly by such persons, and persons and entities acting on their behalf or direction.[72]

In this manner, the international community witnessed the production of global normative standards in the field of counter-terrorism outside the framework of the multilateral treaty. This shift did not go unnoticed by international lawyers, who stressed the Security Council's 'legislative' role.[73] In this context, it has been pointed out that Resolution 1373 is of general and abstract character and does not name a single country, society or group of people;[74] that with Resolution 1373, together with the related efforts of its 1267 Sanctions Committee, the Council is no longer responding with discrete action directed at a particular state because of a concrete threat to peace arising from a specific incident;[75] and that Resolution 1373 imposed general obligations on all states for an indefinite period, while

71 Para.8(c)

72 Para.1(a)–(c).

73 See in particular S. Talmon, 'The Security Council as World Legislature' *American Journal of International Law*, (2005) 99, 175; J.E. Alvarez, 'Hegemonic International Law Revisited' *American Journal of International Law*, (2003) 97, 873.

74 Talmon, fn.73 above, 176–177.

75 Alvarez, fn.73 above, 874.

Resolution 1267 set up a sanctions committee with court-like powers to identify and freeze the assets of individuals, groups, and corporations.[76] This production of normative standards by the Security Council has been criticised as undemocratic on the grounds of the limited transparency of Security Council negotiations,[77] of the adoption of the Resolutions (in particular 1373) speedily as emergency measures,[78] and last, but not least, on the ground of the selective membership of the Security Council. It has been forcefully pointed out that 'a patently unrepresentative and undemocratic body such as the Council is arguably unsuitable for international lawmaking' and that 'Council practice may be criticised as contrary to the basic structure of international law as a consent-based legal order'.[79] It has also been argued that the Resolutions 'circumvent the "vehicle *par excellence* of community interest", namely the multilateral treaty', and that as such they serve to promote the interests of a limited number of state actors.[80] As Cohen has noted, 'the assumption of legislative power and its actual legislation thus have a double status: general laws are being made by an (unelected, unrepresentative) executive body and constitutional change in the allocation of powers is being perpetrated by that same body insofar as it ascribes to itself the competence and capacity to legislate for the world, thereby introducing a radically new way of global law-making.'[81]

It must be noted in this context that the Resolutions not only impose an extensive normative restrictive counter-terrorism framework as such, but also aim to ensure and accelerate the implementation of the enforcement standards adopted in a pre-existing multilateral treaty, the 1999 Convention on terrorist finance.[82] In a departure from the consensus required for the adoption of legally binding provisions in a multilateral international treaty, in the case of the UN Security Council far-reaching norms are produced by a body operating with a limited agenda, membership, transparency or scrutiny. What makes this departure even more striking is that, in the counter-terrorism Resolutions, the individual (targeted by a series of sanctions) enters directly the realm of a system designed to address primarily interstate relations.[83] What renders these Resolutions even more far-reaching is that, in addition to the fact that they target individuals directly, they leave (in particular Resolution 1267) states and international organisations such as the EU with very limited discretion as to how to implement them. As Krisch has noted, insofar as

76 I. Johnstone, 'Legislation and Adjudication in the UN Security Council: Bringing Down the Deliberative Deficit' *American Journal of International Law*, (2008) 102, 275, 283.

77 See in particular Talmon, fn.73 above, 190.

78 See Talmon, fn.73 above, 187, and the detailed analysis of Johnstone, fn.76 above, 284.

79 Talmon, fn.73 above, 179.

80 Alvarez, fn.73 above, 874–875.

81 J.L. Cohen, *Globalization and Sovereignty. Rethinking Legality, Legitimacy, and Constitutionalism* (Cambridge: Cambridge University Press, 2012), 278.

82 See in this context the criticism of Alvarez, fn.73 above, 875.

83 See in this context in particular P.C. Szasz, 'The Security Council Starts Legislating' *American Journal of International Law*, (2002) 96, 901; Johnstone, fn.76 above, 295.

Member State implementation is necessary to give measures effect, states' action is reduced to a subordinate, non-discretionary role in the overall administrative machinery directed by the Council and its committees, resulting in the significant reduction of the distance between national and international law in this domain and leading to an increasing enmeshment between those layers.[84]

Some of the rule of law challenges posed by the production of norms by the Security Council have been addressed by the judiciary, and in particular by the European Court of Justice (ECJ) in its *Kadi* litigation. In the first round of the *Kadi* rulings, referred to in this chapter as *Kadi I*, the ECJ stressed the requirement for the EU to comply with fundamental rights in the implementation of the Security Council Resolutions and found that uncritical automatic implementation ran contrary to the right to judicial protection as enshrined in the EU legal order – and at the same time affirming the autonomy of the EU constitutional order.[85] As in the case of the FATF, the Security Council responded to this criticism by introducing changes to its internal listing processes. Resolution 1822/2008 introduced the requirement for listing proposals to identify those parts of the statement of case that may be publicly released, including for use by the Sanctions Committee for development of the summary described below or for the purpose of notifying or informing the listed individual or entity, and those parts which may be released upon request to interested states.[86] The Resolution also provides that the Sanctions Committee, when it adds a name to its Consolidated List, is to make accessible on its website 'a narrative summary of reasons for listing' and that it is to make accessible on the same site 'narrative summaries of reasons for listing' names on that list before the adoption of Resolution 1822/2008.[87] A further Security Council Resolution, 1904/2009, established an 'Office of the Ombudsperson', whose task is to assist the Sanctions Committee in the consideration of delisting requests. The person appointed to be the Ombudsperson must be an individual of high moral character, impartiality and integrity with high qualifications and experience in relevant fields, including law, human rights, counter-terrorism, and sanctions.[88] A subsequent Resolution, 1989/2011, extended the mandate and support of the Ombudsperson and included detailed provisions on listing and de-listing procedures.[89] The Security Council continues thus to have the ultimate decision-making power on delisting and is not obliged to follow a de-listing recommendation by the Ombudsperson.[90]

84 N. Krisch, *Beyond Constitutionalism. The Pluralist Structure of Postnational Law* (Oxford: Oxford University Press, 2010), 156–157.

85 *Yassin Abdullah Kadi and Al Barakaat International Foundation v Council and Commission*, Joined Cases C-402/05 P and C-415/05 P, [2008] ECR I-6351. From the plethora of commentaries, see V. Mitsilegas, 'The European Union and the Globalisation of Criminal Law' *Cambridge Yearbook of European Legal Studies* (2009)–(2010) 12, 337–407.

86 Para.12.

87 Para.13.

88 Para.20.

89 Paras 12–35.

90 Para.23.

This new scheme of listing was examined by the ECJ in the *Kadi II* litigation.[91] While attempting to accommodate to some extent security considerations, the Court has adopted in *Kadi II* a rigorous, substantive test of judicial review of listing decisions by the European judiciary. The Court reiterated that such a judicial review is indispensable to ensure a fair balance between the maintenance of international peace and security and the protection of the fundamental rights and freedoms of the person concerned, those being shared values of the UN and the EU.[92] While the emphasis on shared values may have been included to diffuse potential tensions with regard to the conflict between EU law and UN Security Council measures, the Court did not hesitate to emphasise the need to protect human rights in the face of a UN framework providing limited safeguards. The Court reiterated the substantial negative impact of sanctions to the affected individuals[93] and went on to say that the improvements at UN level with regard to listing do not provide the guarantee of effective judicial protection to the affected individual.[94] The Court thus confirmed again, as in *Kadi I*, the autonomy of the EU legal order based on the respect for the rule of law and fundamental rights. While the Court's ruling in *Kadi I* has had a noticeable impact in improving listing procedures at UN level, the Court in *Kadi II* sent a clear message that such improvements can by no means equate to effective judicial protection. The Court continued to remind the international community that it is the individual who should be the focus of authorities in the invasive process of the imposition of restrictive sanctions. At the same time, the Court in *Kadi II* sent a clear message with regard to the relationship between the executive and the judiciary: the executive cannot use secrecy and confidentiality to evade judicial scrutiny, especially when the protection of fundamental rights is at stake.[95] However, it must be noted that the Court focused on procedural justice and refrained from ruling on the impact of terrorist listings on substantive human rights of the affected individuals such as the right to property and did not question (perhaps unsurprisingly) the very existence of the sanctions system and the elevation of the UN Security Council into a legislator. This practice is continuing, with the recent adoption of a UN Resolution on 'foreign fighters' being a key example. As with the post-9/11 Resolutions, the 'foreign fighters' Resolutions have gone through a process of legitimisation via the adoption of legislation – in Europe, this has occurred as seen above with the Council of Europe and currently with the European Union.

91 Resulting in *European Commission v Kadi*, Joined Cases C-584/10 P, C-593/10 P and C-595/10 P.

92 Para.131.

93 Para.132.

94 Para.133.

95 V. Mitsilegas, 'The European Union and the Global Governance of Crime' in V. Mitsilegas, P. Alldridge and L. Cheliotis (eds), *Globalisation, Criminal Law and Criminal Justice. Theoretical, Comparative and Transnational Perspectives* (Oxford: Hart, 2015), 153–198.

VI. Conclusion

This chapter has provided a typology of norm-making in the field of transnational criminal law and has painted a complex, multi-layered landscape of global security governance. Traditional forms of international law-making – in the form of UN treaties – have emerged in the past three decades to address major perceived security threats including drug trafficking, money laundering, organised crime and corruption. The more recent treaties – the 2000 Palermo Convention and UNCAC in 2003 – have placed emphasis not only on standard-setting but also on compliance, by establishing a series of monitoring mechanisms albeit on the basis of the principles of equality and sovereignty of States Parties. This model of global law-making has been deemed to be limited by key global players (and in particular the US and the EU). The lack of global consensus has meant that the international community has not managed to reach consensus on all major areas of security concern (terrorism and cyber-crime are examples in this context). At the same time, regulatory and legal responses reflected the need to react to perceived security threats as a matter of urgency (in particular post-9/11) and as a matter of priority and sustained focus (in particular in the development of a global anti-money laundering regime). They also reflected a greater emphasis towards effective implementation and compliance across the globe, in an effort to create a global regulatory and legal level playing field. These factors explain the emergence of forms of governance parallel to the traditional model of international Conventions. These forms of governance have emerged at three levels: at the regional level; at the level of 'soft' or 'informal' law; and at the level of 'global administrative law.' Rather than being mutually exclusive, these levels of governance of transnational crime are interrelated and mutually reinforcing. In all areas of transnational crime examined in this chapter, regulation in one level of governance has resulted in regulation in another level of governance. The emergence of a brand new global framework to counter money laundering and terrorist finance exemplifies this trend: norms have emerged at the UN system (in both the Vienna and Palermo Conventions), at the regional level (in the CoE, the EU and the regional bodies of the FATF), and at the level of the UN Security Council. Global anti-money laundering governance has also witnessed the emergence in the form of the FATF of a new international institution with a single agenda, entrusted specifically to counter money laundering and financing of terrorism.

The emergence of this paradigm of global multi-level governance in the field of transnational crime poses significant challenges for justice and the rule of law. As a starting point, it must be remembered that this is a paradigm centred on enforcement, with the norms adopted having a significant impact on individual rights. In a system of transnational criminal law, the norms adopted at global level have a domestic reach, in creating criminal law obligations at the national level and at times – as in the case of sanctions imposed in the Security Council – having a direct impact on individuals. Both the way in which global norms are produced, and their impact, challenge perceptions and the substance of justice at the international and domestic level. At the international level, a key issue is justice among states, which is an aspect of the principle of equality among states. On a number of occasions – and in particular in cases of less traditional forms of norm-making including by the FATF and the UN Security Council – we have seen that norms are pushed through by a select club of states which then attempt to impose standards globally. This form of governance gives little space to a plurality of voices across the globe. The shift towards regionalism can be explained as an attempt to address this injustice and take into account diversity, but the very foundations and processes of global norm-making have not changed significantly over time. At the domestic level, the issue of justice is linked to the protection of fundamental rights, and in particular the right to judicial protection. The justice deficit in this context has been clearly demonstrated in the case of terrorist sanctions imposed by the UN Security Council, where invasive action has been adopted against specific individuals behind closed doors and with very little transparency or justification. Challenges to justice in this context are inextricably linked to challenges to the rule of law. In its *Kadi* litigation the ECJ has highlighted these challenges for the protection of fundamental rights by insisting on the need for full judicial scrutiny of executive action. But the rule of law challenges are not limited to judicial review. The system of governance established in particular by informal and global administrative law raises major questions of democracy, transparency, accountability and participation in the process of global norm-making in transnational criminal law. Notwithstanding attempts to improve procedures at the FATF and UN Security Council, a plethora of global enforcement standards are being depoliticised and produced behind closed doors by experts from a select group of states – and are then presented as an orthodoxy for the whole world to adopt. Fundamental rule of law requirements and the impact of these measures and transnational criminal law on individual rights makes this form of governance increasingly untenable.

Part II

Chapter 5

Prosecutorial strategies and opening statements

Justifying international prosecutions from the International Military Tribunal at Nuremberg through to the International Criminal Court*

Ron Levi, Sara Dezalay and Michael Amiraslani

I. Introduction

The expansion of a professional field of international criminal law since the 1990s is commonly identified with a trajectory of international justice that gained traction over the course of the twentieth century. This is said to begin at the International Military Tribunal at Nuremberg (IMT) – and to extend to the current International Criminal Court (ICC). This trajectory, thought of by political scientists as a 'justice cascade',[1] is said to have reshaped how atrocities are handled at the international level, by emphasizing individual criminal responsibility as the mode of accountability for war crimes and massive human rights violations.[2] This surge is said to recover the 'legalism' underlying the Nuremberg trials,[3] extending what Sikkink[4] identifies as the 'hard law streambed' of individual criminal accountability globally.

When one contrasts the narrow legal authority of the IMT at Nuremberg with the growth of international criminal law from the 1990s onward, the growth of this field appears, indeed, teleological. Yet as the field of international criminal justice has expanded and solidified, struggles over the *authority* of these courts

* This paper is a slightly expanded version of a paper first published in 26(4) *Comparativ: Zeitschrift für Globalgeschichte und vergleichende Gesellschaftsforschung* (2016) 58–73.

1 K. Sikkink, *The Justice Cascade: How Human Rights Prosecutions Are Changing World Politics* (Norton, New York, 2011).

2 R. Levi and J. Hagan, 'Penser les "Crimes de Guerre"' 173 *Actes de la recherche en sciences sociales* (2008) 6–21; D. Scheffer, *All The Missing Souls. A Personal History of the War Crimes Tribunals* (Princeton University Press, Princeton, 2012).

3 G. Bass, *Stay the Hand of Vengeance: The Politics of War Crimes Tribunals* (Princeton University Press, Princeton, 2000).

4 Sikkink, fn.1 above.

have continued to rage. Despite growing attention to international criminal justice as a broad framework, it is not the case that each of these courts has simply gained greater authority over time. This is partly because these courts have been unable to develop routinized legal strategies that can persist over time.[5] Given the atypical political environments in which these courts operate, and the contentious nature of their operations, their authority is instead derived from the relationship between geopolitical contexts and the capacities of their prosecutors to adapt to these demands. The result is that, despite their formal legal authority, gaining authority in fact – that is, the capacity to generate alliances among wider constituencies and thus being able to effectively launch international legal prosecutions – has rested on the ability of prosecutors to detect these demands, to adapt their strategies for collecting evidence, and to calibrate their bureaucratic processes for indictment and prosecution to varying political circumstances.[6]

As a result, it is prosecutors, rather than judges, who have been at the strategic core of how international criminal courts negotiate external geopolitics. Their attempts to build authority for these courts explain, for example, the documentary strategy at Nuremberg, the media relations strategy of the International Criminal Tribunal for the former Yugoslavia, and the hesitation to engage in on the ground investigations by the Office of the Prosecutor at the International Criminal Court.[7]

Yet prosecutors do more than engage in investigation and the collection of evidence. They ground their interventions by framing their prosecutions in a language aimed at justifying the decision to pursue individual criminal accountability. Thus, there is a *moral grammar* to these prosecutions, through which international prosecutors work to assure other institutional players and external audiences that these prosecutions are 'worth the candle'.[8] We argue that these legal justifications should form part of a broader sociology of practice and of fields. Our claim is that these justifications are particularly relevant to international legal fields *both* because of the centrality of language as a form of symbolic power for law, *and* because the field of international criminal law in particular is a weak and heteronomous field.[9] These justifications are themselves part of the strategic work that prosecutors engage in, with each institution recreating itself and justifying its weak authority rather than relying on a slow accretion of authoritative practice.[10]

In this chapter, we contrast the strategic work of prosecutors at two significant moments of the development of the field of international criminal law: at the stage

5 S. Dezalay, 'Weakness as Routine in the Operations of the International Criminal Court' *International Criminal Law Review* (2016) 1–21.

6 R. Levi, J. Hagan and S. Dezalay, 'International Courts in Atypical Political Environments: The Interplay of Prosecutorial Strategy, Evidence, and Court Authority in International Criminal Law' 78(4) *Law and Contemporary Problems* (2016) 289–314.

7 Levi, Hagan and Dezalay, fn.6 above.

8 P. Bourdieu, *Practical Reason: On the Theory of Action* (Stanford University Press, Stanford, 1998), 77.

9 Levi, Hagan and Dezalay, fn.6 above.

10 Dezalay, fn.5 above.

of the genesis, at the International Military Tribunal at Nuremberg (IMT), and at the International Criminal Court (ICC), the first *permanent* court of international criminal justice. By studying the opening statements in these two instances, our emphasis is on how prosecutors at these two tribunals *justify* these proceedings and the prosecutorial strategies they have elected to pursue. To be sure, the opening statements at Nuremberg reflected the national interests of each of the four states involved.[11] Yet, looking at these statements together is also a way to infer from these justifications the status of the Tribunal more broadly, in its wider context – and we then compare these with the opening statements of the first prosecutions at the ICC. This does not mean that we divorce the study of prosecutors' language from that of context or power. Instead, through an analysis of these justifications we gain insight into the repertoires available to prosecutors and the position-takings of prosecutors in relation to their audiences at both Nuremberg and the ICC. This provides us with a comparative sociology of law in two different eras and geopolitical contexts – the immediate period following World War II on the one hand, and the post-Cold War and post-9/11 context of the creation of the ICC on the other hand – to explain the 'conditions under which different types of evaluation prevail'[12] in international criminal justice, and how legal power is justified in each instance.

In what follows, we expand briefly on our approach to the study of justifications, before turning to our two case studies: the full text of the opening statements of the four different Chief Prosecutors at the IMT at Nuremberg (respectively from the US, France, the UK, and the Soviet Union), and the opening statements for the prosecution in the first three cases of the ICC. In assessing these texts against a range of possible justifications, we find narrower appeals over time and less diversity in the orders of worth to which prosecutors appeal to launch cases. We trace this as a shift from a justificatory model of 'organizational hedging'[13] to a model of unhedged bets, in which we see significant investment in a narrower set of justifications and a move away from broad appeals to justify legal intervention. Combining these findings with interviews and archival data, we conclude that this is part of a broader move toward an investment in 'pure law' at the ICC, embedded in a geopolitical context of comparatively weak – if not waning – political support for its operations and prosecutions, and an ongoing competition between law and diplomacy that threatens the supply of cases and situations to the Court.

11 M. Marrus, *The Nuremberg War Crimes Trial, 1945–46: A Documentary History* (Bedford Press, Boston, 1997).

12 M. Lamont and L. Thévenot (eds), *Rethinking Comparative Cultural Sociology. Repertoires of Evaluation in France and the United States* (Cambridge University Press, Cambridge, 2000), 7.

13 D. Stark, *The Sense of Dissonance: Accounts of Worth in Economic* Life (Princeton University Press, Princeton, 2011).

II. Prosecutorial discourse as practice: studying repertoires, stability, innovation, and change in international legal fields

Perhaps in an effort to distinguish itself from internal and legalistic approaches to studying law, the sociology of international law often defines legal practices as nearly everything *but* the discourse of law itself. Though often decried as an outmoded distinction, this continues to inform polarizing debates in the field. This is illustrated by Bourdieu's view that Latourian research on science (or, presumably, now on law) amounts to mere *textism* because it ignores positions and position-takings, or Latour's opposite response that, for Bourdieu, 'legal form does not add anything, other than the impossibility of criticizing the resources that it hides between its pseudo-rationalizations'.[14] Seeking to go beyond these debates, we combine a focus on prosecutorial opening statements, which we construe, thereby, as themselves a form of *practice*, with parallel attention to the resources and positions available to prosecutors as they develop their strategic statements. In other words, our research strategy relies on an empirical approach to strategic statements that regards international legal practices as themselves embedded within the geopolitical context in which courts operate.[15]

Contrasting how repertoires change over time, and in these two institutional forums, enables us to empirically trace processes of change over time in international legal fields. Focusing on how innovative international legal institutions and processes are justified over time is indeed a way to emphasize processes of stability, innovation, and change in the field of international criminal law.[16] Examining how legal innovation is justified builds on work in comparative sociology and the sociology of culture that examines how, for example, different social groups evaluate 'worth' and 'morality'.[17] The focus is thereby shifted from a sociology exclusively focused on *values* to a sociology of *value* and of *valuation*.[18]

To build this approach, we bring together two related conceptual tools. The first, drawn from the literature on practices in international relations and international law, regards discourse as a form of practice itself (with practices themselves understood as a form of speech act[19]). Yet we also suggest that legal discourse does

14 B. Latour, *The Making of Law: An Ethnography of the Conseil d'Etat* (Polity Press, Cambridge, 2010).

15 K.J. Alter, M.R. Madsen and L. Helfer, 'How Context Shapes the Authority of International Courts' 79 *Law and Contemporary Problems* (2016) 1–36.

16 See generally J. Brunnée and S. Toope, 'Interactional International Law: An Introduction' 3(2) *International Theory* (2011) 307–318.

17 Lamont and Thévenot, fn.12 above.

18 M. Lamont, 'Toward a Comparative Sociology of Valuation and Evaluation' 38(1) *Annual Review of Sociology* (2012) 201–221.

19 E. Adler and V. Pouliot, Adler, 'International Practices' 3(1) *International Theory* (2011) 1–36; J. Meierhenrich, 'The Practice of International Law: A Theoretical Analysis' 76(3–4)

more than this: statements by prosecutors are not only epistemic in the sense of building on a community of practice, they are also fundamentally strategic and justificatory. This echoes Bourdieu's elaboration on law and the state in *Sur l'État*, in which he identified the central importance of the 'capital of words' available to lawyers in the parallel development of legal fields and fields of state power.[20] This capital is what allows lawyers to innovate over time. Thereby, the unique power of jurists to justify is also a power that draws together the political *with* language in order to justify and explain innovative political and social practices.

We rely on these insights to trace change, innovation, and stability over time in international criminal legal institutions, with an emphasis on processes of legitimation and justification. This is particularly critical in the context of international criminal law, given the logic of the 'constant coup' that seems to dominate this field,[21] and the need, therefore, for continued justification and legitimacy. In other words, while the field of international criminal law may appear to have a teleological trajectory from the post-World War II moment through to the present, there is also a sense of constant crises in which lawyers must legitimate and justify their intervention at each turn. In the field of international criminal law, this is illustrated by the protracted tension between international criminal justice and its political alternatives, most prominently manifested in the 'peace-justice tradeoff' that pits lawyers against diplomats for the resolution of violent conflict. This is a classic problem for actors in a weak field, making it a struggle to gain and maintain authority.

III. Prosecutorial opening statements: legal innovation in unsettled times

To study how legal innovation is justified, we rely on the regimes of justification distilled by Boltanski and Thévenot in *On Justification*, in which they classify the chief conventions, or 'orders of worth', that individuals rely on to justify their positions in light of disagreements or contention.[22] As they demonstrate, there is a pluralism to how people justify actions: rather than being limited to justifications from a particular social field, individuals may move from one form of justification to another, and rely on moral principles from an array of ethical spheres. These are 'market performance', 'industrial efficiency', 'civic equality', 'domestic relations', 'inspiration', 'renown', and in more recent literature, 'sustainability'.[23] Each of

Law & Contemporary Problems (2013) 1–83; and see J. Searle, *Speech Acts: An Essay in the Philosophy of Language* (Cambridge University Press, New York, 1969).

20 P. Bourdieu, *Sur l'État. Cours au Collège de France (1989–1992)* (Le Seuil, Paris, 2012).

21 Dezalay, fn.5 above.

22 L. Boltanski and L. Thévenot, *On Justification: Economies of Worth* (Princeton University Press, Princeton, 2006).

23 Lamont and Thévenot, fn.12 above.

Table 5.1 Orders of worth[1]

	Inspired	*Domestic*	*Civic*	*Opinion*	*Market*	*Industrial*
Mode of evaluation (worth)	Grace, nonconformity, creativeness	Esteem, reputation	Collective interest	Renown	Price	Productivity efficiency
Elementary relation	Passion	Trust	Solidarity	Recognition	Exchange	Functional link

1 This table is a condensed version of the table in L. Boltanski and L. Thévenot, 'The Sociology of Critical Capacity', 2 *European Journal of Social Theory* (1999) 359–377, 368.

these categories provides a moral grammar for justifying action, as summarized in Table 5.1.

This moral grammar can be illustrated with a common situation of justification. In his work applying this sociology of justifications to how changes in the economy were articulated and produced in Eastern Europe, David Stark elegantly relies on the example of a faculty reference letter for an academic job candidate.[24] Such a letter would often rely on multiple justifications for why the candidate deserves the position: it may indicate that the candidate is very creative (thus drawing on the world and language of creativity and 'inspiration'), that they are loyal to students (thus drawing on the language of the 'domestic' order and its elementary relation of trust), that they are a good citizen in engaging with their colleagues (thus drawing on the language of the civic and the collective interest), that they are frequently cited (and thus renowned), that they have a strong record of attracting grant funding (or a market justification), and that they are also highly productive and efficient.

Stark's example not only demonstrates these orders of worth in practice: it also underlines that justifications need not be exclusive of each other. Indeed, this becomes part of Stark's analysis of how justifications can reflect and allow for 'organizational hedging'. If an institution is uncertain about the metrics that will be used to evaluate its success, and/or if an institution is looking for opportunities to gain degrees of freedom by *producing* that very uncertainty so as to allow it to act along different paths and meet a variety of requirements, it will develop justifications for contentious action across multiple registers: as he suggests, '[i]n managing one's portfolio of justifications, one starts from the dictum: diversify your accounts'.[25]

In the context of international criminal law, this is a particularly attractive avenue to examine how courts are positioned over time. It is also especially relevant as a method to study prosecutorial practices, since these reflect both the range of the possible (what can be said) and the appeals that can be made (in Stark's terms,

24 Stark, fn.13 above.

25 D. Stark, 'Recombinant Property in East European Capitalism' 101(4) *American Journal of Sociology* (1996) 993–1027.

prosecutors must be attendant to their environment to both react to and at times produce uncertainty through their statements), and on the social skill of prosecutors in developing these frames and aligning their institutions around them in order to induce cooperation as needed.[26]

In this chapter, we focus on the four prosecutorial opening statements at the IMT,[27] and contrast these with the prosecutorial opening statements in the first three cases of the ICC (*Lubanga*,[28] *Katanga*[29] and *Bemba*[30]). We selected these as significant case studies: the ICC's prosecutorial statements in its first three cases provide a current empirical moment for considering the 'Nuremberg legacy', comparing the field's genesis at the IMT with the ICC as the first *permanent* international criminal court.

We coded the prosecutorial statements to identify language, in these prosecutorial statements, that reflected an appeal to the orders of worth distilled by Boltanski and Thévenot: 'industrial', as an appeal to efficiency; 'domestic', as an appeal to domestic practices and national loyalty; 'inspired', as an appeal to humanity; 'opinion', as an appeal to recognition; 'market', as an appeal to economic efficiency; 'civic', as an appeal to collective welfare and society. As we develop below, these empirics across both courts underline clear patterns of position-taking and change in prosecutorial statements between these two institutional settings and over time.

IV. The International Military Tribunal at Nuremberg: hedging across topics and across time

In his opening statement to the Nuremberg trial in 1945, the Chief Prosecutor for the United States, Justice Robert Jackson, emphasized documentary proof in

26 J. Barbot and N. Dodier, 'Rethinking the Role of Victims in Criminal Prosecution' 64(3) *Revue Française de Science Politique* (2014) 23–49; J. Hagan and R. Levi, 'Social Skill, the Milosevic Indictment, and the Rebirth of International Criminal Justice' 1 *European Journal of Criminology* (2004) 445–475; N. Fligstein, 'Social Skill and the Theory of Fields' 19(2) *Sociological Theory* (2001) 105–125.

27 These are available through 'Trial of the Major War Criminals Before the International Military Tribunal, Nuremberg, 14 November 1945–1 October 1946', *The Avalon Project at the Yale Law School.* For discussion see Marrus, fn.11 above.

28 Mr Luis Moreno-Ocampo, Prosecutor of the International Criminal Court, Ms Fatou Bensouda, Deputy Prosecutor of the International Criminal Court. 'The Case of the Prosecutor v. Thomas Lubanga Dyilo. ICC-01/04-01/06. Opening Statement', The Hague, 26 January 2009.

29 Mr Luis Moreno Ocampo, Prosecutor of the International Criminal Court, Ms Fatou Bensouda, Deputy Prosecutor of the International Criminal Court, Mr Eric MacDonald, Senior Trial Lawyer of the International Criminal Court, 'The Case of the Prosecutor v. Germain Katanga and Mathieu Ngudjolo Chui. ICC-01/04-01/07. Opening Statement', The Hague, 24 November 2009.

30 Mr Luis Moreno-Ocampo, Prosecutor of the International Criminal Court, 'The Case of the Prosecutor v. Jean-Pierre Bemba Gombo. ICC-01/05-01/08. Opening Statement', The Hague, 22 November 2010.

the prosecution. 'We will give you undeniable proofs of incredible events', he said, referring among other items to 'hundreds of tons of official German documents', the 'captured orders and captured reports' that provide evidence of atrocities, and the violence and criminal enterprise that 'we will prove from their own documents'.[31] 'There is no count in the Indictment that cannot be proved by books and records', Jackson indicated, emphasizing that '[t]he Germans were meticulous record keepers'. Justice Jackson held this position for months leading up to the prosecution: at the International Conference leading to the trials, he insisted that '[w]e must establish incredible events by credible evidence', underlining that the trial would be 'a drab case' based on documentary evidence of Nazi crimes, but that the documents would render it unchallengeable.[32]

In addition to Justice Jackson's documentary-based strategy, each prosecutor of course also sought to represent their country's own national positions in their opening statements. It is thus not surprising that General Rudenko mainly sought to justify the prosecution in light of the Nazis' crimes regarding the Soviet Union (a 'domestic' justification that represents nearly 60 per cent of all justifications he used in his statement). The prosecutors from France and the United Kingdom each relied on domestic justifications in nearly a quarter of all their justificatory statements: and the US prosecutor, hailing from the most distant of the four countries, only relied on domestic justifications in under 7 per cent of his statements. The opposite occurred with respect to industrial justifications speaking, for instance, to a system of international justice. The US prosecutor relied heavily on this industrial logic (nearly 75 per cent of all his justifications reflected the 'industrial' order of worth); the prosecutors from France and the UK each relied on this for just over half of their justificatory statements; and the Soviet prosecutor relied on industrial justifications for just over one quarter of his justificatory claims at Nuremberg. And in contrast, the US prosecutor was the only one of the four to even briefly invoke a 'market'-based justification for the prosecution, in the name of 'the American dream of a peace-and-plenty economy'. Clearly, national positions made a difference in these prosecutors' justifications.

Yet what is most notable is that, throughout the opening statements, all four prosecutors also invoked nearly all of the justifications identified by Boltanski and Thévenot. All prosecutors spoke across a wide array of orders of worth to justify the Nuremberg Trial: in other words, *each and every prosecutor justified the Nuremberg trial by invoking the worlds of inspiration, the domestic, the civic, opinion, and the industrial* (with a market justification, as noted above, also

31 R. Jackson, Opening Statement Before the International Military Tribunal (22 November 1945), accessed 6 June 2017 at www.roberthjackson.org/the-man/speeches-articles/speeches/speeches-by-robert-h-jackson/opening-statement-before-the-international-military-tribunal/.

32 S. Breyer, 'Crimes Against Humanity: Nuremberg, 1946' 71(5) *New York University Law Review* (1996) 1161–1164.

Table 5.2 Justifications for the IMT Nuremberg prosecution

IMT Prosecutor	*Inspired*	*Domestic*	*Civic*	*Opinion*	*Market*	*Industrial*
Jackson (US)	4.1%	6.8%	10.2%	3.7%	1.35%	73.9%
Shawcross (UK)	6.5%	24.1%	4.3%	8.6%	—	56.5%
de Menthon (France)	7.4%	22.4%	9.8%	5.4%	—	55%
Rudenko (USSR)	1.7%	59.3%	8.7%	2.9%	—	27.3%

invoked by the US prosecutor). So while each national prosecutor placed different *emphasis* on some orders of worth, each of the prosecutors also relied on a *wide array* of these orders of worth in justifying the Nuremberg prosecution. We demonstrate this in Table 5.2.

These findings are illustrated by the following quotes, which demonstrate appeals to each order of worth by different prosecutors.

The Nuremberg prosecution as an appeal to the world of *inspiration*:

> 'We believe that there can be no lasting peace and no certain progress for humanity, which still today is torn asunder, suffering, and anguished, except through the co-operation of all peoples and through the progressive establishment of a real international society' (de Menthon, France, representing 7.4 per cent of his justifications).

The Nuremberg prosecution as an appeal to the world of the *domestic*:

> 'Now, when as a result of the heroic struggle of the Red Arms and of the Allied forces, Hitlerite Germany is broken and overwhelmed, we have no right to forget the victims who have suffered. We have no right to leave unpunished those who organized and were guilty of monstrous crimes' (Rudenko, USSR, representing 59.3 per cent of his justifications).

The Nuremberg prosecution as an appeal to the world of the *civic*:

> 'The day has come when the peoples of the world demand a just retribution and ... when they demand severe punishment of the criminals' (de Menthon, France, representing 9.8 per cent of his justifications).

The Nuremberg prosecution as an appeal to the world of *opinion*:

> 'When Belgium and the Low Countries were occupied and France collapsed in June of 1940, England – although with the inestimably valuable moral and

> economic support of the United States of America – was left alone in the field as the sole representative of democracy in the face of the forces of aggression' (Shawcross, UK, representing 8.6 per cent of his justifications).

The Nuremberg prosecution as an appeal to the world of the *market*:

> 'The American dream of a peace-and-plenty economy, as well as the hopes of other nations, can never be fulfilled if those nations are involved in a war every generation so vast and devastating as to crush the generation that fights and burden the generation that follows' (Jackson, US, representing 1.4 per cent of his justifications).

The Nuremberg prosecution as an appeal to the world of *industry, efficiency, and practicality*:

> 'This Tribunal, while it is novel and experimental, is not the product of abstract speculations nor is it created to vindicate legalistic theories. This inquest represents the practical effort of four of the most mighty of nations, with the support of 17 more, to utilize international law to meet the greatest menace of our times – aggressive war' (Jackson, US, making up 73.9 per cent of his justifications).

How can we understand the wide array of justifications that were deployed by each of the Nuremberg prosecutors? By drawing together the study of justifications with field sociology, we suggest that this wide breadth of justifications can be understood as a strategy of 'organizational hedging' (to use Stark's concept) by Nuremberg prosecutors. This 'hedging' strategy, we suggest, allowed these four prosecutors to shore up the tribunal's authority and legitimacy through the language and moral grammar they deployed. This was particularly important given the skepticism the IMT faced, and the political fields within which the IMT and its prosecutors were embedded.

This was particularly important in the IMT context. First, this was a time- and place-bound tribunal that, while purporting to develop legal rules for possible application to future cases, was more proximately a response to how to deal with Nazi criminality. Yet there was suspicion – both in the US and the UK, and certainly in the USSR – over the very idea of criminal prosecution for Nazi leaders, regarded by many as risky and as an overly soft response by elites and public opinion alike. This was instantiated in the view of Roosevelt's Secretary of the Treasury Henry Morgenthau, who derided the strategy as 'kindness and Christianity' rather than a strategy to deindustrialize Germany and to 'attack [] the German mind' itself.[33] The IMT's comparative lack of early authority was

33 Bass, fn.3 above, 152.

reflected in the views of elite government lawyers such as Joseph O'Connell, who regarded the Tribunal as a fundamentally 'unlegalistic approach' that applies domestic approaches 'to a world situation which has nothing in common with it';[34] or even the view of Henry Stimson, the leading US government designer and champion of the trial-based approach at Nuremberg, who referred to the 'difficult question' of the Nuremberg trials.[35] It was similarly reflected in the early views of President Roosevelt, who sought to emphasize the collective responsibility of the German people, rather than merely that of 'a few Nazi leaders'.[36] Second, among other segments there was criticism over the tribunal's perceived legitimacy,[37] with the trials often derided as 'victor's justice', and the criminal counts enumerated in the Charter of the IMT characterized as ex post facto charges that undercut legal and political legitimacy.[38] Third, the prosecution was internally embattled: each of the Allies were pursuing different goals, and each articulated the rationale for the prosecution differently depending on the degree to which they regarded themselves as victims of the Nazi regime.[39]

This wider context of contestation over the very standing of the Tribunal helps explain the broad appeals being made at various levels of justification, precisely because the IMT at Nuremberg was *both* understood to be operating within a context of high ambiguity over its degree of authority, *and* because its prosecutors – in the US but also in the UK and France – would be invested in keeping a broad rhetorical framework so as to position themselves broadly in their national jurisdictions (Jackson, for instance, had been identified before his departure as a possible Chief Justice of the US Supreme Court).[40]

This perhaps also explains the degree to which the prosecutors, in particular Hartley Shawcross from the UK, but others as well, sought to downplay the degree to which Nuremberg represented a legal innovation. Shawcross, for instance, explicitly positioned the IMT as 'no more than the logical development of the law' rather than an 'innovation', despite 'some small town lawyers who deny the very existence of any international law'. For his part, while underscoring that the IMT prosecutions were 'novel and experimental', Jackson still emphasized

34 Bass, fn.3 above, 179.

35 Bass, fn.3 above, 171–172.

36 Bass, fn.3 above, 154.

37 N. Frei, 'Before and After Nuremberg' 38(2) *Journal of Contemporary History* (2003) 333–343.

38 M. Minow, *Between Vengeance and Forgiveness: Facing History After Genocide and Mass Violence* (Beacon Press, Boston, 1998); but see S. Karstedt, 'The Nuremberg Tribunal and German Society: International Justice and Local Judgment in Post-Conflict Reconstruction' in D.A.B. and T.L.H. McCormack (eds), *The Legacy of Nuremberg. Civilising Influence or Institutionalised Vengeance?* (Brill, Leiden, 2008), 13–35.

39 Marrus, fn.11 above.

40 For a discussion see J. Barrett, 'Bringing Nuremberg Home: Justice Jackson's Path Back to Buffalo, October 4, 1946' 60 *Buffalo Law Review* (2012) 295–321.

that the Tribunal was not 'created to vindicate legalistic theories' or to advance law and legal developments, but was instead a merely technical, practical way to solve problems. Indeed, this emphasis on continuity was central in Jackson's statements, who thereby underlined a strategy that had already been legitimated among the US legal elite who were enrolled into the prosecution. If junior staff filled the prosecutorial ranks, the most senior of the US lawyers at Nuremberg were those who had been instrumental in US antitrust cases in the 1930s. Robert Jackson himself had played a leading role in these cases, and he was joined at Nuremberg by other prominent New Deal veterans of antitrust litigation: William Donovan of the OSS; John Amen of the US Attorney General's Office, who was New York's 'leading "crime buster"' and son-in-law of President Cleveland; and Henry Stimson, the Secretary of War and the leading proponent in the Roosevelt administration for holding war crimes trials. These lawyers had all invested in antitrust litigation strategies for criminal prosecutions domestically, whether dealing with corporations such as the Sugar Trust, or gangsters in New York. Taking this shared domestic legal experience to the international stage – and to a Tribunal that was considered to be without precedent – was a prosecutorial strategy designed to resonate with the existing practices of a powerful constituency of legal experts in the United States.

Finally, this organizational hedging is also mirrored in how all prosecutors deployed *time* in their justifications. As others working on the sociology of conventions and justifications have noted, strategic actors often deploy time in ways to gain adherents and to build their claims, often with an orientation to the future in their justifications.[41] We demonstrate this in Table 5.3.

Indeed, while the Soviet prosecutor, Rudenko, was least strategic in this regard (since of course he did not regard the case as building a set of future-oriented principles), the other prosecutors invoked the future relatively consistently, if not overwhelmingly so. Indeed, the IMT prosecution sought to build authority for the Nuremberg trials – in light of these legal concerns and the wider geopolitical context – by looking to the future and the anticipated legacy of the trial. Notably,

Table 5.3 Temporality at IMT Nuremberg

Prosecutor	*Future*	*Past*	*Neutral/Present*
Jackson (US)	18.5%	11.3%	70.2%
Shawcross (UK)	10.4%	46.6%	42.9%
de Menthon (France)	13.3%	34.0%	52.7%
Rudenko (USSR)	0	69.8%	30.2%

41 N. Dodier, 'Les appuis conventionnels de l'action: Eléments de pragmatique sociologique' 11(62) *Réseaux* (1993) 63–85.

Jackson sought to do so by building an external constituency for the Tribunal by emphasizing the momentum it could spur historically. As Jackson wrote to Henry Stimson, his evidentiary strategy was to produce a case that would be perceived as sound, 'particularly when the record is examined by the historian'. This aimed at bolstering the authority of the IMTs toward the community of elite US lawyers and deflect potential resistance from the start – but this future orientation also appealed to a wider spectrum of constituencies among audiences in the US, and Europe.

As we will see below, on both of these dimensions – organizational hedging and future orientation – the IMT prosecutors stand in stark contrast to the justifications of the first three prosecutions at the ICC.

V. The International Criminal Court: investing in technicality and law as an unhedged bet

The most notable institution in international criminal justice currently is the International Criminal Court. With the ICC being restricted by its own statute to cases where countries are unwilling or unable to conduct their own investigations, and limited to those countries which have joined the Court as States Parties (absent a Security Council referral) – and with atrocities occurring in some African states – the ICC's docket quickly became focused on African conflicts.[42] In light of this, the authority of the ICC has become deeply at stake with the potential withdrawal of African Union states from the Rome Statute, with the African Union expressing concern over the 'politicization and the misuse of indictments against African leaders by the ICC'.[43] As a result, though the ICC enjoys a professionalized base of legal scholarship and practitioners on which to draw – compared to the IMT at Nuremberg – it is also faced with persistent challenges to authority along with charges of politicization.

At one level, the resulting crisis of authority lies in the very mandate of the Court, since the situations and often real-time crimes that the ICC is seized with are deeply enmeshed within ongoing diplomatic, political, and economic struggles. As Alex Whiting, who earlier served in the International Criminal Tribunal for the former Yugoslavia (ICTY) and then as both Investigation and Prosecution Coordinator with the ICC notes, in the ICC 'each investigation is largely shaped by the constraints and opportunities peculiar to the situation at hand'.[44] Commentators also increasingly wonder whether the 1990s which built

42 See A. Branch, 'Neither Liberal nor Peaceful? Practices of "Global Justice" by the ICC', in S. Campbell, D. Chandler and M. Sabaratnam (eds.), *A Liberal Peace? The Problems and Practices of Peacebuilding* (Zed Books, London, 2011), 121–137.

43 Extraordinary Session of the Assembly of the African Union, 12 October 2013, Addis Ababa, Ethiopia, Ext/Assembly/AU/Dev.1-2 (Oct. 2013).

44 A. Whiting, 'Dynamic investigative practice at the International Criminal Court' 76 (3–4) *Law and Contemporary Problems* (2013) 163.

the momentum for the creation of the ICC represented a high-water mark that was unlikely to be sustained, in the post-9/11 era, pointing to perceived bias in prosecutions, and to the failure to deal with the protracted conflict in Syria.[45] The ICC thus finds itself in a paradoxical position in which there is a seemingly strong 'common sense'[46] over international criminal justice as a legitimate response to mass violence – indeed reinforced by the professionalization of the field – but a protracted fragility of the ICC as the institutional forum for this response.[47]

In this context it is perhaps not surprising that the prosecutorial strategy, as illustrated in the first three cases of the ICC, appears to turn more adamantly on a legal framework, with an appeal to 'pure law'[48] that draws on the now more elaborate doctrine of international criminal legal and increasing legal professionalization within the field. This interview with a senior ICC prosecution lawyer adeptly caps this turn to a 'pure law' strategy:

> We have always followed a policy where we do not want to have ICTY type of investigations where we charge basically the history of the Balkans in one case, so that is an attempt to write history in criminal proceedings ... *So what we do is we focus our investigations on a very limited number of crimes, we also focus our investigations on those persons whom we believe bear the greatest responsibility* ...[49]

This focus on pure law was stressed by the first Prosecutor himself: 'International criminal law is so primitive that for us, it's law, but for others, it is just one political option among others.'[50]

This turn to a legal framing can partly be seen as a strategy to deflect criticisms of the politicization of the ICC.[51] It is also likely an outgrowth of the increasing legal professionalization of the field of international criminal law, with new young legal personnel coming through the ICC with academic training and detailed knowledge of international criminal law. This growing expertise is seen – as just one example – in Figure 5.1, which provides a count of the number of faculty members listed as specializing in international criminal law in law schools across the US.

45 D. Bosco, *Rough Justice: The International Criminal Court in a World of Power Politics* (Oxford University Press, New York, 2014).

46 C. Topalov (ed.), *Laboratoires du nouveau siècle. La nébuleuse réformatrice et ses réseaux en France (1880–1914)* (Editions de l'EHESS, Paris, 1999).

47 Dezalay, fn.5 above.

48 Y. Dezalay, 'From Mediation to Pure Law: Practice and Scholarly Representation in the Legal Sphere' 14 *International Journal of the Sociology of Law* (1986) 89–107.

49 Authors' interview with legal officer at the OTP, The Hague, 22 August 2012. Emphasis added.

50 Authors' interview with Luis Moreno Ocampo, Toronto, 8 November 2012.

51 J. Meierhenrich, 'The Evolution of the Office of the Prosecutor at the International Criminal Court: Insights from Institutional Theory, in M. Minow, C. True-Frost and A. Whiting (eds.), *The First Global Prosecutor: Promise and Constraints*' (University of Michigan Press, Ann Arbor, 2015), 97–127.

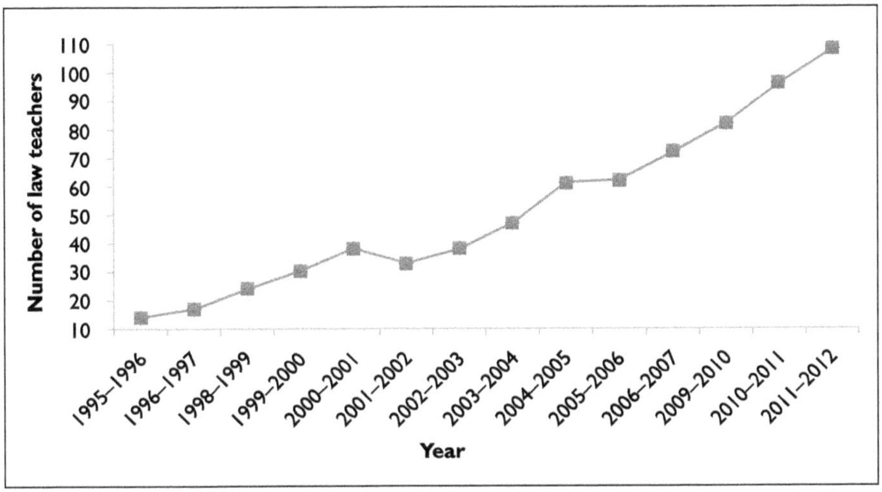

Figure 5.1 Number of law teachers in US law schools specializing in international criminal law.[52]

Note: data unavailable for 1997–1998, 2007–2008, 2008–2009.

This legalization turn has also been reflected in an explicit strategy of the ICC prosecutor, both for the conduct of investigations, and in the professional profiles among the staff at Office of the prosecutor.[53] By 2009, prosecutions were largely overseen from the ICC Office of the Prosecutor in The Hague, with few if any on-the-ground investigations, and by professionals with backgrounds in law more than in police investigation (in contrast to previous tribunals, such as the ICTY). This offshore investigation strategy was driven in part by the difficulty of conducting on-site investigations, compounded by the lack of US support in the first years of operation of the ICC. But it also responded to the prosecutor's strategy of developing cases against top political and military figures, with the stake of establishing the responsibility for command authority over crimes, rather than proving the occurrence of the crimes themselves.

This approach has led to direct criticism of the ICC Prosecutor's Office, thought to unduly rely on investigatory materials and evidence provided by secondary actors, such as pre-positioned NGOs on the ground such as Avocats Sans Frontières.[54] But it has also, indirectly, narrowed the spectrum of possible

52 These data come from the American Association of Law Schools' directory of law teachers for each of the relevant years: AALS. The AALS Directory of Law Teachers. Washington, D.C.: AALS.

53 Dezalay, fn.5 above.

54 Notably in the *Lubanga* case, in which, among the 624 pages of the decision, more than 200 focus on evidence-related issues – not only the investigation strategy, but also a central issue pertaining to this case – and others: that of the selection and roles played by 'intermediaries' on the ground to gather evidence or identify (and vet) witnesses and victims.

justifications once evidence is marshaled, downstream, into the Court, notably regarding the position of victims in prosecutorial justifications. As one interviewee indicated, at the ICC 'they don't see any problem in defending, in given trials, one group and another in another trial, even though they massacred each other. In any case they are victims ... it is a depoliticization of the court ...'[55]

This context of constraint and constant external pressure to not be identified as 'political', along with this prosecutorial strategy of offshore investigations, is directly reflected in the prosecutorial opening statements in the first three cases of the ICC. Indeed, in stark contrast to the organizational hedging model of the IMT prosecutors at Nuremberg, these underline a turn to an unhedged bet of law and legal expertise. There is thus a concentration of justifications across three orders of worth: the 'civic', the 'inspired', and the 'industrial' – and no invocation at all of the 'domestic', 'opinion', or the 'market'. Further, not only is there a substantial growth of appeals to the 'industrial' – but the 'industrial' is also the primary justification – making up over 70 per cent of justifications in all three cases, reaching 84 per cent in the *Bemba* case. While hinging on an appeal to professionalism and efficiency, this further reflects what Bourdieu described as an 'organizational capital with a legal basis',[56] whereby prosecutions are justified on the basis of a legal form of expertise. This is particularly well illustrated in the opening statement in *Bemba*:

> The Rome Statute consolidated customary international law on the topic and specified its dimensions. It does not introduce a new and separate liability of the superior into international law [...] In accordance with this principle and the Pre-Trial Chamber III's decision confirming the charges for trial, the Prosecution will prove the elements required by the law in this specific case.[57]

This turn to 'pure law' is further reflected by the relative change of other orders of worth invoked by prosecutors over the ICC's first three cases. We demonstrate this shift in Table 5.4.

Table 5.4 Orders of worth in ICC prosecutions

	Inspired	*Domestic*	*Civic*	*Opinion*	*Market*	*Industrial*
ICC Lubanga	21.2%	—	5.8%	—	—	73%
ICC Katanga	13%	—	9.8%	—	—	77.2%
ICC Bemba	4%	—	12%	—	—	84%
IMT at Nuremberg (all four prosecutors)	5.2%	29.0%	8.4%	5.2%	<1%	52.3%

55 Authors' interview with victims' lawyer, Brussels, 13 December 2012.

56 Bourdieu, *Sur l'État*, fn.20 above, 524–525.

57 *Bemba*, fn.30 above.

As prosecutors relied ever more heavily on 'industrial' justifications that reflect legal professionalism, expertise, and efficiency, they relied ever less on appeals to the order of 'inspiration'. In the *Lubanga* case, the very first prosecution of the ICC, prosecutors placed significant weight on inspiration in the opening statements. For example: 'The children still suffer the consequences of Lubanga's crimes. They cannot forget what they suffered, what they saw, what they did [...] They will tell the Court what happened to them. They will speak or themselves and for all the other, for those who could not overcome the past or face the present.'[58] Yet over the course of the next two cases, prosecutorial appeals to inspiration fell dramatically, from 21 per cent of all justifications in *Lubanga*, to 13 per cent in the following case of *Katanga*, and down to merely 4 per cent of all prosecutorial justifications in the *Bemba* opening statements. And on the flip side, justifications based on a 'civic' order of worth were deployed by ICC prosecutors to emphasize solidarity with victims and a global community that is built, in the main, through law and legal tools – and these doubled in prominence, from 6 per cent of justifications in *Lubanga*, to 10 per cent in *Katanga*, and 12 per cent of all justifications in the ICC's third case in *Bemba*. Take for example the prosecutorial opening statement in *Katanga*:

> The people from such places as Bogoro, Bunia, Aveba and Zumbe must know that they are not alone, they do not need to resort to violence again ... the people from Ituri, have to feel they are part of a global community, that we are their brothers and sisters. The Rome Statute is building one global community to protect the right of victims all over the world.[59]

In parallel to this narrowing in orders of worth, prosecutorial statements in the ICC have also used ever less of the future tense in their justifications. While more prevalent in the ICC's first case in *Lubanga*, by the ICC's third case in *Bemba*, only the 'industrial' order of worth relies on some future-orientation in its language (at just 5 per cent of these justifications), and the use of future-statements in the context of inspiration and civic orders of worth falls to zero in the prosecutorial statements. This is also in contrast with the opening statements at Nuremberg, where some use of the future appeared across all orders of worth. ICC prosecutors are thus relying both on a narrower set of justifications over time, and on an increasingly presentist (rather than a future-oriented) language. This shift in the use of time is demonstrated in Table 5.5.

Taken together, this evidence suggests that in the ICC there is a growing segmentation of law from diplomacy and from the national context of state politics. This is in favor of an unhedged bet on legalization and professionalism,

58 *Lubanga*, fn.28 above, 2.
59 *Katanga*, fn.29 above, 3.

Table 5.5 Future-orientation of orders of worth

	Inspired	*Domestic*	*Civic*	*Opinion*	*Market*	*Industrial*
ICC: Lubanga	37.90%	—	12.50%	—	—	5%
ICC: Katanga	50%	—	0%	—	—	1.40%
ICC: Bemba	0%	—	0%	—	—	4.80%
IMT at Nuremberg (all four prosecutors)	64.70%	3.10%	15.80%	11.10%	50%	8.20%

aimed at insulating the ICC from criticism and wider contextual constraints – be it a result of being shunned by states, or the difficulties of conducting investigations on the ground.

VI. Conclusion

The moral grammar of international criminal prosecution is, we argue, deeply connected to the position-takings of prosecutors and the geopolitical contexts in which courts are embedded. At any given time, prosecutors are engaging in a strategic approach that engages with the opportunities and constraints of the field: both to deflect concerns over the cases they are prosecuting, and to afford themselves opportunities to recast the debate. Comparing the IMT at Nuremberg and the ICC along these lines, we find markedly different approaches. For a Tribunal in the post World War II context in which there was skepticism over even its *de jure* authority and over the capacity of law to respond adequately to Nazi crimes, IMT prosecutors responded to that uncertainty through organizational hedging that drew on the widest array of justifications available. In contrast, the ICC finds itself on the other end of the continuum: faced with persistent charges of politicization and now beyond the peak of international social movement support, ICC prosecutors have instead invested in an unhedged bet that increasingly privileges a single justificatory language – a technical, legal, and institutional approach – while also refraining from a future-orientation to its prosecutorial claims.

It is here that the focus on prosecutorial statements is brought together with a field theory of international law. Paralleling the professionalization of international criminal law over time, interview evidence suggests that the decision to invest more heavily in a legalization that seeks to deflect politics is as much a reaction to the political context in which the ICC finds itself as it reflects the availability of a professionally and increasingly specialized staff. As Bourdieu's work on the state and the role of jurists indicates, juridical capital here relies on the capacity to rely on words and meaning to both advance the legal cause – both in the IMT and in the ICC – and to legitimate the role of legal institutions as a response to atrocity. This further serves to legitimate the professional expertise and domain of lawyers operating within the ICC. In this way, prosecutors in both eras are seeking to position the courts vis-à-vis its critics, real or anticipated. The entrepreneurial work of prosecutors in these statements is thus to mediate and to present the innovations of these courts – and their own positions within the field as a result – in ways that respond to and shift the terrain to accommodate the dominant values of the field at a given moment in time. This combination of language and rhetorical appeals as both responsive to constraints and an attempt to recast the terrain is, we suggest, core to understanding the juridical capital of prosecutors in international legal fields.

Chapter 6

Red Notices and transnational police practices

Nicola Langille and Frédéric Mégret

Introduction

International criminal law, classically understood, regulates individuals engaging in crimes of a truly international nature. It also, however, concerns itself with the regulation of crime with cross-border elements (or transnational criminal law).[1] By and large, international criminal law is perceived to be a law-oriented field – administered by courts, rule-bound and dominated by states. This is partly a result of the study of the discipline being increasingly dominated by a focus on the centralized practices of international criminal tribunals and their particular approach to international cooperation. Yet international criminal tribunals remain a poor indication of the day-to-day operation of international criminal law, whether seen in its classic or more expansive sense. In many ways, the daily life of international criminal law as a whole is characterized by horizontal exchanges between states in the context of extradition and judicial assistance. Moreover, in the shadow of international criminal tribunals and even state-to-state channels of criminal cooperation lie a number of intriguing transnational practices that are better understood as hybrid: part judicial, part administrative, and part policing. These practices reflect the reality of something that is not always understood to be part of the system of international criminal law, namely transnational policing.

Transnational policing can be defined as the totality of efforts engaged in the effort to maximize the effectiveness of the enforcement of domestic and international criminal law. To be specific, we have in mind the effort of states and policing organizations within them to enhance cooperation in the arrest and surrender of fugitives. To be even more specific, this chapter will be devoted to the study of one particularly emblematic practice that has evolved in the second half of the twentieth century: Interpol Red Notices. Interpol and its practices are much older than the emergence of the current regime of international criminal

1 See e.g. Neil Boister, 'Transnational Criminal Law?' (2003) 14:5 *European Journal of International Law* 953.

law, but they have significant organic and conventional links with it, and constitute one of the backbones of the system of international criminal law. They bring attention to the challenges of enforcing criminal law in a decentralized and plural international system. Interpol is also an interesting case of what Anne-Marie Slaughter has described as a transnational 'government network',[2] one relying on collaboration between civil servants on the basis of a certain professional solidarity and technical know-how, that supposedly transcends national rivalries.

Red Notices specifically are interesting for a number of reasons. First, their operation is relatively little understood beyond specialized governmental and intergovernmental agencies, even though they form a crucial part of the routinized administration and enforcement of international criminal law. Their relatively discreet, specialized and unspectacular character means that they are typically neglected in relation to much more visible forms of international criminal law enforcement. Second, Red Notices operate at the intersection of several fields and logics in a way that makes them sui generis: although they are meant as a prelude to extradition and judicial proceedings, their fundamental logic is administrative or managerial. In that respect, they raise interesting questions for liberties and human rights, but also more generally about the nature of practices that operate in the shadow of more formalized procedures. Third, Red Notices are an interesting case of transnational criminal practice in the making and suggest ways in which policing and police forces can subtly emancipate themselves from the emphasis on the state. They are characteristic of the continued relevance of a horizontal model of cooperation that operates between states but also in practice between policing agencies themselves.

This chapter suggests that a better understanding of neglected mechanisms such as Red Notices can shed light on international criminal law as a discipline that is deeply embedded in transnational policing practices. Transnational policing raises questions about the possibility of an enforcement-focused model of transnational criminal law not falling prey to political manipulation. To analyze the development of Red Notices this chapter first locates the emergence of this technology within the operation of Interpol as a unique form of transnational police cooperation (I). It then highlights the centrality of Red Notices within that institutional context and exposes their basic operation (II). Finally, the chapter reflects from a more critical perspective on the implications of the rise of Red Notices as a preferred mode of law enforcement (III). The argument is that Red Notices are part of an effort to circumvent judicial protections against extradition (and detention pending extradition) in suspect circumstances, for the benefit of aggressive policing and law enforcement aims.

2 Anne-Marie Slaughter, *A New World Order* (Princeton: Princeton University Press, 2004).

Interpol as sui generis international cooperation

Red Notices cannot be understood outside the emergence of a very specific form of cooperation, that is part inter-governmental part professional network. The rise of Interpol is interesting as a transnational phenomenon heavily mediated by police actors seeking to facilitate cooperation between and amongst themselves. While the problem of cross-border crime is not new – nor is the idea of international cooperation with a view to addressing it – the shape that cooperation takes has and continues to change. Interpol represents one such effort.

Origin

Interpol's origins date to the First International Police Congress, held in Monaco in 1914 (the 'First Congress').[3] Prior to the First Congress, efforts at bilateral and multilateral police cooperation were as varied as the histories of the countries and regimes in which that cooperation occurred.[4] While these efforts at informal police cooperation in the nineteenth century laid the groundwork for the development of more enduring forms of police cooperation, it was not until the early twentieth century that international police cooperation began to be structured in a 'more or less' permanent organization.[5]

The First Congress attracted approximately 300 participants from 24 countries, both within and outside of Europe.[6] Participants engaged in four thematic sessions, addressing 'general police questions, means of identification, a central registration system, and extradition procedures'.[7] To fulfill mutual aims relating to the themes discussed at the First Congress, including the dissemination of search warrant information, it was suggested that information be shared directly

3 R.E. Kendall, 'International Co-operation – Extra Territorial Enquiries, Extradition and Surrender of Fugitives, Exchange of Information' (1988) 11:1 *Police Studies: The International Review of Police Development* 18 at 18. According to one commentator, efforts at police cooperation failed in 1914 because the meeting 'was still framed in terms of the provisions of international law rather than the bureaucratic model that police institutions had by then come to adopt': Deflem, 'Wild Beasts Without Nationality: The Uncertain Origins of Interpol, 1898–1910' in Philip Reichel (ed.), *Handbook of Transnational Crime and Justice* (Thousand Oaks, CA: Sage Publications, 2005), 277.

4 Early examples of international police cooperation between German states, for instance, focused on political policing and the repression of loosely labeled 'anarchists': Richard Bach Jensen, 'The International Anti-Anarchist Conference of 1898 and the Origins of Interpol' (1981) *J. Contemp. Hist*, 323.

5 Mathieu Deflem, *Policing World Society: Historical Foundations of International Police Cooperation* (Oxford: Oxford University Press, 2002), 97. See also ch.1, 'The Rise of International Policing'.

6 Deflem, *Policing World Society*, 102.

7 Deflem, *Policing World Society*, 103.

between various police agencies, and a system was proposed for the distribution of an international publication containing such information.[8]

However, the outbreak of World War I effectively sidetracked any progress associated with the First Congress. It was not until 1923 that efforts began to kick-start the project anew. In September of that year, approximately 138 representatives from 21 states and territories met at the headquarters of the Criminal Police of Vienna for the Second International Criminal Police Congress (the 'Second Congress'), and formed what they would call the International Criminal Police Commission (the 'ICPC'), Interpol's predecessor organization.[9]

The participating policing organizations in the ICPC preferred to operate in direct contact with one another, rather than through governments (a preference shared by First Congress participants as well[10]).[11] By working directly through policing agencies, the ICPC sought to circumvent the expressly political in favor of what were thought to be common policing aims. Its logic was therefore functional in a context where the fight against crime was increasingly seen as a universal goal. Indeed, during his opening speech to the Second Congress, Johannes Schober (the Police President of Vienna, who initiated the meeting) stated that police cooperation was 'not a political but a cultural goal'.[12]

As a result, the ICPC was not created through government action – no treaty was ever signed to bring it into being.[13] Instead, its activities were planned and carried out by police organizations without the input or control of their governments.[14] Nonetheless, the participation of police agencies was not intended to signal a sacrifice or denial of national sovereignty. The ICPC 'was set up explicitly ... not as a supranational force but as an inter-national network enabling direct communications between police of different countries'.[15] Membership was and still is on a national basis,[16] though participating police representatives have

8 Deflem, *Policing World Society*, 103.
9 Trevor Meldal-Johnsen and Vaughn Young, *The Interpol Connection: An Inquiry into the International Criminal Police Organization* (New York: The Dial Press, 1979), 34.
10 Deflem, *Policing World Society*, 98. Nonetheless, Deflem has argued that the First Congress 'was still rooted in principles of national politics and formal systems of law'; for instance, it was organized not by police officials or bureaucrats but instead by the Prince of Monaco (Albert I). Moreover, some of the themes discussed at the First Congress – most importantly those concerning extradition – took place within a legal framework rather than a bureaucratic one (Ibid., 107).
11 Michael Barnett and Liv Coleman, 'Designing Police: Interpol and the Study of Change in International Organizations' (2005) 49:4 *International Studies Quarterly*, 593–619.
12 Deflem, *Policing World Society*, 136.
13 This remains true with respect to Interpol: see Matti Joutsen, 'International Instruments on Cooperation in Responding to Transnational Crime' in Philip Reichel and Jay Albanese (eds), *The Handbook of Transnational Crime and Justice*, 2nd edn (Thousand Oaks, CA: Sage, 2014), 255–74.
14 Deflem, *Policing World Society*, 137. Nonetheless, status within the League of Nations was sought throughout the 1920s and 1930s: see Deflem, *Policing World Society*, 138.
15 Deflem, *Policing World Society*, 136.
16 Michael Fooner, *Interpol: Issues in World Crime and International Criminal Justice* (New York: Plenum, 1989), 48.

been able to secure what Deflem terms 'formal bureaucratic autonomy' from their respective governments.[17]

Early on, the ICPC proved to be highly effective at sharing information with respect to criminals. Within the first year of its founding, it began publishing wanted persons notices in its International Public Safety Journal. By 1933, the ICPC's archives had a list of 3,240 internationally wanted criminals, with photographs and fingerprints for a number of them.[18] In 1946, the organization emitted its first 'notice' seeking the arrest, detention, and extradition of a fugitive.[19] These early efforts laid the foundation for Interpol's notices system.

Political co-optation and the emergence of Interpol

In spite of its commitment to political independence (one retained by Interpol to this day), the ICPC has been criticized – to varying degrees and in relation to various acts – for political forays over the course of its existence. According to James Sheptycki, '[o]ne way to view the ... development of Interpol during the 20th century is that it was a transnational organisational entity that was "captured" by certain specific states' interests and that the really significant signposts of its chronology are moments when the captive status was transferred.'[20] In what is universally acknowledged to be a particularly disturbing historical moment the ICPC entered into a period of 'nazification' beginning in 1938.[21] By 1942, it had fallen completely to Nazi control, and its headquarters were relocated to Berlin. In a separate period later on, a former SS officer, Paul Dickopf, ascended to Interpol's presidency.[22]

As another example, the FBI terminated its participation in the ICPC in 1950 in part due to Soviet control over Eastern European nations that were members

17 Deflem, *Policing World Society*, 174.

18 Crime and Justice International (2007) 23: 98.

19 Interpol, *History*, accessed 6 June 2017 at www.interpol.int/About-INTERPOL/History.

20 James Sheptycki, 'The Accountability of Transnational Policing Institutions: The Strange Case of Interpol' (2004) 19:1 *Can. J. of Law and Soc.* 107 at 115 (Sheptycki, *The Strange Case of Interpol*). See also Deflem *Policing World Society*, 175ff.

21 Sheptycki, *The Strange Case of Interpol*, 115. Much has been written about this period of Interpol's history: see e.g. Meldal-Johnsen and Young, *The Interpol Connection*, ch.3 (*The Nazi Take-Over*); M. Deflem 'The Logic of Nazification: The Case of the International Criminal Police Commission ("Interpol")' (2002) 43 *Int. J. Comp. Soc.* 21. According to Sheptycki, Interpol's entire history can be described through political capturing. In his view, Interpol remained almost wholly under French influence from the 1940s until 1986, when a period of 'Anglo-American hegemony' began (*The Strange Case of Interpol*, 115–16). Since then, Interpol has had to manage the rise of other regional powers, as well as the inclusion of several post-colonial nations. For the roots of French influence on international police cooperation, see Deflem, *Policing World Society*, 107–110.

22 Meldal-Johnsen and Young, *The Interpol Connection*, 13ff.

of the organization.[23] While the FBI subsequently re-established formal ties with the organization in 1969,[24] the representativeness of these historic difficulties should not go overlooked. An institutional commitment to political independence has not meant that Interpol has avoided being swept into the political realm. The organization has at times struggled to divorce the aims and politics of its individual members from its broader vision as an organization.

In 1946, following on the heels of World War II, the ICPC was founded anew, and in 1956 the organization changed its name to Interpol.[25] As a result of previous periods of political cooptation, Article 3 of Interpol's Constitution now states, 'It is strictly forbidden for the Organization to undertake any intervention or activities of a political, military, religious or racial character.'[26]

Thus, the ICPC and Interpol emerged out of the aspirations of those who sought to secure international policing efforts without involving the formal mechanics of the state. The organization has always been designed to facilitate communication and the sharing of information directly between policing organizations, while escaping the potentially distorting effect of political influence and involvement. These foundational aims are supposed to continue to lay the groundwork for Interpol in its modern form.

Interpol today

Currently, Interpol boasts a membership of 190 countries.[27] In a number of member states, Interpol's membership is second only to the United Nations.[28] Interpol's stated mission is 'Preventing and fighting crime through enhanced international police cooperation'.[29] Article 2 of Interpol's Constitution states that the organization's aims are:

1 To ensure and promote the widest possible mutual assistance between all criminal police authorities within the limits of the laws existing in the different countries and in the spirit of the 'Universal Declaration of Human Rights';

23 Cyrille Fijnaut, 'The International Criminal Police Commission and the Fight Against Communism, 1923–1945' (1997) *Polic. Polit. Twent. Century Hist. Perspect*, 107.

24 Fooner, *Interpol: Issues in World Crime and International Criminal Justice*, 122.

25 Michael Fooner, *INTERPOL: The Inside Story of the International Crime-Fighting Organization* (Chicago: Henry Regnery Company, 1973), 26–27.

26 Interpol Constitution, Art.3, accessed 6 June 2017 at www.interpol.int/About-INTERPOL/Legal-materials/The-Constitution.

27 Interpol, accessed 6 June 2017 at www.interpol.int/Member-countries/World.

28 Bettina Schöndorf-Haubold, 'The Administration of Information in Interpol Administrative Law – The Example of Interpol' (2008) 9:11 *German L.J.* 1719 at 1720 (Schöndorf-Haubold, *The Administration of Information*).

29 Interpol, accessed 6 June 2017 at www.interpol.int/About-INTERPOL/Overview.

2 To establish and develop all institutions likely to contribute effectively to the prevention and suppression of ordinary law crimes.[30]

Importantly, Interpol does not view global criminality as something limited to interstate crime, or truly international crimes. While Interpol is concerned with both of these phenomena, like its predecessor it mostly implicates itself in fighting domestic crime by seeking to facilitate both the tracking and capture of individuals whose alleged crimes may have been committed entirely within one nation's borders but who have subsequently left that nation, and coordinating cooperation in crime investigation. Interpol's mandate, therefore, focuses squarely on the facilitation of conventional policing and law enforcement aims, practices, and processes.

Interpol's role in accomplishing these aims is largely facilitative. The organization remains a network of policing organizations that enables international contact between police,[31] and it functions mostly by sharing information between member police forces.[32] Interpol provides the infrastructure for international police cooperation, offering a global communication system, compiling databases and distributing wanted notifications. Despite the powerful and popular imagery of a truly international police force, Interpol has not developed – and arguably cannot develop – to assume such a global position.[33] The organization itself has no operational role (in the words of one commentator, '[t]he man from Interpol never arrested anyone').[34] This imposes important limitations on its functions. Interpol cannot and does not conduct its own investigations or intervene in cases on its own. Instead, it should be seen as a tool for international cooperation between the national police authorities that fulfill these tasks.[35]

While membership in Interpol is formally constructed at the state level, domestically it plays out through national policing chapters (National Central Bureaus ('NCBs')). NCBs 'serve as operational centers and linking platforms between the national and the international level'.[36] Much of Interpol's work takes place through the NCBs.[37] Each NCB (and participating member state) is presumed to be an equal participant in Interpol. As one commentator has put it, Interpol conducts its affairs according to the following principles: respect for

30 Interpol Constitution, accessed 6 June 2017 at www.interpol.int/About-INTERPOL/Legal-materials/The-Constitution.

31 Sheptycki, *The Strange Case of Interpol*, 115.

32 Ben Bowling and James Sheptycki, 'Global Policing, Mobility and Social Control', in *The Routledge Handbook on Crime and International Migration* (Sharon Pickering and Julie Ham eds., 2015), ch.4 (unpaginated).

33 See generally Fooner, *INTERPOL: The Inside Story of the International Crime-Fighting Organization*.

34 Sheptycki, *The Strange Case of Interpol*, 116.

35 Schöndorf-Haubold, *The Administration of Information*, 1720.

36 Schöndorf-Haubold, *The Administration of Information*, 1726.

37 Sheptycki, *The Strange Case of Interpol*, 123.

national sovereignty, application of the provisions of Article 3 of the Constitution, universality, equality of all member states, cooperation with other agencies, and flexibility of working methods.[38]

The Red Notice system

In many ways, the Red Notice system is the 'jewel in the crown' of transnational police cooperation governed by Interpol. Understanding its unique functioning opens a window to how inter-professional cooperation between police organizations allows them to manifest their relative autonomy beyond governments.

Foundation

One of Interpol's most powerful communication and coordination tools, in this context, is its notices system. As noted above, the ICPC had from its outset been concerned with facilitating extradition. In fact, according to Deflem extradition was by far the topic most addressed by members of the ICPC during the organization's formative years.[39] In particular, members took issue with what they viewed to be the cumbersome nature of official extradition procedures (especially the 'slow, diplomatic channels' through which the practice traditionally operated).[40] The overwhelming concern was to bring efficiency to the practice. Nonetheless, at least at the time of the founding of the ICPC, it was determined that requests for provisional arrest to a foreign police authority could only be made on the basis of an extradition order.[41] Therefore, it was not yet open to representatives to make direct requests for the arrest of individuals for the purpose of extradition. Instead of interfering with the physical extradition process itself, the ICPC sought to facilitate extradition through the efficient and speedy exchange of information directly between police bureaus.[42] Moreover, Interpol sought to make extradition a multilateral process. From 1936 to 1938, for instance, it collaborated with the International Penal and Penitentiary Commission in the preparation of a draft universal convention on the subject of extradition.[43]

In recent years, however, Interpol's role in facilitating extradition has expanded with the increasing use of the organization's long-standing notices system. This system allows for the dissemination of several types of alerts to member states.

38 R.E. Kendall, 'International Co-operation – Extra Territorial Enquiries, Extradition and Surrender of Fugitives, Exchange of Information' (1988) 11:1 *Police Studies: The International Review of Police Development* 18, 18–20.

39 Deflem, *Policing World Society*, 145.

40 Trevor Meldal-Johnson and Vaughn Young, *The Interpol Connection: An Inquiry into the International Criminal Police Organization* (New York: The Dial Press, 1979), 37.

41 Deflem, *Policing World Society*, 127–28.

42 Deflem, *Policing World Society*, 145.

43 Fooner, *Interpol: Issues in World Crime and International Criminal Justice*, 143.

Interpol issues eight types of notices: orange notices ('[t]o warn of an event, a person, an object or a process representing a serious and imminent threat to public safety'); black notices ('[t]o seek information on unidentified bodies'); yellow notices ('[t]o locate missing persons…'); green notices ('[t]o provide warnings and intelligence about persons who have committed criminal offences and are likely to repeat these crimes in other countries'); blue notices ('[t]o collect additional information about a person's identity, location or activities in relation to a crime'); purple notices ('[t]o seek or provide information on modus operandi, objects, devices and concealment methods used by criminals'); and so-called UN Security Council 'special notices' ('[i]ssued for groups and individuals who are the targets of UN Security Council Sanctions Committees').[44]

Finally, and most importantly for these purposes, Interpol can issue Red Notices '[t]o seek the location and arrest of wanted persons with a view to extradition or similar lawful action.'[45] Red Notices can be issued either prior to a trial or to facilitate execution of a sentence.[46] In brief, a country's police force can request that Interpol issue a Red Notice when an individual wanted for prosecution (or who has otherwise absconded pending a judicial case) is thought to be in another country. A Red Notice is intended to alert other nations that that individual may be found within their territory, and asks the nation that locates that individual to arrest him or her with a view to extradition. Red Notices are not *themselves* arrest warrants, but can, in certain circumstances, be given a similar effect. While the ICPC initially refused to take such a step, Interpol now asks its members to recognize the Red Notice as a valid request for provisional arrest pending extradition.[47] When treated as a request for provisional arrest, a Red Notice can lead directly to the detention of a potential fugitive. It is perhaps for this reason that Red Notices are commonly misconceived as being international arrest warrants, or at least – as the United States Prosecutors' manual states – the closest thing to one that exists.[48]

The operationalization of Red Notices

Practically speaking, the manner in which Red Notices are operationalized is via communication from one NCB to Interpol's General Secretariat. A Red Notice can be emitted after the issuance of a valid arrest warrant or judicial decision

44 Interpol, Notices, accessed 6 June 2017 at www.interpol.int/INTERPOL-expertise/Notices.

45 Interpol, Notices, accessed 6 June 2017 at www.interpol.int/INTERPOL-expertise/Notices. Interpol has also recently commenced a pilot project for the dissemination of 'silver notices', concerning the tracing and recovery of assets.

46 Schöndorf-Haubold, *The Administration of Information*, 1739.

47 Interpol, General Assembly, 80th Session, Hanoi, 31 October – 3 November, 2011 (AG-2011-RES-06).

48 See M. Cherif Bassiouni, *International Extradition: United States Law and Practice* (Oxford: Oxford University Press, 2014), 1065 (United States Attorneys' Manual, s.9-15.635).

having the same effect, coordination between the NCB and the authorities responsible for extradition, and the General Secretariat's approval.[49] The Red Notice/diffusion contains basic information about the fugitive sought and the crime he/she has purportedly committed. If an NCB's request does not qualify for the publication of a notice, however, the underlying information can nonetheless be sent directly to a chosen nation or nations through the use of a 'diffusion'.[50] Diffusions are not 'endorsed' by Interpol, but nonetheless Interpol facilitates their direct dissemination to organizations worldwide.

When deciding whether or not to approve a Red Notice, the General Secretariat must determine whether issuing the notice is 'necessary and advisable with regard to the aims and tasks of the organization, the respect of Human Rights and the required security measures against possible menaces to ... police cooperation, to Interpol itself or to the member states'.[51] The General Secretariat is barred from issuing a Red Notice if the request fails to meet the formal requirements of Interpol's constitution, or other Interpol regulations. Article 83 of Interpol's *Rules on the Processing of Data* establish certain criteria that must be met in order for the Notice to be issued: among other things, the offence concerned must be a 'serious ordinary-law crime', certain minimum penalties must be associated with the offence, and the request must be 'of interest for the purposes of international police cooperation'.[52] However, a Red Notice that does not meet these criteria can nonetheless be published if doing so 'would be of particular importance to international police cooperation'.[53] Article 83 further stipulates that Red Notices may be issued only when sufficient identifying information associated with the subject of the Notice is provided, and when there is sufficient 'judicial data', including a summary of the facts of the case, charge(s), and reference to a valid arrest warrant or judicial decision having the same effect.[54]

Of course, the particular standards applicable to these requirements remain opaque. Interpol is not a judicial body – nor does it pretend to be – of the sort that could make these determinations transparently.[55] Moreover, in spite of these

49 Interpol, *Rules on the Processing of Data*, Art.83, accessed 6 June 2017 at www.interpol.int/About-INTERPOL/Legal-materials/Data-protection.

50 Interpol, *Rules on the Processing of Data*, Arts 97ff. A diffusion 'is circulated directly by an NCB to the member countries of their choice, or to the entire INTERPOL membership': Interpol, 'Notices', accessed 6 June 2017 at www.interpol.int/INTERPOL-expertise/Notices. These two categories of methods by which Notices are diffused are also discussed in Kendall, 'International Co-operation', 26.

51 Schöndorf-Haubold, *The Administration of Information*, 1740.

52 Interpol, *Rules on the Processing of Data*, Art.83(1)(a).

53 Interpol, *Rules on the Processing of Data*, Art.83(1)(b).

54 Interpol, *Rules on the Processing of Data*, Art.83(2).

55 As one Interpol official has stated, 'Interpol is not a judicial body. It is not, nor should it be the responsibility of INTERPOL ... to assess evidence at the national level': *The Guardian*,

formal rules around the dissemination of Red Notices, practically speaking a Red Notice need not be approved by Interpol's General Secretariat for the information it contains to be widely disseminated. Article 77 of Interpol's *Rules on the Processing of Data* permits the publication of the Notices while they are being examined by the General Secretariat. While, in such a case, an additional indication is inserted to alert the viewer that the request has not been approved and is not a published notice,[56] the information contained in the notice is nonetheless disseminated to member nations and entities around the world (according to Interpol, officers in the NCBs and other authorized users are able to access this online database system).[57] Finally, Interpol's diffusion system is almost entirely regulated by the NCBs, without comparable levels of Interpol oversight.[58]

Reception and popularity

Of course, the fact that a Red Notice has been emitted says little about how it will be received in a country in which the subject of the Notice has been located. As stated above, the concrete effect that is given to a Red Notice depends upon the choices made by the state in which the individual subject of the Red Notice is ultimately found. Some member countries (by some estimates, one-third) consider a Red Notice to be a valid request for provisional arrest and will detain its subject if found within their territory. In addition, some bilateral and multilateral extradition treaties now recognize Interpol as an official channel for sending requests for provisional arrest.[59] For example, section 20 of the United Nations' Model Law on Extradition addresses how recipients should respond to requests for provisional arrest, and does not draw a distinction between a request for provisional arrest received directly from the requesting state and one emanating from Interpol.[60]

In other cases, Interpol's mechanisms for disseminating requests for provisional arrest are incorporated directly into formalized extradition arrangements. For example, Article 16.3 of the European Convention on Extradition indicates that a request for provisional arrest should be sent either 'to the competent authorities of the requested Party either through the diplomatic channel or direct by post or

accessed 6 June 2017 at www.theguardian.com/uk-news/2013/nov/27/interpol-accused-red-notice-requests.

56 Interpol, *Rules on the Processing of Data*, Art.77(3).

57 Interpol website, accessed 6 June 2017 at www.interpol.int/INTERPOL-expertise/Data-exchange/I-link.

58 Interpol, *Rules on the Processing of Data*, Arts 77ff.

59 The Law Library of Congress, *Interpol: Red Notices* (July 2010), accessed 6 June 2017 at www.loc.gov/law/help/archived-reports/interpol-red-notices.pdf.

60 *United Nations Model Law on Extradition*, accessed 6 June 2017 at www.unodc.org/pdf/model_law_extradition.pdf.

telegraph or through the International Criminal Police Organisation (Interpol).'[61] Article 22.3 of the Economic Community of West African States' (ECOWAS) Convention on Extradition replicates this language.[62] In sum, Red Notices are being formally legitimated as both a means of spreading information about fugitives, and reliable grounds upon which nations should act once that information is received.

The rapidly increasing use of Red Notices speaks to the increased legitimacy that they are gaining as a means of transmitting requests for provisional arrest. In 2002, for instance, 1,212 Red Notices were issued.[63] By 2015, this number increased almost tenfold to 11,492.[64] Diffusions, for their part, have also greatly increased in use. Whereas in 2002, 7,500 diffusions were issued, in 2015 this number had risen to 22,753.[65] In part, this increase in the use of Red Notices stems from the establishment of a new Command and Coordination Centre ('CCC') following September 11, 2001.[66] The CCC operates 24 hours a day, 365 days of the year, and is therefore at the ready when dissemination of a Red Notice is sought.[67] However, this multiplication of Red Notices also attests to their growing popularity as a way of rapidly obtaining certain effects on the ground, including provisional arrest, even as actual extradition remains a sometimes remote possibility.

Two phenomena characteristic of the explosion of international criminal law in the last 20 years have boosted the relative authority of Red Notices and their tendency to take increased autonomous significance. First, the post-9/11 era has witnessed a considerable boom in the number of Red Notices issued in relation to terrorism offences.[68] Interpol had traditionally been wary of getting involved

61 European Convention on Extradition, accessed 6 June 2017 at rm.coe.int/CoERMPublicCommonSearchServices/DisplayDCTMContent?documentId=0900001680064587.

62 Economic Community of West African States, *Convention on Extradition*, accessed 6 June 2017 at documentation.ecowas.int/download/en/legal_documents/protocols/Convention%20on%20Extradition.pdf.

63 Interpol, 2002 Annual Report, accessed 6 June 2017 at www.interpol.int/News-and-media/Publications2/Annual-reports2.

64 Interpol, 2015 Annual Report, accessed 6 June 2017 at www.interpol.int/News-and-media/Publications2/Annual-reports2.

65 Interpol, 2002 Annual Report; Interpol, 2015 Annual Report, accessed 6 June 2017 at www.interpol.int/News-and-media/Publications2/Annual-reports2.

66 Interpol, 2001 Annual Report; Interpol, 2002 Annual Report, accessed 6 June 2017 at www.interpol.int/News-and-media/Publications2/Annual-reports2. According to Interpol's 2001 Annual Report, the Centre's 'principal aims are the fast-tracking of information which relates directly to an on-going situation, to provide pertinent analysis and facilitate the information flow between affected NCBs. This includes the distribution of watch lists and the use of Interpol notices and diffusions.'

67 Interpol, accessed 6 June 2017 at www.interpol.int/INTERPOL-expertise/Command-Coordination-Centre.

68 See e.g. Mathieu Deflem, 'International Police Cooperation against Terrorism: Interpol and Europol in Comparison' in H. Durmaz et al. (eds.), *Understanding and Responding to Terrorism* (Washington: IOS Press, 2007), 20.

in policing terrorist offences for fear of politicization but significantly altered that stance after 9/11. For example, 55 Red Notices were issued immediately after the attacks alone, several of which led to arrests.[69] INTERPOL decided to give priority to such notices at its Budapest General Assembly, held in 2001. The pressure to arrest those suspected of terrorist activities is considerable and undoubtedly accounts for the increasing fluidity with which Red Notices are treated. Second, the rise of an international criminal law focused on so-called 'core crimes' has given rise to a plethora of Red Notices being issued concerning genocide, crimes against humanity and war crimes. Interpol has cooperated closely with international criminal tribunals, for example honoring Red Notices even in cases where tribunals had not issued an indictment yet. In the case of Milan Likić, for example, Interpol coordinated information exchanges between Chile and Argentina that led to his arrest.[70] Again, the pressure to honor such notices is extremely strong given both the nature of the crimes and the requesting authority, an international rather than merely national actor.

In short, Red Notices are more and more gaining legitimacy as a means of disseminating information about accused persons, and there is an increasing expectation that nations hosting the subjects of Red Notices in their territories will act upon them.[71] It is clear that Red Notices have now become a fixture of the global extradition scene. On a daily basis, NCBs are initiating and disseminating such notices with a view to having those who have committed crimes or escaped punishment caught, arrested, and returned to their territory. Of course, that nations would seek to catch and return international fugitives is no surprise – extradition as an institution has for centuries been a legitimate and entrenched political/legal process. Nonetheless, the Red Notices system may also be a manifestation of deeper illiberal tendencies embedded in transnational cooperation.

69 Mathieu Deflem and Samantha Hauptman, 'Policing International Terrorism' in Francis Pakes (ed.), *Globalisation and the Challenge to Criminology* (London: Routledge, 2013), 72.

70 See e.g. Ilias Bantekas and Susan Nash, *International Criminal Law* (3d edn) (London: Routledge, 2007), 413.

71 For an example of a recent operation in which Red Notices figured heavily, see e.g. US Immigrations and Customs Enforcement, 'ICE, US Marshals arrest 45 international fugitives with Interpol Notices', accessed 6 June 2017 at www.ice.gov/news/releases/ice-us-marshals-arrest-45-international-fugitives-interpol-notices. Many other examples can be cited: see e.g. CSO, 'Police arrest man suspected of LinkedIn's 2012 mega breach', accessed 6 June 2017 at www.cso.com.au/article/608845/police-arrest-man-suspected-linkedin-2012-mega-breach/; The Indy Channel, 'Mexican national wanted by Interpol for murder found working in Indianapolis', accessed 6 June 2017 at www.theindychannel.com/news/crime/mexican-national-wanted-by-interpol-for-murder-found-working-in-indianapolis; *BalkanInsight*, accessed 6 June 2017 at www.balkaninsight.com/en/article/montenegro-extradites-belgian-drugs-trafficing-suspect-11-23-2015; *The Sun Daily*, 'Honduras detains Argentine linked to Sinalao cartel', accessed 6 June 2017 at www.thesundaily.my/news/1747375; *DW*, 'Suspected Israeli organ trafficker arrested in Turkey: reports', accessed 6 June 2017 at www.dw.com/en/suspected-israeli-organ-trafficker-arrested-in-turkey-reports/a-18896905.

Implications of the Red Notice system

In spite of their increased legitimacy, Red Notices are not without controversy, and in ways point to a darker side of transnational cooperation. Several organizations and commentators have already expressed concern about the manner in which they have tended to be used. One of the main concerns seems to be that even as, and perhaps ironically, because transnational police cooperation has sought to transcend governmental cooperation, it has emerged as a tool that is relatively vulnerable to it.

Relationship to extradition

For one, there are reasons to believe that the Red Notice system's professional and managerial emphasis subtly works to undermine the legal framework of extradition in which it is supposed to operate. Of course, it remains possible to challenge one's detention as a result of a Red Notice as part of the contestation of extradition proceedings, and domestic courts have often retrospectively and implicitly at least suggested that Red Notices were illegitimate.[72] The practice of extradition has roots that go much deeper than the Red Notice system. In its earliest form, heads of state acceded to requests to return fugitives on a discretionary basis, and out of comity. No legal obligation existed to return an accused.[73] Often, such individuals were sought on the basis of threats they had posed to the requesting sovereign, rather than for commission of 'common' crimes.[74] As a legal process, extradition became full-fledged and began assuming its modern form in the eighteenth and nineteenth centuries, when the negotiation of extradition treaties with foreign states became more commonplace.[75]

Initially, there was very little judicial oversight of the extradition process. The respect for sovereignty inherent in extradition as it emerged in the eighteenth and nineteenth centuries meant that if any existing legal procedure were satisfied, extradition would proceed. States operated under the assumption that it was their duty to extradite, and not their place to inquire about the validity of the requesting nation's procedures for handling a fugitive. To the extent there was judicial

72 Benoît Vitkine, 'Le Conseil d'Etat annule l'extradition de l'opposant kazakh Moukhtar Abliazov' *Le Monde.fr* (9 December 2016) accessed 6 June 2017 at www.lemonde.fr/international/article/2016/12/09/le-conseil-d-etat-annule-l-extradition-de-l-opposant-kazakh-moukhtar-abliazov_5046666_3210.html.

73 See e.g. *United States v Rauscher*, 119 U.S. 407, 411 (1886).

74 But see Christopher L. Blakesley, 'The Practice of Extradition from Antiquity to Modern France and the United States: A Brief History' (1981) 4:1 *B.C. Int'l & Comp. L. Rev.* 39, 45ff.

75 Nicholls et al. state that between 1174 and 1794, England concluded only five extradition treaties: Clive Nicholls Q.C. et al., *The Law of Extradition and Mutual Assistance* 3rd edn (Oxford: Oxford University Press, 2013), 4.

oversight, courts too made this assumption, in the American case terming their deference the 'rule of non-inquiry', according to which 'the court determining whether a defendant is extraditable may not examine the requesting country's criminal justice system or take into account the possibility that the defendant will be mistreated or denied a fair trial in that country'.[76] In short, extradition emerged as a mode of sovereign cooperation by which states collaborated, on the basis of reciprocity, with a view to the enforcement of each other's sovereign prerogatives.

Nonetheless, even as extradition grew more commonplace, it remained limited by common constraints placed on the practice by the requested state. First and foremost was the very fact that extradition largely remained a *bilateral* practice, which served to protect fugitives from both extradition itself and from potential abuses associated with it (whether in the form of detention prior to extradition,[77] or the attendant punishment once committed for trial). Because nations would only conclude extradition treaties or engage in the practice with nations with which they sought extended reciprocal relations and from which they expected basic – or at least sufficiently parallel – legal and political guarantees, fugitives were unlikely to be extradited to places falling below those standards. In addition, assuming any legal barriers to extradition were overcome,[78] the ultimate decision

76 Jacques Semmelman, 'Federal Courts, the Constitution, and the Rule of Non-Inquiry in International Extradition Proceedings' (1991) 76 *Cornell L. Rev.* 1198. For a discussion of the rule of non-inquiry in the American context, see John Quigley, 'The Rule of Non-Inquiry and the Impact of Human Rights on Extradition Law' (1990) 15 *N.C.J. Int'l L. & Com. Reg.* 401; John T. Parry, 'International Extradition, The Rule of Non-Inquiry, and the Problem of Sovereignty' (2010) 90 *Boston U. L. Rev.* 1973. According to Parry, the rule of non-inquiry was first expressed by the Supreme Court of the United States in the 1901 case of *Neely v* Hankel, 180 U.S. 109 (1901): Parry, ibid., at 1980. Canadian courts have also expressed something akin to the rule of non-inquiry. In *Canada v Schmidt* ([1987] 1 SCR 500 at 522–23), for instance, Justice La Forest stated: 'I see nothing unjust in surrendering to a foreign country a person accused of having committed a crime there for trial in the ordinary way in accordance with the system for the administration of justice prevailing in that country simply because that system is substantially different from ours with different checks and balances. The judicial process in a foreign country must not be subjected to finicky evaluations against the rules governing the legal process in this country. A judicial system is not, for example, fundamentally unjust – indeed it may in its practical workings be as just as ours – because it functions on the basis of an investigatory system without a presumption of innocence or, generally, because its procedural or evidentiary safeguards have none of the rigours of our system.' See also Donald K. Piragoff and Marcia V.J. Kran, 'The Impact of Human Rights Principles on Extradition from Canada and the United States: The Role of National Courts' (1992) 3:2 *Crim. L. Forum* 225, 238–39.

77 Note that provisional arrest did not become a common component of extradition treaties until the 1960s: see Cherif M. Bassiouni, *International Extradition: United States Law and Practice 501* (Oxford: Oxford University Press, 2014), 840 (Bassiouni, *International Extradition*).

78 Many of these common legal barriers to extradition played and continue to play a significant role in the extradition process: to name a few, the rule of 'double criminality' stipulates that

of whether or not to extradite was left in political hands. Extradition has thus historically operated as a bilateral, state-level practice through which individuals can be sought by and from states that have chosen extradition partners that they believed worthy of mutual respect.[79]

Interpol and its associated practices disrupt these traditional relationships. First, the Red Notice system seeks to replace the actors traditionally involved in the extradition process. At its roots, extradition was an interstate practice, conceived of as a matter of foreign policy 'best left to the head of state and his ministers'.[80] Because the purpose of extradition law was seen as vindicating the right of the requesting state to prosecute persons who had violated its laws (that is, it was aimed at 'the facilitation of a foreign state's criminal process'[81]) the legal obligation that emerged as a result remained at the interstate level.[82] At least amongst nations committed to certain basic legal principles, a legal framework was developed to guide the extradition process, but it retained its political roots. Later on, courts would assume an increasingly dominant position in the management of extradition, in ways that limited executive discretion but also whatever autonomous role police bodies might have.

Interpol, by contrast, operates as a communication and coordination network between *policing* organizations. The traditional actors who had driven extradition practices in the past – heads of state (or their delegates), often acting within rigid legal frameworks and courts – do not enter the picture until significant exchanges of information have already occurred between policing organizations around the globe. As Deflem has noted, the techniques adopted by the organization to promote cooperation across national borders were chosen to promote efficiency,

extradition can only proceed if the offence for which the individual's return is sought also constitutes an offence in the requested state (see Bassiouni, *International Extradition*, 501); the doctrine of specialty requires the requesting state to prosecute the accused only for those offences on the basis of which extradition was sought (see e.g. B.A. Banoff and C.H. Pyle, 'To Surrender Political Offenders: The Political Offense Exception to Extradition in United States Law' (1983) 16 *N.Y.U.J. Int'l L. & Pol.* 169); and the notion of 'extraditable offences' delineates the nature of offences for which extradition can be sought (Bassiouni, 507). In addition, according to the 'political offence' exception, extradition should be refused if the underlying offence for which it is sought is political in nature (see e.g. Christine Van Den Wijngaert, *The Political Offence Exception to Extradition: the delicate problem of balancing the rights of the individual and the international public order* (Deventer: Kluwer, 1980)).

79 This is not to ignore the significant rise in multilateral extradition treaties: see e.g. I.A. Shearer, *Extradition in International Law* (Manchester: Manchester University Press, 1971), 22ff.

80 Michael P. Shea, 'Expanding Judicial Scrutiny of Human Rights in Extradition Cases After Soering' (1992) 17 *Yale J. Int'l L.* 85 at 87, citing Shearer, *Extradition in International Law*, 198.

81 Robert J. Currie, *International and Transnational Criminal Law* (Toronto: Irwin Law, 2010), 447.

82 John Quigley, 'The Rule of Non-Inquiry and the Impact of Human Rights on Extradition Law' (1990) 15 *N.C.J. Int'l L. & Com. Reg.* 401.

rather than 'concerns over legality or justice'.[83] From Interpol's perspective, the obvious advantage of the Red Notices system is that it is a fast and effective means of prompting action (i.e., the arrest and detention of suspected criminals) without necessarily having to address or run through the traditional legal channels. Interpol's expediency – its deliberate circumvention of upfront judicial scrutiny – is, on a law enforcement account, its main advantage.

Tensions with human rights

One of the consequences of this efficiency outlook, moreover, is that it may undermine one of the basic premises of the criminal law in any legal system: that individuals should not be deprived of their rights, and have their liberty restricted, without some proof of their involvement in a criminal offence. Individuals who are subject to Red Notices can be detained with a view to extradition absent the traditional protections associated with that practice. Unfortunately, there are many examples of this occurring. While there is no doubt that, as in any sophisticated legal system committed to basic legal rights for the criminally accused, Interpol's member nations must assert some form of criminality to justify dissemination of and acting upon a Red Notice, the degree to which Interpol can consistently regulate this practice is open to doubt in a 190-member organization. And in any event, even before Interpol has a chance to scrutinize the information contained in a Red Notice, it can be disseminated broadly to NCBs.

It is important to note that the relationship between Interpol's member states is not a selective one. The extreme multilateral nature of comprehensive international membership (with equal participation rights for all) extending to 190 members means that many possibilities exist for states to use Interpol's processes to facilitate various illegitimate aims. In fact, the International Consortium of Investigative Journalists has found that of more than 7,600 Red Notices published in 2010, approximately 2,200 emanated from states that, according to Freedom House, placed 'severe' restrictions on political rights and civil liberties. Moreover, approximately half were from countries labeled 'corrupt' according to Transparency International's corruption index.[84] Not all member states share the same concerns around enforcing adequate criminal procedures; many boast dismal human rights records.[85] In light of this, it is unsurprising that one common criticism leveled against Red Notices is that in spite of Interpol's

83 Deflem, *Policing World Society*, 146.

84 See e.g. *The Globe and Mail*, 'Interpol faces scrutiny over its global arrest alerts', accessed 6 June 2017 at www.theglobeandmail.com/report-on-business/industry-news/the-law-page/interpols-widening-net-faces-scrutiny-over-global-arrest-alerts/article26550633/.

85 To take but one example many have surmised that many of those Kazakhstan issues are circulated for political reasons: see e.g. *EUObserver*, 'Kazakhstan using Interpol to chase dissidents in EU', accessed 6 June 2017 at euobserver.com/opinion/121311.

formal commitment to political neutrality, Red Notices are frequently sought by states for political purposes.

Compounding this problem is the fact that Interpol's member states are, in theory, all equal. As discussed above, a Red Notice cannot properly be deemed a Red Notice until its dissemination is approved by Interpol (diffusions, as noted above, do not have this requirement). Interpol, which remains committed to formal equality and non-politicization, is awkwardly placed when evaluating the compliance of Red Notices with its own internal requirements. At the same time, member states join Interpol for their own law enforcement aims. Given the great diversity of national and ideological outlooks amongst the states that have gained entry, it should be no surprise that Interpol itself would demonstrate varying levels of adherence to its founding principles.

There are of course some important practical and legal limitations on the manner in which Red Notices can be disseminated and employed. First are those inherent in the organization's functional capacities: Interpol is not itself capable of effecting detention or extradition. Interpol is and remains largely an information-sharing organization, and 'any enforcement action arising from the issue of a red notice relies on the power of policing authorities within a state and not on the actions of Interpol itself.'[86] Second, extradition, should it follow, remains an interstate legal process controlled by the judiciary. Third, Interpol does take at least formal measures to ensure that its system is not abused and the use of Red Notices does not necessarily mean that human rights concerns will take second place. For example, Article 3 of Interpol's Constitution states: 'It is strictly forbidden for the Organization to undertake any intervention or activities of a political, military, religious or racial character.'[87]

Nonetheless, the operation of Red Notices may well erode legal protections that have come to be entrenched in extradition law. Red Notices have been and continue to be an experimenting ground for interstate practices that largely foreground expediency at the expense of what might be a more thorough examination of the validity of requests. Red Notices are a popular first step in securing detention as a precursor to extradition. A person arrested following a Red Notice is at least physically more susceptible to being extradited than if she had been allowed to go on as a fugitive; she may practically be more vulnerable

86 Ben Bowling and James Sheptycki, 'Global Policing, Mobility and Social Control' in Sharon Pickering and Julie Ham (eds.) *The Routledge Handbook on Crime and International Migration* (Abingdon: Routledge, 2015), ch.4.

87 Interpol Constitution, accessed 6 June 2017 at www.interpol.int/About-INTERPOL/Structure-and-governance. Moreover, Art.83 of Interpol's *Rules on the Processing of Data* stipulates that Red Notices may not be published for offences 'that in various countries raise controversial issues relating to behavioural or cultural norms'; offences 'relating to family/private matters'; or offences 'originating from a violation of laws or regulations of an administrative nature or deriving from private disputes, unless the criminal activity is aimed at facilitating a serious crime or is suspected of being connected to organized crime.'

in that she will have been identified as a person sought and the requested state will already have deferred to that wish.[88]

In sum, Interpol and Red Notices are allowed to operate in a relative grey zone, one in which one may well suspect that even though an arrest occurring as a result of a Red Notice may not lead to an extradition, it will nonetheless be honored in deference to the broad needs of police cooperation. In other cases, a Red Notice and arrest may be the immediate prelude to an otherwise illegal and swift transfer to the requesting state. At the same time, because Interpol is a collaboration of police forces, it is more likely to be driven by an efficiency agenda and less likely to feel formally invested in the duty to account for the rights of the accused. Indeed, efficiency in extradition has been one of Interpol's (and its predecessor organization's) founding aims for almost 100 years. It is hardly surprising that the organization would seek to continue to find ways to promote the prompt return of fugitives.

Potential abuse

In light of the inherent risks pointed to, it is unsurprising that several instances of abuse have occurred.[89] One example is the case of Benny Wenda, the former leader of the West Papuan independence movement. Wenda only discovered he was the subject of a Red Notice issued at the request of Indonesia well after the fact.[90] He lives with his family in exile in the United Kingdom. Wenda had previously been imprisoned in Indonesia, and, after being subject to threats and harassment, he escaped. There is little doubt that the Red Notice requested by Indonesia was politically motivated, contravening Interpol's 'cardinal rule of political neutrality'.[91] While Fair Trials International was able to intervene and successfully lobbied Interpol's Commission for the Control of Files to remove the Red Notice against Wenda, this occurred only after repeated requests for Indonesia and the United Kingdom to act on Wenda's behalf.

Interestingly, examples such as the Wenda case can be found throughout Interpol's history. It is widely known that J. Edgar Hoover made the decision to withdraw FBI participation from the ICPC in 1950 as a result of an apparent violation of the organization's constitutional prohibition on political involvement.[92] That year, Czechoslovak nationals requested political asylum in Allied-controlled

88 See generally Trevor Meldal-Johnsen and Vaughn Young, *The Interpol Connection*, ch. 9 ('The Violation of Human Rights').

89 See also the story of Derek Bond in Ben Bowling and James Sheptyvki, *Global Policing* (London: Sage, 2002), 9–10; Fair Trials International, *The Power of the Interpol Red Notice*, accessed 6 June 2017 at www.fairtrials.org/documents/IELRinterpolfinal.pdf.

90 Alex Tinsley (*The Guardian*), 'Benny Wenda's plight has highlighted the misuse of Interpol', accessed 6 June 2017 at www.theguardian.com/commentisfree/2012/aug/06/benny-wenda-misuse-interpol.

91 Ibid.

92 Fooner, *Interpol: Issues in World Crime and International Criminal Justice*, 41.

Germany after taking control of two aircraft and forcing them to land there. While the US State Department agreed to the asylum request, Czechoslovakia sought notices for their arrest, and these notices were granted by the organization. Hoover – and others – were so opposed to the request having been granted that they terminated participation in the organization.[93] Thus, the tension between Interpol's apparent institutional desire to act promptly and the need to protect against potential abuses has been felt throughout Interpol's history. The present context, one marked by considerable pressure to arrest war criminals and *génocidaires*, has not done away with the risk of politicization altogether, as evident in some Red Notices that Belgrade sought to have circulated by Interpol concerning alleged Bosnian war criminals.[94]

Beyond the possibility of being arrested and extradited as a result of a Red Notice, the inherent harms associated with the instant sharing of information should not go overlooked. Red Notices are published on Interpol's website for public viewing, and disseminated broadly to the NCBs. It bears repeating that in the extradition context, many of the individuals affected have not yet been convicted of the crime for which they are sought. As stated by Meldal-Johnsen and Young, '[i]f an organization such as Interpol handles information on criminal activities and then extends it to "suspected" criminal activities without qualifying the information – as Interpol does not, in spite of its claims to the contrary – then it is leaving itself wide open to abuse, particularly if it is under no government control, as is the case with Interpol.'[95] It has been argued that the mere publication of information concerning individuals on Interpol's website can negatively impact individuals' reputation, in a context where the evidence on which they rest may be flimsy at best.[96] Red Notices can also negatively impact the subject's ability to travel, preventing them from crossing borders and from being issued visas.[97] To take but one example, Shahram Homayoun, an Iranian dissident based in Los Angeles but sought as a result of a Red Notice solicited by the government of Iran, has been virtually unable to travel out of the US, which will not honor the Notice, because of the risk that other countries would.[98]

93 See also the discussion in Deflem, *Policing World Society*, 203.

94 See e.g. Libby Lewis, 'Interpol's Red Notices used to publish political dissenters, opponents', accessed 6 June 2017 at www.huffingtonpost.com/the-center-for-public-integrity/international-police-agen_b_901385.html.

95 Meldal-Johnsen and Young, *The Interpol Connection*, 12.

96 Stephen Bailey, *International Law Observer*, 'INTERPOL: Reckless Arrogance or Simply Naïve?', accessed 6 June 2017 at www.internationallawobserver.eu/2015/10/14/interpol-reckless-arrogance-or-simply-naive-part-ii/.

97 See e.g. *The New York Times*, 'The Misuse of Interpol's Database', accessed 6 June 2017 at www.nytimes.com/2015/11/11/opinion/the-misuse-of-interpols-database.html?_r=0.

98 The International Consortium of Investigative Journalists, 'Interpol's Red Notices used by some to pursue political opponents', accessed 6 June 2017 at www.icij.org/project/interpols-red-flag/interpols-red-notices-used-some-pursue-political-dissenters-opponents.

For these reasons, the Red Notices system has been the object of renewed scrutiny.[99] In 2013, for instance, Fair Trials international published a report documenting shortcomings in the Red Notice system.[100] The report noted that Red Notices 'come with considerable human impact: arrest, detention, frozen freedom of movement, employment problems, and reputational and financial harm.'[101] The report suggested two major areas for improvement: (1) Interpol should not assume that Red Notices are requested in good faith and should review them more rigorously; and (2) Interpol should provide a greater opportunity to challenge the dissemination of information through Interpol's databases.[102] Currently, the only means of challenging the dissemination of a Red Notice is through the Commission for the Control of Interpol's Files (the CCF), but the workings of that body have to date been somewhat opaque.[103] In 2016, however, Interpol reformed the rules governing the CCF, increasing the body's independence, transparency and capacity.[104] Among other things, once the rules

99 See e.g. *The Guardian*, 'Interpol accused of failing to scrutinise red notice requests', accessed 6 June 2017 at www.theguardian.com/uk-news/2013/nov/27/-accused-red-notice-requests; *The Globe and Mail*, 'Interpol faces scrutiny over its global arrest alerts', accessed 6 June 2017 at www.theglobeandmail.com/report-on-business/industry-news/the-law-page/interpols-widening-net-faces-scrutiny-over-global-arrest-alerts/article26550633/; *The New York Times*, 'The Misuse of Interpol's Database', accessed 6 June 2017 at www.nytimes.com/2015/11/11/opinion/the-misuse-of-interpols-database.html?_r=0; *The Telegraph*, 'Interpol accused of using "wanted" alerts to bersmirch [sic.] exiled opponents', accessed 6 June 2017 at www.telegraph.co.uk/news/worldnews/asia/srilanka/10476653/Interpol-accused-of-using-wanted-alerts-to-bersmirch-exiled-opponents.html.

100 Fair Trials International, 'Strengthening Respect for Human Rights, Strengthening Interpol', accessed 6 June 2017 at www.fairtrials.org/wp-content/uploads/Strengthening-respect-for-human-rights-strengthening-INTERPOL5.pdf. See also a 2013 report from the Council of Europe's Committee on Legal Affairs and Human Rights criticizing, in part, Interpol's Notices system, accessed 6 June 2017 at semantic-pace.net/tools/pdf.aspx?doc=aHR0cDovL2Fzc2VtYmx5LmNvZS5pbnQvbncveG1sL1hSZWYvWDJILURXLWV4dHIuYXNwP2ZpbGVpZD0yMDMxMCZsYW5nPUVO&xsl=aHR0cDovL3NlbWFudGljcGFjZS5uZXQvWHNsdC9QZGYvWFJlZi1XRC1BVC1YTUwyUERGLnhzbA==&xsltparams=ZmlsZWlkPTIwMzEw. The Parliamentary Assembly adopted the report in 2014.

101 Fair Trials International, 'Strengthening Respect for Human Rights, Strengthening Interpol', accessed 6 June 2017 at www.fairtrials.org/wp-content/uploads/Strengthening-respect-for-human-rights-strengthening-INTERPOL5.pdf, 4.

102 Fair Trials International, 'Strengthening Respect for Human Rights, Strengthening Interpol', accessed 6 June 2017 at www.fairtrials.org/wp-content/uploads/Strengthening-respect-for-human-rights-strengthening-INTERPOL5.pdf, 3–4.

103 See discussion in Rutsel Silvestre J. Martha, 'Challenging Acts of INTERPOL in Domestic Courts' in August Reinisch (ed.), *Challenging Acts of International Organizations Before National Courts* (Oxford: Oxford University Press, 2010), 206.

104 The new *Statute of the Commission for the Control of INTERPOL's Files* will be effective March 11, 2017. The Statute can be found online at www.interpol.int/About-INTERPOL/Commission-for-the-Control-of-Files-CCF, accessed 6 June 2017.

enter into force the CCF will be required to provide individuals with greater access to information, and to release public reasons for its decisions.

It remains to be seen whether these internal reforms to the CCF will provide effective remedies to those impacted by Red Notices, and discourage their improper dissemination.[105] As it stands, there is reason to believe that many Red Notices fail to adhere to Interpol's own standards. According to one account, while a fraction of Red Notices are ever challenged, of those studied by the CCF in 2014, approximately one-third were found to be noncompliant with Interpol's internal policies.[106] In addition, and perhaps more importantly, even if a successful challenge can be leveled against the Red Notice, in many instances the information will already have been shared and acted upon, and the individual targeted will have already felt its effects.[107]

Interpol has also modified its regime somewhat when it comes to core crimes, deciding that it would continue to honor 'as are' requests submitted by international tribunals but insisting that if a request is submitted by member countries against the national of another member country, the latter may protest such a request within 30 days. Individuals have managed to have Red Notices targeting them rescinded. Nonetheless, potential abuses remain a real risk, in a context where the line between common and political crimes may be a fine one, and in which it is simply implausible for Interpol to assess the potentially political motivations of thousands of requests. For example, in 2015 INTERPOL issued a Red Notice concerning Dmitry Yarosh, a Ukrainian leader who had opposed Russian military action in Ukraine. His name was subsequently taken off Interpol's international wanted list in early 2016, although it is unclear why.

Conclusion

Interpol began as an attempt to streamline police cooperation along largely functionalist lines, in a context where the global goal of crime control was seen as largely consensual. It sought to escape the bad precedents set by nineteenth-century political policing of anarchists, the overtaking of the organization by the SS in the late 1930s and attempts by the Soviet block to use it to pursue dissidents. Yet based on mutual assistance between police forces rather than states, it has

105 Fair Trials International, for its part, appears cautiously optimistic: see Fair Trials International, 'Fair Trials' recommendations inform major INTERPOL reforms', accessed 6 June 2017 at www.fairtrials.org/fair-trials-recommendations-inform-major-interpol-reforms/.

106 *Wall Street Journal*, 'How Rogue Regimes Have Weaponized Interpol', accessed 6 June 2017 at www.wsj.com/articles/how-rogue-regimes-have-weaponized-interpol-1467151465.

107 See e.g. the case of Bahar Kimyongür, highlighted by Fair Trials International, accessed 6 June 2017 at www.fairtrials.org/bahar-kimyongur/. For more on the difficulty of having Red Notices removed, see Mario Savino, 'Global Administrative Law Meets "Soft" Powers: The Uncomfortable Case of INTERPOL Red Notices' (2010) 43 *N.Y.U. J. Int'l L. & Pol.* 263 at 286ff.

paradoxically emerged as a tool for certain states to harass specific individuals or score political points, in a context where the good faith of sovereigns cannot be presumed.

The source of the problem may lie in the political dangers of Interpol's 'depoliticization': in an effort to avoid politicization of policing (which had previously thwarted international multilateral policing efforts), Interpol has remained committed to the notion of formal equality amongst members – each with equal voting status, and countries' internal statuses respected. The result has been that in some instances, the aims of those countries and policing organizations with problematic records have been given effect, to the detriment of individuals targeted by those entities.

Interpol has made some effort to respond to criticisms that have been made of its notices system. In 2015, it met with representatives from Fair Trials International and confirmed that enhanced checks would be conducted prior to issuing Red Notices. It is also worth noting that contentious cases represent only a small fraction of the thousands of unproblematic notices issued each year. Nonetheless, it remains to be seen whether and how Interpol will respond to the legal and political criticisms that have been leveled against it. Clearly, the organization has long sought to promote efficiency in extradition; it should come as no surprise that this entails a corresponding diminution in respect for legal processes and procedures. Moreover, it is interesting to note that as calls for enhanced checks and balances on Interpol's more formalized Red Notices procedures increase, so too does the use of its less formalized information-sharing mechanisms, like diffusions. Paradoxically, though perhaps inevitably, the push for transparency and an approximation of domestic legal processes in the Red Notices system may have the effect of increasing the use of more informal mechanisms for information control. In the end, it can be expected that similar informal mechanisms, however operationalized, will continue to play an important if understated role in international criminal law.

Chapter 7

Trading on guilt

The judicial logic of plea bargains at the ICTY and its transplant to Serbia and Bosnia

Kerstin Bree Carlson

Plea bargaining is the practice of encouraging defendants to plead guilty to a crime, thus invalidating the need to prove the defendant's guilt through a criminal trial. The practice is a prominent element of criminal law practice in the United States, and has been applied, in recent years, by international criminal tribunals. At international criminal law, the most developed plea bargaining practice is that of the International Criminal Tribunal for the former Yugoslavia (ICTY); of the 161 indictments before the ICTY, 20 have resulted in pleas of guilt through a type of 'plea bargaining' procedure developed by the Tribunal. While in the US prosecutors hedge elevated charges and sentences against the uncertainties of trial to bargain with the defendant for a charge and/or sentence he will accept, the ICTY's plea bargaining practice modifies elements of US practice. Centrally, while prosecutors at the ICTY can elect which charges to bring (and can drop charges as well), the sentence length awarded the defendant remains entirely the purview of the judges. Thus the straight 'trade' element central to US practice – where both parties are imagined to have the benefit of a deal constructed beforehand – is modified at international criminal law, where the uncertainty is borne entirely by the defendant.

This chapter traces the transposition of the logic of the trade that characterizes plea bargaining in US practice through a consideration of the 20 guilty pleas before the ICTY, examining how much, and under what circumstances, the 'trade' that animates the practice at US law has taken root in ICTY jurisprudence. The chapter finds that although most ICTY guilty pleas involve some form of a 'trade', the trade is rarely meaningful as a 'defense strategy' in the way that plea bargaining at US law offers a particular pathway to those defendants who engage in it. This chapter argues that the absence of meaningful 'strategy' offered by pleading guilty at the ICTY is centrally due to a combination of continental legal typology's discomfort with 'negotiated justice' (which for jurists trained in a civil law tradition amounts to oxymoron) as well as institutional practices that exhibit discomfort with assisting defendants with 'strategy' in any form. From this jurisprudence, the chapter inquires what we might expect of war crimes cases in Bosnia and Serbia, where newly-drafted, common-law styled criminal procedures have been put into effect. The ICTY is a model and a partner for domestic war crimes chambers operating in the former Yugoslavia, and plea agreements, also sometimes designated as guilty pleas, have exploded in Bosnia-Herzegovina (BiH) and Serbia since the initiation of the new codes. Plea bargains are often constructed as unfair to defendants, even in situations where a meaningful trade is envisioned. How does the absence of a 'trade' impact the fairness of the ICTY and domestic criminal processes in Bosnia and Serbia for defendants?

I. Pleading guilty to war crimes

What to do with those war criminals who admit their guilt? The problem of self-incrimination arose, unexpectedly, remarkably early in the ICTY's jurisprudence, when a young Bosnia Croat soldier who had fought for the Bosnian Serbs at Srebrenica came forward to tell his story. Dražen Erdemović, through his own admission of guilt, became the ICTY's first conviction, in 1996.

Erdemović was a Bosnian Croat who had served in the Bosnian Muslim and Croatian armies before serving in the Bosnian Serb army, where in 1995 he participated in the massacre (genocide) of more than 7,000 Bosnian Muslim men and boys at Srebrenica. By his own testimony, on 16 July 1995, under orders and by threat of death if he disobeyed, Erdemović executed more than 70 civilian prisoners as a foot soldier in a firing squad. In early 1996, after having been released from a Serbian hospital,[1] Erdemović and a friend gave an interview to a foreign journalist regarding atrocities they had witnessed and committed during the war. The tape of the interview was confiscated by Serbian authorities, and Erdemović and his friend were arrested, indicted for war crimes, and scheduled to stand trial in a Serbian court. With international pressure and a public campaign initiated by ICTY Prosecutor Goldstone 'to save [Erdemović's] life' (Hagan 2003: 76), Erdemović was transferred to the ICTY. In The Hague, Erdemović cooperated extensively with the Tribunal, providing evidence and testimony against other indictees. When the ICTY's Office of the Prosecutor (OTP) indicted Erdemović on war crimes charges for his role in the massacre, he pled guilty.

Erdemović came to the ICTY's attention at a time when the institution was remarkably insecure. When the war in Bosnia ended in late 1995, the war crimes court erected under the UN Security Council's 'Peace & Security' mandate,[2] now

1 Erdemović testified that he was shot a few days after the Srebrenica murders, and speculated that the shooting was retaliation for his unwillingness to participate in some of the violence he was ordered to commit, as well as because he was a Bosnian Croat (IT-96-22, Transcript 20 November 1996, 231–233). An excellent consideration of the case is found in Cryer (1997).

2 The ICTY was created in 1993 through United Nations Resolution 808, under the Security Council's Article VII. Security Council Resolution 808 S/Res/808 (22 February 1993).

with no war to end, risked lame-duck status. International political will had faltered over arresting ICTY indictees (who had gone to ground, still heavily armed, in Bosnian locales where they enjoyed local support and loyalty), and a frustrated ICTY Prosecutor Richard Goldstone found himself with tens of indictments issued and no defendants in the dock aside from one low-level thug, Dusko Tadić, extradited from his home in Germany while the war was still raging. Goldstone had further made the ICTY an *institutione-non-grata* by issuing indictments against high-ranking Bosnian officials before the war's end, thus complicating the peace process. In short, in 1996 the ICTY – the first international criminal tribunal since those at Nuremberg and Tokyo, a contemporary experiment in using justice to frame peace – looked set to fail (Bass 2000; Hagan 2003).

In cooperating with the ICTY, Erdemović provided critical confirmation of the events at Srebrenica, events that were powerfully contested at the time. Information regarding the location of massacres, when used in conjunction with satellite imagery, gave ICTY investigators valuable clues which they used to eventually build a jurisprudence around the genocide at Srebrenica, most critically the command structure surrounding the event; the fruit of the seeds planted by Erdemović is the trial against Ratko Mladić,[3] the general who ordered and oversaw the massacre. Moreover, Erdemović became the ICTY's 'star witness' (Chikov 2009) not only for the material facts he substantiated, but also for his expressed contrition. By cooperating with the ICTY, Erdemović provided an exemplar of the transitional justice ideology underwriting the construction of a *court* (as opposed to other institutional methods of fostering reconciliation) to address large-scale social and political violence (Akhavan 1998; Forsythe 2005). The *Erdemović* Sentencing Chamber found that Erdemović's plea of guilty contributed to the discovery of truth, which it then linked directly to reconciliation, arguing, 'Discovering the truth is a cornerstone of the rule of law and a fundamental step on the way to reconciliation.'[4]

Thus the appearance of Dražen Erdemović, in the person of a contrite, cooperative witness, and in the situation of participant in genocide (the crime of crimes which could justify the necessity of a tribunal such as the ICTY) was – to put it crudely – a fantastic stroke of luck for the fledgling institution. Yet when Erdemović cooperated with the ICTY, there was no procedure under the ICTY's Rules that permitted a judicially meaningful admission of guilt. In some jurisdictions, plea bargaining procedures make it possible for a defendant to save the court the trouble of a trial to determine his guilt by admitting his guilt himself (this is the value the defendant can use to 'bargain' regarding the charges and sentence imposed on him). Other jurisdictions reject this possibility, however; at German law, for example, a trial is required regardless of a defendant's confession

3 *Prosecutor v Ratko Mladić*, IT-09-92, trial currently ongoing.

4 *Prosecutor v Erdemović, Sentencing Judgment II*, 5 March 1998, para.21.

(Bohlander 2001). The hybrid procedure employed by the ICTY, while heavily influenced by US legal culture and practice (Hagan 2003), did not originally recognize plea bargaining.

A. Developing plea bargaining at the ICTY: The practice instituted by Erdemović

Erdemović came into ICTY custody in March 1996 and was indicted under two counts: (1) murder as a crime against humanity and, alternatively, (2) murder as a violation of the laws and customs of war. Two months later, Erdemović made his initial appearance before the ICTY Trial Chamber and pled guilty to murder as a crime against humanity. A central problem in the hearing, around which a divided Appeals Chamber later reversed the Trial Chamber judgment, was the question of what crime Erdemović pled guilty to, however. The indictment charged Erdemović with a crime against humanity *or alternatively* a violation of the laws and customs of war. Erdemović pled guilty to the former, and the OTP, in response, dropped the latter at the Trial Chamber's suggestion.[5] The Appeals Chamber would go on to find Erdemović's plea uninformed because he pled guilty to the more serious of the two charges.[6]

Following his guilty plea, the Trial Chamber sentenced Erdemović to 10 years' prison.[7] Erdemović appealed. In addition to the grounds raised by Erdemović, the Appeals Chamber raised a number of issues *proprio motu*, chief among them the validity of Erdemović's guilty plea, given that he had both pled guilty *and* suggested that he acted under duress. In some systems, duress constitutes a complete defense to criminal charges. The Appeals Chamber found that Erdemović's plea was not internally consistent (what at law amounts to 'equivocation') because he could not meaningfully plead guilty while simultaneously maintaining that he acted under duress, which would make him not legally 'guilty'. From the five Appellate judges there issued four opinions. In this plurality decision, the Appeals Chamber found that Erdemović's plea had not been informed because he had not understood which of the two charges – crimes against humanity versus war crimes – was the more serious charge. Two of the five judges (McDonald and Vohra, both hailing from common law systems) additionally considered questions of equivocation in Erdemović's plea, as his claim that he was forced to kill or risk death himself amounted to duress. The Appellate Chamber ultimately held, in a 3:2 decision, that duress was not a complete defense at international criminal law.[8]

5 31 May 1996 Tr. Pg.35:19.
6 *Prosecutor v Erdemović*, Appeals Chamber Judgment, 7 October 1997.
7 *Prosecutor v Erdemović*, Sentencing Judgment, IT-96-22, 29 November 1996.
8 *Prosecutor v Erdemović*, Appeals Judgment, IT-96-22.

B. Plea bargaining post-Erdemović

Following the *Erdemović* Appeals Chamber judgment, the ICTY instituted Rule 62 *bis*, and later Rule 62 *ter*, governing plea bargaining. The text of the first substantial change to the rules, Rule 62 *bis*, was drawn directly from the separate opinion of Judges McDonald and Vohra in the *Erdemović* Appeals Chamber judgment regarding the necessary content and scope for receiving and adjudicating a guilty plea. This general plea bargaining rule, built on a common law foundation, does not in itself constrain the parties regarding the potential for a trade between them. Instead, Rule 62 *bis*, like descriptions of plea bargaining at common law, is centrally focused on protecting the rights of the defendant. While serving to bolster the legitimacy of the process, Rule 62 *bis* is centrally concerned with protecting the defendant by insisting (i) that his plea is his choice; that he (ii) understands its significance; that (iii) the admissions of his plea are consistent and clear (which tend to support points (i) and (ii)); and (iv) that the facts support the defendant's story.

Rule 62 *bis* addresses questions regarding plea bargaining arising at common law, centrally the concern that the uneven bargaining power between the state and an individual accused by the state must be mitigated. It does little to allay the concerns of a civil law audience regarding the practice of plea bargaining, however. Mirjan Damaska's (1986) seminal theorization of 'ideal types' which define the ideological distinctions between civil and common law procedural approaches, under a civil law ideal type, the rights of the defendant are not directly engaged by the question whether he confesses, because, under a civil law rubric, the defendant's confession cannot in itself alter the course of the proceedings against him (Bohlander 2001). Thus, within the civil law typology, the problem of plea bargaining rests in the 'interest' politics between prosecutor and defendant, where plea bargaining is perceived as a political (and therein antithetical to legal) act (Carlson 2016a). Attending to defendants' rights through the four requirements listed in Rule 62 *bis* cannot address the structural concerns inherent in the process from a civil-law-typology informed perspective. For those trained in civil law jurisdictions, the self-interested, case-by-case trade between adversarial parties at the center of plea bargaining is counterfactual to justice itself, which must be predictable and disinterested in order to qualify as justice. This perspective is based in part on the distinct understandings between common and civil law regarding the role of the prosecutor (including and especially the shape of prosecutorial discretion in the two systems). More fundamentally, it derives from a distaste for 'bargaining' or 'negotiation' as a valid element of criminal law, rejecting a regime that would substitute 'split-the-difference for a judicial determination of guilt or innocence' (Alshuler 1983). At civil law, practitioners are required to apply a law determined by the legislature. Justice is practised and protected by professionals applying criminal laws equally and without discrimination. The rule of law consists of this constancy. Thus the idea of 'trading' a charge for information, cooperation, or any institutional benefit strikes many acclimated to civil law jurisdictions as contrary to rule of law, justice, or legal legitimacy. For practitioners of civil law, plea bargaining looks like the antithesis of law: it is political, subjective, and random. Suspicion of plea bargaining before a civil law audience is not therefore just an unfamiliarity with the practice, its processes, or its potential benefits, but rather a more deeply rooted rejection of what the practice represents (Plantz 2004).

Four years after instituting Rule 62 *bis*, to answer concerns regarding how far the parties might take a 'trade' relationship, the ICTY adopted Rule 62 *ter*. Rule 62 *ter* focuses on constraining the parties regarding the content of their trade, and thus directly impacts the capacity for defendants to 'strategize' their defense through a plea of guilt (an essential element of plea bargaining at common law). Following the adoption of Rules 62 *bis* and *ter*, we can speak of an ICTY which engages in both charge and sentence bargaining. Through charge bargaining, the OTP revises the indictment against the accused and drops certain charges in exchange for the accused's plea of guilt.[9] Sentence bargaining is more complex, as in exchange for a plea of guilty, the OTP will recommend a shortened sentence for the accused, sometimes joining with defendant's counsel to agree on a proposed sentence length (the potential significance of this 'alliance' is discussed in Part II, below). ICTY Chambers are not bound by the OTP's suggestion, although in fact, in nearly all cases before the ICTY, the defendant's sentence has followed the OTP's recommendation. ICTY case law has found the defendant's guilty plea and/or statement of remorse as a mitigating factor to be considered in sentencing,[10] ostensibly resulting in shortened sentences.[11] In principle, at least, after confirming the OTP's charges,[12] the Trial Chamber is free to pronounce the sentence it deems fit regardless of what the OTP, defense, or previously decided cases might suggest.[13] And while in the US, a plea of guilt waives the defendant's right to appeal, at the ICTY, defendants may appeal a process they 'agreed to' through their plea, as indeed nearly half of all those who pled guilty have done.

9 Amended indictments must be submitted to the Trial Chamber for approval. Thus far, no indictment has been refused amendment for the purpose of securing a guilty plea. *But see* Judge Schomburg's dissenting opinion in the *Derojnić* case (contesting the OTP's decision only to indict Deronjić only on atrocities committed in the village of Glagova, where Deronjić likely played a significant role in other war crimes, including the organization of the Srebrenica massacres. The *Deronjić* case is discussed further in Part II).

10 *See* e.g. *Prosecutor v Momir Nikolić*, IT-02-60/1 (2 December 2003).

11 *See* Dixon and Demirdjan (2005: 681) (arguing guilty pleas reduce sentences by one-third). Due to the discretionary and highly non-uniform nature of ICTY sentences, however, estimating the impact of plea bargaining on sentence length can only ever be speculative.

12 The Trial Chamber is permitted to enquire into the terms of the plea agreement, and has discretion regarding acceptance of a guilty plea. *See Prosecutor v Nikolić* Sentencing Judgment, para.54, IT-02-60/1 (2 December 2003).

13 Beyond the problems imposed by plea bargains, sentencing at the ICTY is particularly problematic as there are few guidelines or mandates; this has led to an extremely varied and unpredictable sentencing regime.

Thus there are two significant ways in which the ICTY's practice diverges from the US practice upon which it is modeled. First, the chamber (judges) retain the right to determine the defendant's sentence, regardless of what the prosecution, or the prosecution together with the defense, suggest. Second, the defendant retains his right to file an appeal.

It is difficult to find a proponent of plea bargaining trained under a civil law ideal type, where the practice is largely treated with mistrust even by the international judiciary tasked with implementing it. Those common law-trained jurists in favor of plea bargaining before international tribunals argue that it is a win-win situation for prosecution and defense. By offering deals to defendants in exchange for testimony, prosecutors can secure crucial information against 'bigger' criminals, and assure the defendant's cooperation by making it worth his while (Nalepa 2012). This allows prosecutors access to information that they might never otherwise procure, and allows the criminal justice system to focus its resources efficiently (where efficiency can be understood as realized through the capture of 'big fish'). In the case where pleas are offered for reduced charges or dropped charges, proponents of plea bargaining note that this saves system resources, because it obviates the need for expensive, resource-consuming trials. Defendants accept guilt and are punished, which serves the purposes of criminal justice. While such sentences are shorter than they might otherwise have been without the plea bargain, they are nonetheless assured (which is never the case at trial, where prosecutors have the hefty burden of proving the defendant's guilt 'beyond a reasonable doubt'), and society as a whole is served by the assurance that criminals will be put in jail.

Common law-trained opponents of plea bargaining often note the disparity in the power of the two sides: a prosecution with the entire resources of the state behind it facing a lone individual is a highly unequal situation. In such a structural power imbalance, they argue, the idea of a 'fair deal' between these two sides is impossible. Moreover, at common law, prosecutors typically inflate charges against defendants; under such inflated indictments, a plea bargain is no 'bargain' at all, and rather represents the actual charges that a prosecutor could successfully bring against a defendant at trial. Recall that a trial setting at common law, with the prosecutor's high burden and the presence of a non-professional jury, always carries with it the significant possibility of acquittal for the defendant. Thus, in giving up a trial for a deal that is not actually any kind of deal for a defendant, opponents of plea bargaining see a structural power imbalance at work.

Instituting Rule 62 to permit plea bargaining carried the promise of addressing both institutional challenges. Hybridizing plea bargains by maintaining the complete judicial independence of the Trial Chamber regarding sentence length assuaged concerns, most often iterated by civil law jurists, related to justice. And insistence that plea bargains and statements of remorse increased Tribunal legitimacy and social reconstruction (borrowing heavily from the *Erdemović* experience) seemed to answer the concern that plea bargains, entirely foreign to a civil law audience and rejected by judicial professionals hailing from civil law cultures, might threaten the ICTY's legitimacy, not bolster it.

II. Guilty pleas at the ICTY

Erdemović's confession raised the immediate question of how the hybrid ICTY should *process* self-incrimination; the political/institutional question of how the ICTY might eventually *encourage* defendants to admit their guilt was a close corollary. Proponents of plea bargaining before international criminal tribunals argue that it does more than simply relieve congested dockets, but rather that it combats denial and promotes reconciliation (Harmon 2009). Beginning with the *Erdemović* case, there have been 20 guilty pleas before the ICTY. In the following section, the chapter considers these 20 guilty pleas through a 'plea bargaining' lens, inquiring to what extent, and in what way, these 20 pleas evince the 'trade' that characterizes plea bargaining at US law, from whence the practice originated. This analysis concludes that, although most plea bargains at the ICTY consist of some form of trading (for the vast majority, this is a trade wherein the OTP drops charges in return for a plea of guilt), the more substantive, meaningful element of the trade evinced by US law (the way in which the trade might constitute, in the words of the *Erdemović* Trial Chamber, a 'defense strategy') is absent.

A. Plea bargains by numbers

There were 20 guilty pleas obtained by the ICTY between 1996 and 2007. In preparation for closure, the ICTY has issued no new indictments since 2004 and is finalizing the last of its trial proceedings (though appeals will likely continue for several more years). Thus, at this juncture, it is likely that there will not be any more plea agreements at the ICTY.

After *Erdemović* in 1996, the next guilty plea was made by Goran Jelisić in 1999. Jelisić is a highly atypical case in ICTY plea bargaining jurisprudence, where there was no trade, and a very high sentence (40 years, the highest sentence ever passed with the exception of two life sentences, both handed down much later and neither for defendants who pled guilty). Jelisić was a Bosnian Serb serving time in a prison in Bijelina (in Republika Srpska, Bosnia). Acting under the authority of the Brčko police, Jelisić was released from the Bijelina prison, given a weapon, a radio, and a list of people to kill. The ICTY indicted him in 1995 on 32 counts, including genocide. Jelisić pleaded guilty to 31 of the 32 counts (all counts except genocide), and went to trial on the genocide charge. He was acquitted by the Trial Chamber without mounting a defense, as the Trial Chamber found that the OTP had not met its burden of proof with regards to the genocide charge. Nonetheless, based on his plea agreement, the Trial Chamber sentenced him to 40 years based on the 'repugnant, bestial and sadistic nature' of his behavior, and lowered the mitigating weight of his guilty plea because Jelisić 'failed to demonstrate true remorse'. Of all 20 plea bargains heard at the ICTY, Jelisić is only one of four cases where defendants are, as of this writing, still serving time in prison.[14]

14 *Prosecutor v Jelisić*, Sentencing Judgment, IT-95-10 (14 December 1999). Affirmed on Appeal (May 2001).

Jelisić's high sentence may have had a chilling impact, and the next plea agreement was two years in coming. Yet the *Todorović* (2001) process set out the template that the bulk of ICTY plea agreements would follow: a significant reduction in charges by the OTP, and a joint recommendation by the OTP and Defense in terms of sentence length. Plea bargains at the ICTY really took off, however, with the plea agreement of Biljana Plavšić in February 2003. On the eve of her trial, Plavšić pled guilty to one count – prosecutions – and saw the OTP's other seven counts, which had included genocide, dropped. Plavšić, who in her capacity as President of Republika Srpska oversaw a campaign of ethnic cleansing and murder, was sentenced to 11 years. Plavšić's sentence was reviled for its gentleness by Bosnian Muslims, even while the 'remorse' articulated by Plavšić was celebrated by the ICTY as both significant for reconciliation in the Balkans as well as a show of the Tribunal's own growing legitimacy among Balkan populations (Carlson 2016a).

Plavšić's lenient sentence was followed by a rash of plea bargains, and from February 2003, when Plavšić was the eighth person in eight years to plead guilty, to June 2004 and the higher than proposed by the OTP sentence of Milan Babić, nine defendants pled guilty. Thus nearly half of all plea agreements concluded before the ICTY took place within this one-year period, 'bookended' by the judgments against Plavšić and Babić.

B. The 'trade'

The most obvious 'trade' engaged in between OTP and Defense is 'charge' bargaining, where the OTP drops charges in exchange for the Defendant's plea of guilt. The bulk of the 20 plea bargains at the ICTY involve 'trades' of this sort, wherein the OTP reduced counts originally charged in exchange for a plea of guilty. The case of Stevan Todorović, a Bosnian Serb, is illustrative.

Todorović was Chief of Police in Bosanski Šamac. Todorović was indicted in July of 1995 together with several other defendants, and accused of crimes committed in pursuit of a Bosnian Serb 'campaign of terror' that included murder and sexual torture in his treatment of non-Serb prisoners. In becoming the third defendant to plead guilty before the ICTY, Todorović saw 26 of the indictments' original 27 charges against him dropped; his guilty plea contained just one count, 'persecutions'. The OTP recommended a sentence of 5–12 years; Todorović was awarded 10. In its sentencing judgment, the ICTY spoke of the aggravating circumstances of Todorović's case – the cruelty of his actions, and his superior position within the police hierarchy – and opined that had it not been for the mitigating circumstance of his plea of guilty, Todorović would have faced a much higher sentence.[15]

15 *Prosecutor v Todorović* Sentencing Judgment, IT-95-9/1 (31 July 2001). *But see* (Combs 2007: 63), who argues *Todorović* does not constitute 'charge' bargaining because, while 26

At the ICTY, the most direct (and assured) 'trade' in which the OTP and Defense can engage is the trade of charges for plea of guilt. The OTP and Defense can also, however, make an 'alliance' regarding the proposed sentence length. Such a proposal carries no guarantee that the judges will comply: judges at the ICTY retain their absolute capacity to determine and impose sentence length, with the longest permissible sentence being life imprisonment. Yet at the same time, of the 20 plea bargains heard by the ICTY, 17 sentences issued at the Trial Chamber level fell within the period recommended by the OTP. Of the three cases that fell outside the OTP's recommendation, two were 'rectified' on appeal. This leaves the outlier case of Milan Babić (Carlson 2016b), who, because he committed suicide in prison, did not benefit from the early release practice that often sees the convicted serving sentences far shorter than those mandated by the Tribunal.

As an example of an 'alliance' case, the case of Dragan Nikolić is illustrative.[16] Nikolić, a Bosnian Serb, was the commander of the Sušica camp in Eastern Bosnia, and was the first indictment issued by the ICTY. He was arrested by SFOR in 2000, six years after the indictment was issued against him. The prosecution and defense allied to jointly request a sentence not to exceed 15 years. The Trial Chamber's original sentence of 23 years appeared to be designed to recognize that alliance, by taking into account that defendants convicted before the ICTY serve their sentences throughout Europe, where prisoners are generally eligible for parole when two-thirds of their sentence is served. The Appeals Chamber shortened the sentence to 20 years, however, ruling that the Trial Chamber had erred by attaching too much weight to the possibility of an early release.

C. *Plea bargain as 'defense strategy'*

Very few ICTY cases involve defendants eager to cooperate with the ICTY. The majority of plea bargains at the ICTY involve defendants who initially resisted the institution, the charges leveled against them, or both. In such cases, the structure of the 'trade' emerging from common law leads to a consideration of how the 'trade' might construct the defendant's strategy.

The OTP has several tools available to it. Though 'sentence bargaining' is not recognized at the ICTY, and determination of the length of the sentence always resides with the trial chamber, in point of fact almost no plea bargains have resulted in sentences longer than that proposed by the OTP (Combs 2007). The OTP's suggested sentence length, therefore, should be understood as a bargaining chip that the OTP is able to exercise vis-à-vis the defense.

A second bargaining chip that emerged for the OTP in the final years of ICTY indictments was the threat of transfer of cases under the ICTY's Rule 11 *bis*

of the 27 counts were withdrawn, Todorović pled guilty to the most serious charge, and it contained all the factual elements that were covered by all the other charges.

16 *Prosecutor v Dragan Nikolić*, Sentencing Judgment, IT-94-2 (18 December 2003).

procedure to the war crimes court in Bosnia. Combs (2007) finds that three latter plea agreements before the ICTY were encouraged through the threat of transfer. Thus, Rule 11 *bis* constitutes another bargaining chip the OTP possesses.

Finally, and while this has generally been resisted as a judicial tool, the OTP, in constructing its indictment, signals which judicial facts it finds relevant to its charges and the investigation, i.e. the OTP determines which specific elements of history and crime enter into the facts considered within the indictment. Thus, it follows, the construction of the extent of the criminal activity within which the defendant was involved also constitutes a tool available to the OTP. Generally speaking, due to the legitimacy international courts derive as historians (Wilson 2011) or otherwise as 'epistemic engines' (Holtermann 2015), judgments have been loath to represent the factual investigative work performed by the courts as partial, or otherwise as only representing one part of a defendant's guilt. Instead, international judicial actors have sought – often highly problematically, as with the protracted and ultimately failed prosecution of Serbian president Slobodan Milošević, who died while on trial – to make complete representations of a defendant's role and responsibility. Observe, for example, how the OTP, in dropping seven of the eight counts against Biljana Plavšić, highlighted that the *factual basis* of Plavšić's prosecution remained unchanged, all that was altered was the legal classification of her crimes (Carlson 2016b).

The question then is to what extent plea bargains provide a 'strategy' to the defense. An examination of the 20 plea bargains reveals that there is only one recorded case demonstrating successful strategizing with the OTP:[17] the case of Miroslav Deronjić and the 'Agreement between the Parties' Deronjić signed with the OTP, promising that information he provided would not be used to indict him.

Deronjić served as the president of the crisis staff in violence-torn eastern BiH (close to Srebrenica), and in that capacity oversaw some of the bloodiest circumstances of the war. After working with teams from the ICTY for five years, Deronjić was himself indicted in 2002 on the charge of 'persecutions' in regard to the deaths of 65 civilians from the undefended village of Bratunac, razed in May 1992. The OTP recommended 10 years' imprisonment, which a majority of the Trial Chamber awarded.[18]

In an acerbic dissent, however, Judge Schomberg (Germany) contested the OTP's indictment and the legality of the Agreement between the Parties stipulating that material provided by Deronjić to the OTP not be used against the defendant. Judge Schomberg queried the accuracy of the OTP's indictment, not in terms of the charges related to deaths in Bratunac, but rather to the lacunae of other charges. Given his leadership position, what did Deronjić know, and do, for

17 There remains, of course, the problem of measuring an absence, which in this case might consist of the indictments not issued by the OTP in exchange for cooperation.

18 *Prosecutor v Deronjić*, Sentencing Judgment, IT-02-61, (30 March 2004). Affirmed on Appeal 20 July 2005.

example, with regard to the genocide at Srebrenica? Judge Schomberg recommended a sentence of 20 years, and offered strong condemnation of a practice that would detract from the perceived propriety of the OTP.

III. Transplanting the judicial 'trade' to BiH and Serbia: a first analysis

Following the war, both BiH and Serbia instituted elements of common law processes into the criminal procedure used to try war crimes cases. In both countries, a version of plea bargaining has entered into local practice through these modified criminal codes.[19] Given the heavy modifications seen regarding the intent and/or capacity of plea bargains vis-à-vis a trade between OTP and defense as between US practice and ICTY practice, this section queries what elements of the 'trade' that underwrites US plea agreement judicial practice might remain in this new practice instituted under the newly crafted criminal codes of BiH and Serbia, a question which at its base seeks to understand how the practice, as transplanted into BiH and Serbia, might erode defendants' rights.

Both BiH[20] and Serbia[21] codified plea bargaining quite differently than the ICTY. In both countries, the capacity for a 'trade' is preserved at law. In Serbia, the OTP can decline to charge at all in exchange for testimony, 'provided that the significance of his testimony for detecting, proving or preventing the criminal offence he has committed'.[22] In exchange, the accused gives up his right to a trial, as well as his right to appeal (a significant distinction between Balkan and ICTY practice). Similarly, the Bosnian criminal code permits negotiations between defense and prosecution regarding charges and prescribed sentences,[23] and defendants give up their rights to trial and appeal.

Yet while plea bargains have been implemented in both countries, and widely applied in BiH,[24] where plea bargaining is now available for regular criminal acts (and not just war crimes or organized crime, as in Serbia), the logic of the trade,

19 An OSCE report on criminal justice processes in BiH went so far as to call plea bargaining 'one of the core mechanisms within the criminal procedure of Bosnia and Herzegovina since its introduction in 2003': OSCE 2006.

20 Plea bargains are recognized in a general criminal code applicable throughout the country, as well as before the specialized national chamber hearing war crimes and organized crime. I am indebted to Nedzad Smailagić for details regarding the construction of the BiH code of criminal procedure.

21 Plea bargains are permitted under a specific criminal code applicable to war crimes and organized crime only, and tried by a special prosecutor operating within a distinct wing of the Belgrade city courts.

22 Serbia Code of Criminal Procedure Art.320 para.2.

23 Art.231 para.1 CPC BiH; Art.231 para.3 CPC BiH. See also OSCE 2011, p.55.

24 The OSCE has produced several reports regarding justice in Bosnia-Herzegovina. Its 2006 report follows more than 2000 cases of plea bargaining.

which is to say, the trade as defense strategy, is under-developed.[25] This is evidenced through discussion of the problem of 'cooperation agreements' before the Bosnian War Crimes Chamber. So far, the contours of this debate focus on the OTP and concerns that it get the benefit of its bargain, specifically the benefit of testimony from the defendant pleading guilty which can be used to secure the convictions of other defendants. The question of defendant's rights is not central to the agreement, although some examples from the Bosnian jurisprudence indicate that defendants' rights are at risk. The question of defendants' rights under plea bargaining procedures in BiH was the topic of a 2007 OSCE report on challenges to the presumption of innocence before Bosnian courts.

At the time of this writing, 29 plea agreements have been concluded before the Bosnian War Crimes Chamber.[26] The Bosnian War Crimes Chamber was constructed in 2003, part of a wider reform package which also instituted a mixed criminal procedure, adversarial and inquisitorial, throughout BiH (Sijerčić-Čolić 2005). The War Crimes Chamber specifically addresses war crimes and organized crime, although law reforms (including the procedural inclusion of plea bargains) are wider reaching than this one constructed court, touching criminal procedures at the state and entity level in Bosnia (Korner 2016), as well as in the independent Brcko district.

The problem of cooperation agreements concerns the problem of 'enforcement' of the plea bargain. Under the Bosnian CPC, once the court accepts the plea agreement and the proposed sentence, there is no possibility to revisit this decision. This can become an issue in the event a defendant who has agreed to testify retracts such agreement or otherwise fails to fulfill their obligations (this was infamously experienced in the Plavšić case before the ICTY, for example).[27]

25 See, for example, the recommendations from a 2013 conference held by Partners for Democratic Change Serbia. Recommendations from the conference encouraged a focus on the exchange of information between parties made possible by plea bargaining:

> The recommendations emphasized that both sides to the plea agreement should recognize that it is a negotiation, one that may be initiated by either side, and one that will consider the strengths and weaknesses of the case. The participants agreed that the deputy prosecutor should have greater authority and discretion to offer plea agreements, and should be able to arrange a sentence below the specified minimum, that he has authority to amend the indictment to reduce the charges, and that the offer should include specific benefits for the defendant in exchange for waiving his right to trial. The participants also understood that it is necessary to develop a culture of negotiation and direct communication if plea bargaining is to be implemented in Serbia.

13 November 2013 conference, accessed 6 June 2017 at www.partners-serbia.org/en/?p=2729.

26 Indira Arnaut, SLON radio 27 August 2016. '"Izdajnicimia" male kazne za ratni zločin' accessed 6 June 2017 at www.rtvslon.ba/zavrsen-dokazni-postupak-za-zlocine-u-stuparima/.

27 The *Plavšić* case is highly illustrative of trade problems, because Plavšić, represented by the OTP as penitent and remorseful for her role in the Bosnian horror, refused to cooperate with the OTP in any case following her sentence, and ultimately recanted her plea of guilt itself (Carlson 2016b).

At the War Crimes Chamber, the issue has arisen both in defendant retractions of cooperation, as well as in defendant alterations of testimony contradicting the content of plea agreements themselves.

In the case of Gordan Djurić,[28] the defendant pled guilty to crimes against humanity in exchange for a sentence range of 5–8 years. Djurić, who had been standing trial together with several other defendants, saw his case severed through his plea of guilt. As part of his plea, he agreed to testify in the case against his former co-defendants.[29] This testimony, however, contradicted elements of his Plea Agreement. Specifically, while he had originally testified that he was present as men were separated into groups and led away to a chasm to be massacred, at trial he testified that he left the scene before the separation occurred. Based on the inconsistencies in these two stories, the trial chamber, which had been awaiting his testimony before announcing its decision regarding his plea of guilt, rejected his plea. The Prosecutor's office renegotiated a new plea but the sentence range was higher (7–10 years). Djurić was eventually sentenced to eight years.

The *Djurić* case highlights the problematic and uncertain terrain faced by defendants who would negotiate guilty pleas as part of their defense strategy. The OTP, having lost the benefit of its bargain in prior cases where defendants, following pleas of guilt, did not follow through with testimony against their former co-accused,[30] seeks to 'lock in' defendant cooperation and therein fully realize its trade. This cooperation, however, is subject to external interpretation, and leaves the defendant in a grey zone where the value of his trade is subject to the assessment of another party (the trial chamber) which may, or may not, recognize his actions as compliant. In the *Djurić* case, unlike the *Plavšić* case before the ICTY discussed above, the defendant did in fact cooperate with the OTP and testify, as agreed. The testimony, however, did not comport with the factual statement given in the plea agreement in a manner which the trial chamber deemed significant. Specifically, the trial chamber found that:

> because in his testimony as a prosecution witness during the main trial the Accused stated that he had left the location and went in the direction of Travnik on his own initiative, while the statement of facts in the Indictment renders that the Accused was ordered to move away from the location in order to stand guard. Therefore, under the stated Agreement, the Accused admitted his guilt for all the actions alleged in the statement of facts in the Indictment, however in his testimony he departed from the factual allegations of the Indictment describing the manner of perpetration of the criminal offense.

28 Case No. X-KR-08/549-2, Verdict of 10 September 2009.

29 X-KR-08/549 'Koricanske stijene'.

30 Enes Handzic (S1 1 K 005760 11 Krl), in Nisvet Gasal et al. case (S1 1 K 003485 07 Krl).

> Due to the discrepancies between the factual allegations and the accused's witness testimony, the Panel decided not to grant the stated Agreement.[31]

These inconsistencies, which carry legal significance, are arguably insignificant to the lay defendant, who may easily, in good faith, alter a detail such as the one described above as he restates the facts. Such a defendant finds himself suddenly deprived of the benefit of his bargain. Instituting a practice of cooperation agreements, which is the course recommended by external observers such as the OSCE (2011), would officially authorize the War Crimes Chamber to conduct its affairs as the trial chamber did in the *Djurić* case.

Conclusion

Plea agreements are an emerging practice of international criminal law. At the time of this writing, the International Criminal Court has just heard its first plea of guilt.[32] In the case of ICTY plea bargains, the practice constitutes a suggested design for transposition to BiH and Serbia, whose war crimes chambers are taking over the work of the ICTY as that Tribunal closes down. At the ICTY, certain procedural elements of the 'trade' transposed from US law are still intact. Structural and cultural elements of the 'trade' however – elements best understood in terms of how such a 'trade' might meaningfully constitute a 'defense strategy' – are often, although not always, lost in ICTY practice.

In BiH and Serbia, two formerly continentally-styled judicial systems with no historical bargaining practice, plea agreements have been instituted. Concerns that the OTP receive the benefit of its bargain in order to justify the foreign practice of trading charges or sentence time for jurists trained in systems unfamiliar with the practice emerge in Serbia and BiH in forms similar to what is seen in ICTY discussions, as evidenced by the current debate regarding cooperation agreements in BiH. The push to codify cooperation agreements, however, potentially challenges the rights of defendants to enter plea agreements as part of a defense strategy. The discussion over cooperation agreements, and the War Crimes Court's trial chamber's practice in the *Djurić* case, highlights the risks defendants face in making a bargain subject to ongoing court interpretation.

While plea bargaining has been transposed from US jurisprudence to the ICTY and now on to BiH and Serbia, the 'trade' at the center of the US practice is transposed only with difficulty for jurists unfamiliar with common law procedure. The centerpiece of the 'trade' is that both sides should be able to conceive, and realize, a benefit from their bargain. The admission of guilt by defendants, however, appears to skew their bargaining capacity by making them less worthy of

31 *Prosecutor's Office of BiH of Đurić*, Case No. X-KR-08/549-2, Verdict of 10 September 2009, p.5.

32 *The Prosecutor v Ahmad Al Faqi Al Mahdi*, ICC-01/12-01/15 (22 August 2016).

support than the offices of the state seeking to bring their crimes to justice: defendants who admit their guilt before Bosnian and Serbian courts are transformed into convicts, or traitors, or both. Although plea bargaining as 'defense strategy' is still nascent in its development in BiH and Serbia, the signposts suggest that the element at the center of US plea bargaining which seeks to redeem the practice as an element of the justice system – the invitation for parties to the process to negotiate regarding justice while sanctioned by the state – may be lost in translation.

References

Akhavan, Payam, 1998. 'Justice in The Hague, Peace in the Former Yugoslavia? A Commentary on the United Nations War Crimes Tribunal' *Human Rights Quarterly* 20(4), 737–816.

Akhavan, Payam, 2012. *Reducing Genocide to Law: Definition, Meaning, and the Ultimate Crime* (Cambridge, UK: Cambridge University Press).

Alshuler, Albert W., 1983. 'Implementing the Criminal Defendant's Right to Trial: An Alternative to the Plea Bargaining System' *University of Chicago Law Review* 50(3), 931–1050.

Ambos, Kai, 2003. 'International Criminal Procedure: "Adversarial", "Inquisitorial" or Mixed?' *Third International Criminal Law Review* 3, 1–37.

Bass, Gary Jonathan, 2000. *Stay the Hand of Vengeance: The Politics of War Crimes Tribunals* (Princeton: Princeton University Press).

Bassiouni, M. Cherif, 2012. *Introduction to International Criminal Law* (Dordrecht, the Netherlands: Nijhoff/Brill).

Bassiouni, M. Cherif, and Peter Manikas, 1996. *The Law of the International Criminal Tribunal for the Former Yugoslavia* (Transnational Publishers).

Bohlander, Michael, 2001. 'Plea-Bargaining Before the ICTY' in Richard May, et al. (eds), *Essays on ICTY Procedure and Evidence in Honour of Gabrielle Kirk McDonald*, International Humanitarian Law Series (The Hague, the Netherlands: Kluwer Law International).

Boll, Matthias, 2009. *Plea Bargaining and Agreement in the Criminal Process: A Comparison Between Australia, England and Germany* (Hamburg, Germany: Diplomica Verlag).

Carlson, Kerstin Bree, 2016a. 'Post Rule of Law: The Structural Problem of Hybridity in International Criminal Procedure' *Italian Law Journal* 2(1), 33–64.

Carlson, Kerstin Bree, 2016b. 'Reconciliation Through a Judicial Lens: Competing Legitimation Frameworks in the ICTY's Plavšić and Babić Judgments' *Denver Journal of International Law and Policy* 44(2), 281–322.

Cassese, Antonio, 1998. 'On the Current Trends Towards Criminal Prosecution and Punishment of Breaches of International Humanitarian Law' *European Journal of International Law* 9, 2–17.

Cassese, Antonio, 1998. 'Reflections on International Criminal Justice' *Modern Law Review* 61, 1–10.

Civikov, Germinal, 2009. *Srebrenica: Der Kronzeuge (Srebrenica: The Star Witness)* (Vienna, Austria: Promedia).

Clark, Janine Natalya, 2009. 'Plea Bargaining at the ICTY: Guilty Pleas and Reconciliation' *European Journal of International Law* 20(2), 415–36.

Combs, Nancy, 2006. 'Procuring Guilty Pleas for International Crimes: The Limited Influence of Sentencing Discounts' *Vanderbilt Law Review* 59(1), 69.

Combs, Nancy, 2007. *Guilty Pleas in International Criminal Law: Constructing a Restorative Justice Approach* (Stanford, CA: Stanford University Press).

Cryer, Robert, 1997. 'One Appeal, Two Philosophies, Four Opinions and a Remittal: The Erdemović Case at the ICTY Appeals Chamber' *Journal of Conflict and Security Law* 193–208.

Damaska, Mirjan, 2004. 'Negotiated Justice in International Criminal Courts' *Journal of International Criminal Justice* 2, 1018–1039.

Dixon, Rodney and Demirdjan, Alexis, 2005. 'Advising Defendants about Guilty Pleas before International Courts' *Journal International Criminal Justice* 3, 680–94.

Dongois, N., and B. Viredaz, 2007. 'De l'américanization des sciences pénales europééenees' in *Melanges Offerts à Raymond Gassin: Sciences Penales et Sciences Criminologiques* (Marseille: Presses Universitaire d'Aix-Marseille), 216.

Feeley, Malcolm, 1979. 'Perspectives on Plea Bargaining' *Law & Society Review* 13(2), 199–209.

Hagan, John, 2003. *Justice in the Balkans: Prosecuting War Crimes in the Hague Tribunal* (Chicago: University of Chicago Press).

Harmon, Mark, 2009. 'Plea Bargaining: The Uninvited Guest at the International Criminal Tribunal for the Former Yugoslavia' in Jose Doria, et al. (eds), *The Legal Regime of the International Criminal Court: Essays in Honour of Prof. I. P. Blishcenko*, International Humanitarian Law Series, (Leiden, the Netherlands: Koninklyke Brill), 163–82.

Henham, Ralph and Drumbl, Mark, 2005. 'Plea Bargaining at the International Criminal Tribunal for the Former Yugoslavia' *Criminal Law Forum* 16(1), 49–87.

v. H. Holtermann, Jakob, 2017. '"One of the Challenges that Can Plausibly Be Raised Against Them?" On the Role of Truth in Debates About the Legitimacy of International Criminal Tribunals', in Nobuo Hayashi and Cecilia Bailliet (ed.), *The Legitimacy of International Criminal Tribunals* (Cambridge: Cambridge University Press), 206–227.

Human Rights Center and International Human Rights Law Clinic, 2000. 'Justice, Accountability and Social Reconstruction: An Interview Study of Bosnian Judges and Prosecutors' *Berkeley Journal of International Law* 18, 102–64.

Johnson, Scott T, 1998. 'On the Road to Disaster: The Rights of the Accused and the International Criminal Tribunal for the Former Yugoslavia' *International Legal Perspectives* 10, 111.

Korner, Joanna, 2016. 'Processing of War Crimes at the State Level in Bosnia and Herzegovina' OSCE Mission to Bosnia-Herzegovina (16 June 2016), accessed 6 June 2017 at www.osce.org/bih/247221?download=true.

Langbein, John H., 1974. 'Controlling Prosecutorial Discretion in Germany' *University of Chicago Law Review*, 439–67.

Langbein, John H., and Lloyd L. Weinreb, 1978. 'Continental Criminal Procedure: "Myth" and Reality' *The Yale Law Journal* 87(8), 1549–69.

Langer, Maximo, 2004. 'From Legal Transplants to Legal Translations: The Globalization of Plea Bargaining and the Americanization Thesis in Criminal Practice' *Harvard Law Review* 45(1), 29.

Langer, Maximo, 2005. 'The Rise of Managerial Judging in International Criminal Law' *Bepress Legal Series*, 343, 1–64.

Mundis, Daryl A, 2001. 'From "Common Law" Towards "Civil Law": The Evolution of the ICTY Rules of Procedure and Evidence' *Leiden Journal of International Law* 14(2), 367–82.

Mégret, Frédéric, 2009. 'Beyond Fairness: Understanding the Determinants of International Criminal Procedure' *UCLA Jounral of International Law and Foreign Affairs* 14, 37.

Meron, Theodor, 1997. 'Answering for War Crimes: Lessons from the Balkans' *Foreign Affairs* 76, 2–8.

McMahon, Patrice C, and David P Forsythe, 2008. 'The ICTY's Impact on Serbia: Judicial Romanticism Meets Network Politics' *Human Rights Quarterly* 30(2), 412–35.

Nalepa, Monika, 2012. 'Reconciliation, Refugee Returns, and the Impact of International Criminal Justice: The Case of Bosnia and Herzegovina' in Melissa S. Williams, et al. (eds), *Transitional Justice: Nomos Li* (New York: NYU Press), 316–60.

Ohlin, Jens, 2011. 'Proportional Sentences at the ICTY' in Bert Swart, Göran Sluiter, and Alexander Zahar (eds), *The Legacy of the International Criminal Tribunal for the Former Yugoslavia* (Oxford: Oxford University Press).

OSCE, 2011. 'Delivering Justice in Bosnia and Herzegovina: An Overview of War Crimes Processing from 2005 to 2010' accessed 6 June 2017 at www.osce.org/bih/108103?download=true.

OSCE, 2007. 'The Presumption of Innocence: Instances of Violations of Internationally Recognized Human Rights Standards by Courts of Bosnia and Herzegovina' accessed 6 June 2017 at www.osce.org/bih/110246?download=true.

OSCE, 2006. 'Plea Agreements in Bosnia and Herzegovina: Practices before the Courts and their compliance with international human rights standards' accessed 6 June 2017 at archive.oscebih.org/documents/osce_bih_doc_2010122311061412 eng.pdf.

Pargendler, Mariana, 2012. 'The Rise and Decline of Legal Families' *American Journal of Comparative Law* 60, 1043–74.

Rauxloh, Regina E., 2010. 'Negotiated History: The Historical Record in International Criminal Law and Plea Bargaining' *International Criminal Law Review* 10, 739–70.

Rauxloh, Regina, 2012. *Plea Bargaining in National and International Law, a Comparative Study* (Abingdon: Routledge).

Sijerčić-Čolić, Hajrija, 2005. Komentari zakona o krivičnom/kaznenom postupku u Bosni i Hercegovini. Sarajevo: Vječe Evrope: Evropska komisija.

Swart, Mia, 2010. 'Judicial Lawmaking at the Ad Hoc Tribunals: The Creative use of the Sources of International Law and "Adventurous Interpretation"' *Zeitschrift für ausländisches öffentliches Recht und Völkerrecht* 70(3), 459–86.

Vogel, Mary E., 2007. *Coercion to Compromise: Plea Bargaining, the Courts, and the Making of Political Authority* (Oxford: Oxford University Press).

Wilson, Richard A., 2011. *Writing History in International Criminal Tribunals* (Cambridge: Cambridge University Press).

Chapter 8

The making of international criminal justice

Towards a sociology of the 'legal field'

*Kirsten Campbell**

I. The problem of legal practice

The pass is a small pink slip with 'VISITOR' in large letters across it, issued by the UN security officer in a small room set apart from the large white building behind it. With this pass, I can enter the building. First into the lobby area, a sweeping corporate reception area troubled only by the court hearings broadcast on large screens, and, from there, up side stairs into the courtroom itself. There is a thick glass screen between the small public seating area and the court. Behind this screen, the trial of Naser Oric, who was previously the Senior Commander of Bosnian Muslim forces in Bosnia and Herzegovina in 1992, is proceeding. I have followed my pink slip into the world of the International Criminal Tribunal for the former Yugoslavia (ICTY), the first international criminal tribunal established by the United Nations in 1994.

There is now a rich strand of socio-legal scholarship studying such new 'global' forms of law. One strand of this work is the 'emerging sociology of international criminal courts' (Christensen 2015). This work primarily draws on the work of Bourdieu, and focuses upon the study of legal institutions and practices (such as John Hagan and Ron Levi).[1] However, to explain the making of international criminal justice requires further engagement with two conceptual problems in this idea of law as practice, which are not yet sufficiently addressed within these sociological studies. The first concerns the operation of 'legal norms and practices as structured forms of social action' (Campbell 2007). This is the key question of the 'specifically legal dimension of this field', and the associated issue of *legal*

* Kirsten would like to thank Suki Ali, David Oswell, and Kate Nash for their comments on earlier drafts of this paper. The research leading to these results has received funding from the European Research Council under the European Union's Seventh Framework Programme (FP7/2007–2013)/ ERC grant agreement No. 313626, 'Gender of Justice' project.

1 Another strand of studies draws on Latourian science and technology studies (STS) by anthropologists such as Annelise Riles and Sally Engle Merry, and focuses upon transnational commercial law and human rights.

practice (Megret 2016: para.4). The second problem concerns how gender shapes patterns of legal practice (Campbell 2007). This problem concerns how hierarchical systems of gender relations structure social action within this field, and, ultimately, shape the making of the field of international criminal law itself.

Problem one: concepts of legal practice in Bourdieu and Latour

Latour's anthropology of law and Bourdieu's sociology of the juridical field offer important accounts of practice and law, but limited explanation of legal practice as such. At a descriptive level, both Latour and Bourdieu identify three distinct categories of practice as legal. Latour describes these as 'modes' or regimes' of practice, while Bourdieu describes them as 'forms', proposing three broadly similar categories of legal practice. The first category consists of practices of the legal claim. This is the lawsuit or juridical problem in Bourdieu, or the claim that initiates the legal process in Latour. The second is the practices of the legal institution. This includes Bourdieu's description of the class-background and structure of the legal profession, and Latour's discussion of the characteristics of the court as a social institution. The third category consists of practices of legal reasoning. This includes what Bourdieu calls juridical rhetoric and discourse, and Latour terms legal judgements and statements. At a conceptual level, these categories of legal practice reflect their underlying modes of law as practice.

For Bourdieu, these 'social practices of the law are in fact the product of the functioning of a "field"' (1986: 817). The field is a 'relatively autonomous' social space, which structures practices according to its particular logic, regulative principles and values. Bourdieu names this legal logic, together with its associated principles and values, the 'juridical field'. The juridical field structures the regular and iterated social actions of law so that it functions as a field of action for the actors operating within it. It thus forms a distinct set of structured forms of social action, which consist of legal practices. The underlying logic of the field structures these seemingly diverse and multiple practices (Bourdieu 1984: 101). The specific logic of the juridical field is determined by two facts:

> on the one hand, by the specific power relations which give it its structure and which order the competitive struggles (or, more precisely, the conflicts over competence) that occur within it; and on the other hand, by the internal logic of juridical functioning which constantly constrains the range of possible actions and, thereby, limits the realm of specifically juridical solutions.
>
> (1986: 816)

The juridical field, like other fields, is a space of conflict and competition over capital according to the specific logic of the field. The participants in this conflict 'occupy objective positions in structures of power, with varying amounts of capital (economic, cultural, social) whose possession enables access to the specific profits that are at stake' by the conversion of that capital into profit through the operation of the field (Nash 2009: 30). For Bourdieu, 'juridical capital' is 'an objectified and codified form of symbolic capital, which emerges with the genesis of the modern European state (1994: 9). Law has an 'essentially conservative function of legitimating the established order' through its function as legitimated state (symbolic) violence (1986: 852). For Bourdieu, 'it thus legitimizes victories over the dominated, which are thereby converted into accepted facts' (1986: 817).

However, the difficulty of this reflexive sociology of law as account of legal practice is that it does not appear to allow for the 'relative autonomy' of the legal. Instead, the juridical 'in the last instance' becomes an expression and effect of the social. For this reason, Latour argues that in Bourdieu's work: 'at the end of the day, the law only possesses an arbitrary force of domination which it does no more than "legitimate" ... [and] legal form does not add anything'. This vision of law 'would compel us to leave the winding path of practice in order to focus on another reality, one that is invisible to the actors themselves but which is supposed to explain their behaviour [that is] the true reality of society and social violence' (2010: 141). Latour's critique reflects his wider rejection of 'critical sociology' in general, and of Bourdieu in particular as its representative. It also caricatures Bourdieu's account of law. Nevertheless, it is also true that law *is* an 'instrument of domination' for Bourdieu (Villegas 2006). How can we retain Bourdieu's insightful notion of the field of law as a distinctive and differentiated social space of regular and repeated action, while also staying on the 'winding path of practice'?

In contrast to Bourdieu, Latour insists that our analysis should not begin with 'the social' as the source of explanation of legal practice. Instead, following actor-network theory, we need to ask how the 'social' is made and remade through networks of association (2007: 8). The Latourian model of law attempts to shift from using the sociology of Durkheim, in which 'society was treated as an existing and tangible domain, [and] allowed from a neat division of "law" from "society"' (Levi and Valverde 2008: 806). Latour instead draws on the sociology of Tarde, with its emphasis upon process, movement, and association (Toews 2003). This approach understands the social not as substance, but as the actions (movements, displacements, translations, mediations and so on) that make social connections (Latour 2007: 8).

Latour sets out his detailed ethnographic study of legal practices in the French administrative court, the Conseil d'État in *The Making of Law* (2010). He seeks to understand law as a network of heterogeneous associations that build 'the social', describing it as a 'vehicle, a movement of aggregation' that assembles entities through semiotic and material associations. 'Association' is a form of action, in which 'to do is to make happen ... [w]hen one acts, others proceed to action'. Critically, one can only act by association with others. For Latour, those others are both human and non-human entities (1996: 237). Consequently, he understands law as 'a situated material practice that ties a whole range of heterogeneous phenomena in a certain specific way' (2010: x). Latour argues that law 'circulate[s] throughout the landscape to associate entities in a legal way' (2007: 239). Law is a chain of these practices, as 'making these connections, linking up these elements, weaving the social: all this is law itself' (2010: 261). Latour offers general statements describing law as a mode of disinterested and disattached objectivity, an 'enunciation regime', and a metalanguage, a 'transparent network', and a 'factish' (2010). Legality is a process in which particular practices organize social relations. These practices associate actants, and form the legal through their assembly. The 'legal' describes particular and peculiar kinds of associations, those that construct the *vinculum juris*, the chain or tie of legal obligation or relation (2010: 261). Law is a specific way of composing associations in particular forms, which are made of 'obligations' (2010: 6).

We learn little more about what constitutes legal practice as such, beyond his detailed description of the 'legal way' of association in the Conseil d'État. These specific claims about legal practices are based on his particular case study of a unique administrative judicial body, and do not carry well across to criminal law. Ellen Hertz points out that 'Latour's formulation applies particularly well to the kind of legal institution he has chosen to study [but] had Latour been observing a trial court, he would have observed an entirely different logic of linkage between what *the law takes as law* and what *the law takes as society*' (2003: 115). Similarly, Bourdieu (2004: 33) argues that Latour generally fails to engage with the 'structure of objective relationships' that governs or orients practice and actors' capacities for action. Again, Bourdieu's critique reflects his vehement rejection of Latour's work as representative of a certain kind of sociology of science. He, too, caricatures the theory itself. However, it is also true that Latour's account insists upon the irrelevance of the problems of the power of law and of power upon law, an exclusion that is highly problematic for any account of legal practice in international criminal justice.

These theories of law, then, provide important but insufficient conceptual resources for understanding legal practice as such. Moreover, both these accounts of legal practice presume national legal systems – in this case, France – with specific legal cultures tied to nation states. As a result, their accounts cannot simply be transposed to the international level.[2] The first challenge, then, is how to develop these powerful accounts of law as a theory of legal practice in international criminal law.

Problem two: gender and legal practice in international criminal law

There is now an extensive body of feminist scholarship pointing to the centrality of gender issues to international criminal law.[3] However, the gendered shaping of legal practice has been given little attention in the new sociology of international criminal courts. Latour and Bourdieu themselves do not offer gendered accounts

2 For further discussion of this issue, see Campbell (2013).

3 For an overview of this work see Buss (2016). See also Brammertz and Jarvis (2016).

of legal practice, despite the well-established critiques of the gendered nature of laws of nation states, such as the French legal system that they analyse. Moreover, their work cannot simply be applied to explain gender and legal practice in international criminal law. While Bourdieu (2001) recognises the importance of understanding 'masculine domination' in social life, his account of gender as such has been widely critiqued.[4] In contrast, Latour rejects 'gender' as a social category through which to understand practice (Campbell 2004).[5] For these reasons, again, it is not possible simply to apply Latour or Bourdieu's theories of legal practice as accounts of gendered legal practice in international criminal law. The second challenge, then, is how to provide a feminist account of the gendered shaping of the legal field.

II. Towards an account of the making of the legal field

To develop an account of how gendered legal practices shape international criminal justice, I use the new concept of the 'legal field'. The concept of the legal field brings together Latour's insights regarding the assemblage of law in associative practices, and Bourdieu's argument that power shapes particular patterns of practice in any given field of social action. In developing this concept, I do not follow Bourdieu in assuming 'society' is an already existing and 'external' fact that produces the juridical field (in contrast to current 'relational' approaches). The idea of 'the social' at the international level – including its sociological (and empirically descriptive) sense of a complex 'international' world of governments and non-governmental organisations, actors, and institutions – remains highly problematic. Instead, I build on my earlier exploration of Latour to frame this concept of the legal field (Campbell 2014). This approach follows Latour in examining how legal practices assemble the legal field. It does not assume that law and society are given phenomena that then act upon each other, but rather asks how actions and associations operate to make 'the legal' and 'the social'. It examines how the legal way of associating entities makes international criminal justice, asking how distinct categories of legal practices assemble this field.

To build this idea of the legal field, I trace the ongoing process of making the legal field of the ICTY. This aims to describe the assemblage of 'law' (in Latour's terms), and draws on extensive interviews and participant observation over five years in the ICTY and the former Yugoslavia.[6] I adapt actor-network theory

4 See, for example, the work of Bev Skeggs on Bourdieu (e.g L. Adkins and B. Skeggs (eds) *Feminism After Bourdieu* (2004)).

5 See also the important work of Donna Haraway on Latour and gender (e.g. *Modest witness@second-millennium.femaleman©-meets-oncomouse™* (1997)).

6 This research builds upon a broader set of empirical projects concerning transitional justice in the former Yugoslavia. It includes 90 rolling in-depth personal interviews conducted with key

(ANT) methodology and use *The Prosecutor v Oric* as a methodological device to understand the legal case as Latourian 'black box' (rather than to provide an ethnography of the *Oric* proceedings as such). The 'black box' is a cybernetics term, which indicates a complex phenomenon about which nothing needs to be known other than its input and output (Latour 1987: 3). In ANT, the black box represents an accepted fact or claim, which is the outcome of a set of stabilized relations of networks. The ANT methodology aims to reopen the black box through description. This description traces the networks that transform the input – a controversy – into the output – the accepted claim and the credible fact. To do this, as Latour suggests, I follow the actor to trace the unfolding of their actions of association. However, I extend the legal chain past the court, the 'site of law' for Bourdieu and Latour. Following Latour (2010: 138), I analytically extend the legal chain by increasing the number of actors, expanding the range of agencies making the actors act, multiplying the number of objects active in stabilizing groups and agencies, and mapping the controversies about matters of concern.

This extension of our analysis past the courtroom is made possible by including a modest witness in my description of the making of this legal field. For Donna Haraway, the modest witness is a figure of how gender and ethnicity shapes who is able to witness what and how persuasively, and hence shows how these social hierarchies are integral to the assembling of actor-networks in particular ways. The modest witness is also a figure of the perspectives of those whose accounts of the world have not been persuasive because of their different (incompatible, weaker) positions in an 'inhomogeneous gendered social space' (Haraway 1991: 195).[7] The modest witness provides a feminist analytic to examine the differential forms of practice in the legal field. Including a modest witness in my description of the making of international criminal law gives another perspective of the way in which this field is assembled, including through the practice of gender.

This reinscription of a feminist politics is not only a question of including or adding women (Bell and O'Rourke 2007: 42). Rather, it necessarily involves asking about how gender shapes legal practice. Posing the problem of differential positioning and resources also makes Bourdieu's work a useful tool in our analysis of the making of international criminal justice, as it provides an important account of power in the legal field. This account, in turn, provides a stronger and better account of the assembling of networks, as it reinscribes the problems of an unequal social space and of change in the practices that produce it (Haraway 1992).

ICTY and defence staff, as well as the War Crimes Chamber ('WCC') and transitional justice NGOs in Bosnia and Herzegovina ('BiH'). It was carried out with my co-investigator, AAA from 2005 to the present. I would like to thank all the informants for their time. Due to the sensitive nature of this research, references to interviewees have been anonymised as 'I'.

7 Haraway calls this position the 'mutated' modest witness to indicate that it operates against the racial and gendered assumptions of what it is to be a persuasive witness. However, I want to retain both elements of this figure, drawing attention to both this agency and the moderated, small, and limited speaking position of the witness.

This 'modest witness' is Ms Edina Karic, a witness in the *Oric* case, who I follow through the legal field. *The Prosecutor v Oric* concerned the command responsibility of Naser Orić, Senior Commander of Bosnian Muslim forces in municipalities in eastern Bosnia and Herzegovina, including Srebrenica, from 1992 until the fall of the Srebrenica enclave in 1995. Karic was one of 30 witnesses called by the Defence. Her testimony was intended to raise reasonable doubt of the charges against Oric by providing evidence of Serbian military dominance in Eastern Bosnia. She testified to her detention, rape, and assault by Serbian Bosnian soldiers when aged 15. Karic speaks as a witness. She is neither accused (charged with crimes) nor prosecutrix (on whose behalf the prosecutor brings those charges). She is not a legal subject in the technical sense (Campbell 2012). At the same time, Karic acts as an agent, insisting on her right to be heard and her claim to justice for her harm. For these reasons, she occupies a position of modest witness in this legal case.

The social wrong: from social conflict to legal controversy

> We also heard a distressing testimony of Edina Karic, the then 15-year-old girl. She was raped, inter alia, by the Serb soldiers from Bjelovac. She had identified them many years before this case.[8]

The blackbox of the *Oric* case (the legal decision regarding the accepted claim and the credible fact) may appear to begin with the controversy or dispute that this legal case seeks to settle. However, the *Oric* case in fact begins with multiple conflicts and controversies. These controversies circulated within the conflictual space of the former Yugoslavia, and continually re-emerged during the trial itself (Sadović 2006). Numerous people claimed that Oric committed atrocities against them, or that his military actions saved them. Mass graves were found, and their bodies disinterred. Were they Serbian or Bosnian? Did Serbs or Bosnians murder them? Statements of the living and the dead testifying to military activities of Serbs and Bosnians circulate through the files of UN investigators, journalists, NGOs. Pro-Serbian political parties claim that the ICTY did not prosecute Oric because of its pro-Muslim bias, while Bosniak war veteran and survivor associations campaigned against his arrest. Despite their differing content, these controversies shared a similar structure: a claim of injustice, and a claim for justice.

How can we trace this complex movement from the claim of injustice to the legal claim? The question of issue formation is not well developed in ANT methodology (Marres 2007). Moreover, Latour acknowledges that the ethnographer cannot easily glimpse the 'long history' that precedes the legal claim (2010: 73). However, this history is crucial, because it raises the unavoidable question of the beginning and end of the legal chain of obligation (Barry 2001). So where

8 *The Prosecutor v Oric*, Transcript, 5 April 2006, 16312.

is the beginning of this legal chain? Bourdieu offers a helpful argument that the operation of law begins with 'the conversion of direct conflict between directly concerned parties into juridically regulated debate between professionals acting by proxy' (1986: 831). Following this argument, the constitution of the legal chain of obligation begins with the conversion of a social controversy into a legal problem. The process of conversion of social conflict into juridical debate can be seen as similar in its operation to Andrew Pickering's idea of the 'mangle of practice' in his social study of science. The material-semiotic mangle of law transforms and structures social controversy into a legal problem.[9]

In the case of the ICTY, this mangle of law needs to be built. This field of 'international criminal justice' begins with the UN establishing the legal institution and the statute setting out its crimes and procedures. To have a juridically regulated debate requires a physical court (which had to be built in the Hague), as much as it requires a statute that defines which crimes it can hear (which had to be drafted and agreed by the UN Security Council). This process involved the stabilisation of complex networks of actants stretching from New York to the Hague. So, for example, campaigns by Yugoslavian and international feminist activists for the prosecution of the widespread sexual violence in the conflict were crucial to the establishment of the ICTY (Gardam and Jarvis 2001: 44). With the building of this 'mangle' of legal practice, the armed conflict in the former Yugoslavia became the object of juridically regulated debate. Accordingly, the legal chain of obligation begins with this creation of this material-semiotic juridical device, which transforms social conflict into an object of legal regulation.

With the building of this 'mangle' of legal practice, the social conflict can become a legal controversy. This organizes '*the public representation* of social conflicts according to established forms' (Bourdieu 1986: 830–1). These established forms are practices that seek to *appropriate* conflict to law by characterizing it as an object of juridical debate; that aim to *neutralize* this conflict by having legal professionals decide its outcome according to given norms and procedures, and claim to *universalize* these norms and procedures across all legal controversies (Bourdieu 1986: 819–20). These practices of formalization and codification using legal conventions and rules are part of the process of assembling legal associations. These are practices of appropriation, neutralization, and universalization, which transform social conflict into a legal controversy. This is not just that armed conflict, such as the war in the former Yugoslavia, becomes the object of legal regulation. Rather, it also refers to the process by which particular social claims of injustice become (or not) subject to legal decision, once this mangle of law is built.

These practices that transmute a social controversy into a conflict subject to juridical decision may be formal, such as prosecution strategies, or informal, such

9 For further discussion of this idea, see A. Pickering, *The Mangle of Practice* (Chicago: University of Chicago Press, 1995).

as patterns of investigation, charging, or arrest. For example, the change in formal ICTY Office of the Prosecutor (OTP) policy from prosecution of so-called 'lower level' to 'higher-level' leadership cases has led to a change in the kinds of claims of injustice being heard before the court. Similarly, at an informal level, concerns regarding gaps in jurisprudence, or whether cases can represent particularly affected regions of the conflict or particular 'situations' of conflict have also shaped which claims have been taken up by OTP.[10] However, what is clear from informant interviews is that the successful claim multiplies its actants through these practices, often in surprising and contingent associations. These range from regional NGOs, media, police, victims and war veterans associations; to the OTP, which decides to investigate, send its investigators to the region, and whether to prosecute; and to the complex political entities of the European Union and Bosnia and Herzegovina, which range from the Office of the High Representative to the NATO troops arresting the accused.

However, our modest witness reminds us that many social conflicts do not become legal controversies. In her testimony in the *Oric* case, Edina Karic gave evidence of her rape by named Serb soldiers, which she had already provided to Bosnian authorities nearly ten years earlier.[11] However, her claim was not considered as a legal claim in this or any other case. It had not become part of a chain of legal obligation. The issue here is not whether law can capture the 'full event' of conflict. After all, this impossibility is not the aim or practice of the ICTY. Nor is it a question of the 'exigencies' of the particular case. Legal practices constitute 'facts' and 'witnesses'. Rather, we need to be able to explain why Nedeljko Radić, a Serb detainee, 'named in the indictment against Oric as one of a number of specific Bosnian Serbs who were subject to "physical abuse" and "serious suffering" at the hands of his men' and the first prosecution witness to appear in court, becomes part of the legal chain, whereas the crimes against Edina Karic did not (Sadović 2005).

To address this issue requires engaging with the incompatibility of certain actants with others, and the weakness of certain associative links. Unlike Latour, Bourdieu acknowledges the potential failure of the social harm to become a juridical problem because of the unequal positions of actors.[12] He reminds us that actants are differentially situated in social space: some are more compatible with legal associations, and have more compelling narratives and resources to deploy in making those associations. So, for example, the claim may not become a juridical problem, because harms to a certain category of persons are not

10 Senior Trial Attorneys A and B, OTP, 2007.

11 *The Prosecutor v Oric*, Decision On Alleged Prosecution Non-Compliance With Disclosure Obligations Under Rules 66(B) And 68(I), 29 September 2005.

12 From his earliest to most recent work, Latour insists that just as we should not use 'the social' as a causal explanation, so too we should not use the black-box concepts of 'power' and 'domination', or identity. This approach is also the reason for much feminist critique of his work, most notably by Donna Haraway.

recognized as an injustice. It was not until the early 1990s that sexual violence in armed conflict as such was unquestionably recognized as an international crime.[13] Even if accepted as an object of juridical regulation, particular types of social claims to injustice may not enter the legal field. For example, claims concerning sexual violence may not become subject to juridical dispute because of gendered practices concerning investigation, charging or witnessing (Mischkowski and Mlinarevic 2009). The ICTY's record in this area has been problematic, with clearly different patterns in relation to male and female victims (Campbell 2007). For this reason, we must consider not only whose accounts win and become recognized as legal claims, but also whose accounts lose and do not.

Legal claims

> 26. **Naser ORIC** from about September 1992 to August 1995 knew or had reason to know that his subordinates were about to plan, prepare or execute the imprisonment, killing and/or cruel treatment of Serbs detained at the Srebrenica Police Station
>
> By these acts and omissions **Naser ORIC** committed:
>
> **COUNT 1:** MURDER, a **VIOLATION OF THE LAWS OR CUSTOMS OF WAR.**[14]

The next link or association in the legal chain of obligation is the process of modifying the social controversy by 'translating' it into the form of a legal claim (in Latour's terms). This process involves taking the complex networks around the displacement from the social to the legal controversy, and inscribing the legal controversy in the form of a legal and factual claim. This inscription connects the legal chain to the social controversy, or the claim of injustice. The legal issue concerns the elements of the crimes to be proven, and the factual issue concerns the submission of evidence to prove those crimes. For example, the judicial 'ordeal' in the Oric case begins with the indictment above, which is the key transcription device in this set of legal practices. The indictment sets out the material facts on which the prosecution will rely ('**Naser Oric**, from about September 1992 ... '), together with the alleged crimes that the accused is charged with ('**COUNT 1**: MURDER . . .'). It takes the complex multiple social and legal controversies concerning Oric, and rearticulates them as material facts and charges of crimes.

In this process, a 'complete retranslation of all of the aspects of the controversy is necessary in order to, as the Romans said, *ponere causam* (to 'put' the case), that

13 Rape had previously been recognised as a war crime subject to national prosecution, or where connected to the international crime of aggression. For further discussion, see Kelly Askin's classic work, *War Crimes Against Women* (1997).

14 *The Prosecutor v Oric*, Case No IT-03-68-T, Third Amended Indictment, 30 June 2005.

is to institute the controversy *as a lawsuit,* as a juridical problem that can become the object of juridically regulated debate' (Bourdieu 1986: 833). In the ICTY, this process rearticulates a harm or wrong in terms of the legal components (or elements) of a crime. This is not understood as a right of the victim as such, but rather as a serious violation of international humanitarian law. It is this violation that constitutes an international crime. So, for example, the *Oric* case arose from allegations of the international crimes of violations of the laws or customs of war. This re-articulation of a harm or wrong in terms of the legal elements of these crimes transformed a grievance into a crime contrary to international humanitarian law, and therefore a legal wrong recognized by substantive law. This process makes it into a juridical problem, establishing it as a legal claim that the court can adjudicate. In contrast, the rape to which Ms Karic testified remains a personal harm, and was not rearticulated as a legal wrong.

If we consider the performative nature of law as a semiotic practice, then we can better understand this process. In this re-articulation of the harm as a crime, 'the law becomes a form *par excellence* of symbolic power – and of symbolic violence – given the possibilities possessed by its practitioners to create institutions and with them historical and political realities through [an] act of naming' (Villegas 2004: 60). These international rules operate as semiotic practices, which name the harm as a criminal offence, and represent this harm according to their norms. For example, in technical terms, the Geneva Conventions 1947 define whether Oric's conduct was legitimate military action or the destruction of undefended villages without military justification. These rules define who is a victim of that harm and who is not; together with who is a perpetrator and who is not. For example, the doctrine of command responsibility defines whether or not Oric was legally liable for the cruel treatment of Serb detainees by his subordinates. In this way, legal rules work as the:

> quintessential form of the symbolic power of naming that creates the things named, and creates social groups in particular. It confers upon the reality which arises from its classificatory operations the maximum permanence that any social entity has the power to confer upon another, the permanence which we attribute to objects.
>
> (Bourdieu 1986: 840)

Legal rules operate as performative semiotic practices. It is not simply that actors deploy more or less persuasive rhetorical strategies. Rather, this legal power to name constructs specific kinds of legal subjects and relations, which in turn permits the constitution of particular chains of legal obligation to certain social groups and not others.

However, these semiotic practices construct gendered legal subjects and relations. The definition of sexual violence in international criminal law is ostensibly gender-neutral, since it is intended to refer to violence of a sexual nature against either women or men (Campbell 2007). However, our modest witness offers us another perspective. Her testimony reminds us how the harm of sexual violence in legal rules is given content by particular understandings of gendered bodies, acts, and sexuality, both in terms of what is suffered and who suffers it. The 'sexual' in crimes of sexual violence is always already gendered.[15] It constitutes victims and perpetrators as gendered persons, and invariably involves ideas of gendered bodies of men and women.[16] These narratives shape legal harms, persons, and liabilities, such as who is harmed, which harms are legally recognized as crimes to be prosecuted before the court, and who should be prosecuted for them. They construct the tie of legal obligation in gendered terms, and thereby create differential patterns of claims of injustice within the legal field.

Legal proceedings

> THE WITNESS: [Interpretation] I solemnly declare that I will speak
> the truth, the whole truth, and nothing but the truth.
> WITNESS: EDINA KARIC[17]

Edina Karic appeared as a witness for the Defence in the legal proceedings against Oric. The OTP needed to prove their charges against Oric 'beyond reasonable doubt' to Judge Agius and his colleagues, and the Defence to raise reasonable doubt. Ms Karic's evidence was intended to raise this doubt. These legal proceedings function as 'an *epistemic* engine' for determining facts and norms (Laudan 2006: 2). This process of constructing credible legal facts and accepted legal norms is the next link in the legal chain of obligation. In trial proceedings, each party seeks to enrol new actants to their claim, both human and non-human, of which I, with my visitor's pass, am one. Each legal argument and evidential submission seeks to add another actant, and thereby to extend the legal network. For example, the Defence does not call Edina Karic so that she may testify to the wrong against her. Instead, she is called to testify to the actions of Serb soldiers in the eastern Bosnian region, so as to provide empirical evidence of Oric's justification of military necessity in his armed defence of Bosniaks in this area.

The legal trial operates as the legal equivalent of the experiment seeking to establish the scientific claim. As I can see in the courtroom before me, each party seeks to demonstrate their legal claim by connecting argument, documents, videos, statistical analyses, bodies, forensic reports, texts, and victim-witnesses. Establishing this claim involves enrolling human actants, such as lawyers, witnesses, judges, translators, as well as non-human actants, such as court buildings, databases, and Serbian televisions. Like the laboratory, the courtroom becomes the site of fact and

15 For the classic outline of this theory, see Butler, *Gender Trouble* (2004).

16 For further discussion, see Campbell (2007).

17 *The Prosecutor v Oric*, Transcript, 14 September 2005, 10969.

norm construction. These include the structure of trial proceedings, the parties and their role in those proceedings, which change the form of fact-finding. It also includes practices of evidencing harms, such as evidential rules, forms of witnessing, and types of evidence given, which shape the judicial finding of facts. The legal practices of the courtroom include the rules and conventions that formalize and systematize norms. In Bourdieu's terms, they operate to construct law as an autonomous, neutral, and universal space of arbitration for conflict. The ICTY claims its legitimacy on the basis of its operation as a neutral legal space, which converts social conflict into legal conflict by the use of the norms and conventions of trial proceedings. This is reflected in the physical layout of the courtroom itself.

However, the position of Edina Karic as witness in this world of law is not neutral. So, for example, legal practices construct the prosecution of sexual violence in differential patterns depending upon the gender of the claimant. Edina Karic's testimony is typical of the gendered patterns of witnessing before the ICTY. As a woman, she is more likely to appear to testify to sexual violence. As a woman appearing as a witness in a so-called leadership case, she is less likely to give evidence against those who actually harmed her, or to have that harm be the subject of distinct charges (Mischkowski and Mlinarevic 2009).

These legal practices do not simply reflect men's domination of the legal field, or women's complicity with it, as Bourdieu's account can be read as implying (Fowler 2003, Adkins and Skeggs 2005). Rather, these practices produce 'gender' itself. For example, this gendered pattern of witnessing constructs women as visible victims of sexual violence, but not as the subject of legal wrongs. This creates a pattern of testimony in which men appear to testify to conflict and women testify to rape, such that men appear as active agents in the conflict and women as passive victims of sexual violence. It thereby operates as a 'practice of gendering' that figures masculinity as active and femininity as passive (Loizidou 2007: 124). Our modest witness, Karic, resists this gendered practice. At trial, she refuses the repeated offer to give evidence in private session, insisting that she has nothing to be ashamed of. However, the bench also insists that they may decide to go into private session, 'in the best interests of the witness to do so, whether or not she has asked for it'.[18] The bench did not decide to do so, other than at the request of the witness to prevent identification of other victims with her at the time.

Settling a controversy

> 3. The Takeover of Srebrenica by Bosnian Serb Forces and its Recapture by Bosnian Muslims.
>
> 100. On 18 April 1992, after shelling, Srebrenica fell to the Bosnian Serbs. Following the takeover, a Serb flag was paraded through town. Serb forces,

18 *The Prosecutor v Oric*, Transcript, 5 April 2006, 10972–73.

accompanied by paramilitaries, plundered goods, damaged houses, and killed many of the remaining Bosnian Muslims.[213]

213 James Gow, T. 1965; Hakija Meholjić, T. 6741–6742; Ibrahim Bečirović, T. 7411; Bečir Bogilović, T. 6223, 6380; Kada Hotić, T. 9664–9665, 9668; Sabra Kolenović, T. 10056–10057, 10060–10061, 10063–10064, 10068–10071; Nesib Burić, T. 10585–10587; Edina Karić, T. 10987–10990; Suad Smajlović, T. 1447[19]

Edina Karic reappears in the judgment of the Trial Chamber in the *Oric* case, when her testimony is used as evidence to support judicial findings of fact. The Chamber's guilty verdict on the basis of superior responsibility for two charges of war crimes was reversed on appeal, with Oric acquitted on all counts. The *Oric* case ends with decisions: determinations of fact, law, liability, and punishment. As Latour describes, 'a case has to be concluded' (2010: 221). The *Oric* judgment exemplifies the legal practice of judgment, with its 'rhetoric of autonomy, neutrality, and universality', and its claim to the rational, consistent, and coherent application of norms to the case before it.[20]

This legal judgment creates another link in the chain of legal obligation. The process of judgment aims both to settle the legal controversy of fact and law and the social controversy of the injustice. To do this successfully, the judgment must construct two chains of legal obligation. First, it needs to tie together the legal determination of facts with the occurrence of an event. Latour suggests that the legal decision has no relation to its object or truth. However, that decision must be able to link its determination of what happened to the 'empirical' event that is re-presented in evidence in the courtroom. Otherwise, it fails to function as a 'reasonable trier of fact' as the ICTY appellate jurisprudence puts it. The judgment inscribes a series of fact-finding practices, which serve as the epistemic foundation of legal determination of 'fact'. 'Evidence' serves as the link between this fact-finding of the law and the external world of the event. This chain constructs the legal fact as a social fact. Second, the judgment must tie together the legal determination of wrongs and the social controversy of the wrong. As Latour acknowledges, *res judicata* 'has to produce justice and declare the law' (2010: 241). The judgment must link the just and the wrong together in its decision to create a legal chain to the social controversy. If it succeeds in constituting this chain of obligation, then it 'settles' the dispute.

If we follow Latour in understanding law as a vehicle or 'a movement of aggregation', then we can see that the success of the legal construction of these chains depends on its ability to link fact and event, justice and wrong. So, for example,

19 *The Prosecutor v Oric*, Case No IT-03-68-T, Judgement, 2006.

20 Bourdieu has an extensive discussion of the function of precedent and judicial interpretation, which technically is not applicable to the ICTY (or any other international body). However, the use of authority to legitimate legal argument remains an important technique of judgment. See Bourdieu (1986: 820).

the claim of the wrong moves through a series of displacements, translations, and modifications through Bosnia, through the legal institution, process, and proceedings in the Hague, and then back to 'the region' following judgment. These chains can be longer or shorter, or be part of wider or smaller networks. For the ICTY, a key problem has been how to extend their legal chains of obligation, how to enrol more actants, and how to create new forms of association, and accordingly, to generate new forms of the social between the Hague and the former Yugoslavia.[21] The ICTY seeks to remake the 'social' of the former Yugoslavia by constructing new chains of legal obligation that can 'assemble' a post-conflict societies (Campbell 2014). However, the settlement of controversy by the ICTY judgment also constitutes certain forms of the social, rather than others, by virtue of the kinds of chains of legal obligations that it builds. For example, what form of the 'social' does the ICTY assemble when chains of legal obligation do not extend to victims of sexual violence? From the perspective of our modest witness, this settlement (re)produces differential and unjust legal obligations, which reassemble a gendered and unjust 'social' within law.

III. Legal practices and the legal field

From this description of the making of the legal field of the ICTY, legality is a process that assembles chains of legal obligations through particular practices. These legal practices are semiotic and material actions that work to assemble entities of human and non-humans into new forms of association and relation. The legal world I can see before me in Courtroom 1 is an assemblage of persons and things, and operates as an effect of the practices of both animate and inanimate entities. The case only proceeds with the security guard, judge, witness, and translator. Similarly, it has been necessary to build the courtroom in which they stand, the databases that they consult, the camera that broadcasts their testimony, and the transcription software that converts their testimony in one language to a transcript in another. All these practices are necessary for 'the law' to be enacted and to remain in place.

Bourdieu reminds us that practice, in its broadest and most abstract sense, is a meaningful practical activity that consists of regular action that unfolds over time and space. Practice is systematic (forming regular patterns of action) and temporal (repeated action over time). Following this idea, legal practices are regular patterns of action that are repeated over time. In this sense, 'law' is a series of repeated techniques and performances, which are composed of actions that are both meaningful and material. My description of the making of international criminal justice shows that there are four key distinctive categories of such practices. These categories of practice:

1 transform the social controversy into a legal concern;
2 translate claims of injustice into the legal rules that symbolize harms;

21 See, for example, 'Outreach', accessed 7 June 2017 at www.icty.org/sections/Outreach.

3 construct credible facts and accepted norms through legal proceedings; and
4 settle the legal issue through judgment.

These are repeated and regular actions, which form distinctive and distinct categories of practice. These distinctive categories of actions associate entities in 'a legal way', thereby creating the legal chain of obligation. We can describe these new forms of association as 'legal'. This should not be taken to imply that there is a 'legal substance', which differentiates law from other social practices. Rather, it is that there is a set of practices that we can name 'legal', because they assemble the legal chain of obligation. To follow Latour, '[l]aw is defined ... by a marker that qualifies a given enunciation as an element of law and not of some other mode of existence' (Pottage 2012: 174). However, as Latour himself notes, such an approach may return us to the classical jurisprudential problem, in which the attempt 'to define Law ... always ends up resorting to the adjective "legal" to qualify it'. In his important intervention, Pottage argues that Latour in fact fails to deal with this 'legal tautology' because his account does not engage with the 'first and most basic feature of law [which] is to decide on the difference between the legal and the non-legal' (2012: 177). Without acknowledging how this distinction produces 'law', Latour can only describe law as a 'dematerialised structure' rather than grasping its material form. However, my account of legal practices offers a means of addressing this problem. It insists that a specific set of practices make 'law' by constructing the distinction between the legal and the non-legal. These practices qualify 'events or enunciations as legal in the first place' by assembling particular material-semiotic networks in chains of legal obligation (Pottage 2012: 177). Like the making of science in STS laboratory studies, we see the making of law in the materiality of the court, in 'its apparatuses, its physical organisation, and its practices' of constructing credible facts, accepting claims, and settling controversies (Law 2008: 631).

Framed in this way, the regular and repeated patterns of action of legal practices can be understood as constructing the field of international criminal justice in time and space. International criminal justice is not a 'given' social substance, understood in the sense of an already existing and 'external' social fact. Instead, legal practices assemble this world of law, and sustain it in time and space through repeated performances of material and semiotic actions. Latour suggests that the legal 'resembles delicately knitted lace' forming fine filaments of association (2010: 264). However, his suggestive analogy of the legal chain is more useful. If, as in the OED, we describe a chain as 'a connected flexible series of metal links used for fastening or securing objects and pulling or supporting a load', then we can understand the legal chain as a flexible series of links, connecting actants through legal practices, and fastening and securing these links to claims and decisions. The legal field operates not so much as a fine lace, but rather as a mesh of interlinked chains of legal practices. This mesh is not above the 'social', but forms a net of support for the social assemblage, holding its elements together, and hence working as a reinforcing structure of the field. This mesh spreads through time and space, constituting its networks through chains of associations or relations, which are assembled through legal practices.

The legal field thus forms a net of relational forces, 'within which an effect of field is exercised, so that what happens to any object that traverses this space cannot be explained solely by the intrinsic properties of the object in question' (Bourdieu 1992: 100). This net of practices captures the object, diffracting it through new relations to other entities and practices, and meanwhile attributing particular properties and qualities to that object. For example, what happens to Edina Karic as she traverses the legal field cannot be explained solely by her intrinsic or 'ontological' qualities. Rather, it is explained by her constitution as a claimant and a witness in relation to other entities and practices, and the construction of her harms as non-justiciable and her claims as unpersuasive (Campbell 2002). This field is not flat (contra Latour), but is unevenly constituted through differential relations, practices, and objects, including gender (pace Bourdieu). However, it is also important to recognise that the object is agentic, in the sense that it is able to intervene in these associations by engaging with different chains of obligations, and thereby enrolling itself in new relations. For example, Edina Karic intervenes in the making of the chain of legal obligation between Oric and his alleged victims by testifying to her own harms at the ICTY. In this way, she seeks to make another legal chain of obligation by articulating a claim of injustice and hence making a claim to justice.[22]

Legal practices produce this mesh of law, and circumscribe its boundary in time and space. The *legal field*, then, is a bounded configuration of particular and related forms of material and symbolic practices. As Bourdieu puts it, '[t]he limits of the field are situated at the point where the effects of the field cease' (1992: 100). A chain is not only the flexible link that connects entities, since it also works as a fetter, or restraining force. The legal chain also closes the boundaries of the field by delineating the entities within it. For example, the operation of the legal field restrains the testimony of Ms Karic in particular ways by rearticulating her claim of a wrong as evidence supporting the Defence's case. However, this boundary is not a spatial fact that has social consequences, but a sociological fact that is formed spatially and temporally (to paraphrase Simmel). This shifts our model of the legal field from being a topological space of positions that set a boundary. Instead, legal practices construct the boundary of the field by demarcating the legal from the non-legal. By making this boundary in time and space, they construct the 'inside' and the 'outside' of the law, and the beginning and end of the legal chain.

The 'social' that is assembled in this legal chain of obligation appears as the neutral, legitimate and just settlement of the controversy. It seeks to appear as though it is outside the effects of power and domination. But what if the law simply reproduces the older political settlements that produced the wrong in the first instance? If Edina Karic's harm is not addressed, then the political settlement founded upon violent collectivities of gender and ethnicity remains in place, and with it the very inequalities that produced her harm. This leaves us with the problem of justice, and, by extension, of value. In the legal field, 'everything is

22 *The Prosecutor v Oric*, Transcript, 5 April 2006, 16312.

not *equally possible or impossible*' (Bourdieu 1986: 241). Some claims and claimants are more persuasive than others because the world of law is not flat, neutral, or equal. For this reason, we need to engage with 'neglected things', 'counting in participants and issues who have not managed or are not likely to succeed in articulating their concerns, or whose modes of articulation indicate a politics that is "imperceptible" within prevalent ways of understanding' (Bellacasa 2011: 94–6). Reframing our understanding of legal practice through the position of the modest witness 'counts in' participants and issues that otherwise remain imperceptible with current sociological approaches. This provides another perspective on the politics of gendered legal practice in the field.

The settlement of a social controversy in international criminal law may restore 'equilibrium', as Latour claims (2010: 243). For both Bourdieu and Latour, law is fundamentally conservative, since the legal settlement of disputes sustains, rather than disrupts, the existing order. However, this is not a necessary condition of such a settlement, or its only form, as the development of legal practices in the area of conflict-related sexual violence shows. Instead, settlement of a dispute may involve the invention of legal practices that can generate new facts, laws, and justices. These innovations in turn have the capacity to create forms of association and new forms of the social by offering *a new settlement of a controversy.* International criminal law can translate new claims to injustice into legal concerns, and inscribe these new injustices into the legal rules symbolizing harms, and thereby change that naming of wrongs. It can construct new credible facts and new epistemic norms for determining a claim. Finally, it can develop new norms of judgment.

This is law at its most inventive: 'making the connection, linking up these elements, weaving the social' (Latour 2010: 261). In this mode of making the social, international criminal law can 'encompass transformative justice or challenge fundamentally unjust power relations within society; power relations that are often at the heart of the conflict itself' (Valiji 2007: 3). A transformative settlement of a controversy takes law's material and symbolic power, and seeks to deploy it to generate more equitable collectives. Ultimately, this political process requires the generation of new legal practices, and a remaking of the legal field of international criminal law itself.

References

Adkins, L. and Skeggs, B. (eds.) (2004) *Feminism After Bourdieu* (Oxford: Blackwell).

Bell, C. and O'Rourke, C. (2007) 'Does Feminism Need a Theory of Transitional Justice?' *International Journal of Transitional Justice* 1(1), 23–44.

Bourdieu, P. (1984) *Distinction* (Cambridge, MA: Harvard University Press).

Bourdieu, P. (1986) 'The Forms of Capital' in J. Richardson (ed.), *Handbook of Theory and Research for the Sociology of Education* (New York: Greenwood).

Bourdieu, P. (1986–7) 'The Force of Law: Toward a Sociology of the Juridical Field' *Hastings Law Journal* 38, 814–853.

Bourdieu, P. (2001) *Masculine Domination* (Cambridge: Polity).
Bourdieu, P. (2004) *Science of Science and Reflexivity* (Cambridge: Polity).
Bourdieu, P., Wacquant, L. and Farage, S. (1994) 'Rethinking the State' *Sociological Theory* 12(1), 1–19.
Bourdieu, P. with Wacquant, L. (1992) *An Invitation to Reflexive Sociology* (Chicago: University of Chicago Press).
Brammertz, S. and Jarvis, M. (eds.) (2016) *Prosecuting Conflict-Related Sexual Violence* (Oxford: Oxford University Press).
Buss, D. (2016) 'International Criminal Courts' in Jill Steans and Daniela Tepe-Belfrage (eds.), *Handbook on Gender in World Politics* (Cheltenham, UK and Northhampton, MA: Edward Elgar).
Campbell, K. (2002) 'Legal Memories' *Signs* 28(1), 149–176.
Campbell, K. (2004) 'The Promise of Feminist Reflexivities' *Hypatia* 19(1), 162–182.
Campbell, K. (2007) 'The Gender of Transitional Justice' *International Journal of Transitional Justice* 1(3), 411–432.
Campbell, K. (2011) 'Victims and Perpetrators of International Crimes: The Problem of the "Legal Person"' *Journal of International Humanitarian Legal Studies* 2(2), 325–351.
Campbell, K. (2013) 'The Making of Global Legal Culture and International Criminal Law' *Leiden Journal of International Law* 26(1), 155–172.
Campbell, K. (2014) 'Reassembling International Justice: The Making of "The Social" in International Criminal Law and Transitional Justice' *International Journal of Transitional Justice* 8(1), 53–74.
Christensen, M. J. (2015) 'The Emerging Sociology of International Criminal Courts' *Current Sociology* 63(6), 825–849.
Fowler, B. (2003) 'Reading Pierre Bourdieu's Masculine Domination' *Cultural Studies* (3–4), 468–494.
Garcia Villegas, M. (2004) 'On Pierre Bourdieu's Legal Thought' *Droit et Société* 56–7, 57–81.
Garcia Villegas, M. (2006) 'Comparative Sociology of Law' *Law and Social Inquiry* 31(2), 343–382.
Haraway, D. (1997) *Modest witness@second-millennium.femaleman©-meets-oncomouse™: Feminism and Technoscience* (New York and London: Routledge).
Hertz, E. (2003) 'Compte-rendu de La Fabrique du Droit: une ethnologie du Conseil d'Etat (B. Latour, 2002)' *Political and Legal Anthropology Review* 26(1), 113–115.
Latour, B. (1987) *Science in Action* (Cambridge, MA: Harvard University Press).
Latour, B. (1996) 'On Interobjectivity' *Mind, Culture, and Activity* 3(4), 228–245.
Latour, B. (2007) *Reassembling the Social* (Oxford: Oxford University Press).
Latour, B. (2010) *The Making of Law: An Ethnography of the Conseil d'État* (London: Polity).
Laudan, L. (2006) *Truth, Error, and Criminal Law: An Essay in Legal Epistemology* (Cambridge: Cambridge University Press).
Law, J. (2008) 'On Sociology and STS' *Sociological Review* 56(4), 623–649.
Levi, R. and Valverde, M. (2008) 'Studying Law by Association' *Law and Social Inquiry* 33(3), 805–825.
Mégret, F. (2016) 'International Criminal Justice as a Juridical Field' *Champ pénal/Penal field*, 13, http://champpenal.revues.org/9284; DOI: 10.4000/champpenal.9284 (accessed 7 June 2017).

Pottage, A. (2012) 'The Materiality of What?' *Journal of Law and Society* 39(1), 167–183.
Puig de la Bellacasa, M. (2011) 'Matters of Care in Technoscience' *Social Studies of Science* 41(1), 85–106.
Sadović, M. (2005) 'Oric Praised by Prosecution Witnesses', 17 November, *Institute for War and Peace Reporting*.
Sadović, M. (2006) 'Oric Trial Drama', 10 April, *Institute for War and Peace Reporting*.
Toews, D. (2003) 'The New Tarde: Sociology After the End of the Social Theory' *Culture and Society* 20(5), 81–98.
Valverde, M. (2006) 'The Sociology of Law as a "Means of Struggle Against Itself"' *Social Legal Studies* 15(4), 591–597.

Chapter 9

Extracurricular international criminal law

*Mark A. Drumbl**

Introduction

Domestic criminal law informs the register of international criminal law, whether formally through the development of general principles of law or informally through experience and analogy. Reciprocally, international criminal law also informs the register of domestic criminal law, whether formally through incorporation of treaty and custom or, once again, informally through experience and analogy. Circulation thereby arises within the curricular sphere of penal responsibility.

Might international criminal law nonetheless, and perhaps unexpectedly, stray elsewhere in domestic law? When it comes to municipal legal practice, might international criminal law cast a somewhat longer shadow, travel a bit farther, or leave a somewhat haler legacy?

This chapter assesses the jurisprudential impact of international criminal courts and tribunals on domestic civil litigation in the United States for gross human rights abuses, specifically in Alien Tort Statute (ATS)[1] claims brought in US federal courts. The ATS allows victims of human rights abuses to file tort-based lawsuits for violations of the laws of nations (a phrase taken to mean customary international law).

This chapter begins with the International Criminal Tribunal for Rwanda (ICTR). It undertakes a search of references to ICTR case law and materials in ATS judgments and identifies a set of ATS judgments containing such references. Overwhelmingly, these judgments also include references to the work product of other international criminal courts and tribunals. US judges who cite to ICTR

* I extend my appreciation to Cody Philips and Annie Cox for research assistance, to the Frances Lewis Law Center for resource support, and to Sergey Vasiliev for helpful comments. This chapter is excerpted from a much longer piece to be published under the same title in 16:3 *International Criminal Law Review* 412–447 (2016). I thank Brill Publishers and Caroline Fournet for permission to use herein an abridged version of this article. Readers seeking details regarding research methodology or extensive citations to the jurisprudence are encouraged to consult the longer piece.

1 28 U.S.C. § 1350 (2012). The ATS is also known as the Alien Tort Claims Act (ATCA) or Alien Tort Act (ATA).

work product to determine the rule of application in an ATS dispute frequently invoke the case law and materials of the International Criminal Tribunal for the former Yugoslavia (ICTY), International Criminal Court (ICC), the International Military Tribunal at Nuremberg (IMT) and the American Military Tribunal at Nuremberg (AMT). Hence, this chapter references these cases and materials as well. The entangled nature of these citations suggests that US judges perceive international courts and tribunals as constituting some form of system.

This chapter therefore interrogates the migration of substantive criminal law from the public international domain to private municipal tort law. It investigates judicial method and the role of transnational legal migrations therein.

Assuredly, the ATS retains key aspects of penal and international law, in that the tort claim hinges upon finding a breach of a customary international criminal norm. What is more, governmental and political entities, notably the US State Department, may express firm opinions regarding ongoing litigation – for example, how it interfaces with international comity – and may actively share that opinion with the deciding judges. On the other hand, ATS litigation departs from international criminal proceedings when it comes to venue (civil litigation at the national level), remedy (monetary damages), burden of proof (balance of probabilities), goals (compensation rather than incarceration), standing (private plaintiffs), actionability (only definable, universal, and obligatory customary international norms are enforceable), and management (national judges in courts of general jurisdiction).

ATS verdicts are infrequently enforced. Victims rarely collect. Individual defendants often are impecunious or outside the jurisdiction. At times, to be sure, cases are settled and compensation will pass hands as part of that settlement. That said, ATS litigation triggers expressive effects. It ventilates obscured tragedies and empowers victims who initiate claims. ATS litigation also educates the public.

This chapter does not deliver quantitative or empirical results beyond the most rudimentary tabulations; it simply identifies cases in which US federal judges adjudicating ATS disputes have relied upon ICTR cases and ICTR materials, and discusses how and for which purposes these materials – along with those of other international institutions – have been received. The research is best described as qualitative. These modest research findings nonetheless evoke a fascinating story of legal transplant, migration, digestion, legacy, and professionalism – on this latter point, the relationship of national judges with international law.

In light of the sharply limited capacity of international criminal courts and tribunals, domestic tort claims as avenues for redress of systematic human rights abuses will likely grow in number. The experiences of US courts of general jurisdiction as 'receivers' of international criminal law reveal broader patterns of transnational legal migration and a largely unanticipated legacy of the work product of international criminal courts and tribunals. Distortions may nonetheless arise when international norms migrate into legal practices at the national level, in particular, when they do so in cognate legal regimes. These migrations constitute national practices indicative of 'comparative international law', namely, that international legal norms may take shape differently among, and within, various national jurisdictions. While international criminal lawyers may welcome the broad diffusion of international norms, including extracurricularly from the criminal to civil context in a rich array of venues, concerns emerge should the content of the norms fragment and, thereby, weaken international law's purported universality. The US experience is thereby instructive in terms of striking the appropriate relationship between national courts and international law. Should national courts serve as dispassionate law enforcers, as translators of law, or engaged law creators? Should international judges be mindful of the at times unforeseen afterlife of the jurisprudence they create? Obversely, the US experience also raises questions as to whether the specialized, and at times inconsistent, work-product of the international criminal courts and tribunals is even suitable for broader dissemination and incorporation at the national level.

Part I briefly introduces the ATS and its legal elements. Part II sets out the research methods and some preliminary findings. Part III discusses substantive aspects of citation by US judges to ICTR materials. Part IV places these citations within the broader framework of judicial recourse to ICTY, ICC, IMT, and AMT materials in the adjudication of ATS disputes. At times, US judges replay amongst themselves debates that roil international judges and institutions regarding the correct interpretation of a point of substantive criminal law. Part V concludes.

I. The Alien Tort Statute

The ATS dates from the First Congress (1789). It is a succinct instrument that reads as follows:

> The district courts shall have original jurisdiction of any civil action by an alien for a tort only, committed in violation of the law of nations or a treaty of the United States.

The ATS has limited legislative history. Its brevity nonetheless belies the tremendous jurisprudential complexity it has sired.

The ATS lay largely dormant for two centuries. Beginning in 1980, however, plaintiffs turned to the ATS to pursue redress in US courts for atrocity crimes. Plaintiffs did so in a broad variety of factual circumstances, including when allegations involved abuses committed outside the United States by non-US nationals against non-US nationals. By definition, plaintiffs pursuing ATS claims will be foreign nationals. In many instances, however, plaintiffs present some connection to the United States, either because they are physically present in, had moved to, or are non-residents living in the US.

The initiation by plaintiffs, often with the support of sophisticated activists, of ATS litigation has obliged US courts to determine whether a broad array of impugned acts actually constitute violations of the laws of nations. In its 2004 opinion in the *Sosa* case, the US Supreme Court ruled that, while the identification of substantive causes of action under the ATS should proceed cautiously, the statutory remedy is not to be limited only to those violations of the laws of nations acknowledged in 1789.[2] Rather, the remedy covers violations extant today that bear comparable universality and specificity to those that had been recognized in 1789. Courts are to invigilate this process of trans-historical analysis. Actionable contemporary norms must be of sufficiently definite, obligatory, mutual, and universal character. Although the 'law of nations' is taken by US courts to mean customary international law, the importation of these criteria qualifies traditional understandings of the elements of customary international law.

A first generation of ATS claims pursued individuals based on their alleged direct involvement in atrocity crimes. A second wave that began in the 1990s targeted corporations on theories of aiding and abetting in the commission of atrocity crimes. This latter wave proved more controversial jurisprudentially (i.e. regarding modes of liability) as well as politically (i.e. risking a chilling effect on investment in developing nations, dragging US courts into disputes that lacked connections with the jurisdiction, and interfering with the conduct of US foreign relations).

These controversies suffused the *Kiobel* case, decided in April 2013 on jurisdictional grounds regarding the extraterritorial application of US statutes. Here, the US Supreme Court sharply curtailed the scope of future ATS claims by requiring proof of a compelling nexus with the United States:

> [E]ven where the claims touch and concern the territory of the United States, they must do so with sufficient force to displace the presumption against extraterritorial application. Corporations are often present in many countries, and it would reach too far to say that mere corporate presence suffices.[3]

The facts of *Kiobel* involved Nigerian citizens, albeit long-time legal residents of the United States on asylum grounds, who pleaded that Dutch, British, and Nigerian oil exploration and extraction corporations aided and abetted the Nigerian government in committing systemic human rights violations during the 1990s. All nine judges dismissed the case, holding that the factual context was too remote from the United States to justify allowing the claim to continue. Chief Justice Roberts – writing for a five-justice majority – robustly applied the presumption against extraterritoriality to the ATS. Justice Kennedy and Justice Breyer (writing for himself and three others) gestured in separate concurrences towards a slightly more generous approach to jurisdiction. Justice Alito, in contradistinction, drew a line that was even firmer than that of Chief Justice Roberts.

Following *Kiobel*, Circuit Courts of Appeal have dismissed ATS claims based on extraterritoriality concerns. But other claims have survived extraterritoriality

2 *Sosa v Alvarez-Machain*, 542 U.S. 692 (2004).
3 *Kiobel v Royal Dutch Petroleum Co.*, 133 S.Ct. 1659, 1669 (2013).

challenges. While *Kiobel* restrained ATS litigation, it did not close the door on it.[4] One probative example is that of a District of Columbia district court in a long-standing dispute regarding injuries allegedly inflicted upon plaintiffs by Indonesian soldiers employed by corporate defendants to provide security at a natural gas facility in Aceh.[5] In an exhaustive analysis, this district court emphasized that the extraterritoriality bar will be displaced when the claims sufficiently touch and concern the United States because of: (1) substantial and specific domestic conduct relevant to the ATS claims; (2) US citizenship or corporate status of the defendant; and (3) the presence of important US national interests.[6] Applying this test to the facts at hand, the presiding judge ascribed considerable probative value to the allegations that corporate executives in the US received briefings on rape, torture, unlawful detention, assault, and killings committed in Aceh; that decision-making was US-based; that the defendant was incorporated in the US with a principal place of business in the US; and that security personnel were committing violations through the use of defendant's equipment.

The Fourth Circuit in *Al-Shimari* permitted claims to proceed against US defense contractor CACI for abuse and detention at Abu Ghraib.[7] The Fourth Circuit found that ATS claims related to the alleged torture at Abu Ghraib sufficiently touched and concerned the United States because of the defendant corporation's US status, the US citizenship of the defendant's employees, defendant's status as a contractor of the US Government, the location where contracts were made, and allegations that the wrongful conduct in question occurred domestically in the United States (i.e. approving, encouraging, and covering up the alleged torture). In yet another dispute – the *Lively* case – a United States district court in Massachusetts denied a motion to dismiss in September 2013.[8] This case involved an ATS claim against Scott Lively, a pastor, brought by a Ugandan non-governmental organisation (NGO), Sexual Minorities Uganda, alleging violations of the laws of nations regarding the infliction of persecution against LGBTI persons in Uganda. Lively, a US citizen, allegedly fomented and attempted to foment these persecutory acts. In this case, the district court distinguished the facts from *Kiobel* because the defendant was an American citizen residing within his venue and the alleged tortious acts took place to a substantial degree within the United States over many years with only 'infrequent actual visits' to Uganda.[9]

In sum, ATS claims will continue, in particular, where the underlying conduct (including manufacture, financing, managing, or developing) occurs in the

4 For significantly more detailed discussion, *see* Drumbl in 16:3 *International Criminal Law Review* 412–447 (2016).

5 *Doe v Exxon Mobil*, 2015 WL 5042118 (6 July 2015) (D.D.C.).

6 Ibid., *7.

7 *Al Shimari v CACI Premier Tech. Inc.*, 758 F.3d 516 (4th Cir. 2014).

8 *Sexual Minorities of Uganda v Lively*, 960 F. Supp. 2d 304 (D. Mass. 2013).

9 Ibid., 321.

United States, where the conduct was intended to impact the United States, and where the United States may be harboring an alleged wrongdoer.

In any event, many years of ATS litigation offer a fascinating laboratory into the deployment of international criminal judgments and materials in domestic civil litigation for gross human rights abuses. It is towards this laboratory that this chapter now turns.

II. International materials in ATS litigation: sources and research methods

ICTR case law and materials are understood to mean: (1) judicial decisions of both the ICTR Trial Chambers and the Appeals Chamber; and (2) the ICTR Statute itself. A search of US federal judgments was initiated through the *WestlawNext* database platform in the summer of 2013. This search generated an opening sample baseline of federal judgments. Judgments decided since 2013 were subsequently integrated into the analysis, albeit on a piecemeal basis, in an effort to qualitatively assess the case law. A second database search was undertaken in the summer of 2015 to consolidate the findings. The initial set of federal judgments generated by the search for references to ICTR cases and materials in ATS litigation was notable in the sense that, with only one exception, each of the federal judgments also contained a reference to the materials of one of the ICTY or the Nuremberg-era tribunals, often both, and also at times to the materials of other international criminal courts or tribunals (ICC, for example).

One immediate observation is that ICTR case law and materials appear only in a modest number of ATS cases. A number of caveats, however, pertain to this observation. Many cases that pop up in a search for ATS may only involve incidental reference thereto without necessarily involving litigation thereunder; others may involve strictly extraterritorial questions, to which the substantive law of the international tribunals is not germane, or invocation of *forum non conveniens* or political question doctrine (same irrelevance). Since ATS claims began in earnest in the early 1980s, over a decade of ATS litigation preceded the creation of the ICTR and nearly two decades of this litigation took place prior to consistently produced ICTR case law. Finally, it is plausible that a percentage of results yielded by the acronym ATS (or ATCA) involve totally unrelated subject matter.

Citations to the case law and materials of international criminal courts and tribunals in ATS litigation may be modest in number but they are neither sporadic nor intermittent. Nor are they thoughtless. International case law and materials are deliberately invoked when it comes to determining the content of the law of nations. US federal courts appear to consider the case law and materials of international criminal courts and tribunals alternately as *sources* of international law or as *evidence* of customary international law. Although these materials help identify and legitimate a rule of decision, this vacillation among US judges generates some doctrinal confusion. Furthermore, those courts that view these materials as sources hedge as to whether these are primary or subsidiary sources pursuant to Article 38 of the Statute of the International Court of Justice. The most representative way to typologize the approach of US federal judges, however, is that they turn to international case law and materials (notably ICTR, ICTY, Nuremberg-era tribunals, and the ICC) as authoritative evidence of the existence and content of a customary rule (in other words, of the state of customary international law).

For the most part, references to ICTR materials in domestic ATS litigation primarily reinforce or confirm the existence of certain substantive rules of customary international law. At times, however, these references are jurisgenerative in that they establish new law, applicable directly at the national level, which may in fact be more progressive than the extant rules as generally understood. For example, *Lively* references ICTR judgments (and other international sources) to support the proposition that an orchestrated campaign of intimidation of LGBTI persons constitutes persecution as a crime against humanity.[10] A review of ATS jurisprudence reveals the tendency of certain US judges to tread cautiously with regard to the content of customary international law while other judges proceed quite audaciously. This observation gestures toward the attitudinal diversity among US federal judges.

In a number of instances, inconsistent treatment of the same putative rule arises among the differing judicial Circuits. This fragmentation may vex outside readers, but it actually is somewhat uneventful within the US federal system insofar as the different Circuits can proceed in their own directions. In situations of serious Circuit splits, the US Supreme Court is supposed to step in to resolve the *différends*. That said, this variability among judges and Circuits with regard to content and meaning might pose a *sui generis* set of challenges when it comes to international law as a rule of decision in light of international law's universalizing aspirations as well as the ongoing relevance of positivistic notions of state consent. This variability may be problematic when it occurs *within* a national jurisdiction; as it may be problematic when it occurs as *among* different national jurisdictions. In both instances, courts, either within or among national systems, may seek to create international law rather than simply apply international law.

The fact that many ATS cases are initially adjudicated on motions to dismiss or summary judgment motions – in which the facts are taken in the most favorable fashion for the plaintiffs and the legal standard of pleading is one of plausibility – may encourage a slightly more purposive or elastic view of the content of customary international law. Many ATS judgments also arise on motions for leave to amend existing complaints. If and when matters go to trial, it is readily foreseeable that more restrictive interpretations would emerge.

10 Ibid., 310 ('[M]any authorities implicitly support the principle that widespread, systematic persecution of individuals based on their sexual orientation and gender identity constitutes a crime against humanity that violates international norms').

A number of ATS cases involve the same disputes that sinuously wend their way up the judicial system, then are remanded back pursuant to interlocutory motions, only to wend their way up again. Litigation rotates around some epic claims: for example, *Khulumani* (South Africa), *Mujica* (Colombia), *Doe v Exxon* (Indonesia), *Doe v Nestle* (Côte d'Ivoire), *Presbyterian Church* (Sudan), and *Kiobel* (Nigeria). These disputes last for many years. The findings presented in this chapter include references to international materials in the same dispute as it works its way up and down varying trial and appellate levels of the federal judicial system, and then following appeal once again to remand at the trial level. In these situations, each individual court's discussion is included separately. This chapter discusses judgments even if subsequently overturned on points of law by an appellate circuit court. What is more, *en banc* appellate decisions may overturn (and vacate) decisions previously rendered by three-member appellate panels: in these instances, which may occur in ideologically fraught Circuits, this chapter includes both the initial appellate decision and the *en banc* decision. This chapter also discusses citations in dissenting opinions. The bottom line is to offer a qualitative snapshot of the various ways US judges rely on ICTR materials specifically and international materials generally.

Another complicating issue arises when international materials inform an initial determination of a substantive rule of customary international law, but then the US court opinion that effected the initial international citation itself becomes the ongoing point of reference to justify the existence of the substantive rule. In other words, court X comes to conclusion Y based on international materials. Then court A cites to conclusion Y, justifying the decision based only on the precedent of court X instead of the international materials. Here, international law enters the domestic legal lexicon, but then sheds its international provenance. In a telling trend, several of the more recent ATS appellate opinions cite less frequently to international materials than had been the case in earlier opinions. In US courts, apparently, the legitimacy of a Circuit Court of Appeals citation (or even that of a district court) on a point of law tends to exceed what may be seen as the more *shaky* reliance on international sources, although international sources may have generated the initial substantive rule. In other national jurisdictions, *a contrario*, citation to an international source may be seen as conferring greater legitimacy or credibility to the assertion of the existence or content of a specific substantive rule of customary international law.

Which ICTR materials receive the most attention? The ICTR Statute is frequently cited. Citations also are made to a number of cases. When it comes to case citation, a fairly scattershot approach is taken. Citations are broadly dispersed and not clustered into one or two cases alone. On the other hand, some advantage emerges in terms of subsequent citation frequency for early adjudication in ICTR history.

III. ICTR citations and ATS litigation: substantive aspects

Which of the ICTR's work has had the greatest impact in US courts, and in which areas of customary international law?

Citations to ICTR materials are diverse but cluster around three substantive areas: (1) aiding and abetting as a mode of liability; (2) the definition and legal elements of genocide and crimes against humanity; and (3) corporate liability. This Part considers each of these three areas in greater depth. In addition, stray references in ATS litigation to ICTR materials touch upon some residual issues, such as exhaustion of local remedies and conspiracy as applicable only to genocide or aggressive war. Other occasional ICTR citations appear on the issue of command responsibility, for example as a liability theory in cases of failure to prevent the commission of crimes or to punish subordinates following the commission of crimes, or, in addition, when contemplating the extension of command responsibility into the context of private companies.

III.1 Aiding and abetting

Establishing the availability and parameters of aiding and abetting liability under customary international law became particularly salient to ATS litigation once plaintiffs targeted corporations as defendants insofar as corporations could only be accessorily linked to the wrongdoing. ICTR materials inform judicial conversations about the existence of aiding and abetting liability under customary international law and, secondly, help delineate the required elements of such liability (i.e. addressing whether a defendant need act only with knowledge of the criminal goals or must purposefully intend to facilitate those goals). The existence of aiding and abetting liability is settled in ATS jurisprudence. Considerable fractiousness, however, emerges regarding the elements that a plaintiff must establish both in pleading and subsequently at trial. This fractiousness matches the reality that these questions are far from resolved in and among the practices of the various international criminal courts and tribunals.

The *actus reus* of aiding and abetting requires proof of providing assistance or other forms of support to the commission of a crime. This assistance must be substantial. Controversy arises, however, over whether international law imposes the additional requirement that assistance must be specifically directed towards the commission of the crime. In 2014, the ICTY resolved quarrels regarding proof of specific direction in *Šainović*[11] when, overturning its own antecedent case law, the ICTY Appeals Chamber ruled in favor of rejecting the specific direction requirement as part of the *actus reus* in contexts where the defendant is remote

11 *Prosecutor v Šainović*, 12 January 2014, ICTY, Case No. IT-05-87-A, Judgment, paras 1617–25.

from the crimes. In December 2015, the *Šainović* approach was affirmed by the ICTY Appeals Chamber in its judgment in *Stanisić & Simatović*.[12] The ICTY's retreat from the specific direction requirement has nonetheless not defused this controversy within ATS adjudication. While noting the rejection of the specific direction test by the Special Court for Sierra Leone (SCSL) and some ICTY judgments (though not the repudiation of the test in *Šainović*), the Ninth Circuit nonetheless refused to formally relax the specific direction requirement for domestic purposes.[13] The District of Columbia Circuit, on the other hand, remains unflagging in its view that specific direction is not an element of aiding and abetting liability under customary international law.[14]

In addition, US courts have turned to ICTR authority to determine whether the *actus reus* of aiding and abetting requires practical assistance, encouragement, or moral support which has a substantial effect on the perpetration of the crime.[15] In 2015, citing the ICTR appeals judgments in *Ndahimana* and *Nzahonimana*, a district court judge ruled that while a link or connection must be established between the aider and abettor's actions and the underlying crime, a 'cause-effect relationship' between the two is not required.[16]

The standard for *mens rea* in aiding and abetting triggers additional debate, notably, whether knowledge alone, given proof of the substantial effect of the defendant's acts upon the commission of the crime, suffices or whether purpose must be shown. US judges split when it comes to the knowledge or purpose element. Some rely on knowledge alone.[17] These judges, for example on the District of Columbia Circuit, have invoked ICTR materials.[18] The jurisprudence

12 *Prosecutor v Stanišić & Simatović*, 9 December 2015, ICTY, Case No. IT-03-69-A.

13 *Doe v Nestle*, 766 F.3d 1013 (9th Cir. 2014).

14 *Doe* 2015, *10. This judgment reviewed a series of ICTR cases (*Ndahimana*, *Ntawukulilyayo*, *Kalimanzira*) which it interpreted as invoking the specific direction requirement, but then discounted their interpretive value on a variety of grounds including lack of clarity and reliance on other international precedent that had since been superseded.

15 *Almog v Arab Bank*, 471 F. Supp. 2d 257, 286 (EDNY 2007).

16 *Doe* 2015, *8.

17 See, e.g., *Romero v Drummond*, 552 F.3d 1303 (11th Cir. 2008); *Sinaltrainal v Coca-Cola Co.*, 578 F.3d 1252 (11th Cir. 2009).

18 *Doe VIII v Exxon Mobil Corp.*, 654 F.3d 11, 30 (D.C. Cir. 2011), vacated in part, 527 Fed. Appx. 7 (2013) (mem), remanded to 69 F.Supp.3d 75 (D.D.C. 2013); *Doe* (2014), 1023 (citing to ICTY cases, the ICTR's *Kayishema* Judgment from 1999, and also the SCSL's Appeals Judgment in *Taylor*). Although the 2011 Circuit Court of Appeals opinion in *Doe VIII* has been vacated, the reasons for *vacatur* and the course of subsequent proceedings in the litigation reaffirm the legal analysis of the Court of Appeals on the critical points of jurisdiction, corporations as defendants, methodological recourse to international materials, and aiding and abetting liability. Manuel Ventura argues that purpose does not reflect customary international law. Manuel J. Ventura, 'Farewell "Specific Direction": Aiding and Abetting War Crimes and Crimes Against Humanity in Perišić, Taylor, Šainović et al., and US Alien Tort Statute Jurisprudence', in Stuart Casey-Maslen (ed.), *The War Report: Armed Conflict in 2013* (Oxford: Oxford University Press, 2014), 511–553 at 513.

of the ad hoc tribunals is generally taken to affirm a knowledge standard. Other US judges, however, require the higher bar of intentionality. On this note, in the Second Circuit the appropriate test is whether the defendants acted with the purpose to aid and abet the violations of customary international law committed by someone else. The Fourth Circuit approaches the question similarly. As discussed in detail *infra*, judges who prefer this option look beyond the ad hoc tribunals for support, and incline toward the Rome Statute as an authoritative source. The Ninth Circuit for its part has declined to formally establish whether a purpose or knowledge standard applies to aiding and abetting ATS claims.[19]

In addition, considerable confusion persists within ATS jurisprudence whether specific direction and purpose are *mens rea* or *actus reus* requirements. At times, specific direction may be deployed as a proxy for purpose; *ipso facto*, then, a retreat from specific direction could be seen as a move towards knowledge. This malleability is unsurprising in light of just how complex the determination of these modes of liability has become under international law.

In sum, when it comes to aiding abetting liability, fragmentation at the international level appears to replicate itself nationally.

III.2 Existence of genocide and crimes against humanity under customary international law and identification of elements thereof

US judges consult ICTR materials in support of the prohibition of genocide and crimes against humanity as customary international law and, as a secondary matter, to clarify key elements thereof. The majority of these citations cluster in determining crimes against humanity to be proscribed by customary international law. An impulse may arise to cite to the ICTR (and the ICTY and Rome Statute) because of the absence of a comprehensive treaty prohibiting crimes against humanity, unlike the case with genocide. These judicial references intimate that the work of international criminal courts and tribunals can fill gaps when treaty law is unavailable to constitute first-best evidence of a rule of customary international law.

ICTR sources also help elucidate the elements of these crimes. ICTR materials have clarified the definition of genocide, of an enumerated group, and of the requisite level of specific intent;[20] and have legitimized the inference of genocidal intent from facts and circumstances. ICTR materials have been invoked to assess the meaning of ‘widespread’ and ‘systematic’ attack for the purposes of the *chapeau* requirements of crimes against humanity,[21] along with the meaning of

19 *Doe* 2014, 1023–24.

20 *Abagninin v AMVAC Chem. Corp.*, 545 F.3d 733, 739 (9th Cir. 2008).

21 *Bowoto v Chevron Corp.*, 2007 WL 2349343, *3 (N.D. Cal. 14 August 2007). This opinion turned to the ICTR’s *Akayesu* judgment to define widespread as ‘massive, frequent,

'attack' generally[22] and the level of knowledge of an accused to establish liability.[23] ICTR materials are also cited to define elements of persecution as a crime against humanity, including the purposive finding of protected groups in the *Lively* trial judgment (citing to *Nahimana*). The *Lively* court held that '[t]o properly plead persecution as a crime against humanity, Plaintiff must allege both the proper *actus reus* – denial of fundamental rights – and *mens rea* – the intentional targeting of an identifiable group'.[24] While recognizing that 'many of the international treaties and instruments that provide jurisdiction over crimes against humanity list particular protected groups without specifying LGBTI people', the district court also noted that 'international courts have interpreted the identity of the group requirement broadly to encompass persecution of a discrete identity'.[25] This is a strikingly purposive use of ICTR case law as persuasive authority to substantiate the existence of a substantive rule that exceeds what is commonly accepted as the content of customary international law. US judges adjudicating ATS claims also have faced the challenge of identifying whether a food or medical blockade constitutes a crime against humanity.[26]

US courts have also turned to ICTR materials where a non-state actor is alleged to commit crimes against humanity, in particular, regarding the question whether the non-state actor must exercise a level of *de facto* control over territory in order to be held responsible.[27] In *Krishanthi v Rajaratnam*, a district court found that the LTTE met this burden for the purposes of plausibility pleading. Whether the *de facto* control requirement firmly exists as an element of the plan or policy aspect of crimes against humanity under customary international law remains unclear.

large-scale action, carried out collectively with considerable seriousness and directed against a multiplicity of victims' but, interestingly, also observed in a footnote that 'case law from the ICTR provides little guidance for the application of the *chapeau* elements, apparently because there was little dispute that the mass slaughter of Tutsis and their sympathizers constituted a widespread or systematic attack on a civilian population'. Ibid., *3 n.2.

22 *Lively*, 319. This opinion invoked *Akayesu* to hold that an attack, for the purpose of a crime against humanity, may be non-violent in nature. The Court quoted extensively from *Akayesu*, and noted that 'imposing a system of apartheid … or exerting pressure on the population to act in a particular manner, may come under the purview of attack, if orchestrated on a massive scale or in a systematic manner'. Ibid.

23 *Mehinovic v Vuckovic*, 198 F. Supp. 2d 1322, 1354 n.50 (N.D. Ga. 2002).

24 *Lively*, 317.

25 Ibid., 317–18.

26 *Sarei v Rio Tinto*, 671 F.3d 736, 767–68 (9th Cir. 2011) (determining that deprivation of food or medicine owing to a blockade does not constitute actionable extermination or 'another inhumane act' under the *Sosa* test), *vacated*, 133 S. Ct. 1995 (2013) to follow *Kiobel*, *remanded to* 722 F.3d 1109 (9th Cir. 2013).

27 *Abagninin*, 741 (9th Cir. 2008); *Krishanti*, *10.

III.3 Corporate liability

ICTR materials have been interpreted as germane to the question whether corporations can be found criminally liable under international criminal law and, hence, by analogy to the question whether they may incur civil liability for violations of the laws of nations. US courts have failed to achieve consensus on these questions. Considerable fragmentation and vivid contestation persist. While ICTR materials are seen as helpful to these debates, judges have drawn strikingly different inferences from them.

The District of Columbia Circuit in *Doe VIII v Exxon* (2011),[28] and the Seventh Circuit in *Flomo* (2011),[29] each has held that corporations can be sued under the ATS. The *Doe VIII* litigation, staccato in nature because of appeals, reversals, *vacaturs*, and remands, continues: in July 2015, the district court allowed some of the ATS claims to continue because they displaced the presumption against extraterritoriality and because the law in the D.C. Circuit is clear that corporations can be sued under the ATS.[30] In *Doe VIII*, Judge Kavanaugh dissented in the Circuit Court of Appeals. He opined that the ATS did not reach corporate actors.[31] To buttress his conclusion, he referenced the ICTR as only having jurisdiction over natural persons. In this regard, the establishment of international tribunals to punish individuals may paradoxically crimp the ability of the law to reach entities or collectivities. The expansion of a system of international law that individualizes guilt may narrow the range of appropriate defendants.

On the other hand, other judges have turned to the same set of ICTR materials and reached an opposite conclusion. For example, Judge Cote, in dismissing the motion for judgment on the pleadings in *Presbyterian Church*, held:

> [That] the ICTY and ICTR Statutes do not provide for corporate criminal liability for genocide and other atrocities carries very little weight as those Statutes were devised in the context of ethnic and tribal warfare where atrocities committed by private individuals, not corporations, loomed large. Such an argument is akin to claiming that a rule governing the law of the sea has not reached the status of customary international law because a number of landlocked States have not accepted it.[32]

28 *Doe VIII* 2011, 57 ('Given that the law of every jurisdiction in the United States and of every civilized nation, and the law of numerous international treaties, provide that corporations are responsible for their torts, it would create a bizarre anomaly to immunize corporations from liability for the conduct of their agents').

29 *Flomo v Firestone National Rubber Company*, 643 F.3d 1013, 1019 (7th Cir. 2011).

30 *Doe* 2015.

31 *Doe VIII* 2011, 83–84 (Kavanaugh, J., dissenting).

32 *Presbyterian Church v Talisman*, 374 F. Supp. 2d 331, 336 (S.D.N.Y. 2005) (motion for judgment on the pleadings).

That said, and to be very clear, Judge Cote's view is no longer good law in her own court, the Second Circuit. In 2010, the Second Circuit ruled that corporations may not be held liable for violations of international law under the ATS.[33] This 2010 ruling arose in the *Kiobel* litigation that eventually went to the Supreme Court. While it was widely anticipated at the time that the Supreme Court would decide *Kiobel* on the question whether corporations can be sued under the ATS, in part because of splits among lower courts, the Supreme Court subsequently ordered the case to be newly briefed and approached it from the unanticipated perspective of extraterritoriality and jurisdiction. The Supreme Court's opinion in *Kiobel* did not address corporate liability. Interestingly, in the 2014 *Mastafa* case, the Second Circuit did not seize the opportunity to dismiss the complaint because of the corporate nature of the two defendants.

In September 2014, in *Doe v Nestle*, the Ninth Circuit ruled that there is no categorical rule of corporate immunity or liability under the ATS. In this regard, the Ninth Circuit explicitly reaffirmed the corporate liability analysis it had previously reached pre-*Kiobel* in *Sarei v Rio Tinto*.[34] This analysis requires that a court look, in each claim, to international law and determine whether corporations are subject to the norms underlying that specific claim. Claims in the *Doe v Nestle* litigation – brought by former child slaves forced to harvest cocoa in Côte d'Ivoire – involved allegations that defendant corporations aided and abetted child slavery by providing assistance to the Ivorian farmers. The Ninth Circuit Court of Appeals held that the prohibition against slavery was universal and could be asserted against the corporate defendants. The Ninth Circuit had previously held in *Sarei* that the norms against genocide and against war crimes were applicable to corporations. In *Sarei*, in fact, the Ninth Circuit had held that a norm could form the basis for an ATS claim even in the absence of a decision from an international tribunal enforcing that norm against a corporation. Returning to the *Doe v Nestle* litigation, the Ninth Circuit held that 'corporate liability under an ATS claim does not depend on the existence of international precedent enforcing legal norms against corporations'.[35] Of significance is that the Ninth Circuit in *Doe* buttressed its finding with reference to Article 3(c) of the ICTR Statute. The Ninth Circuit noted that, pursuant to the ICTR Statute, the condemnation of 'persons

33 *Kiobel v Royal Dutch Petroleum Co.*, 621 F.3d 111, 120 (2d Cir. 2010) (relying on the lack of corporate liability in international tribunals as evidence of customary international law disfavoring corporate liability).

34 *Doe* 2014, 1021–22 (affirming the three principles about corporate liability: no categorical immunity, liability under the ATS is independent of international norms of enforcement, and universal norms can provide the basis for an ATS claim against a corporation) (citing to *Sarei v Rio Tinto, PLC*, 671 F.3d 736, 747–65 (9th Cir. 2011), vacated, 133 S. Ct. 1995 (2013), remanded to 722 F.3d 1109 (2013)).

35 *Doe* 2014, 1021 (noting also that 'the absence of decisions finding corporations liable does not imply that corporate liability is a legal impossibility under international law' and 'that the lack of decisions holding corporations liable could be explained by strategic considerations').

responsible' for enslavement of civilian populations was 'broadly phrased', which it took as evidence that 'the prohibition against slavery applied to state actors and non-state actors alike, and there are no rules exempting acts of enslavement carried out on behalf of a corporation'.[36]

Circuit Court splits persist on the question whether corporations can be liable for ATS violations. Corporate liability under the ATS remains unresolved. This dissensus perhaps reflects – and contributes to – the ongoing (and seemingly intractable) debates under international law regarding corporate responsibility generally.

IV. ICTR citations within the broader corpus of international criminal law materials

The search of the US federal judgments database organizes itself around a search for ICTR cases and materials. Twenty-four of the 25 cases in the 2013 baseline sample that reference ICTR cases and materials also reference ICTY materials. The work product of other international courts and tribunals also surfaces. To be clear, no independent search for ICTY, ICC, or Nuremberg-era materials was ever undertaken. The search was only for ICTR case law and materials. In order to obtain a probative picture of the volume of references to other international institutions, searches with those institutions as the search term would have to be undertaken. It may well be that the number of ATS cases that reference ICTY case law and materials while making no reference to ICTR materials is significant. The fact, however, that so many other international materials come up in a search for ATS judgments that reference ICTR materials demonstrates the entangled nature of these citations. The results of the ICTR search, notwithstanding their modesty, portend fascinating vignettes of authority, systematicity, legitimacy, and fragmentation within the work product of international criminal courts and tribunals.

The case law and materials of the ICTY and ICTR overall tend to be cited by US judges in complementary, and often perfunctory, string fashion to support the same substantive legal rule. This methodology suggests that US federal courts view the ICTR and ICTY outputs as confirmatory of each other or, perhaps, that they determine the existence of a substantive legal rule of customary international law to emerge when the jurisprudence of the two ad hoc tribunals is aligned. Ordinally, the palpable practice is to more prominently feature the ICTY's work. In this regard, the ICTR lurks somewhat in the shadows, so to speak. It is the less visible of the two: it is routinely there – to be sure – but in the distance.

US federal courts also cite to the Rome Statute and to the 'Nuremberg' proceedings (both the IMT and the AMT). On rare occasion, the International

36 Ibid., 1022 (citing also to Art.5(c) of the ICTY Statute).

Court of Justice also surfaces.[37] Within the text of ATS opinions, the Nuremberg-era sources typically precede discussion of the materials from the contemporary international tribunals. US courts thereby approach the development of a customary norm somewhat longitudinally, with citation to the ad hoc tribunals crystallizing the current status of the norm. On the other hand, at times a perceived lack of clarity or continuity in the international jurisprudence militates in favor of US courts' finding that the norm lacks the requisite definiteness and universality. This occurred, for example, when one court faced the question whether 'moral support' and 'tacit encouragement and approval' could be included within the scope of aiding and abetting.

The frequency of citation to the IMT and the AMT is noteworthy, in part simply because international criminal law has evolved so much since their operation 70 years ago. The IMT and AMT, nonetheless, greatly appeal to US judges and carry considerable legitimacy. One may speculate why this is so: certainly, the iconicity of Nuremberg within the American vision of international justice looms large. From an instrumental litigation strategy, in any event, Nuremberg references fare as well as or better than citations to contemporary institutions. ATS litigants would be well advised to reference the work product of the AMT and IMT in their pleadings.

US courts cite to the Rome Statute as well. They do so despite the obvious reality that the United States is not a party thereto and, under President Bush, had in fact renounced its signature on the treaty. References to the Rome Statute are often made to consolidate, buttress, or support interpretations of the laws of nations grounded in citations to the ad hoc tribunals and Nuremberg-era institutions. References to the Rome Statute, however, also arise in contexts of dissonance and fragmentation, typically with regard to the requirements for aiding and abetting liability where the approach of the Rome Statute may be contrasted to that attributed to the ICTR and ICTY. Whereas the Rome Statute's approach is seen as propounding a specific intent requirement for aiding and abetting, ICTR and ICTY materials tend to be understood to support a knowledge requirement. So, for example, in *Doe VIII* it was held that the ad hoc tribunals 'have declared the knowledge standard suffices under customary international law'.[38] This means that the aider and abettor does not need to share the *mens rea* of the perpetrator but, rather, must only have knowledge that his or her actions will assist the perpetrator in the commission of the crime. The *actus reus* will be

37 See e.g., *Doe v Nestle*, 748 F. Supp.2d 1057, 1068–69, 1083, 1126 (C.D. Cal 2010), rev'd in part and vacated in part, 766 F.3d 1013 (9th Cir. 2014).

38 *Doe VIII* 2011, 36; see also ibid., 34 n.19 ('The knowledge standard appears to conform with the standard for aiding and abetting liability in many other countries, including France, Germany, England, Canada, Australia, and Switzerland'). Principally, the *Doe VIII* court relied on the work of the ICTY in this context, but cited to the *Ntakirutimana* Appeals Judgment (2004) and the *Musema* Trial Judgment (2000) as well. Ibid., 34.

practical assistance, moral support, or encouragement which has a substantial effect on the perpetration of the crime.

In the Second Circuit Court of Appeals opinion in *Presbyterian Church* and Judge Katzmann's concurrence in *Khulumani* it was held that liability may arise when a defendant provides practical assistance to the principal that has a substantial effect on the perpetration of the crime and does so purposefully to facilitate the commission of that crime. In reaching this conclusion, Judge Katzmann gestured towards the language of the Rome Statute and found it weightier because, in his view, the Rome Statute constitutes an authoritative expression of the legal views of a great number of states.[39] He did note, to be sure, that there was 'some support' for a 'definition of aiding and abetting that would lead to liability where an individual provides substantial assistance "with the knowledge that the acts performed by the aider and abettor assist the commission of the specific crime of the principal"'.[40] Notwithstanding these fissures, Judge Katzmann saw the purpose standard as 'well-established' and 'core'.[41]

The District of Columbia Circuit Court of Appeals in *Doe VIII*, on the other hand, rejected the Rome Statute as a source of the *mens rea* standard for aiding and abetting liability.[42] It did so because, in its opinion, the Rome Statute is a treaty and not customary international law. This Circuit Court of Appeals added that, in its view, the Rome Statute and the practice of the ICC was not unequivocal on the centrality of purpose as a legal element. Interestingly, in the *Aziz* case, the Fourth Circuit criticized the District of Columbia Circuit Court of Appeals for its treatment of the Rome Statute. The Fourth Circuit agreed that the Rome Statute was not customary international law, but rejected the notion that its status as a treaty favors a preference for the approach of the ad hoc tribunals to aiding and abetting liability. The Fourth Circuit held that:

> We have no quarrel with the view of the *Doe VIII* majority that the Rome Statute does not express a rule of customary international law. We simply find the Rome Statute's *mens rea* standard for aiding and abetting liability, reached after prolonged negotiations among delegates from over 100 signatory nations, to be a more authoritative barometer of international expression on the subject.[43]

39 *Khulumani v Barclay Nat'l Bank Ltd.*, 504 F.3d 254, 276 (2d Cir. 2007) (reporting that the Rome Statute has been signed by 139 countries, including 'most of the mature democracies of the world').

40 Ibid., 278 (citing to an ICTY judgment).

41 Ibid., 276 n.12.

42 *Doe VIII* 2011, 36 ('[T]he Rome Statute was not meant to affect or amend existing customary international law'); *Doe* 2015, *3 ('The Court of Appeals has held that the Rome Statute is not a persuasive source as to the content of customary international law').

43 *Aziz v Alcolac, Inc.*, 658 F.3d 388, 400 n.12 (4th Cir. 2011).

In *Aziz*, the Fourth Circuit also found that the fact that the 'Rome Statute is not binding on the United States ... does not lessen its import as an international treaty and, thus, a primary source of the law of nations'.[44] The *Aziz* opinion held that defendants must be plausibly alleged to have the purpose of facilitating the violations. *Aziz* involved plaintiffs of Kurdish descent who were harmed by Iraqi government chemical weapon attacks or were relatives of those killed in such attacks. The defendant was a British company that sold a chemical which could be used to make mustard gas to another company that was a shell corporation facilitating acquisition of that chemical for the Iraqi company in violation of US law. The claim was dismissed because intentional conduct was insufficiently pleaded. In *Aziz*, the Fourth Circuit considered the fragmentation among international criminal courts and tribunals and sources on this point as an indication of the vacillating and indeterminate nature of customary international law (i.e. calling customary international law an 'elusive system' for which the 'difficulties in appli[cation] ... are manifest').[45]

The Ninth Circuit Court of Appeals distinguished the facts pleaded in the Ivorian child slavery case (*Doe v Nestle*) from those in *Aziz* even within the legal context of a purpose standard. The Ninth Circuit was drawn to the inference 'that the defendants placed increased revenues before basic human welfare, and intended to pursue all options available to reduce their cost for purchasing cocoa [... noting that] the use of child slavery benefited the defendants and furthered their operational goals ...'.[46] The Ninth Circuit also noted the defendants' alleged lobbying efforts to defeat federal legislation that would have required chocolate importers and manufacturers to certify and label their chocolate as 'slave free'.[47]

Insofar as the substantive rule of international law determines the rule of decision to be applied in ATS litigation, as the ICC remains and the ad hocs (and now the Mechanism (MICT)) wind down their work, it may be that the purpose requirement prevails over time. Treaty law can inform customary international law and can become compelling evidence thereof. On the other hand, actual ICC jurisprudence might incline away from the purpose requirement even if textually this language derives from Article 25(3)(c) of the Rome Statute.

V. Conclusion

This chapter opens two little windows. One window looks out to the relationship between penal law and tort law in redressing human rights abuses. The view from this window, to be sure, is limited by the fact that the ATS encases what is fundamentally a penal violation and attaches tort responsibility thereto rather

44 Ibid., 400.
45 Ibid.
46 *Doe* 2014, 1024.
47 Ibid., 1017, 1025.

than incarceration. It is for this reason, perhaps, that recourse to international criminal law materials remains largely uneventful in ATS tort-based litigation.

The second window, however, gives way to a much wider expanse. The landscape from this window is one of movement of international norms to the national level in different but cognate legal regimes. This chapter thereby identifies a new usage – in the case of the ad hoc tribunals, moreover, an after-life – of the work product of the international tribunals, to wit, international criminal law straying in extracurricular fashion into the domain of national tort law and directly into the hands of national judges of general civil jurisdiction. US courts, and thus US judges of general jurisdiction, engage, and remain engaged with, nettlesome questions central to the practice of international criminal law. They approach the subject matter creatively, and give life to international authorities in unexpected ways unforeseen to international criminal lawyers.

What to make of this extracurricular movement? On the one hand, these migrations facilitate wider awareness, recognition, and internalization of international criminal law. It is not assured, however, that the content of the law thus diffused is accurately appreciated by national judges, or is even capable of predictable appreciation, thereby imperiling international law's general aspirations of doctrinal consistency, universalism, and legitimacy. International jurisprudence – no different from any sources of law or precedent – may be misapplied, or wishfully applied, in national contexts. International judgments involving the specifics of a conflict or of a state with which national judges may have little familiarity may be particularly susceptible to error in terms of subsequent extracurricular application.

The turn by US judges to international materials in ATS litigation represents an example of what Anthea Roberts identifies as 'comparative international law', that is, the reality that national courts are more than just international law enforcers, but may also serve as international law creators, and that national variations in the judicialized domestication of international law is a subject worthy of study.[48] International law as shaped and created by national courts, which may lead to divergent results dependent on the court or jurisdiction in question, is, according to Roberts, a reality that ought to be central to any discussion of international law's sources. While the *Lively* court may be chastized for creating a new rule of international law, it may simply be unwise to expect a national court to exercise greater restraint in applying customary international law than national constitutional or human rights law. Acting in such a fashion might excessively prioritize the place of legislatures and executives in the process of incorporating international law. Drawing from the work of Karen Knop, who posits national

48 Anthea Roberts, 'Comparative International Law? The Role of National Courts in Creating and Enforcing International Law' 60 *International and Comparative Law Quarterly* (2011) 57–92, 60. Comparative international law studies how actors in different national and regional systems interpret, understand, and apply international law.

courts as translators of norms rather than mere enforcers of norms, Roberts observes that 'even if national courts attempt to faithfully enforce international law, its domestication requires them to simultaneously assert their own legal language'.[49]

As among courts of various states, then, questions arise as to 'what extent national courts engage in strategic interpretation' of customary international law, rather than interpretation 'based on prevailing practice and *opinio juris*'.[50] Within the courts of a specific state, divergent understandings among national judges as to the substantive content of international law may reflect the most prosaic insights of legal realism: that is, the availability of international law may simply accord judges another tool or device to achieve what they already wish to achieve within the often fraught indeterminacy and selectivity of judicial method, in particular, in common law jurisdictions.

The purposes of tort law may differ so significantly from those of criminal law, either in general or specifically the case of massive human rights violations, that movement from one realm to the other should best be viewed cautiously. Extracurricular application could therefore be dissuaded. International criminal tribunals, on this note, might *ex ante* preempt such movement by declaring that their work product ought to have limited reach. Judges on international tribunals might thereby disclaim the possibility that their national counterparts operating in courts of general jurisdiction pick up their work product and apply it to private law disputes.

Care should be taken to differentiate legal migration from legal circulation. Circulation connotes an iterative cycle of refreshment and depletion and return; migration, the term I have deployed in this chapter, may readily be taken to mean a unidirectional move to take root elsewhere, but migration might also imply a return of sorts, albeit not an iterative or routine one. In this latter regard, then, it might be of interest to systematically examine whether ATS jurisprudence informs, or even arises, in the judgments of the international criminal tribunals.

Manuel Ventura is one scholar who has considered this issue. He has not done so systematically, to be clear, but his work on aiding and abetting liability provides some valuable insights. Ventura notes that defense teams at the ICTY and SCSL have relied on ATS cases, notably *Presbyterian Church*, in arguing for an enhanced purpose requirement for aiding and abetting liability. He laments, however, that when the SCSL and ICTY judges came to visit, and then revisit, the specific

49 Ibid., 74; see also ibid., 76 ('The repeated application of international law by the national courts of particular countries may, over time, lead to distinct dialects developing that exist somewhere between international and national law, and between law enforcement and creation').

50 Pierre-Hugues Verdier and Mila Versteeg, 'International Law in National Legal Systems: An Empirical Investigation' 109:3 *American Journal of International Law* (2015) 514–533, 531.

direction requirement they failed to appreciate the pertinent analyses of US courts. The movement of new practices, therefore, seems to be one-way. Ventura suggests that the debate over the *mens rea* requirements that plague ATS litigation is a 'mirror image' to the debates over the requirements of the *actus reus* in cases of remoteness of the accused; yet, the international tribunals have failed to learn from the robust conversations that have occurred within the ATS context.[51]

Hence, while international norms may have extracurricular application in this specific instance at the domestic civil level, debates within the domestic civil level inspired by the international migration may simply stop there. A lack of endogeneity arises. As Ventura aptly notes, while US courts 'are cognisant of the discussions and debates in ICL', even in extracurricular contexts, 'international lawyers should also be similarly aware that there is more to ICL than the four corners of The Hague'.[52] Ventura's admonition is pertinent. International law happens in many places far removed from its venerated centers. A new wave of scholarship is emerging which explores the diverse historical hinterland of international criminal law and hence epistemologically pluralizes the roots from which we as international lawyers imagine our own discipline to grow.[53] As a profession, we would do well to embrace the diverse and disconnected venues – and the clever yet on occasion clumsy ways – in which international law is manufactured, often by *bricolage*. Fetishizing the reified, and often languid, vortices of the high-profile international tribunals belies the vivacity and eclecticism of the places that make, apply, and chide international law.

51 Ventura, *supra*, fn.18, 512.

52 Ibid., 548.

53 Kevin Heller and Gerry Simpson (eds.), *The Hidden Histories of War Crimes Trials* (Oxford: Oxford University Press, 2013); Mark A. Drumbl, 'Stepping Beyond Nuremberg's Halo: The Legacy of the Supreme National Tribunal of Poland' 13:5 *Journal of International Criminal Justice* (2015) 903–932.

Part III

Chapter 10

Criminal investigation and prosecution by a European public prosecutor's office in the EU

Shared enforcement without procedural safeguards and judicial protection?[1]

Michiel Luchtman and John Vervaele

I. Introduction

The European Union is an entity of particular interest when it comes to the development of innovative ways and institutions to deal with new forms of transnational crime. It is different from the intergovernmental development of internationalisation of criminal justice – as for instance through suppression treaties, treaties of mutual legal assistance or Security Council resolutions. The EU Member States agreed to establish, in the words of the EU Court of Justice, a new legal order, with its own institutions. The Member States have limited their sovereign rights for it, also in the area of criminal justice. The EU's legal order comprises not only those states, as in international law, but also their nationals.[2] Indeed, it grants its citizens access to an Area of Freedom, Security and Justice (AFSJ), in which they can move freely and in which innovative ways of law enforcement are needed to deal with crime. The Treaty on the Functioning of the European Union (TFEU) provides for the legal framework in this regard.

One of the most prominent examples of such new supranational investigative and prosecutorial powers of a criminal nature can be found in the proposed European Public Prosecutor's Office (EPPO).[3] It cannot easily be compared to

1 This chapter is partially based on M.J.J.P Luchtman and J.A.E. Vervaele, 'European agencies for criminal justice and shared enforcement' (Eurojust and the European Public Prosecutor's Office), *Utrecht Law Review*, 10 (5), December 2014, 132–150.

2 Opinion 2/13 of 18 December 2014 on the accession of the European Union to the European Convention for the Protection of Human Rights and Fundamental Freedoms, para.157.

3 COM (2013) 534.

the more traditional forms of mutual legal assistance in criminal matters, and not even to the more recent, enhanced modes of cooperation, including those under the principle of mutual recognition. Neither can it easily be compared to the Office of the Prosecutor (OTP) of the International Criminal Court (ICC). The EPPO is a new *European* institution of criminal justice. It is a single authority which is not part of any national system of criminal justice, with a specific mandate. It may investigate, prosecute and bring to trial alleged offences against the EUs financial interests in any of the participating Member States. In doing so, it is in principle no longer dependent on the traditional forms of bi- or multilateral cooperation. To the contrary, it's *raison d'état* was precisely to avoid the often cumbersome operation of mutual legal assistance. Yet by consequence, this may also mean that other principles of international criminal law no longer fit the specific setting of the EPPO. For instance, where there is the tendency in many national legal orders not to engage in an inquiry of the legality of foreign investigative acts, this approach is certainly not self-evident in the EPPO setting.

On the other hand, however, there is no doubt that even the EPPO would still need to be embedded in the national justice systems. The reasons for this shared enforcement design are multiple. In criminal justice, the adjudication of alleged offences is the exclusive competence of the Member States and that remains the case under Article 86 TFEU, EPPO's legal basis. This means that all prosecutions and trial procedures are national. Even during the investigations, the EPPO will continually interact with the national investigative authorities, through an exchange of information, delegated investigative acts, the ex-ante authorization of coercive measures, et cetera. To a certain extent this could be compared with UN-agreed prosecutorial bodies that investigate and prosecute serious crimes in some central American countries, like for instance CICIG (International Commission against Impunity in Guatemala).[4] CICIG was established as an independent, international body designed to support the Public Prosecutor's Office and the National Civil Police in the investigation of crimes committed by members of illegal security forces and clandestine security structures. CICIG, however, does not function in a context of an integrated legal order as the EU and its AFSJ.

Important conceptual questions therefore arise. How should shared criminal enforcement in the AFSJ be designed and implemented to achieve the goals of the AFSJ? To what extent must domestic enforcement be harmonized in order to achieve equivalent standards and core values? Are European powers available to the Delegate Public Prosecutors, or national powers, or a mix? What does this mean for the applicable human rights standards in the AFSJ? Are they defined at the European or at the national level? Is there a joint responsibility by Member States and the EU for guaranteeing the rights of the defence and fair trial rights in relation to the pre-trial investigation? Who is competent for the ex-ante and ex-post judicial review? What does it mean for the admissibility of any evidence obtained?

4 See www.cicig.org/index.php?page=home (accessed 8 June 2017).

In this chapter, we will proceed with these questions through the lens of an age-old debate on criminal law. Ever since the Age of Enlightenment and the rise of the nation state, the latter is considered to be the main vehicle for administering criminal justice on a certain territory, over a certain group of individuals. States possess the competences to define the legal framework and rules for the functioning of society, to enforce those rules and to take action against citizens in case of non-compliance. This triple jurisdiction includes the nation state's monopoly over the use of power, including the power to punish (*ius puniendi*). State actors may not exercise this power in an arbitrary manner. Their actions must therefore have a sound legal basis in the law and respect the separation of powers, judicial independence, as well as fundamental rights and liberties. In that way, the nation state guarantees the liberty, equality *and* the security of its citizens. This basic scheme reflects the very essence of the rule of law (or *Rechtsstaat*).

The question is how this basic scheme of criminal law doctrine influences the notion of shared enforcement, and how, in turn, it is itself influenced by that notion. By focusing on the legal regime for the EPPO that is currently on the legislative table, this chapter will in essence deal with (parts of) the rule of law debate in criminal law, but now in the unique multilevel institutional setting of the European Union. As the emerging EU criminal justice system is far from harmonized and depends heavily on its interaction with the national legal orders of the Member States, the proposed decentralized structures of the EPPO will result in a mixture of applicable European and national law with respect to:

(a) The applicable law for the substantive competence dealing with offences and penalties (*substantive dimension*)
(b) The applicable law for the definition and scope of the powers, including civil rights and liberties and procedural rights (*procedural dimension*);
(c) The applicable law for the judicial control (*institutional dimension*);
(d) The applicable law for the admissibility of evidence (*evidence dimension*).

We will proceed in the following by focusing, first, on the institutional basis for the EPPO (Part II), followed by an initial analysis of its proposed institutional design in light of the four dimensions just mentioned (Part III). From thereon, we will focus in more detail on the position of the citizen vis-à-vis the proposed new player at the European level (Part IV).

II. Shared enforcement by the EPPO: the institutional framework

II.1 The Treaty framework

Under the Lisbon Treaty, the Union has set as a key objective to maintain and develop the Union as an area of freedom, security and justice in which both the free movement of persons and the prevention and combating crime are assured (Article 3(2) Treaty on the European Union (TEU)).

Under Chapter 4 of Title V of the Lisbon Treaty, on judicial cooperation in criminal matters, the missions and competences of the EPPO are an integral part of the AFSJ. Article 86 TFEU provides a legal basis to establish the European Public Prosecutor's Office (EPPO) and also elaborates on the regulatory specifications when it comes to the investigation, prosecution and adjudication of crimes affecting the financial interest of the European Union (PIF crimes) or, if extended by the European Council, serious crimes having a cross-border dimension.

II.2 The proposal on the European Public Prosecutor's Office (EPPO)

In June 2013, the Commission submitted to the Council its proposal for a regulation.[5] The EPPO will not deal with the horizontal judicial cooperation between national judicial authorities, as Eurojust does, but its essence is that it will act through a vertical setting as an investigative and prosecutorial office in the combined territory of the Union's Member States, being a single legal area (Article 25(1) of the proposed regulation). Fourteen chambers of 11 national parliaments[6] have meanwhile sent reasoned opinions to the Commission, thus triggering the subsidiarity control mechanism, also called 'the yellow card', provided for in Article 7(2) of Protocol No 2. The threshold of Article 7(3) of Protocol No 2 (14 Member States) to trigger a review has, however, not been reached. The Commission confirmed that its proposal complies with the principle of subsidiarity as enshrined in the EU Treaties and decided to maintain its proposal explaining the reasoning behind this decision.[7] Nonetheless, under the subsequent Greek, Italian, Luxemburgish and Dutch Presidency the text and approach have substantially changed.

In the original proposal, the central office of the EPPO consisted of the European Public Prosecutor with Deputies, but also of European Delegated Prosecutors who would act (only) within their national jurisdictions.[8] Only in specific circumstances was the European Public Prosecutor allowed to lead the investigation himself/herself.[9] The revisions by the Presidencies have changed the proposed structure of the EPPO and decentralized it even further. It now includes a new governing structure within the EPPO, whereby the vertical

5 Proposal for a Regulation on the establishment of the European Public Prosecutor's Office, COM(2013) 534.

6 See www.ipex.eu/IPEXL-WEB/home/home.do (accessed 8 June 2017).

7 COM(2013) 851 final, accessed 8 June 2017 at ec.europa.eu/justice/criminal/files/1_en_act_part1_v4.pdf.

8 Art.6(4) of the proposed regulation.

9 Art.5 of the proposed regulation.

structure (a centralized European Public Prosecutor's Office and decentralized Delegated Public Prosecutors) is replaced by a College of European Prosecutors of all Member States and by Permanent Chambers. Under that model, the College would be responsible for the policy and strategic management, but with no powers of instruction in individual cases. Several Permanent Chambers, composed of a Chair and two permanent members of the College, would become responsible for monitoring the investigations and prosecutions by the European Delegated Prosecutors and the coordination of cross-border cases. They are also responsible for decisions on the reopening of investigations, the dismissal of cases (including transactions), referrals and the like. They may further instruct Delegated Prosecutors on the commencing and evocation of investigations, as well as on case allocation. The Permanent Chambers act through the European Prosecutor from the state where the investigation is conducted. The investigations and prosecutions themselves will be conducted in the Member States by Delegated Prosecutors, who shall have the same powers as national prosecutors (Article 12). Articles 22(4–6), 26, 28 and 30(2–3) make arrangements for coordination where multiple Member States are involved in the investigation and prosecution phases.

II.3 The applicable law for the substantive competence dealing with offences and penalties (substantive dimension)

Article 86 TFEU is silent on the precise scope of the competence *ratione materiae* of the EPPO, as it contains a limited reference to a basic mandate to combat crime affecting the financial interest of the EU (PIF offences) or, after a unanimous decision in the Council, to an extended mandate to combat serious crimes having a cross-border dimension. It is also unclear if the substantive competence can or must be included in the EPPO regulation(s). From the recitals and the text of the EPPO proposal it is clear that the Commission is aiming at a material scope of competence limited to PIF offences, which would be defined by the proposed Directive on the fight against fraud on the Union's financial interests by means of criminal law,[10] and thus by the implementation legislation under national law. Do we really know today which offences fall within the ambit of crimes 'affecting' the financial interests of the Union? And will the EPPO and the citizen (suspect, victim, etc.) know tomorrow for which offences the EPPO can search and seize and can prosecute and which penalties could be applied? Although the directive will harmonise the constitutive elements of some offences, it only contains references to serious offences. Whether an offence is serious is defined according to national law, having regard to all relevant circumstances, such as the value of any damage done or advantages gained, or the damage to the integrity of confidence

10 COM (2012) 363 final.

in systems for managing the Union's financial interests (recital 16). The scope of EPPO's powers in relation to VAT is unclear.[11] Concerning the sanctions, minimum sanctions are not included and the harmonization of maximum sanctions is limited to their minimum thresholds. This, occasionally, may also have consequences for the availability of investigative powers in the EPPO framework.[12]

Whatever the end result might be of the actual 'trilogue' negotiations on the draft, it is clear that the material competence of the EPPO will depend on the implementation of partial harmonization through a directive and thus depend upon the patchwork of implementation provisions in every single Member State.

II.4 Applicable law for the definition and scope of the enforcement powers

Given the institutional design of the EPPO, it is of crucial value to know which law does apply to the powers of the EPPO. Notions of integrated administration, shared enforcement and legal pluralism are common terminology in the governance discussion on EU institutions and agencies, but they do not solve the important legal question: what are the functions and competences of the EPPO, what are the legal consequences of its actions and what are the procedural safeguards for persons concerned (defendants, victims, third parties)?

When it comes to the opening and closing of the investigation and the decision to prosecute or to drop the case, there is no doubt that these decisions are taken by the EPPO on the basis of European law.[13] However, when it comes to the operational powers of the EPPO, the situation was rather unclear and complex in the Commission proposal. In the actual text under negotiation these powers would be carried out by European Delegated Prosecutors in the Member States on the basis of national law. For this reason, the listing of investigative powers of the EPPO (and related procedural safeguards) has been replaced by partial harmonization of the investigative measures in the Member States. However, even in that very decentralized design the permanent chambers act and instruct under European law and can also, in exceptional cases (Article 23(4)), approve the European Prosecutor to conduct the investigation himself/herself.

The overall picture is that (already to a certain extent under the original proposal, but certainly after its modifications)[14] the EPPO will be, apart from in exceptional circumstances, fully dependent on the delegates in the national legal order for conducting the investigation. Those delegates will apply the (partially harmonized) national criminal procedures. Moreover, the Delegated Prosecutors will wear a double-sided hat. They will have exclusive competence for EPPO

11 See *Taricco*, Case C-105/14, ECLI:EU:C:2015:555 and Council document 14281/15 of 24 November 2015.
12 See Art.25(1) of the proposal.
13 This is also the case under the Greek proposal.
14 See Council document 13658/14, of 30 September 2014.

offences, but they can also exercise their function as national prosecutors. This can result in an investigative and prosecutorial outcome that is not very different from the actual situation, which has been qualified as not achieving effective enforcement. Moreover, there is the risk that the national authorities will face an unclear division of labour, allowing them to hide behind national priorities and obstacles, or not preventing an overlap of enforcement efforts. Even in cases with a clear EU-dimension, for instance related to corruption in the EU institutions, the EPPO cannot act alone and has to rely on the European Prosecutors in the College.

Finally, for cross-border investigations (Article 26), the modified text relies completely on the coordination and cooperation between the European delegated prosecutors in a design that resembles a joint investigation team. This means that the applicable law remains the national law of the jurisdiction where the investigative acts are performed,[15] and that judicial ex-ante authorizations, when needed under the national law of the handling state, have no EU-wide effect under the principle of mutual recognition, as several judicial ex-ante authorizations might be needed. To that extent, the original design of EPPO has been reduced to a large extent to a model based on national investigations with a horizontal cooperation model without mutual recognition. Only the arrest and surrender of persons take places on the basis of the mutual recognition scheme of the European Arrest Warrant (Article 28); however, the European Delegated Prosecutor will have to rely on the issuing of an order by the national competent authority.

II.5 Legal consequences for safeguards, judicial control and the admissibility of evidence

When it comes to the applicable procedural safeguards and human rights standards the recitals of the original EPPO proposal contain several references. The Preamble of the original proposal enshrined the full application of the Charter of Fundamental Rights (CFR), especially Articles 47–48 and 50. Moreover, the harmonized procedural safeguards under Article 82 TFEU also apply. Thirdly, the Preamble referred to extra guarantees in the proposed regulation. Yet in the recent draft, most references to procedural safeguards have been removed from the proposal, together with most of the attempts to ensure a certain level playing field of investigative measures.[16]

In Article 35 of the recent proposal references are made to the harmonized defence rights under the Roadmap, including, inter alia, the rights to interpretation, translation, information and access to the case file and access to a lawyer, as well as the right to remain silent and the right to be presumed innocent as well as the

15 Including the national laws implementing instruments on mutual recognition and cross-border cooperation; Art. 26(5a).

16 Sections 1a and 3 of Art. 25 include references to professional secrecy, whatever that may mean under national law, and the principles of proportionality and subsidiarity.

right to legal aid. However, these instruments do not deal explicitly with the transnational application of these fair trial standards. As most of the human rights standards will apply when applying coercive measures or at the trial setting, they will inevitably apply through national applicable law.

From the point of view of the EPPO's investigative and prosecutorial interests this is without any doubt a complex patchwork. By consequence, the EPPO can optimize enforcement through its choices of the territorial jurisdictions. The free choice of the applicable laws and the inherent possibility of forum shopping is poorly conditioned by legal consequences when it comes to the admissibility of evidence. Article 31 of the recent proposal merely stipulates that evidence presented by the prosecutors of the European Public Prosecutor's Office or the defendant to a court shall not be denied admission on the mere ground that the evidence was gathered in another Member State or in accordance with the law of another Member State, though this does not do away with the responsibility of the trial state to respect the fairness of the procedure and fundamental rights, nor with the power of the trial court to freely assess the evidence presented by the defendant or the EPPO.

III. A closer look at shared enforcement from the perspective of European citizens

It is clear that the proposed framework for the EPPO gives rise to many questions, which are ultimately all related to the fact that the rules on the determination of the applicable legal regimes are unclear. The focus on the integration of both EU bodies into the national legal orders of the Member States is so strong that the EU legislator seems to have lost sight of the inherent transnational setting. In the remainder of this chapter we will therefore go into the question of how this decentralized setting influences the proper operation of the fundamental rights and liberties that are related to criminal justice, such as the right to privacy (Articles 6 and 7 CFR), to a fair trial and an effective remedy (Articles 47 and 48 CFR).

III.1 Determining the applicable legal regime: accessibility and foreseeability revisited

It is a common feature of every criminal justice system of the Member States of the European Union that government action that interferes with the civil rights and liberties of its citizens needs a sound legal basis in the law. According to standard Strasbourg case law, and in order to pass the test of the rule of law, interferences with such rights and liberties must have a sound legal basis and must meet minimum requirements of accessibility and foreseeability.[17] There is no

17 See ECtHR, 24 April 1990, *Kruslin and Huvig v France*, appl. nos. 11801/85 and 11105/84.

reason to doubt that this is any different for an EU system of criminal justice, as is also apparent from Article 2 TEU.

We noticed in the previous section that the proposal would vest the EPPO with powers to deploy intrusive coercive and covert investigative measures. However, the proposal refers back, as a general rule, to the legal order where those measures are to be deployed for their precise scope and content, including the available safeguards. The question that interests us here is whether and how this decentralized system meets the requirements of accessibility and foreseeability in a transnational common enforcement area in which the free movement of citizens is strongly promoted. From the perspective of citizens (suspects, but also others), such a decentralized system has a series of disadvantages. As said, the combination of a regime that largely refrains from rules on where to locate investigative and prosecutorial activities ('forum choices') and a mixture of EU and divergent national rules on investigative powers will lead to a situation in which citizens have great difficulty in assessing the scope of investigatory powers and their legality. Or, from the reverse angle, such a combination leads to situations in which executive powers enjoy great discretion in determining the applicable legal regime.

The question is therefore whether and how a patchwork of EU and diverging national legal rules relates to the fundamental rights standards that we mentioned. There are roughly two opposite approaches to this. The first position takes the stance that interstate differences are an intrinsic part of the EU's legal order, and that, in any case, all versions of the EPPO proposals more or less introduce a series of safeguards that ought to be in place in any event and which will guarantee a certain level playing field concerning procedural safeguards. In such a context, it is precisely because all legal orders adhere to certain standards of fundamental rights, that mutual trust is justified in each other's legal orders and, therefore, evidence may be mutually declared admissible.[18] A much heard related argument in that regard is that the forum shopping argument has a reverse side. Free movement rights can be abused by citizens: 'Criminals must find no ways of exploiting differences in the judicial systems of Member States.'[19] Certainly, then, the EU's shared legal order is not under a legal obligation to allow its citizens to assess under which legal order they are most likely to evade justice.

We have difficulty in accepting this position and propose an alternative, second approach.[20] In our opinion, the former position provides citizens with no answer

18 Cf. one of the options presented by the Commission in its Green paper on criminal-law protection of the financial interests of the EC and the establishment of a European Prosecutor, COM (2001), 715, p. 67.

19 Tampere Conclusions, sub.5.

20 Incidentally, we are not the only ones; see, among others, K. Ligeti (ed.), *Toward a prosecutor for the European Union – Volume 1* (Oxford: Hart 2013); M. Delmas-Marty and J.A.E. Vervaele (eds.), *The implementation of the Corpus Juris in the Member States – Volume I* (Antwerp; Groningen; Oxford: Intersentia 2000); A. Klip, *European criminal law – An integrative approach* (Antwerp: Intersentia 2012).

as to the question of on which of the potential applicable legal regimes they should rely for effective judicial control. Obviously, as the European Court of Human Rights (ECtHR) has also held on many occasions, the goal of the safeguards of Article 8 (or 5) European Convention on Human Rights (ECHR) is not to allow citizens to predict with great precision under which circumstances certain measures will be deployed; rather, the goal is to give citizens an adequate indication of the conditions and circumstances in which the authorities are empowered to resort to any such measures.[21] That goal not only serves the purposes of legal certainty, but also, and perhaps even more, the purpose of legal protection, as it allows for *ex ante* and *ex post* control of the executive.

Now, the problem in our case is not the absence or vagueness of a (single) law that offers such a point of reference, but the presence of a multitude of diverging applicable laws, all of which in themselves may be perfectly in line with Articles 8 ECHR/6 and 7 CFR. Nonetheless, can we really say that in such a decentralized system, which provides the executive with an almost unlimited choice between multiple applicable legal regimes, an *adequate* indication to citizens is offered, as to the scope of intrusive investigatory and prosecutorial powers? The aforementioned first position offers no conclusive answer to this problem, mainly emphasizing that all legal orders in themselves indeed meet the requirements of the ECHR and the Charter.

The same question is on the table with respect to the applicable substantive norms of EPPO competence. It is questionable if the inherent systemic flexibility meets the standards of accessibility and foreseeability under Article 7 ECHR (substantive legality). The ECtHR ruled in *Camilleri v Malta*[22] on the discretion of the public prosecutor to decide on the forum court in a domestic proceeding. Interesting in the case is that, under Maltese law, the discretion of the prosecutor to go for the Criminal Court or to the Court of Magistrates does not affect the definition of the offence and its constitutive elements of the offence (unlawfulness), but that it does alter substantially the punishment. The Court of Magistrates may impose custodial sanctions of 'only' six months to ten years, but the Criminal Court four years to life imprisonment. Camilleri was prosecuted before the Criminal Court and then sentenced to fifteen years' imprisonment. Yet could the defendant foresee the choice of jurisdiction and the applicable penalties? Given the absence of legal provisions or other accessible and binding guidelines on the choice of jurisdiction, the Court comes to the conclusion that the law did not provide for any guidance and that the Attorney General had in effect an unfettered discretion to decide on which minimum penalty would be applicable with respect to the same offence. The Court concludes that the relevant Maltese legal provision failed to satisfy the foreseeability requirement and provide effective

21 Standard case law, cf. *Uzun v Germany*, ECtHR, 2 September 2010, appl. no. 35623/05, para.61.

22 *Camilleri v Malta*, ECtHR, Judgment 22 January 2013.

safeguards against arbitrary punishment as provided in Article 7.[23] Precisely this problem also arises with the prosecutorial decision of forum choice, as the minimum and maximum punishments, even with harmonized offences, vary from Member State to Member State.

Admittedly, it is unlikely that the ECtHR would apply the same reasoning to the transnational setting, as the ECHR applies to the individual territories of states (cf. Article 1 ECHR). The specific setting of the EPPO calls for a 'transnationalisation' of the ECtHR standards in the AFSJ.[24] It is not enough to have mutual trust in the legal systems of all EU Member States. We are in an unprecedented situation in which a single authority will be given the power to operate under more than 20 diverging (national) systems of criminal procedure. Instead of accepting that additional measures, inevitably influencing national laws further, would be 'disproportionate' (as the European Commission),[25] we argue that those mechanisms are, to the contrary, essential for the EU's ambition to establish an AFSJ, because they offer this single authority 'adequate' guidance on how it will make use of its discretionary powers that are capable of interfering with fundamental rights.

III.2 Assuring effective judicial control in pre-trial proceedings

It has been a deliberate choice that judicial protection against (operational) decisions of the EPPO in the pre-trial stage is located at the national level, with the competences of national courts to ask the Court of Justice (ECJ) for preliminary rulings. Though the review of some of the procedural measures of the European Public Prosecutor's Office (it is unclear which ones precisely) has been 'given back' to the ECJ, the main rule remains that the national courts are competent to review other procedural decisions taken by the EPPO. This means that the EPPO is considered as a national authority for the purpose of judicial protection. As such, this is a significant departure from the ground rule that EU courts control the legality of actions by EU bodies, whereas national courts exert control over the actions of national authorities.[26] The Court of Justice held in *Foto Frost* that this system guarantees the coherence and uniformity of EU law, by preventing, inter alia, national courts from delivering contradictory rulings on

23 See also *Maktouf and Damjanovic v Bosnia and Herzegovina* ECtHR, Judgment 18 July 2013.

24 See the debates on safeguards and transnational criminal justice in the recent Utrecht law special on 'Law should govern. Aspiring general principles for transnational criminal justice', 2013.

25 See the original EPPO proposal, COM 2013 (534), preamble, recital 19.

26 See notably A. Meij, 'Some explorations into the EPPO's administrative structure and judicial review', in L.H. Erkelens, A.W.H. Meij and M. Pawlik (eds.), *The European Public Prosecutor's Office: An Extended Arm or a Two-Headed Dragon?* (The Hague: TMC Asser Press, 2014).

Union acts.[27] The Explanatory Memorandum to the EPPO original proposal justifies this departure with reference to the specific nature and different position of the EPPO (compared to other EU bodies and agencies), as all of its (investigative and prosecutorial) acts are closely related to the trial stage before national courts and its effects will therefore be felt mainly within the legal orders of the Member States.[28] What presumably also plays an important role here is that, although it is not explicitly stated, national criminal courts are not (primarily) seized to rule on the validity of actions by EU bodies, but on the guilt or innocence of alleged offenders.[29] The legal basis for this departure from the EU's judicial organization is then found in Article 86(2) and (3) TFEU, stipulating, inter alia, that EPPO regulations determine the rules which are applicable to the judicial review of procedural measures taken by it in the performance of its functions.

Be this as it may, we are not so convinced that these reasons are satisfactory. No matter how much it is stressed that the legal consequences of EPPO activity are *ultimately* felt within the legal orders of the Member States, the fact remains that the EPPO is a European body, which is entrusted with a series of tasks that – by their very definition – cannot be clearly attributed to a single Member State. The development of prosecutorial policies, the decision to start investigations, the decisions to deploy certain investigative measures in a particular state and/or to bring criminal charges in another, are all decisions which involve multiple Member States. The question therefore is to what extent individual national courts are in the position to effectively exert control, now that the regulation does not offer them much guidance. For instance, (how) do we prevent EPPO officials, after having unsuccessfully tried to obtain judicial authorization for a certain measure in one Member State, consequently trying their luck in another state? How do we prevent contradictory rulings being given by different national courts on the legality of a certain investigative measure? Are courts at liberty to refuse to hear a case, if they think that a trial in their jurisdiction is not in the best interest of justice? What criteria do they apply for that? What remedies are available for alleged offenders who may have a legitimate interest in a prosecution in Member State other than the one that was chosen by the EPPO? The proposal is silent on all of these issues. In addition, EPPO investigations may not even reach the trial stage.[30] Which legal order is competent in those instances?

One would have expected that, in order to justify such a clear deviation from *Foto Frost*, these issues would have been explicitly addressed in the proposal. The

27 *Foto Frost*, Case 314/85, [1987] ECR 4225; see also *Reynolds Tobacco and Others v Commission*, Case C-131/03 P, [2006] ECR I-7823, para.80.

28 See the original proposal COM 2013 (534), p.7.

29 Cf. A. Meij, 'Some explorations into the EPPO's administrative structure and judicial review', fn.26 above.

30 As is rightly pointed out by A.H. Klip, 'Een Europees Openbaar Ministerie', *Delikt en Delinkwent* 2013.

problems occur precisely because investigative and prosecutorial decisions are taken by a body that is not national but European, and which has been given powers to operate on a European scale.[31] It is for that reason that the system of EU judicial organization seeks to exclude gaps in judicial protection by introducing a limited, but exclusive jurisdiction to European courts where the Treaties so provide. It is therefore equally difficult to accept Article 86(3) TFEU as the legal basis for such a departure.[32]

Having said that, the challenge remains how to reconcile the need for coherent and uniform (*ex ante* and *ex post*) judicial control on the validity of EPPO actions (opening of investigations; investigatory measures; exercise of prosecutorial discretion) by national and/or European courts with the tasks of national courts to determine the guilt or innocence of alleged offenders in fair proceedings, as attributed to them by Article 86(2) TFEU. This requires not only a certain degree of harmonization of the tasks and powers of national courts, but also the presence of effective remedies at the European level.[33]

With respect to the latter, it must be noted that the current European system may not be quite satisfactory either. Particularly with regard to annulment actions under Article 263 TFEU, the Luxembourg Court will only review measures that are capable of bringing about a distinct change in the legal position in the case of an act or decision against which an action for annulment may be brought.[34] With respect to the exercise of procedural rights, it is well known that the court has been very reluctant to hear cases where it is not clear that procedures will indeed follow. However, that is not to exclude the possibility that actions for annulment may never be successful in other cases,[35] such as unwarranted infringements of civil liberties (for instance the rights to privacy, liberty or property), or situations of forum shopping.[36] Regarding the latter, Inghelram has pointed to *Rendo and Others v Commission*, a competition law case also involving certain import and export restrictions,[37] in which the Commission decided to suspend proceedings under Article 85 EEC with respect to certain import restrictions and to proceed

31 Cf. J.F.H. Inghelram, *Legal and institutional aspects of the European Anti-Fraud Office (OLAF)* (Groningen: Europa Law Publishers 2011), 263–264.

32 A. Meij, 'Some explorations into the EPPO's administrative structure and judicial review', fn.26 above, 266.

33 See, for instance M. Böse, 'Ein europäischer Ermittlungsrichter – Perspektiven des präventiven Rechtsschutzes bei Errichtung einer Europäischen Staatsanwaltschaft', *Rechtswissenschaft – Zeitschrift für rechtswissenschaftliche Forschung* 2012, with interesting suggestions on the matter.

34 Cf. *Gómez-Reino v Commission*, Case T-215/02, [2003] ECR-SC I-A-345; and *Gómez-Reino v Commission*, Case C-417/02 P(R), [2003] ECR I-3207, para.65.

35 That is confirmed by the Court itself, see *Commission v Violetti a.O.*, Case T-261/09 P, 20 May 2010, para.71.

36 Cf. J.F.H. Inghelram, 'Judicial review of investigative acts of the European anti-fraud office (OLAF): A search for a balance' *Common Market Law Review*, 49 (2), 2012 601–627.

37 *Rendo a.O. v Commission*, Case T-16/91, [1992] ECR II-2420.

under Article 169 EEC. That also meant that the procedural rights of the former (Article 85) proceedings were (temporarily) no longer available to the applicants in the latter (Article 169). The General Court held that: 'Since the Commission's deferral has the effect of interrupting the procedure initiated under Regulation No 17 for a considerable period, it must be stated that consideration of some of the issues raised by the applicants in their complaint […] has been taken out of that procedure, in which the applicants have specific procedural rights, and left to proceedings under Article 169 of the Treaty in which the applicants have no such rights. Whilst the procedure under Regulation No 17 is held over, the complainants will be deprived of the effective exercise of their procedural rights.'[38]

It is difficult to determine whether this particular case provides us with an argument for the thesis that forum choices (in a decentralized system of EU and – divergent – national rules) do bring about direct changes in the legal position of the persons concerned. What may have influenced the outcome in *Rendo* could have been that the Commission unilaterally 'switched' procedures – the applicable law – 'during the game'. *Reynolds Tobacco*, however, reveals that 'forum choices' as such will certainly not always fall within the scope of Article 263 TFEU, even where cases are transferred outside the legal order of the EU.[39] Ultimately, what remains to be seen is therefore how the EU courts will appraise the opening of criminal investigations, forum choices and choices on the applicable law, in light of their capacity to bring distinct changes in the legal position of the person affected. We are sympathetic to the idea that prosecutorial bodies should not be able to influence the scope of the rights and duties of their adversaries, or other parties concerned, such as victims. That brings us to the following point of interest: the position of European citizens, particularly defendants, during the trial stage.

III.3 Testing the evidence in a fair trial

One of the main problems in international criminal cooperation is the use of evidentiary materials that were collected abroad.[40] Despite all of the efforts that were put into increasing transnational cooperation with respect to the *gathering* of evidence, international or supranational rules with respect to their *use* barely exist. This is not only due to the complications that are related to the harmonization of the laws on evidence,[41] there are also doubts as to the necessity of such an exercise, at least as long as the scope of such a rule of 'free movement of evidence'

38 *Rendo a.O. v Commission*, Case T-16/91, [1992] ECR II-2420, paras 53–54.

39 *Reynolds Tobacco and Others v Commission*, Case C-131/03 P, [2006] ECR I-7823.

40 See, inter alia, S. Gleβ, *Beweisrechtsgrundsätze einer grenzüberschreitenden Strafverfolgung* (Baden-Baden: Nomos 2006); A. Ryan, *Towards a system of European criminal justice: the problem of admissibility of evidence* (Abingdon: Routledge, 2014).

41 See for an interesting comparative oversight, Ryan, fn.40 above.

is not clearly demarcated and defined.[42] Spencer has noted, for instance, that '[b]roadly speaking, it is surely up to each Member State to frame its own rules as to the admissibility of evidence in criminal cases; and it is not the business of the EU to tell Member States what types of evidence should or should not be admissible in their criminal courts, unless there is some compelling practical reason to require this.'[43] Indeed, if taken to the limit, the free movement of evidence could mean that 'a written statement taken by a *juge d'instruction* from a witness in France (and as such admissible in French criminal proceedings) would be automatically admissible at a trial in England, irrespective of the hearsay rule, which would normally require the witness to give evidence orally; and similarly, it would be automatically admissible in Germany, in contradiction of the German counterpart of the hearsay rule, the 'Grundsatz der Unmittelbarkeit'.[44] Under such a broad interpretation, the admissibility rule would cover not only the *gathering* of materials, but also their *transfer*, as well as their *use as evidence* in court.

Article 86(1) TFEU stipulates that the EPPO shall exercise the functions of a prosecutor in the competent courts of the Member States in relation to such offences. Therefore, the regulations must also contain the rules of procedure applicable to its activities and those governing the admissibility of evidence (cf. Article. 86(3) TFEU). The current proposal reads in Article 31 that evidence presented by the prosecutors of the European Public Prosecutor's Office or the defendant to a court shall not be denied admission on the mere ground that the evidence was gathered in another Member State or in accordance with the law of another Member State. Where the law of the Member State of the trial court requires that the latter examine the admissibility of evidence, it shall ensure it is satisfied that its admission would not be incompatible with Member States' obligations to respect fundamental rights. However, section 2 also stipulates that the power of the trial court to freely assess the evidence presented by the defendant or the prosecutors of the European Public Prosecutor's Office shall not be affected by this Regulation. As suggested by the proposed recital to this provision, this means that, unlike in the original proposal,[45] the Regulation may not be interpreted as prohibiting the trial court from applying fundamental principles of national law on fairness of the procedure, as they apply in common law systems such as in the framework of a trial by jury. This suggests that, though admissible as such, written

42 Incidentally, the 'mutual admissibility of evidence between Member States' is explicitly mentioned in Art.82 TFEU itself.

43 J.R. Spencer, 'The Green Paper on obtaining evidence from one Member State to another and securing its admissibility: the Reaction of one British Lawyer', *ZIS* 2010, 604–605.

44 Spencer, fn. 43 above, 605.

45 The original proposal stipulated in Art.30: 'Evidence presented by the [EPPO] […] shall be admitted in the trial without any validation or similar legal process even if the national law of [the trial] court provides for different rules on the *collection* or *presentation* of such evidence [our italics].'

statements by a French investigating judge would not pass the test of the hearsay rule in the UK and that the witness needs to be heard in court.

Therefore, the current Article 31 obliges courts to accept materials gathered abroad, but not to lower (either because the case has been re-allocated, or in the setting of cross-border investigations) national evidentiary standards. Simultaneously, it largely refrains from a harmonization of procedural safeguards. The national law of the state where the evidence was collected is still the main point of reference, though Article 27 does stipulate that formalities and procedures expressly indicated by the handling European Delegated Prosecutor shall be, in principle, complied with (*forum regit actum*). In addition to the problem that materials can still not be used as evidence in another state, this situation makes the EPPO proposal susceptible to the same criticism that we have seen in the previous sections. There is a risk of forum shopping and of deliberate circumventions of the evidentiary standards of a particular legal order.[46] Gleβ, for instance, has pointed out that defence rights may fall between two stools in cases of interaction between a legal order (where the materials are used during trial) that puts strong emphasis on defence rights at the pre-trial stage, and another other legal order (where the evidence was originally gathered), which relies on the trial stage for this.[47]

Finally, how does the proposal guarantee that those rights are effectuated during the trial stage? In other words, how does the EPPO proposal ensure that foreign witnesses are indeed present during the trial, or that they are otherwise heard under the standards of the Strasbourg Court? The EPPO proposals are completely silent on the powers of the trial courts in this regard. May they use the EPPO structures for that, by instructing the competent officials? Otherwise, should the trial courts use their own Mutual Legal Assistance (MLA) arrangements, evidence warrants, or, in due time, investigation orders, in order to hear the experts or witnesses they think are necessary? If so, what should be done in cases where refusal grounds apply? May the requested/executing national authorities, for instance, refuse to execute MLA requests, because national investigations on related offences are ongoing?[48] May trial courts in turn accept a certain mitigation of fair trial standards and refrain from hearing a witness or only under restrictive

46 See Đurđević, 997–998, in K. Ligeti, *Toward a prosecutor for the European Union – Volume 1* (Oxford: Hart 2013); S. Gleβ, *Beweisrechtsgrundsätze einer grenzüberschreitenden Strafverfolgung* (Baden-Baden: Nomos 2006), 173, 138–139.

47 Gleβ, fn.46 above, 139.

48 A telling sign in that regard is Art.26 (4) of the Italian proposal, stating that 'the executing State may postpone the execution of the [investigative] measure where: – its execution might prejudice an ongoing criminal investigation or prosecution until such time as the Delegated Prosecutor deems reasonable; – the objects, documents, or data concerned are already being used in other proceedings until such time as they are no longer required for this purpose.'

conditions, because transnational cooperation is still time-consuming and slow?[49] Or, on the contrary, do the concepts of the free movement and admissibility of evidence have as their corollary that evidence that cannot be tested by the defence (and is important to the case) may not be used in trial proceedings? The EPPO proposal is silent on all of these issues.

In our opinion it is rather inconsistent to advocate the free movement of evidence and fair proceedings, while simultaneously accepting that the courts of the trial state lack the power to assure, for instance, the presence of witnesses during trial on grounds that are essentially related to the interests of the nation-state and national sovereignty.

IV. Concluding remarks

The vesting of a European agency with operational powers in the criminal judicial area is a new phenomenon. Its added value lies in the fact that it is able to deal with issues that national authorities are unwilling or unable to deal with. Its unique institutional design allows it to operate on a European scale and to develop its own investigative and prosecutorial policies. All these features are very different from the Office of the Prosecutor of the ICC that must rely on mutual legal assistance treaties or other international prosecutorial UN bodies, like CICIG, that operates in one single jurisdiction.

From our preceding analysis, we can deduce that the establishment of EPPO in the AFSJ and its institutional design and governance does not result automatically in a European agency that applies European law in an European common area, the AFSJ. When it comes to the legislative design of the empowerment of the EPPO, in particular the definition of its substantive competence and of its investigative and prosecutorial powers, they are highly decentralized and integrated in the institutions and regulatory regimes (the applicable law) of every single Member State. EPPO would act through its Delegates in the Member States that would apply mostly national law.

The emphasis that is put on integration into the national legal orders of the Member States begs the question whether the inherent European dimension of the EPPO is lost out of sight. The national empowerment of the EPPO is, first of all, problematic from the point of view of the authority itself, as it has to address

49 There are cases where the ECtHR accepted such a reasoning; with respect to witnesses, see *P.V. v Germany*, EComHR 13 July 1987, appl. no 11853/85. With respect to the right to be tried within a reasonable time, see *Sari v Turkey and Denmark*, ECtHR 8 November 2001, appl.no 21889/93. See further A.A.H. Van Hoek and M.J.J.P. Luchtman, 'Transnational Cooperation in Criminal Matters and the Safeguarding of Human Rights' *Utrecht Law Review* 2005, 19; Vogler, 27–40, in S. Ruggeri (ed.), *Transnational Inquiries and the Protection of Fundamental Rights in Criminal Proceedings* (Berlin; Heidelberg: Springer, 2013); L. Bachmaier Winter, 'Transnational Criminal Proceedings, Witness Evidence and Confrontation: Lessons from the ECtHR's Case Law', *Utrecht Law Review* 2013, 135–136.

transnational crimes, but also the increase in national crimes that need transnational cooperation. The EPPO has to work with a patchwork of national regimes and cultures, which easily results in a great legal uncertainty as to the enforcement powers that can be used and their modalities. Transnational problems in the common AFSJ are still addressed – just as under the traditional instruments for mutual legal assistance in criminal matters – by an accumulation of approaches under national jurisdictions.

The national empowerment of the EPPO is also problematic from the point of view of the addressees of the enforcement in criminal matters: witnesses, victims, third parties, and certainly also defendants. Their civil rights and liberties depend on discretionary choices in a regulatory patchwork, which can end up in forum shopping and a run to the bottom of the lowest protective denominator of safeguards. If so, citizens will have great difficulties in defending their rights in court, because national court organizations are not apt to their European dimension and because defence rights and procedural safeguards are still designed to be applied within the national context. Procedural safeguards have only be harmonized by EU law to a limited extent.

The problems that we have identified cannot be solved without more detailed regulations at the European level, not only with respect to the substance of the material competence and of the procedural rights themselves, but also with respect to the mechanisms that allow all parties involved to have an adequate indication as to which rules apply to a certain case.

Obviously, these developments do not only have a European dimension. There is also a national one, which may call upon Member States to address the question of how their criminal justice systems can be of use to the common European goals (that they themselves defined in the Treaties, particularly in Article 3(2) TEU). That European dimension may even urge them to align the cornerstones of their respective criminal justice systems with it and to modify them. We are well aware that our conclusions are diametrically opposed to the position of a significant number of national parliaments and governments. In turn, we are puzzled by the question of how one can promote the establishment of an AFSJ on the one hand, while simultaneously defending national sovereignty in the area of criminal justice. We fear that the consequences of that position will ultimately be paid by those whose interests are said to be defended, i.e. the European citizens. The current proposals leave (too) much to be desired, both in terms of effective law enforcement for the common good, but certainly also in light of an adequate level of legal protection.

Chapter 11

Virtual trials revisited

The shifting politics of state cooperation from the UN ad hoc tribunals to the International Criminal Court

Victor Peskin

I. The enforcement problem and obstructions of justice

The substantial power deferential between the post-World War II Nuremberg and Tokyo Military Tribunals and their modern-day successors highlights the enduring problem that confronts today's global justice project. The contemporary international tribunals' lack of enforcement powers has created a twofold threat of state obstruction and manipulation.

By withholding cooperation or threatening to do so, external actors can obstruct the course of accountability at the UN ad hoc tribunals and the International Criminal Court (ICC). Moreover, targeted states and influential international actors often seek to manipulate international criminal tribunals by bartering their cooperation in exchange for co-opting the tribunals. Tribunal chief prosecutors may grow interested in direct or indirect bartering to secure promises of state cooperation, thereby guaranteeing successful cases and institutional viability. A central focus of co-optation for a targeted state is to gain influence over a chief prosecutor's indictment or case selection decisions. Control over the prosecutorial agenda can reap important political benefits by enabling targeted states to shift the glare of legal scrutiny to the criminality of their enemies. The ad hoc international tribunals and the ICC need not be powerless in the face of attempted obstruction and manipulation, however.

A central aim of this chapter is to demonstrate, through an analysis of the virtual trials framework, how the contemporary international tribunals and their chief prosecutors act strategically to obtain the state cooperation needed to bring suspects into the dock and to deliver courtroom justice. My argument regarding tribunal autonomy and agency poses a challenge to common realist and human rights perspectives on global criminal justice. On the one hand, a typical realist perspective discounts the tribunals' independent means to undertake effective action to fulfill their mandate of delivering impartial accountability. This assumption of the tribunals' innate powerlessness fosters predictions that these international courts will inevitably succumb to powerful states. On the other hand, one type of pro-tribunal human rights perspective tends to exaggerate the tribunals' capacity for independent action. Such a perspective regarding the tribunals' inherent power fosters predictions that these international courts, or at least the larger global justice movement, will inevitably overcome the resistance of powerful states.

One strand of realist thinking posits that the more powerful the external actor the better positioned they are to exert influence over an international tribunal. A salient example of this thinking is seen in the African Union's repeated criticism – and the realist-inspired criticism of some scholars[1] – that powerful Western countries have wrested control of the ICC chief prosecutor's indictment decisions in order to target African leaders and thwart African sovereignty. A different realist perspective argues that international tribunals can be perverted into weapons of 'lawfare'[2] on behalf of relatively less powerful states and non-state actors. Under certain conditions, the less powerful may be able to leverage their weakness by exploiting prevalent international perceptions of their victimization in asymmetric armed conflict. This can then reap legal and political dividends for these weaker actors by helping to trigger scrutiny from high-profile UN commissions of inquiry and possibly even international tribunal prosecutors. This realist perspective is expressed by Israeli government officials in regard to their vigorous opposition to Palestinian efforts to trigger ICC scrutiny of Israeli military conduct in the recent Gaza wars and the government's settlement policy in the West Bank. Palestinian Authority officials and Palestinian activists argue that the use of international law for just political ends is preferable to resorting to actual warfare.[3] Both the African Union critique castigating the ICC as a weapon of the strong and the Israeli critique anticipating the ICC as a weapon of the weak share a common denominator: the belief that international courts can be easily subverted by the power of outsiders.

External attempts to control the contemporary international tribunals have reaped success for some states. Yet, the last two decades have also demonstrated that the international tribunals do possess agency. At times, key tribunal officials have exercised this agency within and beyond the courtroom to advance their impartial judicial mandate. At the ad hoc United Nations International Criminal Tribunals for the Former Yugoslavia and Rwanda and the ICC, chief prosecutors have devised strategies to prod external actors to arrest and transfer suspects, safeguard witnesses and facilitate their travel, grant access to state archives and crime scenes, and provide other forms of cooperation necessary to keep the

1 Mahmood Mamdani, 'The New Humanitarian Order' *The Nation*, September 10, 2008.

2 Consider the claims made by various pro-Israel groups, for example, 'What is Lawfare?' The Lawfare Project: The Legal Arm of the Pro-Israel Community; accessed 8 June 2017 at thelawfareproject.org.

3 Author interviews, May–June 2014.

wheels of justice turning. At the same time, tribunal chief prosecutors have at times skillfully safeguarded their independence by insulating investigation indictment decisions from the appearance and reality of external influence.

That tribunals can act autonomously has led some observers to overstate the potential of these courts to do so.[4] Whereas realists tend to diminish the tribunals' influence over garnering state cooperation and safeguarding institutional control, some human rights champions of the tribunals have taken the opposite position. These voices emphasize how the tribunals have successfully challenged the long-standing impunity paradigm, sparking a legal and normative revolution that has taken on a powerful life of its own.[5] Human rights advocates acknowledge that a chief prosecutor may fail to break this vise when the power of a targeted state is too great. But even in defeat the chief prosecutor and the tribunal itself are redeemed by their moral confrontation with impunity.

In sum, neither the pro-tribunal human rights perspective nor the realist worldview discussed here adequately captures the range of tribunal-state engagement in two key dimensions of strategic action: 1) the tribunals' bid to obtain much-needed state cooperation; and 2) the states' bid to obtain much desired influence over a tribunal's prosecutorial agenda.

To develop a clearer understanding of the dynamics of and prevalent trends in the politics of international criminal justice, this chapter employs the virtual trials framework.[6] This conceptual framework was originally devised to illuminate the new politics of global justice that emerged with the Security Council's establishment of the Yugoslavia and Rwanda tribunals, the first international criminal courts since the Nuremberg era. This chapter employs the virtual trials framework to explain the politics of global justice in the context of these two UN ad hoc tribunals as well as in the context of the permanent ICC. This framework analogizes the political interactions between these tribunals and the ICC, targeted states, and key international community actors to an actual courtroom trial. At its core, the framework focuses on the tribunal-targeted state relationship, but it also incorporates the crucial role played by influential international community actors.

Section II provides a broad overview of the virtual trials framework, drawing on examples from the international tribunals to demonstrate the causes and consequences of prosecutorial confrontation and conciliation with targeted states and key international community actors. This section begins by explaining the deep potential for conflict between international tribunals and targeted states (defined as

4 Rachel Kerr, *The International Criminal Tribunal for the Former Yugoslavia: An Exercise in Law, Politics, and Diplomacy* (Oxford: Oxford University Press, 2004).

5 Kathyrn Sikkink, *The Justice Cascade: How Human Rights Prosecutions are Changing World Politics* (New York: W.W. Norton and Company, 2011).

6 Victor Peskin, *International Justice in Rwanda and the Balkans: Virtual Trials and the Struggle for State Cooperation* (New York: Cambridge University Press, 2008). This chapter develops ideas from this book, particularly pp. 7–13; 238–243.

states whose nationals are implicated in wartime atrocities). Section II is entitled Virtual Trials 2.0 to foreshadow the ways in which the framework has been updated in this chapter by incorporating virtual 'plea bargaining', an image that illuminates the paradigm shift toward highly conciliatory relationships with targeted states in the context of the ICC. Section III explains how certain structural and political factors have helped shape the two ICC chief prosecutors' decisions to engage in virtual plea bargaining as seen in charting a markedly conciliatory course in their external relations with states as well as in their decisions regarding whom to target for investigation and trial. Prosecutorial deference at the ICC has been demonstrated by a general practice of avoiding harsh criticism of non-cooperation by certain targeted states as well as by case selection decisions that have so far avoided (in six of the eight ICC situation countries, but not in Sudan and Kenya) charging suspects belonging to a current government's ethnic, political, or religious group.

II. Virtual trials 2.0

A. The origins of tribunal-state conflict

Tribunal-state confrontation is typically rooted in one of two types of fundamental conflict over international justice. The first conflict arises when a tribunal chief prosecutor decides to investigate suspects who belong to a targeted government's political, ethnic, or religious group. The prosecutor will aim to downplay a targeted state's brewing discontent by reminding state leaders that international indictments only focus on individuals and do not constitute accusations against the state or nation. But charging individuals tied to state-sponsored atrocities can quickly incur the wrath of governments. When it comes to international war crimes indictments, the stakes are great, not only for individuals but for states and societies that perceive themselves threatened with being placed in the figurative dock. An international indictment of a head of state only deepens the tribunal-state conflict.

The clash between a tribunal and targeted state is often characterized by the state's early mobilization to undermine war crimes investigations to preempt tribunal indictments. Efforts by states for impunity may begin well before a tribunal is established because this is a ripe opportunity for states to lobby for a jurisdictional arrangement that dilutes a tribunal's authority to scrutinize state-sponsored atrocities. Some states implicated in violations of international humanitarian law may also mobilize to scuttle international commissions of inquiry in order to avert the establishment of an ad hoc tribunal or referral to the ICC. On this point, the actions of Sri Lanka[7] and North Korea[8] come to mind, as

7 Nick Cumming-Bruce, 'Sri Lanka: Government Rebuked over Stalled Inquiry' *New York Times*, November 8, 2014.

8 Rick Gladstone, 'North Korea Asked to Stop UN Resolution on Rights' *New York Times*, November 18, 2014.

does Israel's intense challenges mounted against the Goldstone and Schabas UN commissions of inquiry into the armed conflicts in Gaza.

The second type of tribunal-state conflict arises when both the tribunal and the state seek to prosecute the same suspect or suspects. In this scenario, both the tribunal and the state have a shared interest in delivering criminal accountability, but each seeks to take ownership of justice by asserting its legal right to carry out prosecutions. Conflict will ensue unless or until one party prevails in the contest over obtaining custody of the suspects or both parties strike an agreement regarding the division of labor for war crimes prosecutions. At the UN ad hoc tribunals, the principal of primacy grants the tribunals the right to prevail in the legal tug-of-war over where particular war crimes suspects should be prosecuted. But experience demonstrates that politics can trump law. At the ICC, the principle of complementarity should dissipate the intensity of competition with the state over a suspect of mutual interest because of the mandated deference given to states to undertake domestic war crimes prosecutions unless they are deemed unable or unwilling to do so. But even in the ICC context, conflict over ownership of justice may occur as we have seen in the Libya situation.[9]

B. *Virtual 'prosecutions' and the politics of confrontation*

Both an actual international trial and the metaphorical one waged over the state cooperation issue are often centered on a clash of opposing narratives. In the actual courtroom trial, the prosecution is pitted against the individual defendant over his alleged guilt for war crimes. The prosecutorial strategy is to build a convincing narrative of the defendant‘s guilt, while the defense seeks to tell a persuasive counter-narrative of innocence. In this virtual trial – also referred to as a 'trial of cooperation'[10] – the tribunal chief prosecutor, in her diplomatic actions beyond the arena of the courtroom, builds a narrative of state responsibility for willfully violating its legal obligation to arrest suspects and facilitate war crimes investigations.

In the trials of cooperation, it is incumbent upon tribunal officials to persuade international community actors to intervene on their behalf against defiant states. Building a credible case of state noncompliance is key to this effort. Strong evidence that reveals state intent to withhold cooperation – for example, by shielding fugitives and destroying evidence – is the foundation upon which tribunal officials can then launch effective virtual 'prosecutions of noncompliant states in the diplomatic arena. In the virtual trial, the state often counters the tribunals' charges

9 Victor Peskin and Mieczyslaw P. Boduszynski, 'The Rise and Fall of the ICC in Libya and the Politics of International Surrogate Enforcership' *The International Journal of Transitional Justice* (2016), 1–20.

10 Peskin, *International Justice in Rwanda and the Balkans* (New York: Cambridge University Press, 2008).

of obstruction of justice to avoid the ostracism of being cast as an international outlaw.

In these trials of cooperation, influential international community actors play a role that can be likened to judges in an actual courtroom trial. These international players – such as the UN Security Council, the US, the European Union, and the African Union (AU) – sit in unofficial but influential judgment of whether states are fulfilling or violating their legal commitments to the international tribunals. An international organization's declaration of state noncompliance can lead to political pressure on the state to reverse its defiant stance toward the tribunal. But the international community's silence can enable a targeted state to continue to obstruct the work of an international tribunal without political cost. The AU's political attacks against the ICC and its political support of President Omar al-Bashir of Sudan, who faces an ICC arrest warrant, demonstrates how the actions of a regional organization can embolden state defiance of an international court.

It has generally been difficult for the ICC to generate global attention to its fight for state cooperation when it has come to the country situations not referred to the court by the Security Council. In these six country situations (Uganda, Democratic Republic of Congo, Central African Republic, Kenya, Côte d' Ivoire, and Mali), the Rome Statute only provides the ICC recourse to lodge complaints of state noncompliance with the Assembly of States Parties (ASP). But the ASP is no match for the Security Council when it comes to projecting global prominence, political clout, and the shadow of enforcement. The ASP, which currently has 124 members, does not include three of the UN's Permanent Five (the US, Russia, and China) or numerous other states (such as Turkey, India, and Pakistan). By and large, the ASP has proven itself an ineffective forum in which the ICC can galvanize punitive action against state noncompliance.

If tribunals seek 'surrogate enforcers'[11] in order to compel noncompliant targeted states, then targeted states seek 'surrogate obstructers' to provide political cover and justification for the state's defiance or dilatory approach in meeting their legal duty of compliance. In the virtual trial between the tribunal and targeted state, both parties have their eye on eliciting a favorable political judgment from key international community actors.

When a state's intransigence becomes enduring, a chief prosecutor may call out the state for allegedly sheltering war crimes suspects, hiding evidence, or tampering with witnesses. Taking a page out of the human rights activist playbook, chief prosecutors will seek to shame a noncompliant state for its alleged violation of international law in the court of international public opinion. In these situations, the confrontational quality of the tribunal-state relationship reminds us of the adversarial drama of the courtroom.

11 Ibid., 12.

C. Counter-shame and the politics of state resistance

If the chief prosecutor's aim is to put the noncompliant state on virtual trial and to 'prosecute' it as an international outlaw, the state's aim is to wage a strong defense directed at instilling reasonable doubt as to whether it has actually failed to cooperate or to argue that its noncooperation is justified by extenuating circumstances. Targeted states deploy a range of strategies to counter tribunal accusations of noncompliance as well as to carve out political exemptions to their legal obligation to cooperate. A common strategy is to advance 'good-faith' justifications for not fulfilling tribunal requests for cooperation. For instance, Serbian officials in the post-Milošević era and Croatian officials in the post-Tudjman era repeatedly invoked the specter of domestic backlash if they moved to arrest high-level suspects heralded at home as wartime heroes. By playing the 'stability card', Serbian and Croatian officials hoped to forestall international pressure to hand over indicted war criminals to The Hague.

Targeted states have also sought to counter tribunal accusations of willful noncompliance by claiming a lack of sufficient law enforcement capacity to track down wily fugitives. In some cases, a state will try to demonstrate its cooperativeness by announcing an 'action plan' for arrests and publicly touting police efforts to locate fugitives and conduct arrest raids. Serbian officials employed the strategy in 2006 amid intensifying EU pressure to arrest former Bosnian Serb General Ratko Mladić.

Targeted states facing accusations of shielding war criminals will often go on the offensive against an international tribunal. The state's strategy is to shift attention away from its alleged noncompliance and toward the question of the tribunal's alleged politicization and malfeasance. Thus, just as tribunals can seek to shame non-cooperative states, states fight back by employing 'counter-shaming',[12] a process in which states try to delegitimize a tribunal by knocking it off its moral pedestal. Neither the tribunal nor the state has a monopoly on deploying shame. The effectiveness of tribunal shaming campaigns and state counter-shaming campaigns depends on the presentation and substance of the criticism launched against the other and the extent to which the tribunal is held in high esteem globally and whether the state is viewed internationally as a victim or perpetrator.

All noncompliant states try their hand at counter-shaming tribunals in the court of international public opinion, but not all succeed. During Serbia's authoritarian and democratic eras, politicians sought to counter-shame the UN Yugoslavia tribunal by vilifying the court for injustices allegedly perpetrated against individual ethnic Serb defendants and, by extension, the Serbian people. This anti-tribunal campaign has resonated loudly at home but not internationally, given the widely-held perception that Serbian forces, being implicated in the majority of wartime

12 Ibid.

crimes, were deserving of so much tribunal scrutiny. The Rwandan government's counter-shaming attacks against the UN Rwanda tribunal point to the ways that some well-positioned states can effectively delegitimize international justice. In its trials of cooperation with the Rwanda tribunal, the Tutsi-led Rwandan Patriotic Front (RPF) government enjoyed a strong political foundation from which to launch its counter-shaming attacks against the Rwanda tribunal. This foundation stemmed from three key factors: 1) the lack of international sympathy for a tribunal that stumbled early on in its genocide trials; 2) the RPF government's dual success in exploiting international guilt and casting itself as a victim state abandoned by the world in order to win international forbearance for the government's own human rights abuses; 3) the RPF's forging of strong alliances with the US and Britain in the aftermath of the genocide. Moreover, the RPF's political acumen enabled it to shift international attention away from its non-cooperation by shining a harsh light on the tribunal's alleged malfeasance that purportedly deprived genocide survivors of justice and dignity.[13]

Kenya provides a more recent example of how a targeted state, with the strong backing of a regional organization, can mount an effective counter-shaming campaign that can damage an international court's legitimacy through repeated criticism of its alleged bias and politicization. To undermine international support for the ICC's ultimately unsuccessful bid to prosecute President Uhuru Kenyatta, he and his allies in Kenya and in the African Union leadership sought to shame the court for being a neocolonial institution. To back up this claim, Kenyatta and his backers pointed to the ICC prosecution's exclusive targeting of Africans for trial. Key to the counter-shaming has been the strategic use of incendiary rhetoric to garner global media attention. A good illustration comes from the attention given to Ethiopian Prime Minister Hailemariam Desalegn's 2013 accusation that the ICC 'process has degenerated into some kind of race hunting'.[14] African criticism of the ICC's disproportionate focus on Africa has hurt the court's image. This 'seems the most critical issue confronting the International Criminal Court in its early years', acknowledged Aryeh Neier.[15] Both the Kenyan and Rwandan counter-shaming campaigns share a common strategy of seeking to cloak their own government's bid for impunity in principled arguments of fairness.

Alongside counter-shaming campaigns, targeted states will often wield the threat of withholding cooperation to exact tribunal concessions. Some states are positioned to up the ante by threatening to effectively shutter an ad hoc tribunal or withdraw its membership in the ICC. The RPF government's 2002 decision to block Tutsi genocide survivors from traveling to testify in genocide trials at the Tanzanian-based UN Rwanda tribunal imperiled the tribunal given its reliance on

13 Ibid., 195–206.

14 'African Union Accuses ICC of "hunting" Africans' *BBC News*, May 27, 2013.

15 Aryeh Neier, *The International Human Rights Movement: A History* (Princeton: Princeton University Press, 2012), 275.

prosecution witnesses to run trials. By contrast, none of the states of the former Yugoslavia could wield a similar threat because the tribunal was not dependent on a single state for witnesses (or arrests). The Kenyan government's 2013 initial parliamentary vote to withdraw its membership from the Rome Statute signals how the ICC is vulnerable to the threat of exit from States Parties displeased with court policies. Just as states can choose to join the court, they can also choose to leave it, as stipulated by Article 127 of the Statute.

D. Virtual 'plea bargaining' and the politics of conciliation

A chief prosecutor's recourse to trying to shame a targeted state for its failure to cooperate will rarely soften state defiance overnight. But it may begin to trigger a process of mounting international pressure on the state. Yet, the celebrated strategy of shaming has clear drawbacks. First, targeted states and influential international actors such as the Security Council may be impervious to shame. Beyond that, repeated reliance on shaming without an increase in state cooperation can magnify the tribunal's weakness by publicly highlighting how easily cooperation can be held without consequence. Moreover, an adversarial approach can trigger cycles of confrontation with the targeted state that can foreclose future opportunities for a softening of state recalcitrance. Finally, a chief prosecutor who relies too much on shaming a non-cooperative state may actually undermine progress by leaving the state little maneuvering room to reverse course without being seen by domestic constituencies as capitulating to a foreign court.

The limitations of confrontation often necessitate a shift toward prosecutorial conciliation with a non-cooperative state. In the virtual trials, as in an actual courtroom trial and the larger legal process in which it is embedded, conciliation and bargaining can become important modes of strategic action to accomplish one's goals. In the context of the virtual trials framework we can think of negotiations between chief prosecutors and targeted states over the terms and timing of state cooperation as a virtual form of plea bargaining.

Virtual plea bargains, like the real ones, constitute a means to keep a judicial system running efficiently.[16] In a virtual plea bargain, as in an actual one, negotiation occurs in the shadows and can be unregulated by any judicial or political actor. In domestic as well as international legal systems, prosecutors and defense attorneys often share a common interest in reducing the uncertain outcomes of a courtroom trial. In order to diminish the prospect of outright defeat in the courtroom and the expense of the trial process both parties may have an incentive to negotiate a plea bargain on mutually beneficial terms. In a virtual

16 For a discussion of plea bargaining in the context of international criminal trials, see Mark A. Drumbl, *Atrocity, Punishment, and International Law* (New York: Cambridge University Press, 2007), 163–169.

plea bargain, a chief prosecutor and targeted state may also recognize the advantages of striking a deal to diminish the negative political consequences of prolonged confrontation over the state's refusal to cooperate. Such a deal can center on the state providing the tribunal with at least some cooperation in exchange for a political or legal concession sought by the state. For example, a prosecutor may decide to forgo indicting high-level political and military leaders in exchange for the state's agreement to hand over low-level suspects.

The politics of virtual plea bargaining is shaped by the parties' relative power and the skill with which they deploy it. In US criminal cases, prosecutors often wield enormous power in the plea bargaining relationship because of defendants' well-founded fear that courtroom convictions will lead to lengthy sentences dictated by mandatory minimum legislation. In the virtual plea bargains at the international tribunals, chief prosecutors tend not to wield such a heavy stick. However, they may wield such a stick when their tribunals receive robust political backing from international actors, as occurred in key instances during the tenure of the Yugoslavia tribunal. In the tribunal-state relationship the balance of power often shifts to the state given its ability to obstruct the legal process. In dealings with targeted states, chief prosecutors may therefore come to realize that the best course of action is to eschew confrontation, forgo accusations of state noncompliance, and de-emphasize the tribunals' foundational claim of non-negotiable rectitude.

In some circumstances, external political actors can impose a bargaining paradigm on the chief prosecutor. A call for a prosecutor and state to settle their differences through negotiation can come from the tribunal's judiciary, an influential state, or an international organization such as the Security Council. In the Rwandan context, for example, US officials pressed Chief Prosecutor Carla Del Ponte in 2003 to strike a deal with RPF officials whereby the Rwandan courts, and not the tribunal, would take sole responsibility for prosecuting RPF war crimes. The RPF and Washington eventually prevailed. This is seen in the subsequent failure of Del Ponte's bid to issue indictments against RPF suspects and in the decision by her successor, Hassan Jallow, to defer the matter of RPF trials to the Rwandan courts. Washington's push for a negotiated resolution – that would benefit its ally, the RPF government – bolstered the state's leverage by signaling that its binding legal obligation to cooperate with the prosecutor's decisions was actually open to compromise.

A central aim of prosecutorial conciliation in the virtual trials is to render the prospects of cooperation more palatable for states. In the context of the UN ad hoc tribunals, legal obligation binds all UN Member States to provide full and immediate cooperation. But the ability of states to frequently violate this obligation with little political cost points to the limits of a prosecutorial strategy that fails to move beyond an adversarial mode of complaint and condemnation. 'The only way the court efficiently operates is if the prosecutor in particular successfully negotiates their way to cooperation state by state,' David Scheffer, the former US Ambassador-at-Large for War Crimes Issues, has observed. 'What is unrealistic … is for the prosecutor to deign to assume that he or she can order the states to do anything.'[17]

By opening up dialogue, chief prosecutors and their political advisers can come to learn that the state may be amenable to cooperating on matters that may not incur significant political cost. 'Dialogue' can involve explicit and implicit discussion of mutual compromise. In one scenario, a targeted state might signal its readiness to hand over a member of the state's own ethnic group, especially if that suspect is low-level and has fallen out with the state leadership. In such a situation, diplomatic engagement might lead to an implicit or an explicit agreement whereby the state facilitates the arrest and transfer of certain low-level suspects to win a reprieve of tribunal pressure to relinquish higher-level suspects. Del Ponte's visit to Belgrade in early 2001 underscores this prosecutorial approach. Del Ponte asked the authorities to provide at least some cooperation, indicating that she would delay pressure for the immediate transfer of Slobodan Milošević if other ethnic Serb suspects were delivered to the tribunal in the near term.[18]

Key to Del Ponte's strategy during this period was an effort to demonstrate her responsiveness to the domestic controversy surrounding Serbian leaders moving to arrest influential war crimes suspects. The prosecutor's conciliatory approach toward Zoran Đinđić, the cooperative Serbian prime minister, contrasted sharply with her combative relationship during the same period with Vojislav Koštunica, the obstructionist president of the rump Yugoslavia. The prosecutor's diplomatic engagement with Đinđić highlights one way in which prosecutors and political leaders can negotiate the terms of state cooperation. Del Ponte took a conciliatory approach when it came to Đinđić's request to delay publicly pressuring him to arrest Ratko Mladić in early 2003. The prosecutor granted him this breathing room because of the domestic difficulties he faced both in making such a high-profile arrest and in his larger bid to crack down on other war crimes suspects, many of whom were implicated in organized crime. Moreover, the prosecutor and prime minister had developed a strong basis of trust following the latter's move to arrest and transfer Milošević to the tribunal in 2001.[19] Some observers contend that Del Ponte failed to be conciliatory enough to Đinđić, given the intense nationalist resistance in Serbia to cooperating with a despised international court. Indeed, many argued that she failed to protect the prime minister and thus shares in the blame for his assassination in March 2003 at the hands of Serbian nationalists. Nevertheless, Del Ponte's granting Đinđić a reprieve from pressure represents an important way that a chief prosecutor can use compromise to leverage state cooperation without acquiescing to the state.

Repeated prosecutorial conciliation with little or no increase in state cooperation can progressively undermine a tribunal's legal authority by demonstrating that the

17 Author interview with David Scheffer, September 2004.

18 Douglas Hamilton, 'Give Us Mladic as Marker, Tribunal Tells Belgrade' *Reuters*, February 19, 2001.

19 Author interview with Carla Del Ponte, December 2003.

state's binding legal obligation can be diluted time and again. Prosecutorial concessions for targeted states can also set in motion a cycle of compromise that risks exposing as empty rhetoric the tribunal's legitimating claim to act above politics. Unrestrained conciliation can imperil tribunal impartiality when a prosecutor implicitly or explicitly barters limited state cooperation in exchange for a promise not to bring indictments against members of a government's own ethnic, national, or political group. Chief prosecutors defend a one-sided indictment policy as being based strictly on legal considerations, typically invoking the higher gravity of one side's atrocities and limited tribunal resources as justifications. But the perception of illegitimate prosecutorial deal-making – at times fostered by the lack of transparency surrounding tribunal meetings with high-level state officials – can generate deep skepticism about the politicization of prosecutorial indictment decisions.

If closed-door meetings create a perception problem for a chief prosecutor, the problem by no means disappears when he engages state leaders in public. This is illustrated by the fallout from ICC Chief Prosecutor Luis Moreno-Ocampo's decision to appear at a joint January 2004 press conference with Ugandan President Yoweri Museveni to announce the opening of an ICC investigation into atrocities committed by the Lord's Resistance Army (LRA) in northern Uganda. The sight of prosecutor and president side by side – announcing a one-sided investigation of the state's enemies – cast an indelible image of prosecutorial deference to state power. The prosecutor's office subsequently declared that its investigation would not be limited to alleged LRA crimes. However, more than a decade later, the ICC has only brought charges against rebel suspects.

Chief prosecutors have become keenly aware of the dangers of confronting states over the cooperation issue. This point is borne out by the Rwanda tribunal's bruising confrontation with the Rwandan government over the question of potential international indictments of its RPF suspects implicated in atrocities against Hutu civilians. In the face of Rwandan retribution and international pressure to forgo indictments, Del Ponte did not fulfill her pledge to indict RPF suspects. Del Ponte subsequently explained that lack of Rwandan cooperation blocked these indictments, though sources close to the prosecution maintain she had sufficient evidence to seek RPF indictments but chose not to do so under intense political pressure.[20] The political crisis triggered by Del Ponte's investigation of RPF atrocities played a major role in the Security Council's August 2003 decision not to renew her term as chief prosecutor at the Rwanda tribunal.

The failure of the RPF investigations and the termination of Del Ponte's tenure at the Rwanda tribunal were closely watched by the new ICC prosecutor (who had just taken up his post in The Hague in June 2003) and foreshadowed his own

20 Author interviews with Carla Del Ponte and Rwanda tribunal prosecution sources, December 2003 and March 2005.

conciliation with Uganda and other African situation states. In contrast to Del Ponte, who initiated but ultimately dropped investigations of Rwandan suspects connected to the government in power, Moreno-Ocampo did not target political or military officials from the regimes in power in Uganda, Democratic Republic of Congo, Central African Republic, and Côte d'Ivoire. The current ICC Chief Prosecutor, Fatou Bensouda, has initiated a new country investigation in Mali, but so far has only publicly issued a single arrest warrant for a jihadist who fought with an Al Qaeda-linked group. The ICC chief prosecutors' case selection decisions in a majority of the court's African situation countries suggest a pattern of shielding suspects tied to state-sponsored atrocities from prosecutorial scrutiny.[21] When it has come to the selection of new country situations, the ICC prosecutor also proceeded with great caution, 'avoiding confrontation and entanglement with major powers'[22] by (as of August 2016) not initiating formal investigations of the Israeli-Palestinian conflict as well as the war in Afghanistan. However, Bensouda received judicial approval in January 2016 to open a formal investigation into the Russian-Georgian conflict of 2008. The ICC prosecution's case selection approach appears to constitute a form of preemptive conciliation and what I call virtual plea bargaining because it has had the effect of avoiding the type of damaging conflict that led to a severe crisis in the Rwanda tribunal's relationship with the RPF government.

III. Shaping the context for conciliation at the ICC

This section provides an overview of key factors that have magnified the ICC's dependence on states, leading to the prevalence of virtual plea bargaining in the chief prosecutors' interactions with African situation countries. While all of the contemporary international criminal tribunals are heavily reliant on states, the ICC's dependence is even greater. This dependence stems from: 1) the court's difficult bid for universal state membership; and 2) structural and legal dimensions of the Rome Statute that weaken the ICC's leverage in the quest for state cooperation. These dimensions include the ICC's limited legal authority vis-à-vis States Parties and non-State Parties, the court's frequent lack of recourse to the

21 This analysis of prosecutorial strategy and situation and case selection decisions is informed by the growing scholarship on this topic, including: William A. Schabas, 'Prosecutorial Discretion v. Judicial Activism at the International Criminal Court' *Journal of International Criminal Justice* (2008) 6 (4), 731–761; Matthew R. Brubacher, 'Prosecutorial Discretion within the International Criminal Court' *Journal of International Criminal Justice* (2004) 2, 71–95; Kevin Jon Heller, 'Situational Gravity Under the Rome Statute' in Carsten Stahn and Larissa van den Herik (eds), *Future Directions in International Criminal Justice* (Cambridge: Cambridge University Press, 2009); David Bosco, *Rough Justice: The International Criminal Court in a World of Power Politics* (New York: Oxford University Press, 2014).

22 Bosco, fn.21 above, 160.

Security Council, and the frailty of the Assembly of States Parties as a 'surrogate enforcer' on behalf of the court.

The ICC's marked reliance on states originates in part from its grand vision of growing a worldwide normative movement 'to guarantee lasting respect for and the enforcement of international justice'.[23] This imperative presents a formidable challenge for the court and, in turn, creates a strong incentive for the chief prosecutor to garner promises of state cooperation and buy-in for the ICC. Therein lies the prosecutorial logic of encouraging State Parties to make self-referrals and non-State Parties to accept the jurisdiction of the court. Central to this effort has been a prosecutorial discourse recognizing the privileged place of states in the ICC system.

The ICC aims not only for state support in its ongoing cases but also to advance the campaign for universal state membership. At the ICC, therefore, the quest for state cooperation reaches well beyond the ad hoc tribunals' central task of enlisting states to aid in the matter of arrests and the facilitation of investigations.

Despite the triumphant mood that accompanied the adoption of the Rome Statute, the court has faced a future with uncertain state support. For States Parties and non-State Parties, doubts focused on how the chief prosecutor's exercise of his legal authority might roil international relations, specifically in regard to the sensitive diplomatic task of negotiating cease-fires and peace treaties. Other concerns centered on the prosecutor's prospective approach to whom he would target for investigation and indictment. These questions of prosecutorial country and case selection were the heart of the matter for many states because of the real and imagined scenarios in which a state's nationals could come under ICC scrutiny.

During the first term of the George W. Bush administration, as has been thoroughly documented, the US issued shrill warnings of prosecutorial overreach. The Bush administration's broad assault against the ICC – characterized by one commentator as 'a baptism of fire'[24] – helped to shape Moreno-Ocampo's conciliatory diplo-macy. Indeed, the new chief prosecutor could ill afford to ignore the US.[25] Although there was no chance that the US would ratify the Rome Statute, assuaging Washington's fears might in time lead it to selectively lend support to the ICC. Therein lay the incentive of the prosecutor to establish his credibility as a responsible legal official. In regard to States Parties and non-State Parties alike, the bid for global political support for the ICC has rested on cultivating an image of a bureaucratically effective though self-restrained chief prosecutor.[26]

23 Preamble to the Rome Statute of the ICC.

24 Gareth Evans, *The Responsibility to Protect: Ending Mass Atrocity Crimes Once and for All* (Washington DC: Brookings Institution Press, 2008), 99.

25 Bosco, fn.21 above.

26 Benjamin N. Schiff, *Building the International Criminal Court* (New York: Cambridge University Press, 2008), 165.

This campaign for political consensus has been so important because the ICC rests on a less robust political foundation than that which undergirds the UN Yugoslavia and Rwanda tribunals. This weaker foundation is in part the result of the decision of the US, and other states, to exercise their right under the Rome Statute to remain outside the ICC system as non-States Parties. Thus, what was ostensibly given to the Yugoslavia and Rwanda tribunals – by virtue of their Security Council mandate that legally binds all UN Member States to support these tribunals – must be earned by the ICC through its campaign for universal ratification of the Rome Statute.

The preferential status afforded to state sovereignty in the Rome Statute constitutes another contextual factor that weakens the chief prosecutor's leverage, potentially influencing a preference to avoid confrontation with states. The court-state relationship is shaped by the principle of complementarity and the consent-based nature of state participation in the Statute and the ICC itself. At the UN ad hoc tribunals, as just mentioned, state cooperation is a legal obligation for all UN Member States. But at the ICC, such obligation is undertaken voluntarily by states, except when the Security Council makes a referral of a non-State Party. Crucially, however, a Council referral does not obligate UN states that are not members of the court to honor requests for cooperation or even contribute fiscal resources to support ICC investigations. This loophole is one of a number that diminish the court's legal authority.

The Statute provides weak ground from which court officials can launch a virtual prosecution of a noncompliant State Party. The ICC does not have the recourse to the Security Council – to issue regular reports on state cooperation and to lodge complaints against uncooperative state – enjoyed by the Yugoslavia and Rwanda tribunals. The only exception occurs when the Council makes referrals as in Darfur and Libya. This structural feature of the ICC usually removes the Security Council as a potential surrogate enforcer and denies the court access to this UN arena where prosecutorial condemnation of state noncompliance can receive global attention and potentially harm the state's international standing. The Council has not been a panacea for the Yugoslavia and Rwanda tribunals or for the ICC in the Darfur and Libya situations. But recourse to the high-profile Council may provide the chief prosecutor with an incentive to launch virtual prosecutions and issue strong appeals for international enforcement. Instead, the ICC (in six of its eight current situation countries) has to turn to the ASP, which has proven to be a weak and bureaucratic institution reluctant to deal firmly with noncompliant States Parties.

Another structural feature of the Rome Statute that can fuel state intransigence and prosecutorial caution is the provision allowing States Parties to exit the Statute for any reason. While no State Party has yet to revoke its membership, the Kenyan parliament's 2013 preliminary vote to do so signaled how easily States Parties can withdraw their consent and ultimately tear down the court. The ICC's worst-case scenario is that a cascade of state withdrawals will reverse the gains of 'the justice cascade'.[27] The next worst scenario is that states leveraging the threat of exit will further entrench the logic of negotiated justice at the ICC and give yet more momentum to the shift toward virtual plea bargaining.

Our discussion of the structural and political features of the ICC system has had two aims: first, to point to some of the main ways in which the balance of power in the virtual trials has shifted significantly toward states; and second, to show how this development has influenced the ICC chief prosecutors' conciliatory orientation toward states, particularly in the matter of who faces investigation. This drift toward a virtual plea bargaining model that pays deference to states – while emphasizing the prosecution of non-state actors and those individuals from the defeated side of a conflict – threatens to undermine the ICC's foundational claim of impartiality.

IV. Conclusion

Although the ICC can reach much further than any of the contemporary ad hoc tribunals – now casting a shadow of potential adjudication in non-States Parties such as Israel, Sri Lanka, and North Korea – the court suffers from a greater powerlessness vis-à-vis states. This powerlessness has been reflected – and perhaps even further aggravated – by the prosecution's cautious approach toward a majority of the African situation states. In Uganda, Democratic Republic of Congo, Central African Republic, Côte d'Ivoire, Libya, and Mali, the prosecution has appeared to anchor its bid for state cooperation in its own display of cooperation with the state. The result has been a pattern of prosecutorial case selection decisions in which, so far at least, political and military leaders of regimes currently in power who are implicated in state-sponsored crimes have not been targeted for international prosecution.

Whether these ICC selection decisions are warranted under the prosecution's malleable gravity criteria is an important question worthy of ongoing examination. Nevertheless, this pattern of deference to these states has pre-empted one of the two fundamental types of conflicts that can arise between an international criminal court and a targeted state. It is this fundamental conflict that has been at the heart of the contentious relationship between the Yugoslavia and Rwanda tribunals and their respective targeted states. And it is because of this fundamental conflict that the virtual trials have often been so adversarial in the context of these UN tribunals. Indeed, the virtual trials framework was devised, in large part, to explain the contentious battles over state cooperation that have pitted the Yugoslavia tribunal against the states of the former Yugoslavia and the Rwanda tribunal against the RPF government.

While the virtual trials framework originally emphasized conflict, it also recognized the prevalence of compromise in the court-state relationship. Even at

27 Sikkink, fn.5 above.

the Yugoslavia tribunal – the international tribunal that enjoyed the greatest international political backing – the logic of prosecutorial compromise served as an important tool for persuading targeted states to provide some cooperation rather than none at all. At the ICC, however, prosecutorial conciliation has reached even deeper than what occurred at the Yugoslavia tribunal or the Rwanda tribunal, where Carla Del Ponte tried but failed to hold RPF suspects accountable. At the ICC, the negotiated justice of virtual plea bargaining has become dominant, underscoring a paradigm shift in the nature of court-state relations and in the politics of global justice. With the important exceptions of its case selection approach in Sudan and Kenya, where Presidents Bashir and Kenyatta have faced indictment, at the ICC we see a prosecution that invokes the battle cry of 'the fight against impunity', but has not vigorously taken on the fight of confronting impunity when it comes to the scourge of atrocities allegedly committed by those currently in power. Perhaps this practice of deference toward state power might change if and when the ICC moves beyond investigating intra-state wars. The ICC might then have incentive to investigate state crimes – rather than only the crimes of rebels, militias, and deposed leaders – if and when it obtains jurisdiction over countries involved in interstate war or in a country like North Korea where the state is the only perpetrator. Time will tell whether the current trend of virtual plea bargaining in the ICC's trials of cooperation will become the new normal and spawn a new global norm of one-sided justice.

Chapter 12

Rwanda's Kabgayi Trial between international justice and national reconciliation

Sigall Horovitz

'It was not a war – it was a genocide!' was the fierce reaction of a high profile Rwandan figure when I asked about his whereabouts during what I termed 'the war'.[1] Other elite Rwandans I interviewed expressed similar sentiments. For them, referring to Rwanda's conflict of 1990–1994 as a 'war' was a form of denying or trivializing the genocide against the Tutsis. War is a concept that may confer agency – and a certain measure of responsibility – on all parties involved, whereas genocide has a clear perpetrator side and a clear victim side. Nevertheless, the genocide was committed in the course of the civil war fought between the extremist Hutu government of the time and the Tutsi-dominated Rwandan Patriotic Front (RPF). The RPF eventually won the war and turned from a rebel group into Rwanda's ruling political party, a position it holds until today. In the last two decades the RPF-led government has been encouraging a binary understanding of the events of 1990–1994, where Tutsis are victims and Hutus are perpetrators. The one-sidedness of Rwanda's genocide trials helped reinforce this understanding, and has contributed to the unwillingness of certain sectors of the Rwandan society to recognize that some Hutus were victims and some Tutsis were perpetrators.

However, in 2008–2009, Rwanda held its first trial where Hutus were recognized as war victims and Tutsis as perpetrators – the so-called 'Kabgayi Trial'. In this trial, four RPF officers were charged with war crimes for massacring 15 civilians, mostly Hutus, near the town of Kabgayi in southern Rwanda in June 1994. Thirteen of the victims were clergy, including Rwanda's Archbishop and two other bishops. The Kabgayi massacre has been described as the conflict's 'most widely known and condemned of executions by RPF soldiers'.[2] The massacre was investigated by the Prosecutor of the International Criminal Tribunal for Rwanda (ICTR), who eventually allowed Rwanda to adjudicate the

1 Interview with Rwandan activist (19 April 2013).

2 Alison Des Forges, *Leave None to Tell the Story* (1999), 547, accessed 8 June 2017 at www.hrw.org/report/1999/03/01/leave-none-tell-story/genocide-rwanda.

case and explained that domestic proceedings would be more conducive to national reconciliation.[3]

The ICTR, established by the UN Security Council in November 1994, was mandated to prosecute the major architects of Rwanda's atrocities of 1994 and thereby 'contribute to the process of national reconciliation'.[4] The Tribunal operated for two decades, during which it tried 73 persons, including the most senior leaders of the genocide, and convicted 61 of them.[5] In this period, Rwanda has embarked on a process of national reconciliation.[6] It is unclear whether and to what extent these two processes are linked. Beyond the Rwandan context, there is a debate on the normative level regarding whether international tribunals should be expected to promote national reconciliation. Another debate revolves around their practical ability to do so.

According to Hannah Arendt's famous critique of the Eichmann and Nuremberg trials, criminal trials (whether national or international) jeopardize their ability to establish the guilt or innocence of suspected perpetrators when they pursue broad social goals.[7] Other commentators, however, differ on this point. For example, Antonio Cassese argued that war crimes trials promote reconciliation by dissipating calls for revenge, individualizing the guilt, establishing the truth and dispensing justice.[8] He also theorized that such trials should be held before international tribunals as these are more impartial than national courts and attract less resistance.[9] The creators of the ICTR (and other modern international tribunals) have

3 The ICTR had jurisdictional supremacy over Rwandan courts but the Tribunal's Prosecutor had discretion not to proceed with a case before it reached the indictment stage.

4 UNSC Res. 955 (1994), preambular para.7.

5 The ICTR tried 73 defendants for international crimes (it additionally tried two persons for contempt of court). See Report on the completion of the mandate of the International Criminal Tribunal for Rwanda as at 15 November 2015, UN.Doc.S/2015/884 (17 Nov. 2015) available at http://unictr.unmict.org/sites/unictr.org/files/legal-library/151117_ictr_final_report_en.pdf.

6 Immediately after the genocide, national reconciliation became a state policy. Numerous institutions and programs were created to promote reconciliation, including the National Unity and Reconciliation Commission (NURC), gacaca court system, community service scheme, demobilization programs, and ingando solidarity retreats. In addition, the post-genocide constitution refers to reconciliation as a national value.

7 Hannah Arendt, *Eichmann in Jerusalem: A Report on the Banality of Evil* (originally 1963; reprinted by Penguin, NY, 2006), 253 ('The purpose of a trial is to render justice, and nothing else; even the noblest of ulterior purposes – "the making of a record of the Hitler regime which would withstand the test of history", as Robert G. Storey, executive trial counsel at Nuremberg, formulated the supposed higher aims of the Nuremberg Trials – can only detract from the law's main business: to weigh the charges brought against the accused, to render judgment, and to mete out due punishment').

8 Antonio Cassese, 'Reflections on International Criminal Justice', 61 *Modern Law Review* 1 (1998), 5–6.

9 Ibid., 6–8. Cassese partly relies on H. Kelsen, *Peace through Law* (Chapel Hill: University of North Carolina Press, 1944), 115 ('The punishment of war crimes by an international

embraced Cassese's position when they mandated the Tribunal to promote national reconciliation.[10] ICTR proponents explain that the Tribunal has helped Rwanda's reconciliation process through establishing individual criminal responsibility for the genocide and producing a historical record of the crimes.[11] Nevertheless, these claims lack empirical support. Furthermore, their validity depends on how we conceptualize national reconciliation, a term for which there is no generally accepted definition and which was not defined by the ICTR's constitutive instruments.[12] If reconciliation requires holding major perpetrators accountable, or establishing the truth about past violent events, then the ICTR may have contributed to reconciliation. Without clarifying which conception of reconciliation the ICTR was meant to promote, it will be difficult to assess the Tribunal's contribution to reconciliation in Rwanda.

For present purposes, I draw on a theory developed by Louis Kriesberg, who posits that reconciliation takes place when the groups that have experienced conflict acknowledge the injustices that occurred, redress these injustices, recognize each other's suffering and humanity, and look forward to a shared future of security and

tribunal, and particularly the punishment of crimes which have the character of acts of State … would certainly meet with much less resistance [than national punishment], since it would hurt national feelings much less').

10 Not only the ICTR but also other international tribunals were expected to promote national reconciliation (in addition to their more conventional criminal justice goals of retribution and deterrence). See United Nations Security Council Resolution 1315 (14 Aug. 2000), UN Doc. S/RES/1315, preambular para.7 (mandating the Special Court for Sierra Leone to contribute to national reconciliation); United Nations General Assembly Resolution 57/228 (18 Dec. 2002), 'Khmer Rouge trials', UN Doc. A/RES/57/228 (distributed on 27 Feb. 2003), preambular paras 2–3 (mandating the Extraordinary Chambers in the Courts of Cambodia to contribute to national reconciliation); *Prosecutor v Thomas Lubanga Dyilo*, ICC Case No. ICC-01/04-01/06, 'Decision Establishing the Principles and Procedures to be Applied to Reparations' (7 Aug. 2012), paras. 177, 179 and 193 (highlighting the role of the International Criminal Court in promoting reconciliation); Payam Akhavan, 'Justice in the Hague, Peace in the Former Yugoslavia? A Commentary on the United Nations War Crimes Tribunal', 20 *Human Rights Quarterly* 737 (1998) (reconciliation goal of the International Criminal Tribunal for the former Yugoslavia).

11 See, e.g., Timothy Gallimore, 'The Legacy of the International Criminal Tribunal for Rwanda (ICTR) and its Contributions to Reconciliation in Rwanda', 14 *New Eng. J. Int'l & Comp. L.* 239 (2008), 255–256 (claiming that the ICTR contributed to Rwandan reconciliation by individualizing criminal responsibility); Erik Møse, 'Main Achievements of the ICTR', 3 *Journal of International Criminal Justice* 920 (2005), 938 (explaining that the ICTR contributed to reconciliation because 'the judgments provide a broader picture of the events in 1994 and the period preceding them').

12 While UNSC Resolution 955 mandated the ICTR to contribute to national reconciliation in Rwanda, it did not define reconciliation or clarify how the ICTR was meant to contribute to it. The Statute of the ICTR also fails to define national reconciliation (or to even mention the term).

wellbeing.[13] Kriesberg considers all these dimensions essential for reconciliation but stresses the importance of justice, explaining that 'without some measure of justice, the resulting outcome may be the imposition of injustice and a relationship that is far from equitable and therefore also is prone to renewed destructive struggle'.[14] I thus understand reconciliation as involving both justice and psychological components: it demands that injustices be acknowledged and repaired but also depends on the re-humanization of the other. These processes are interrelated, as the pursuit of conflict-related justice can humanize both victims and perpetrators. For example, when victims testify in court about their fears and experiences of atrocities, they may become more human in the eyes of members of the perpetrator group. Defendants might also appear more human in the eyes of their victims and society at large if they express remorse during the judicial process. Importantly, by attributing guilt to specific individuals trials may clarify that other members of the perpetrator group are innocent, which in turn could promote their acceptance as humans by members of the victim group. The justice component of reconciliation is naturally more directly served by conflict-related trials: in establishing the guilt or innocence of the accused the trial process and findings can acknowledge the truth about past injustice, provide redress, and promote fairness and equality before the law.

Under the above understanding of reconciliation, it is easy to see how atrocity-related trials can help reconciliation. However, justice must be perceived as administered fairly and equitably, as to not amount to an 'imposition of injustice' of the sort that Kriesberg warns could refuel the conflict. To have a humanizing effect, trials must also be deemed relevant and legitimate by the affected population. But experience over the last two decades shows that international tribunals have often been considered irrelevant or even harmful by their target populations because they are run by foreign judges, follow foreign procedures and are held abroad. Furthermore, local leaders sometimes delegitimize international tribunals, either because they fear being caught in their net or because the truth established by the tribunals may not be convenient for politicians who want to promote other 'truths' about the past. A case on point is the Rwandan government's delegitimization campaign of the ICTR, which has caused many Rwandans to perceive the ICTR negatively and outright reject its messages without even trying to assess the Tribunal on its merits. In the face of such 'hostile' political environments, any international tribunal, even with the best outreach program, will find it difficult to garner local support or even inform target populations about its work. This, in turn, may reduce the ability of international tribunals to directly affect reconciliation in their target country.

13 Louis Kriesberg, 'Coexistence and the Reconciliation of Communal Conflicts', in Eugene Weiner (ed.), *The Handbook of Interethnic Coexistence* (Continuum, 1998), 185.

14 Louis Kriesberg, 'Reconciliation: Aspects, Growth, and Sequences', 12 *International Journal of Peace Studies* 1 (2007), 17.

At the same time, empirical research suggests that international tribunals have encouraged legal or judicial developments in their target countries. For example, Diane Orentlicher found that the International Criminal Tribunal for the former Yugoslavia (ICTY) had generated positive impacts on the rule of law in Bosnia and Serbia, especially by strengthening judicial institutions and triggering domestic war crimes prosecutions.[15] This conclusion was also confirmed by Lara Nettelfield, who has shown, based on extensive in-country fieldwork, that the ICTY had positive effects on the rule of law and democratic development in Bosnia, and strengthened local judicial capacity.[16] Ten case studies conducted under the 'DOMAC Project', including one addressing Rwanda, also demonstrate that international tribunals encourage legal developments in the countries they address, including domestic criminal trials.[17] It accordingly seems that international tribunals, despite being negatively perceived by local populations, may still strengthen the rule of law and encourage local trials in their target countries. This begs the question: could international tribunals (indirectly) contribute to national reconciliation when they promote judicial developments on the domestic level?

This chapter seeks to answer this question by focusing on the case of the Kabgayi Trial. In particular, the chapter assesses the impact of the Kabgayi Trial on national reconciliation in an effort to better understand the (indirect) effects of the ICTR on reconciliation in Rwanda. My point of departure is that since we can attribute the domestic trial to the ICTR, the trial's subsequent effects on the local population can also be (indirectly) attributed to the ICTR. It is noted at the outset that although the Kabgayi Trial addressed only one incident, its potential to contribute to national reconciliation lies in its recognition of Hutu victimhood and Tutsi accountability and its message that all conflict-related victims have an equal right to justice. However, the discussion below suggests that this potential was not met.

15 Diane Orentlicher, *Shrinking the Space for Denial: The Impact of the ICTY in Serbia* (OSJI, 2008), 42–43 (suggesting that the ICTY encouraged the creation in 2003 of a War Crimes Chamber in the District Court of Belgrade and strengthened its capacity to investigate and prosecute war crimes); Diane Orentlicher, *That Someone Guilty Be Punished: The Impact of the ICTY in Bosnia* (OSI, 2010), 107 ('the Tribunal has played a distinctive role in spurring and shaping a major transition within Bosnia's domestic system for prosecuting wartime atrocities ... [and] helped launch a specialized war crimes chamber within the newly established Court of Bosnia and Herzegovina').

16 Lara Nettelfield, *Courting Democracy in Bosnia and Herzegovina* (Cambridge UK: CUP, 2010).

17 The case-studies conducted under the DOMAC Project assess the impacts of various international tribunals on legal developments in their target countries. These studies are available at www.domac.is/reports (accessed 8 June 2017). It is noted that five of the DOMAC case studies were a product of my own field research and authorship, including the one concerning Rwanda (which is one of a handful of empirical assessments of the ICTR's actual impacts in Rwanda).

The chapter draws on 65 interviews conducted in various parts of Rwanda in 2012–2013.[18] In considering whom to interview among the over 10 million Rwandans, given my objectives, I decided to speak with direct 'beneficiaries' of the Kabgayi Trial but also with other Rwandans who were involved in the reconciliation process. The interviewees can be roughly divided into three groups: insiders to the trial (the insider group), individuals associated with the Kabgayi massacre victims (the victim group), and Rwandans who had no direct link to the trial (the outsider group). The insider group included six lawyers who worked on the case (representing both the prosecution and defense), two prosecution witnesses, and one defendant. The victim group included three relatives and two close colleagues of the Kabgayi massacre victims. The 14 individuals belonging to the insider and victim groups were interviewed because they were likely to experience more intensely than others the effects of the trial. Through discussing their own experiences, however, I expected to gain insights into the broader societal effects of the proceedings.

The rest of the interviewees belonged to the outsider group. Since reconciliation is understood here as a collective societal process, it was important for me to include in the research perspectives of Rwandans who had no direct links to the trial. The outsider group included 10 'elite' Rwandans and 39 'ordinary' non-elite Rwandans. The elite interviewees included political and religious leaders as well as professional elites, who were interviewed for their overview perspectives. The 39 non-elite Rwandans who were interviewed belonged to groups that presumably face more than others the need for and challenges of reconciliation, rendering their perspectives particularly valuable for present purposes. They include convicted genocide perpetrators (9), relatives of convicted genocide perpetrators (14), genocide survivors (9), and other ordinary Rwandans who witnessed the genocide (7).[19]

In addition to interview data, the research also draws on the Kabgayi Trial pleadings and judgments, as well as other relevant documents. Before delving into the assessment, the chapter provides background on the Rwandan genocide and related accountability processes, and a description of the Kabgayi Trial.

18 A total of 63 Rwandans were interviewed (two of them were interviewed twice). The interviews were conducted under Rwandan Ministry of Education Research Permit No. MINEDUC/S&T/0078/2012, in connection with my PhD research on the ICTR's impact on reconciliation in Rwanda.

19 I interviewed most of these non-elite outsiders in connection with another study I conducted in parallel to the present one. Since I conducted both studies simultaneously, and both were associated with my PhD dissertation, I asked both sets of interviewees about the Kabgayi Trial. The other study assessed the impact of Rwanda's abolition of the death penalty on reconciliation. See Sigall Horovitz, 'International Criminal Courts in Action: The ICTR's Effect on Death Penalty and Reconciliation in Rwanda', 48 *Geo. Wash. Int'l L. Rev.* 505 (2016).

I. Background: genocide, war crimes and accountability

Between April and July 1994, approximately 800,000 Rwandans were slaughtered in what has been considered the fastest genocide in modern history.[20] The genocide targeted the Tutsi ethnic minority group, as well as ethnic Hutus who were considered 'moderate' (i.e. sympathetic to the Tutsis). Victims were hacked to death with machetes, many tortured and raped before they were killed. Besides the mass killing, atrocities committed during the genocide included the most gruesome forms of torture, mutilation, and sexual violence. The perpetrators were mostly of Hutu ethnicity and included soldiers, militia members, and civilians who were mobilized by Hutu extremist leaders.[21] Given the extensive popular participation in the genocide, and the many individuals who had killed their own colleagues, neighbors and relatives, Rwanda's genocide has been labeled 'participatory'[22] and 'intimate'.[23] The genocide was perpetrated towards the end of a four-year civil war between Hutu-dominated government forces and the Tutsi-dominated RPF rebel group. During the conflict, serious crimes were also committed by RPF members against Hutu civilians, although these were less severe than the genocide committed against the Tutsis.[24]

In July 1994, the RPF won the war, ended the genocide, and established a government of national unity. The new RPF-led government adopted a policy of maximum accountability for genocide-related crimes, implemented through criminal trials in both conventional courts and community-based 'gacaca' courts.[25] Gacaca courts concluded their work in June 2012, after prosecuting approximately 400,000 mainly low and mid level suspects. Rwandan national courts have handled slightly over 10,000 genocide cases and have recently begun adjudicating genocide cases transferred from abroad.[26] The Rwandan government also requested that an

20 Samantha Power, *Bystanders to Genocide*, The Atlantic, (1 Sept. 2001, 12:00pm), accessed 9 June 2017 at www.theatlantic.com/magazine/archive/2001/09/bystanders-to-genocide/304571/.

21 Des Forges (fn.2 above), 8–12.

22 Scott Straus, 'Rwanda and Darfur: A Comparative Analysis', 1 *Genocide Studies and Prevention* 41 (2006), 44 ('The violence in Rwanda was faster, more exterminatory, and more participatory – that is, it involved the participation of far larger numbers of civilians – than in Darfur').

23 Fergal Keane, *Season of Blood: A Rwandan Journey* (Penguin, 1995), 82 ('Back in the North of Ireland I had reported on numerous cases of people being murdered by men who worked with them or who bought cattle and land from them. In Rwanda that intimate slaughter was multiplied by tens of thousands').

24 Preliminary Report of the Independent Commission of Experts (29 Sept. 1994), UN Doc. S/1994/1125, paras 146–48, accessed 9 June 2017 at www.un.org/Docs/secu94.htm.

25 William A. Schabas, 'Genocide Trials and Gacaca Courts', 3 *J. Int'l Crim. Just.* 879 (2005).

26 Sigall Horovitz, 'How International Courts Shape Domestic Justice: Lessons from Rwanda and Sierra Leone', 46 *Israel L. Rev.* 339 (2013), at notes 24–25 and sources referenced therein.

international tribunal be established to prosecute genocide perpetrators who escaped Rwanda. In contrast to its ambitious attempt to prosecute all those involved in the genocide, the government had almost no political will to prosecute RPF members for conflict-related crimes. This is despite the fact that a UN Expert Commission that investigated the 1994 events in Rwanda concluded that crimes committed by the RPF were serious enough to warrant international prosecutions.[27] Rwanda expert Allison Des Forges referred to an estimate that up to 60,000 Hutus were killed by the RPF during the conflict.[28] According to Human Rights Watch, 32 RPF soldiers were tried in Rwanda for conflict-related crimes. Fourteen of them were convicted and received light sentences. The defendants were low-ranking soldiers (except one major) and the trials together addressed fewer than 100 victims.[29] Even if the sentences were heavier, these trials do not seem to reflect the extent of the war crimes committed by RPF members in 1994. Moreover, the crimes were adjudicated as ordinary offenses, which do not carry the serious stigma of war crimes. In light of Rwanda's almost exclusive focus on genocide accountability, despite the perpetration of atrocities by RPF members, the country is often criticized as practicing 'victor's justice'.[30]

In November 1994, the UN Security Council established the ICTR to prosecute the major perpetrators of the atrocities committed in Rwanda in 1994.[31] The ICTR operated until December 2015 and prosecuted 75 persons.[32] Although its jurisdictional powers were crafted to allow the Tribunal to prosecute both genocide perpetrators and RPF members, the ICTR only tried genocide cases. Nonetheless, in December 2000, its then Prosecutor Carla Del Ponte announced that her office would investigate serious crimes committed by RPF members, including the Kabgayi massacre.[33] This led to serious tensions with Rwanda and its president Paul Kagame, as Del Ponte recalls in her memoirs:

> Once again, I informed Kagame that we needed the files of the military prosecutor's investigations of the killings of the archbishop and the other clergymen and other alleged atrocities committed by the RPF in 1994... 'No,' he declared. 'Absolutely not.'... 'You are destroying Rwanda,' Kagame

27 UN Doc. S/1994/1125 (n. 11), paras 79, 82, 146–148.
28 Des Forges (fn.2 above), 18. She adds, however, that this number is likely to 'include persons killed in the course of combat, both civilians and militia'.
29 Human Rights Watch, Law and Reality: 'Progress in Judicial Reform in Rwanda', 25 July 2008, 90, 103–109, accessed 9 June 2017 at http://www.hrw.org/en/reports/2008/07/24/law-and-reality-0.
30 HRW 2009 World Report; AI 2009 World Report; Nicholas Jones, *The Courts of Genocide: Politics and the Rule of Law in Rwanda and Arusha* (Oxford: Routledge, 2009), 100.
31 UNSC Res. 955 (1994).
32 UN Doc. S/2015/884, 17 Nov. 2015
33 ICTR Press Release of 13 Dec. 2000, accessed 26 June 2017 at unictr.unmict.org/en/news/prosecutor-outlines-future-plans.

> charged. 'You must investigate and prosecute the genocide. You haven't gotten Kabuga, go and get him. Don't look into the military. We have done this, and we will do this.' By now, he was fuming: 'You will disrupt the reconstruction of the nation ... I'm rebuilding this country ... I have to maintain internal order ... If you investigate, people will believe there were two genocides ... All we did was liberate Rwanda.'[34]

In an interview from 2012, a Rwandan political scientist explained how (certain) Rwandans viewed Del Ponte's move:

> It was not understandable how the ICTR will prosecute the people who stopped the genocide before prosecuting those who planned and executed the genocide ... It is very discomforting to compare the crimes committed by genocide planners with crimes that were committed by former RPF combatants.[35]

Del Ponte was removed from the position of ICTR Prosecutor in August 2003, before issuing any indictments against RPF members.[36] Her successor as ICTR Prosecutor, Hassan Jallow, continued investigating RPF crimes, including the Kabgayi massacre, but his manner of handling these investigations did not provoke a strong reaction from Rwanda. This could be attributed to a combination of several factors. First, Jallow was not rushing to indict RPF members. Secondly, of all the alleged RPF crimes he seemed to pursue only the Kabgayi massacre. Thirdly, Jallow was keener than his predecessor to hand over to Rwanda the task of prosecuting RPF members.[37] Indeed, in 2008, Jallow announced that he would not prosecute the case if it were genuinely prosecuted in Rwanda.[38] The Rwandan government was not interested, to say the least, in the ICTR prosecuting RPF members, and was therefore quick to try the case domestically.

Jallow justified the transfer of the case to Rwanda by referring to its expected contribution to national reconciliation:

> It is my strong belief that the prosecution of cases of crimes committed by the members of the RPF, where amply supported by concrete evidence, have

34 Del Ponte, *Madam Prosecutor* (Other Press, 2009), 225.

35 Interview with Rwandan political scientist (15 Aug. 2012).

36 Victor Peskin, 'Victor's Justice Revisited: RPF Crimes and the Prosecutorial Endgame at the ICTR' in Scott Straus and Lars Waldorf (eds.), *Remaking Rwanda: State Building and Human Rights after Mass Violence* (Madison: U. Wisconsin Press, 2011), 178 (explaining that pressure from Rwanda led to Del Ponte's removal from office).

37 Ibid., 179.

38 UN Doc. S/PV.5904 (4 June 2008), Speech by Hassan Jallow, 11, accessed 26 June 2017 at www.un.org/en/sc/meetings/records/2008.shtml.

> a potentially greater impact on national reconciliation if conducted effectively and in accordance with fair trial procedures by the Rwandan authorities themselves.[39]

It has been claimed that the real reason behind Jallow's move was that pursuing the case at the ICTR would have meant losing Rwanda's cooperation, which the ICTR depended on for running its cases.[40] It has also been suggested that the ICTR Prosecutor and Rwanda agreed on the case transfer because they both wanted to be seen to be responding to RPF crimes.[41] Rwanda's willingness to try the case has furthermore been attributed to the fact that the Kabgayi massacre was the most notorious RPF massacre (due to the victims' high profile), that it was small and unique, and that the trial gave the government a chance to blame the Catholic Church for supporting the genocide.[42]

But regardless of Rwanda's motivations for holding the trial, and the ICTR Prosecutor's motivations for deferring jurisdiction to Rwanda, a Rwandan war crimes trial against RPF officers (including a high ranking commander) is a significant event that merits evaluation on its own terms. Besides, the threat of international prosecutions is a legitimate means by which international tribunals can encourage national trials. For example, the Rome Statute's principle of complementarity was designed to encourage states to prosecute atrocities in order to avoid proceedings before the International Criminal Court (ICC). In this sense, the Kabgayi Trial is significant precisely because it was encouraged by the ICTR. Prosecutors of other international tribunals are likely to act similarly in similar situations, as they too need to maintain cooperative relations with their target countries while pursuing justice and their own legitimacy. Downplaying the significance of outcomes such as the Kabgayi Trial may discourage important inquiries into the mechanisms by which international tribunals generate such outcomes, and the subsequent impacts of these outcomes on the relevant societies.

II. The Kabgayi Trial

The Kabgayi Trial commenced on 19 August 2008. The proceedings were held in public, before a military tribunal which sat in a civilian courthouse in Kigali's

39 Letter from ICTR Prosecutor Hassan Jallow to Executive Director of Human Rights Watch, 22 June 2009, 2, accessed 9 June 2017 at www.hrw.org/sites/default/files/related_material/2009_06_Rwanda_Jallow_Response.pdf.

40 Peskin fn.36 above, 181.

41 Lars Waldorf, '"A Mere Pretense of Justice": Complementarity, Sham Trials, and Victor's Justice at the Rwanda Tribunal', 33 *Fordham International Law Journal* 1221 (2010), 1246–1247.

42 Ibid. Waldorf also notes that the trial helped Rwanda blunt criminal proceedings that Spain initiated against RPF members, and allowed Rwanda to demonstrate that it was able to prosecute international crimes and was therefore worthy of receiving genocide cases from the ICTR. Ibid., 1239–1244.

Nyamirambo neighborhood.[43] The defendants were Brigadier-General Wilson Gumisiriza, Major Wilson Ukwishaka, Captain John Butera, and Captain Dieudonné Rukeba. The four RPF officers were charged with war crimes under the Geneva Conventions for killing 15 civilians, mostly Hutus, in what was known as the Kabgayi massacre of June 1994. The victims were the Archbishop of Rwanda, the Bishop of Byumba, the Bishop of Kabgayi, ten Catholic priests, a seminarian, and a young boy.[44] At the time of the massacre, defendants Butera and Rukeba were RPF foot soldiers (sergeants) fighting in the Kabgayi area. Ukwishaka was their platoon commander and Gumisiriza was the battalion's intelligence officer. Gumisiriza was a major at the time, and was promoted over the years to the high rank of Brigadier-General.[45] During the trial, the prosecution called four witnesses and the defense called eight. Although the Rwandan legal system allows victims and their relatives to participate as 'civil parties' in criminal proceedings (including military trials), there were no civil parties in the Kabgayi Trial. The evidentiary phase was concluded on 24 September 2008, after five days of hearings. The trial judgment was issued on 24 October 2008.[46] Both parties appealed, and the appellate court issued its judgment on 25 February 2009.[47]

Kabgayi was historically the center of the Catholic Church in Rwanda. It hosts the oldest cathedral in the country, Catholic seminaries, schools and a hospital. As a religious center, Kabgayi attracted clergy and seminarians from different parts of Rwanda. It also attracted scores of Tutsis who fled there when the genocide broke out in April 1994 to seek refuge in the town's religious centers. While many of these Tutsis survived, thousands of them were killed in Kabgayi during the genocide. In early June 1994, the RPF took over Kabgayi. According to the Kabgayi Trial judgments, the RPF evacuated everyone they found at the Kabgayi cathedral, including the clergy who were later massacred, and transferred them to a safer area for their own protection.[48] As the RPF soldiers were escorting the clergy, they heard bystanders identify the clergy as members of the Interahamwe

43 A Rwandan prosecutor explained that the trial was held in that location in order to accommodate the many people who were expected to attend it. Interview with Rwandan prosecutor (8 Aug. 2012).

44 One of the victims, brother Jean Baptiste Nsinga, was a Tutsi. See Juzgado Central de Instrucción No. 4, Audiencia Nacional, AUTO, 6 Feb. 2008, 113, accessed 26 June 2017 at www.veritasrwandaforum.org/dosier/resol_auto_esp_06022008.pdf.

45 *Military Prosecutor General v Brig. Gen. Wilson Gumisiriza et al.*, File no. RAM 0212/KN/05/08, Indictment, 25 May 2008 [Rwanda], English translation certified by the Rwandan Military Prosecution (copy with author).

46 The Military Tribunal in Kigali, *Military Prosecutor General v Brig. Gen. Wilson Gumisiriza et al.*, Case No. RP 0151/08/TM, Trial Judgment, 24 Oct. 2008, English translation certified by the ICTR (copy with author).

47 The High Military Court in Kigali, *Military Prosecutor General v Brig. Gen. Wilson Gumisiriza et al.*, Case No. RPA 0062/08/HCM, Appeals Judgment, 25 Feb. 2009, English translation certified by the ICTR (copy with author).

48 Ibid., paras 1, 10.

(an extremist Hutu militia that played a major role in perpetrating the genocide).[49] Three days later the RPF agreed to move the clergy, upon their request, to the convent of Gakurazo.[50] At the convent the RPF soldiers invited the clergy to a meeting to discuss their concern. During this meeting four RPF soldiers (including Butera and Rukeba) entered the room and shot dead the 15 victims.[51] Other RPF soldiers arrived quickly after the massacre and shot dead one of the killers.[52]

Butera and Rukeba admitted to having shot the clergy without the latter posing a threat, but invoked the defense of provocation. They explained that a fellow sergeant, Déo Nyagatare, had told them that the clergy were responsible for the deaths of his relatives who perished in Kabgayi in connection with the genocide. Butera and Rukeba agreed to help Nyagatare kill the clergy to avenge his relatives' deaths. Together with Nyagatare and another soldier, they entered the room where the clergy gathered and shot them dead. The defendants argued that seeing the many corpses of genocide victims in Kabgayi had affected them psychologically. Given their state of mind, they were provoked to shoot the clergy when they learned that their colleague's relatives perished in the genocidal killings in Kabgayi and that the clergy participated in these killings. In light of the admissions, the judges focused on the provocation defense rather than the facts surrounding the shooting. They rejected the provocation defense, finding no factual link between the Accused and the alleged acts of the victims, and convicted Butera and Rukeba of violating Article 3 of the Geneva Conventions.[53] However, the judges found that the killings were committed under duress, which they considered a mitigating circumstance.[54] The defendants' guilty pleas, request for pardon, and the fact that they were first-time offenders were considered as additional mitigating circumstances.[55] The court sentenced them to eight years' imprisonment.[56] The appellate court also rejected the provocation defense,[57] but found additional mitigating circumstances and reduced the defendants' imprisonment sentences to five years.[58]

Gumisiriza and Ukwishaka, as superiors to Butera and Rukeba, were charged with indirect responsibility under the doctrine of command responsibility. They pleaded not guilty. To convict under the doctrine of command responsibility, it must be shown that the defendant (1) had a superior-subordinate relationship with the direct perpetrator; (2) knew or should have known that the crime would

49 Ibid., paras 1–2, 10; Trial Judgment (n. 33), paras 17–18, 21–22.

50 Appeals Judgment (n. 34), paras 1, 10; Trial Judgment (n. 33), paras 17–18.

51 Appeals Judgment (n. 34), para.1; Trial Judgment (n. 33), para.21.

52 Appeals Judgment (n. 34), para.2; Trial Judgment (n. 33), para.22.

53 Appeals Judgment (n. 34), para.47; Trial Judgment (n. 33), paras 165–167.

54 Trial Judgment (n. 33), para.168.

55 Ibid., para.169.

56 Ibid., para.202.

57 Appeals Judgment (n. 34), para. 7.

58 Ibid., para. 50. In mitigation the court considered the defendants' admissions, request for forgiveness, expression of remorse, and emotional distress at the time of the massacre.

be committed; and (3) failed to prevent or punish the crime.[59] According to international jurisprudence, a major way of establishing that a superior 'should have known' about the crimes is to prove the existence of similar contemporaneous crimes that were either known to the superior or were notorious or widespread and thus presumably known to him. However, the prosecution in the Kabgayi Trial did not argue that similar contemporaneous crimes were committed by the RPF. Instead, the prosecution claimed that the commanders knew that bystanders told the RPF soldiers about the clergy's involvement in the genocide, and, consequently, the commanders should have suspected that the soldiers would kill the clergy. Since the commanders did nothing to prevent the crime, the prosecution argued, they should be held accountable. The judges rejected the prosecution theory. They found that Gumisiriza and Ukwishaka were unaware of similar contemporaneous crimes and could not be presumed to know of such crimes, as the prosecution did not establish their existence. The two commanders were accordingly acquitted.[60] The acquittal was upheld on appeal.[61]

In writing about this case, legal scholar Lars Waldorf observes that the acquittal of Gumisiriza and Ukwishaka 'rests on the falsehood that RPF soldiers had not already committed similar massacres throughout Rwanda in 1994'.[62] He criticizes the prosecution for failing to bring evidence about other atrocities committed by the RPF, for bringing evidence that the Kabgayi massacre was not planned, and for presenting only four witnesses who ended up helping the defense.[63] Nonetheless, the ICTR Prosecutor, who monitored the trial, stated that the proceedings complied with fair trial standards.[64] Waldorf, in response, suggests that an assessment of the trial should consider not only its procedural fairness but also what is included in the prosecution case.[65] The narrative of the judges is also worth considering in this context. For example, at the very outset, the judgment refers to the conflict as 'the war aimed at stopping the genocide perpetrated against the Tutsis'.[66] Thus, before assessing the evidence, the judges situate the allegations against the defendants in the context of their morally justified battle against genocidal forces. As shown above, the judges also portrayed the RPF forces as generally respectful and generous towards the victims. Even when the judgment affirms that four RPF soldiers killed the clergy, it adds that other RPF soldiers immediately intervened. The judgment thus presents the massacre as an unexpected act that was not condoned by the RPF. The judgment further diminishes the

59 See, e.g., Art.6(3) of the ICTR Statute; Arts 86 and 87 of Additional Protocol I to the Geneva Conventions of 1949.
60 Trial Judgment (n. 33).
61 Appeals Judgment (n. 34).
62 Waldorf, *A Mere Pretense*, fn. 41 above , 1253.
63 Ibid., 1249–1253.
64 Letter from Jallow (n. 25), 2–3.
65 Waldorf, *A Mere Pretense*, fn. 41 above, 1253.
66 Appeals Judgment (n. 34), Charges, para.1.

severity of the massacre by discussing the participation of the Catholic Church in the genocide, thus creating an impression that the victims, as Catholic leaders, supported the genocide. While the judgment does not make conclusive findings on this point, it refers to the parties' extensive arguments about the Church's involvement in the genocide and provides no counter narrative.

III. Local understandings of the Kabgayi Trial

The present section discusses the meanings given to the Kabgayi Trial by the Rwandans I interviewed. It is recalled that the interviewees belong to three groups: insiders to the trial such as lawyers and others who were involved in the proceedings; relatives and professional colleagues of the Kabgayi massacre victims; and Rwandans who were outsiders to the trial in the sense that they lacked a direct link to the case. Through analyzing the various perspectives, this section attempts to shed light on whether and how the trial affected reconciliation in Rwanda. As the discussion below illustrates, there are great divergences in how each group perceived the trial. The discussion also demonstrates that the issue of RPF accountability for war crimes remains highly contentious in post-genocide Rwanda, which may explain the approach of the judges and prosecutors in the Kabgayi Trial (e.g., not discussing other non-genocidal massacres, praising RPF conduct). This also suggests that in the present political environment the Kabgayi Trial could not have promoted a broad societal recognition of Hutu suffering and Tutsi accountability, even if the judges had been more far-reaching in their findings.

One last comment should be made at this point: the interviewees differ not only in the meanings they attribute to the Kabgayi Trial but also in their understanding of the concept of reconciliation. However, for purposes of this chapter, I adopt the definition of reconciliation I discuss in the opening.

Views from outside the court

As noted above, the Kabgayi Trial was conducted in public in a civilian courthouse in Kigali. Still, many of the interviewees who were not involved in the trial reported that they knew little about the process. One Hutu interviewee noted that the Kabgayi Trial had no relevance to his life even though he considered his mother to have been unlawfully killed by the RPF in 1994. He noted that the Kabgayi Trial took place while other RPF crimes were not adjudicated because of the high profile of the victims.[67] Other Hutus I interviewed made comments such as: 'I don't know [about the Kabgayi Trial] but I heard on the radio that some bishops were killed';[68] 'I heard about this trial but didn't follow to know what

67 Interview with son of convicted genocide perpetrator (1 Sept. 2012).
68 Interview with sister of convicted genocide perpetrator (28 July 2012).

happened';[69] 'I was busy with my problems, I didn't get time to follow that [trial]';[70] 'I remember [the Kabgayi Trial] was being broadcasted on the radio but I didn't hear about the verdict'.[71] A Hutu priest noted that 'people think many things [about the Kabgayi Trial] but they keep silent [as these are] political issues'.[72] Thus, perhaps some of the interviewees knew about the trial but preferred not to discuss it. Still, it seems that the trial was far from having major effects on their lives.

It is noted in this context that some Hutu interviewees complained about the failure to recognize Hutu victimhood in Rwanda, noting that this was a major impediment to national reconciliation. For example, a Hutu village leader complained that:

> Hutus who died in the war are not remembered, they are not given value… [the authorities] think that only one side was exterminated but they forget about the other side so that affects reconciliation.[73]

Another interviewee, a Hutu priest who heads a church-based reconciliation organization, suggested that the lack of recognition of victimhood entailed the inability to properly bury the victims:

> RPF victims are scared [that] if they ask the authorities to bury their loved ones, the authorities will look at them in a bad way … You still have many people in mass graves [who are] RPF victims. If they could be buried with respect, this would help a lot the reconciliation process.[74]

Tutsi interviewees who were not directly involved in the Kabgayi Trial also knew little about the proceedings. When asked about the trial, their responses included: 'we don't know about the trial of the bishops';[75] 'I don't know anything';[76] 'I don't have much details'.[77] One of them however explained that 'these Bishops were perpetrators of genocide too, mostly the one of Kigali'.[78] This last quote suggests that the interviewee considered the Kabgayi massacre as a mere act of revenge against clergymen who participated in the genocide. This view is consistent with responses I received from elite Tutsi interviewees. For

69 Interview with wife of convicted genocide perpetrator (29 July 2012).
70 Interview with wife of convicted genocide perpetrator (31 July 2012).
71 Interview with son of convicted genocide perpetrator (9 Aug. 2012).
72 Interview with Rwandan priest (21 Jan. 2012).
73 Interview with Rwandan local leader (5 Sept. 2012).
74 Interview with Rwandan Catholic Church leader (17 April 2013).
75 Interview with genocide survivor (31 July 2012).
76 Interview with genocide survivor (31 July 2012).
77 Interview with genocide survivor (28 July 2012).
78 Interview with genocide survivor (27 Jan. 2012).

example, a Rwandan political scientist noted that the Kabgayi Trial was 'just one of the cases' where RPF members were tried for revenge crimes.[79] Similarly, the former Justice Minister explained that the Kabgayi Trial was one of 45 cases where RPF soldiers were tried for revenge crimes.[80] Another senior government official indicated that the trial was 'not isolated from other acts of justice' regarding revenge crimes, adding that the RPF's 'no-revenge' policy was critical to achieving reconciliation.[81] However, the tendency of the Tutsi interviewees (both elite and non-elite) to deprive the massacred clergy of the acknowledgement that they were victims of war crimes suggests that the trial may not have contributed towards reconciliation.

Views from inside the court

A former RPF soldier who testified as a witness in the Kabgayi Trial expressed a similar view to that of the above Tutsi interviewees, noting that 'the trial contributed to reconciliation because members of the military and the population in general learned that revenge is not good, and that there is justice'.[82]

But some of the legal professionals involved in the trial suggested that the proceedings promoted reconciliation in other ways. One of them stressed the trial's value in establishing the truth.[83] Another considered that it benefitted reconciliation by showing 'that justice is for everyone [as] it is not only one part of the community that was judged'.[84] Yet another legal professional explained that the trial was important for reconciliation as it satisfied Hutus beyond those related to the victims,[85] and a fourth one added that the proceedings represented a gesture towards the Catholics of Rwanda:

> If we're talking about reconciliation, we cannot leave behind another group of Rwandans who are Catholics, who are the biggest number of believers in Rwanda. So [the fact that the killing of] the clergy has been prosecuted, to me, it also contributes to reconciliation ...[86]

As the discussion below illustrates, the church leadership did not share this view, and the victims' relatives did not consider the trial to have provided them with justice.

79 Interview with Rwandan political scientist (15 Aug. 2012).
80 Interview with Rwandan Justice Minister Tharcisse Karugarama (16 Aug. 2012).
81 Interview with senior Rwandan official (30 April 2013).
82 Interview with former RPF soldier (10 Aug. 2012).
83 Interview with Rwanda legal expert (17 Aug. 2012).
84 Interview with Rwandan legal expert (30 Aug. 2012).
85 Interview with Rwandan prosecutor (8 Aug. 2012).
86 Interview with Rwanda legal expert (16 Aug. 2012).

The victims' perspective

The perspectives of the relatives and Church colleagues of the Kabgayi massacre victims contradict the above quoted views. As explained by a senior Rwandan Catholic leader I interviewed:

> In our opinion justice was not achieved ... I know how operations are carried out in the military – you cannot say that soldiers came and took the bishops 80km away and killed them without having received orders from their superiors ... It was good that [the Kabgayi Trial] took place but I wish that Rwandan judges were accompanied by foreign judges ... It would have helped to get justice, as the law would have been followed.[87]

He also complained that the church was not informed about the trial:

> We were aware of the trial, but we were not informed about [it] ... we don't know who pressed charges so we decided to remain a bit silent ... They never bothered to ask our opinion. We think we were not considered at all.[88]

The interviewee added that 'we wanted to bury the bishops in their respective dioceses, but we were never allowed to do that. They are still in Kabgayi, and we were never allowed to bury them'.[89]

Another Catholic leader was also critical of the Kabgayi Trial, although he acknowledged its virtues:

> The fact that the trial took place shows that the government doesn't support the culture of impunity, but the sentences they got don't match the crimes they committed. I think it was more of a show because of the pressure of foreign countries ... [However], we were happy that it happened and there was recognition that these bishops died ... many people were happy about the trial and that some of the criminals were convicted, even though the sentences were not fair.[90]

Like the previous one, this interviewee also invoked the issue of the burials:

> We went to visit the place where they buried them, and we wanted to bring the body here [to the diocese] but we were not allowed. Even now we are waiting for them to let us bring the body here. Q: Why aren't they letting you? A: I think there is a negative attitude from the side of the government because

87 Interview with Rwandan Catholic Church leader (16 April 2013).
88 Ibid.
89 Ibid.
90 Ibid.

> they think the Bishops who died were working hand in hand with the previous government and did not do anything to help people during the war.[91]

A third Catholic leader I interviewed addressed the burials as well, but was more empathetic towards the government:

> Usually, [bishops] should be buried in their respective diocese. And up to now [the massacred bishops] are buried in Kabgayi. The government says this is not yet the time to move them, as it will cause tensions. You know people are still fragile. When [the RPF] killed [the bishops] they said they were Interahamwe, so now if they will be buried in their dioceses, also relatives of other people who were killed by the RPF would request that their relatives be brought here for burial and this can lead to claims of 'double genocide' ... The government is still dealing with the issues of genocide. That's the priory. To bring in another issue may destroy what [they] are working on ... They say it is two different things: Genocide is one thing, and the war is another thing.[92]

At the same time, he did not consider the trial to be genuine:

> It was a show off. Think about the crimes! Killing these Bishops! ... The sentences did not reflect the crimes. For us, the law was not applied. A father can only hit his child softly; he cannot hit him hard. This is the same. The trial had to be held because Human Rights Watch and the international community wanted it.[93]

The victims' relatives were also critical of the Kabgayi Trial. One of them explained that the trial was held only because of international pressure and called it 'a joke' and 'a play' intended 'just to show that something was happening'.[94] The interviewee felt that the victims' families were denied justice, as they were not invited to participate in the trial or informed about its progress:

> If justice played its role, they could have invited the members of the family to come and participate in [the trial] but we didn't know anything, we listened like other people who had no profit in that trial...[95]

He explained that participation entailed compensation and burial rights: 'my family was supposed to participate in terms of asking for compensation and we

91 Interview with Rwandan Catholic Church leader (17 April 2013).
92 Interview with Rwandan Catholic Church leader (17 April 2013).
93 Ibid.
94 Interview with relative of Kabgayi massacre victim (4 Sept. 2012).
95 Ibid.

were supposed to be given the right to bury our people'.[96] They were afraid to request these rights because 'when you want to challenge the government about crimes [they] committed, it is a problem for you'.[97]

Another relative of a Kabgayi massacre victim expressed similar views:

> It was a 'so called' trial ... They only picked the simple soldiers to try, but senior officers that were involved in these killings were not tried ... This is a cliché, a cover up ... We don't have justice in this country... [The trial] was broadcast on the radio so we followed [but] we were not happy with the results ... Can someone kill you and be the same person who is judging your trial?[98]

The interviewee explained that she and her relatives did not attend the trial out of fear of being identified by the authorities as relatives of a Kabgayi massacre victim: 'we made sure that we stayed behind so that no one would know that we were related to the victims ... because they kept accusing [the victim who was my relative] of being among the planners of genocide'.[99] A third relative I interviewed explained why the victims' relatives did not get involved in the proceedings:

> We didn't want to implicate RPF soldiers as this could risk our lives ... A relative in 2007 raised this issue in a village meeting and he was arrested and put in prison later ... [Even in gacaca] the issue of the bishops could not be dealt ... People were afraid to raise the issue because RPF is ruling now.[100]

These views suggest that the Kabgayi Trial actually prevented Hutus from receiving acknowledgement of their suffering and kept them stigmatized as perpetrators, in effect legitimizing the officially imposed binary version of the past.[101] However, as discussed in the following section, the Kabgayi Trial and its judgment may have meanings and effects beyond those considered by the interviewees.

IV. Analysis

The Kabgayi Trial of 2008–2009 was Rwanda's first (and so far only) case where war crimes charges were brought and confirmed against RPF members in

96 Ibid.
97 Ibid.
98 Interview with relative of Kabgayi massacre victim (29 Aug. 2012).
99 Ibid. Like the previous one, this interviewee also attributed the holding of the trial to international pressure.
100 Interview with relative of Kabgayi massacre victim (18 Aug. 2012).
101 Also see Waldorf, *A Mere Pretense*, fn.41 above, 1248 (considering that the trial eventually reinforced the official narrative about the massacre, i.e. that some soldiers lost control and took revenge).

connection with the killing of Hutu civilians in 1994. Although the trial addressed only one incident, it had potential to contribute to national reconciliation by publicly acknowledging that some Hutus were victims of war crimes, that some Tutsis had committed war crimes, and that all conflict-related victims have an equal right to justice. However, the parameters of the contestation were significantly narrowed by the parties' submissions that RPF members committed no atrocities besides the Kabgayi massacre. While the judges could have considered additional evidence about other atrocities committed by RPF members, for example in assessing the commanders' responsibility, they preferred to stick to the parties' arguments. Moreover, the judges left the public guessing whether the victims were personally involved in the genocide. Thus, they limited the recognition of Hutu victimhood to the 15 victims of the concrete case and even then questioned whether they were genuine victims. The failure to involve the victims' families in the process further restricted the scope of acknowledgement of Hutu suffering.

Criminal trials can affect reconciliation not only by establishing accountability and recognizing victimhood but also by re-humanizing (or de-stigmatizing) one group in the eyes of the other. For example, by holding specific perpetrators accountable, trials 'individualize' the guilt and thus discourage collective blaming of one group by another.[102] In cases like the Kabgayi Trial, where the victims belong to the stigmatized group, trials can help re-humanize the victims through giving them a voice and by portraying them positively in the judgment.[103] In Rwanda, almost all genocide trials have placed the victims at the center. This is most obvious in gacaca trials, where the absence of prosecutors placed the victims and their relatives in the role of accusers. But it is also the case in Rwanda's conventional courts, where genocide victims and their relatives were extensively involved as witnesses and civil parties. In sharp contrast to those cases, the Kabgayi Trial left the victims out of the process, thus missing an opportunity to re-humanize and de-stigmatize them and those affiliated with them. While the prosecution is generally presumed to represent the victims, in the Kabgayi Trial it refrained from doing so possibly because it would have meant adopting perspectives that challenge the legitimacy of the RPF's struggle in 1994 and its current claim to power. The prosecutors, after all, were RPF soldiers. The judges were also RPF soldiers, and indeed, they refrained from taking the initiative of considering evidence that could have represented the victims' narrative. The interviews suggest that, as a result of excluding the victims' perspective, the trial is considered by Hutus as illegitimate or irrelevant at best. But more importantly, without addressing the victims' perspectives, the court reduced its ability to affect *Tutsi*

102 Cassese, *Reflections* fn.8 above, 5–6.

103 See, e.g., Leora Bilsky, *Transformative Justice: Israeli Identity on Trial* (Ann Arbor, MI: University of Michigan Press, 2004). In ch.7, Bilsky shows that the narrative of the Kufr Qassem judgment treated the Arab victims in a manner which re-humanized Arab citizens of Israel in the eyes of Israeli Jews.

perceptions of Hutus, perceptions that might be crucial for national reconciliation in Rwanda.

The judgment's disregard to the victims' perspective is further emphasized when considering its treatment of the perpetrators. As noted above, the judgment refers to the conflict as a counter-genocide operation. It portrays the RPF as considerate and even generous towards the clergy: the RPF evacuated the clergy from the battle zone, led them to a safer area, and then agreed to move them to a convent of their choice, where they were given an opportunity to discuss their problems. When certain RPF soldiers had unexpectedly attacked the clergy, their colleagues tried to intervene. This emphasis on the humanity of the RPF is a clear example of how criminal trials can exonerate collectives by individualizing the guilt. However, in this case, the perpetrators belonged to the group that needed no exoneration. On the contrary, to promote national reconciliation in Rwanda the Kabgayi Trial should have humanized the *victims* of the Kabgayi massacre and their larger circles. However, the judges make no such attempt.

Finally, as discussed above, the judgment refers to the victims as 'clergy' rather than Hutu civilians. The judgment incorporates the parties' extensive arguments about the Catholic Church's involvement in the genocide, and makes no reference to alternative narratives that could reflect the views of Hutus or the Catholic Church. In this light, designating the victims as clergy 'dilutes' their victimhood, even if no conclusive findings were made about their guilt. Writing about the Kabgayi massacre, Alison Des Forges notes that 'Archbishop Vincent Nsengiyumva was known for his closeness to Habyarimana (Rwanda's president in the lead up to the genocide), but not all in the group held such a position. Bishop Thaddée Nsengiyumva, who was also murdered, had favored political reform and had sought to distance the church from Habyarimana's government.'[104] According to Prunier, another expert on Rwanda, some of the victims of the Kabgayi massacre had actually saved Tutsis.[105] Furthermore, one of the massacred priests was a Tutsi.[106] Including these details in the judgment could have promoted reconciliation by stressing the victims' solidarity with Tutsis. However, the judges chose to further stigmatize Hutus by leaving open the possibility that the massacre was an act of revenge against inhuman genocide perpetrators. The interviews support this conclusion: Tutsi interviewees associated the trial with revenge crimes, while the victims' fellow clergy considered it a show trial and the victims' relatives refrained from attending the proceedings out of fear of being harassed.

Still, as was stressed by some interviewees, the judgment made important normative statements about the impermissibly of revenge crimes, the scope of

104 Des Forges, fn.2 above, 547.

105 Gérard Prunier, *The Rwanda Crisis: History of a Genocide 1959–1994* (New York: Columbia University Press, 1995), 270. This claim was also made in Waldorf, *A Mere Pretense*, fn.41 above, 1248.

106 See note 44 above.

commanders' duty to prevent them, and the subordination of the RPF to the rule of law. While the application of these norms in the Kabgayi Trial fell short of challenging the official binary narrative of the past, the value of the trial may be in its normative message that justice for victims of non-genocidal atrocities can be attainable in Rwanda, even if in a limited form. Furthermore, by applying international principles and jurisprudence pertaining to command responsibility and war crimes, as well as drawing on the Geneva Conventions and international case law, the judgment provides a rich source of jurisprudence on the relationship between Rwandan law and international law.[107] From this perspective, the judgment may have some value as a precedent in future litigation or as a didactic tool in future public discussions on Hutu victimhood.

Since international law does not recognize a statute of limitations for international crimes, it may be possible for Rwanda to hold more such trials in the future. Given the participatory nature of the genocide, it is likely that many of the Hutus targeted by the RPF during the conflict were legitimately killed while participating in the genocide. However, without investigating these crimes, we may never know how many of those killed by the RPF in 1994 were innocent civilians who did not participate in the genocide. A societal reckoning of this aspect of Rwanda's history could satisfy Hutus who seek justice and recognition, and re-establish their confidence in society by demonstrating that all Rwandans are equal before the law. Public acknowledgement of Hutu suffering may also contribute to reconciliation by humanizing (certain) Hutus in the eyes of (certain) Tutsis. The Kabgayi Trial still has the potential to promote reconciliation by triggering such developments. Nonetheless, as of the time of writing, this chapter suggests that the trial had little to no impact on reconciliation.

V. Concluding remarks

Modern international criminal tribunals are expected to promote national reconciliation in their target countries. However, they are not given any guidelines on how to attain this goal. Existing arguments about their effects on reconciliation share a problematic underlying assumption that there is a direct and linear relationship between the outputs of international tribunals (such as their factual or legal findings) and the societies which are expected to reconcile, downplaying the intervening role of the domestic political environment in which these outputs operate.[108] In practice, however, the ability of an international tribunal to promote

107 This is particularly important given that prior to the Kabgayi Trial, Rwandan case law on international crimes primarily concerned factual rather than legal issues. Schabas, fn. 25 above, 889.

108 Another problem is that national reconciliation is defined in many different ways. The term can be defined in a manner that helps sustain the claim that ICTs promote reconciliation, or in a manner that helps prove the opposite.

reconciliation in its target country through its findings largely depends on how these findings (or lack thereof) are interpreted (or misinterpreted) by local elites and explained to the affected society. Moreover, international tribunals may not be equipped for directly affecting highly politicized domestic processes such as national reconciliation in post-conflict environments. Nonetheless, by doing what courts do best – applying and legitimizing legal norms – international tribunals can generate domestic legal developments in their target countries that could, in turn, affect national reconciliation. Understanding how these domestic legal developments influence national reconciliation can help us develop a richer and more nuanced view of the reconciliation impacts of international tribunals. Even if this impact is indirect, it can still be significant in terms of the number of people it affects and length of time it can continue to affect the relevant society.

The Kabgayi Trial, it is recalled, took place because of the ICTR. It can therefore be claimed that the ICTR failed to promote reconciliation in Rwanda when it referred the Kabgayi case to Rwanda (in contradiction to the expectation of the ICTR Prosecutor). However, the Kabgayi Trial was one of several legal developments that the ICTR encouraged in Rwanda.[109] While the Kabgayi Trial did not promote national reconciliation in Rwanda, other legal developments that the ICTR encouraged in Rwanda may have faired better in this sense.[110] An assessment of the reconciliation impact of each of these developments will teach us more about the ICTR's contribution to reconciliation in Rwanda.

109 For a discussion of these developments see Horovitz, fn.26 above.

110 Indeed, as I show elsewhere, the ICTR encouraged Rwanda to abolish the death penalty, a development that had a positive impact on national reconciliation. See Horovitz, fn.19 above.

Chapter 13

As the pendulum swings – the revival of the hybrid tribunal

Mark Kersten[1]

Introduction

Reflecting on his six years as US Ambassador-at-Large for War Crimes Issues, Stephen Rapp recently concluded that 'there isn't a global system of justice, just some cases in The Hague and a few other places'.[2] Rapp's assessment likely comes as a surprise to many proponents of international criminal justice. The 2002 establishment of the permanent International Criminal Court (ICC) was intended to entrench and consolidate a global system of international criminal law which had, until then, been piecemeal and unstable. A series of prior, ad hoc war crimes tribunals, such as the International Criminal Tribunals for the former Yugoslavia (ICTY) and Rwanda (ICTR), the Extraordinary Chambers in the Courts of Cambodia (ECCC), and the Special Court for Sierra Leone (SCSL), relied on the periodic and sporadic confluence of political interest and will to permit their establishment and functioning. They each focused on specific theatres of mass atrocity and were restricted to examining crimes perpetrated in particular windows in time. In sharp contrast, the ICC was intended to be a 'world court', a promise of universal justice, and thus a provider of a permanent, reliable and consistent response to international crimes irrespective of where they occurred. As then-United Nations Secretary General Kofi Annan declared at the conclusion of the Rome Statute negotiations: 'The establishment of the Court is still a gift of hope to future generations, and a giant step forward in the march towards universal human rights and the rule of law. It is an achievement which, only a few years ago, nobody would have thought possible.'[3] According to Human Rights Watch, the

1 The author would like to thank Ron Levi and Mikkel Jarle Christensen for inviting me to write and publish this chapter. Many thanks also to Shehzad Charania for his invaluable comments on an early draft of the chapter.

2 See Simons, Marlise, *Veteran International Prosecutor Foresees War Crimes Trials for ISIS*, *New York Times*, 26 December 2015, accessed 9 June 2017 at www.nytimes.com/2015/12/27/world/europe/veteran-international-prosecutor-foresees-war-crimes-trials-for-isis.html.

3 United Nations, *Secretary-General says Establishment of International Criminal Court is Gift of Hope to Future Generations*, Press Release SG/SM/6643 L/2891, 20 July 1998, accessed 9 June 2017 at www.un.org/press/en/1998/19980720.sgsm6643.html.

ICC represented a promise to 'transform the human rights landscape'; it demonstrated that 'the international community of states [had] agreed ... to embrace this essential institution for bringing the world's worst human rights criminals to justice'.[4]

The ICC was seen as a means to replace a fragmented approach to international criminal justice with a permanent system of global accountability. Yet renewed interest in establishing hybrid tribunals, evident by the remarkable uptick in the number that have been created over last two years, suggests that this is far from the case. There is still a place for hybrid courts as part of the international criminal justice network.

This chapter examines the recent resurgence of hybrid tribunals and seeks to explain why they have 'returned' as a viable model of international criminal justice. It proceeds as follows. The first section of the chapter briefly defines and describes hybrid tribunals before illustrating the resurgence in their use since 2015. A number of recently established and proposed hybrid courts are outlined. The second section of the chapter seeks to explain the reasons behind the 'rebirth' of hybrid tribunals. It situates their re-emergence amidst the confluence of three broad factors: the increasingly evident limitations of the ICC; the waning view that the Court must be the only purveyor of international criminal justice; and the ongoing utility of hybrid tribunals. The chapter then argues, in section III, that hybrid courts should form an important part of a 'network' of international criminal justice alongside, rather than in competition with, the ICC or domestic judiciaries. The section also offers the creation of a permanent hybrid tribunal as a means to consolidate such a network of global justice. Finally, the chapter concludes by arguing that the revival of hybrid tribunals is unlikely to be ad hoc and that, even if they eventually fall out of fashion again, proponents of international criminal justice would do well to study and understand their benefits and advantages.

It should be stressed that the chapter should not be read as an argument in favour of or against hybrid courts as such. It is, rather, intended to offer an explanation of their re-emergence as well as to propose that, in the absence of a consolidated system of global justice, a stronger network of international institutions and organizations can and should be constructed around both hybrid tribunals as well as the ICC.

I. The re-emergence and revival of hybrid and ad hoc tribunals

Since 2015, there has been a sharp growth in interest in establishing ad hoc and hybrid tribunals as a means to deliver justice and accountability in the wake of

4 Human Rights Watch, *Summary of the Key Provisions of the ICC Statute* (1 December 1998), accessed 9 June 2017 at www.hrw.org/news/1998/12/01/summary-key-provisions-icc-statute.

violent political conflicts and instances of mass atrocity. This section outlines a number of hybrid tribunals that have been created or proposed since 2015. First, however, the section briefly defines hybrid tribunals in contrast to ad hoc tribunals and outlines their re-emergence as popular tools in the global justice toolkit.

1.1 All hybrid tribunals are ad hoc, but not all ad hoc tribunals are hybrid

All ad hoc tribunals share certain qualities. For one, ad hoc tribunals are generally established in response to a specific instance of criminality, mass atrocity or a particular conflict situation. The ICTY's mandate was to investigate and prosecute crimes perpetrated in the former Yugoslavia. For the SCSL, its remit was limited to atrocities committed in Sierra Leone. Some, like the Special Tribunal for Lebanon (STL), which is mandated to investigate the 2005 assassination of Rafic Hariri as well as related killings and bombings, are limited to investigating and prosecuting those responsible for a singular criminal event.

As their name suggests, ad hoc tribunals are also temporary responses to mass atrocities. Moreover, their temporal jurisdiction is limited. For example, the ICTR can only investigate crimes perpetrated between 1 January and 31 December 1994, and thus neither the lead-up to nor aftermath of the 1994 Rwandan Genocide.[5] The ECCC is mandated to investigate allegations of war crimes, crimes against humanity, and genocide committed by the Khmer Rouge between 17 April 1975 and 6 January 1979. Unlike the ICC, no ad hoc tribunal or hybrid tribunal has a limitless, forward-looking jurisdiction.

However, ad hoc tribunals are not all alike. In particular, ad hoc tribunals can be distinguished on the basis of whether they are internationalized or hybridized. Internationalized tribunals such as the ICTY and ICTR, both of which were established under Chapter VII of the UN Charter, were constituted by international judges and staff. Hybrid tribunals, such as the ECCC and SCSL, include judges and staff from *both* the situation country in question (i.e. Cambodia and Sierra Leone) as well as foreign personnel. Insofar as they can be seen as rule of law demonstrators and local judicial capacity builders, hybrid tribunals are preferable to purely internationalized ad hoc tribunals. In the case of the ICTY, the widespread recognition that justice needed to be done closer to the situation countries and where victims and survivors resided, led to the 2005 establishment of the War Crimes Chamber in Bosnia, whose numbers of international staff were gradually replaced by domestic prosecutors and judges as the institution matured.[6]

5 The restriction of the ICTR's temporal jurisdiction has come under scrutiny and criticism from some scholars. See, e.g., Lanegran, Kimberly, 'Truth Commissions, Human Rights Trials, and the Politics of Memory', *Comparative Studies of South Asia, Africa and the Middle East* (2005), 25(1), 114.

6 As the ICTJ observers: 'The War Crimes Chamber was intended to give the national judiciary the capacity to conduct war crimes trials according to international standards... The

While there is no consensus view of what a hybrid tribunal should look like, some distinguishing features are shared by all such institutions. Sarah Williams' observations are instructive:

> While there is no definition, such tribunals tend to apply a mix of national and international law (both procedural and substantive) and feature a blend of international and national elements, in particular international and national judges and personnel. While there is some disagreement as to those institutions that are properly considered hybrid or internationalized, the following tribunals are generally included in this category: the Special Court for Sierra Leone (SCSL), the Extraordinary Chambers in the Courts of Cambodia (ECCC), the Special Panels for Serious Crimes in Timor Leste (SPSC), the International Judges and Prosecutors Program in Kosovo (IJPP, or Regulation 64 Panels), the War Crimes Chamber in the State Court of Bosnia and Herzegovina (WCC), and the Special Tribunal for Lebanon (STL).[7]

It is notable that all institutions outlined in Williams' commentary were established in the 2000s. More specifically, all were established between 2000 and 2007 – and no additional hybrid courts were established until 2015. Perhaps this is unsurprising. Despite holding out the promise of creating an effective middle ground between fully domestic and fully international tribunals, the performance of hybrid courts has been widely seen as underwhelming, if not disappointing.[8] In more recent years, however, there has been a resurrection of interest in consecrating additional ad hoc war crimes tribunals. The chapter now describes a number of cases in which the creation of an ad hoc tribunal has been considered.

I.2 The resurgence of ad hoc and hybrid tribunals

The resurgence of interest in hybrid courts is evidenced by those tribunals that have been created and proposed since 2015. Delving into any significant depth into any of these institutions is well beyond the remit of this chapter. This section

establishment of the BWCC was intended primarily to provide the national judiciary with the capacity to run war crimes trials according to international standards.' Importantly however, the ICTJ also notes that there were also other motives: 'perhaps the key factor leading to the creation of the War Crimes Chamber was the necessity for the ICTY to comply with deadlines endorsed by the UN Security Council for the completion of its mandate.' Accessed 19 June 2017 at www.ictj.org/sites/default/files/ICTJ-FormerYugoslavia-Domestic-Court-2008-English.pdf, pp.1, 6.

7 Williams, Sarah, *Hybrid International Criminal Tribunals*, Oxford Bibliographies (28 April 2014), accessed 19 June 2017 at www.oxfordbibliographies.com/view/document/obo-9780199796953/obo-9780199796953-0069.xml.

8 For a good overview, see Kerr, Rachel and Erin Mobekk, *Peace and Justice – Seeking Accountability after War* (UK: Polity Press, 2007), 80–103.

nonetheless outlines three hybrid tribunals that have been established since 2015 as well as a number of proposed hybrid institutions that have, to varying degrees, the potential to be created in the coming years. As will become clear, all face challenges. But, together, they demonstrate a significant uptick in the level of interest in establishing hybrid courts.

Central African Republic: the Special Criminal Court

With support from the United Nations, in 22 April 2015 the National Transitional Council in the Central African Republic (CAR) approved the creation of a Special Criminal Court (SCC). The SCC is mandated to investigate and prosecute international crimes committed in CAR since 2003, including mass atrocities and human rights violations perpetrated by recent bouts of violence between anti-Balaka and Séléka militants.[9] The SCC will be housed within CAR's national judiciary and likely be located in the capital, Bangui. It will include a mix of domestic and international staff. Specifically, and according to Simo Vaatainen, a member of the UN Team of Experts that has assessed the requirements and possible budget of the SCC,

> The Court will be composed of 13 national and 12 internationally recruited magistrates. The prosecution office will be headed by an international prosecutor. While the Court will generally apply Central African laws, the death penalty has been excluded. The law does not provide for amnesty or immunity in cases involving crimes against humanity, war crimes or genocide.[10]

How the SCC will be funded once operational remains unclear. However, given the paucity of resources available to CAR's government, funding is likely to come almost exclusively and entirely from the international community.

Challenges in operationalizing the SCC remain, including sustaining political will in CAR, establishing an effective witness protection programme in the country, and filling in staff positions of the institution. As of writing, the SCC 'exists only on paper'.[11] Nevertheless, the establishment of the SCC is notable for

9 See MINUSCA, *Justice and Corrections Section – Mandate, Activities, Achievements and Perspectives*, accessed 9 June 2017 at minusca.unmissions.org/en/justice-corrections; Human Rights Watch, *Central African Republic: Progress on Special Court* (23 December 2015) accessed 9 June 2017 at www.hrw.org/news/2015/12/23/central-african-republic-progress-special-court.

10 Vaatainen, Simo, 'Establishment process of the National Special Criminal Court in the Central African Republic – Key Challenges', presentation given to Wayamo Foundation (18 March 2016), copy on file with author.

11 Human Rights Watch, *Central African Republic: Prioritize Protection, Justice* (20 March 2016), accessed 9 June 2017 at www.hrw.org/news/2016/03/29/central-african-republic-prioritize-protection-justice.

the fact that it marks the first time that a hybrid tribunal has been created in a country concomitantly under investigation by the ICC. CAR authorities have insisted that the SCC will complement rather than compete with the ICC, which currently has two ongoing investigations in CAR.[12] Officials have also intimated that they would like to 'learn lessons' from the experience of other tribunals, including the Dakar-based chambers that prosecuted former Chadian despot, Hissène Habré.[13]

Chad: the Extraordinary African Chambers

In 2015, Hissène Habré, the former President of Chad, became the firstever former head of state in Africa to be put on trial by another African state. Habré was prosecuted in the Extraordinary African Chambers (CAE) in Senegal, where the former Chadian leader had resided in exile for 17 years.[14] The CAE forms part of the Senegalese national court system and was set up with cooperation from the African Union. It was mandated with the express aim of prosecuting Habré for international crimes and human rights abuses perpetrated during his rule over Chad. In addition to the African Union, Chad, and the European Union (EU), the CAE was funded by France and the United States, both of which had backed Habré during his rule.[15] Habré was in power from 1982 to 1990. As such, his crimes fall far outside of the temporal jurisdiction of the ICC. The staff of the tribunal are also mixed. Senegal's Minister of Justice nominated the EAC's prosecutors and judges, who were subsequently appointed by the African Union Commission's chairperson.[16]

In May 2016, 26 years after Habré fled Chad, the former President was sentenced to life in prison for crimes against humanity, summary execution,

12 See Kersten, Mark, *Why Central African Republic's Hybrid Tribunal Could be a Game-Changer*, Justice in Conflict (14 May 2015), accessed 9 June 2017 at justiceinconflict.org/2015/05/14/why-central-african-republics-hybrid-tribunal-could-be-a-game-changer/.

13 See Hirondelle News Agency, *CAR Wants to Learn Lesons from Habre Trial* (25 May 2015), accessed 9 June 2017 at www.hirondellenews.com/other-courts/35051-250515-carjustice-car-wants-to-learn-lessons-from-habre-trial.

14 The acronym 'CAE' reflects the French name of the institution. See Chambres Africaines Extraordinaires website, accessed 9 June 2017 at www.chambresafricaines.org/.

15 On the relationship between Western states, and especially the US and Habré, see Bronner, Michael, 'Our Man in Africa', *Foreign Policy* (1 January 2014), accessed 9 June 2017 at foreignpolicy.com/2014/01/24/our-man-in-africa/. See also Human Rights Watch, *US, France Backed Convicted Chad Dictator* (28 June 2016), accessed 9 June 2017 at www.hrw.org/news/2016/06/28/us-france-backed-convicted-chad-dictator.

16 For a useful overview, see Human Rights Watch, *Q&A: The Case of Hissène Habré before the Extraordinary African Chambers in Senegal* (3 May 2016), accessed 9 June 2017 at www.hrw.org/news/2016/05/03/qa-case-hissene-habre-extraordinary-african-chambers-senegal#20.

torture and rape. Despite requests from victims and survivors that other senior members of Habré's regime be prosecuted, no other prosecutions of senior figures are planned at the CAE.[17] Some commentators, nevertheless, have argued that the CAE, as a hybrid tribunal, represents a precedent for other African states to emulate. Jason Burke, for example, has argued that the Habré trial is 'an important model of how hybrid courts can reconcile the often conflicting demands of international law and local sovereignty'.[18]

Kosovo: the Kosovo Relocated Specialist Judicial Institution

The Kosovo Relocated Specialist Judicial Institution (KRSJI) was promulgated in 2015, and became a functioning reality in early 2016.[19] The KRSJI is mandated to investigate and prosecute crimes perpetrated between 1 January 1998 and 31 December 2000.[20] Notably, it was set up to investigate crimes alleged to have been perpetrated by the victors of the war in Kosovo and, in particular, members of the Kosovo Liberation Army (KLA) suspected of perpetrating mass atrocities. This makes the KRSJI the first tribunal to be established with the specific aim of prosecuting the victors of a war.[21]

The government of the Netherlands has stressed that because the KRSJI 'is to be established under Kosovan law ... it will not be an international tribunal, but a Kosovan national court that administers justice outside Kosovo'.[22] The reluctance to describe the institution as a hybrid tribunal is notable. But the KRSJI has the traits of a hybrid institution. Due to the political sensitivity of the institution's mandate (many KLA members are seen as war heroes and in senior positions of power), the KRSJI is housed in The Hague. All of its judges will be internationals and the EU will fund the entire venture. Any and all individuals convicted will serve their sentences in The Netherlands. It is thus hard to deny that the KRSJI

17 Some members of his security agents were, however, convicted in Chadian courts. See Human Rights Watch, *Chad: Habré-era Agents Convicted of Torture* (25 March 2015), accessed 9 June 2017 at www.hrw.org/news/2015/03/25/chad-habre-era-agents-convicted-torture.

18 Burke, Jason, 'Hissène Habré Trial Provides Model for International Justice', *The Guardian* (30 May 2016), accessed 9 June 2017 at www.theguardian.com/world/2016/may/30/hissene-habre-trial-provides-model-for-international-justice.

19 See Republic of Kosovo Assembly, Law No.05/L-053, *On Specialist Chambers and Specialist Prosecutor's Office* (3 August 2015), accessed 9 June 2017 at www.kuvendikosoves.org/common/docs/ligjet/05-L-053%20a.pdf.

20 Ibid., Art.8, Territorial Jurisdiction.

21 See Kersten, Mark, 'The New Kosovo Tribunal – Turning Victors' Justice on its Head?', *Justice in Conflict* (18 January 2016), accessed 9 June 2017 at justiceinconflict.org/2016/01/18/the-new-kosovo-tribunal-turning-victors-justice-on-its-head/.

22 The Government of The Netherlands, 'Kosovo Court to be Established in The Hague' (15 January 2016), accessed 9 June 2017 at www.government.nl/latest/news/2016/01/15/kosovo-court-to-be-established-in-the-hague.

is a hybrid court. If it is designed like a hybrid tribunal, staffed like a hybrid tribunal, and funded like a hybrid tribunal, it is a hybrid tribunal.

Hybrid tribunals moving forward

In addition to the CAR's Special Criminal Court, Senegal's Extraordinary African Chambers, and the Kosovo Relocated Specialist Judicial Institution, a number of other hybrid and ad hoc tribunals have recently been proposed. The feasibility of their creation and the potential of their success varies but, together, they provide additional evidence for the growing interest in establishing such institutions in response to ongoing violent political conflicts and instances of mass atrocities.

Ad hoc and hybrid tribunals have primarily been proposed for situations that fall outside the ICC's jurisdictional reach. Both the KRSJI and the CAE deal with crimes outside of the ICC's temporal jurisdiction. In Syria, a civil war has raged since 2011 at the cost of hundreds of thousands of lives.[23] Nevertheless, attempts by members of the United Nations Security Council to refer the situation in Syria to the ICC have failed, primarily due to clashing geopolitical interests among Council powers.[24] The prospects of local justice in the near future are dim – at best. In this accountability vacuum, some have proposed the creation of a hybrid tribunal to deal with war crimes and crimes against humanity perpetrated during the civil war. In March 2016, the US Congress passed a bill urging the creation of such a tribunal.[25] Given ongoing violence in Syria, the proposed tribunal would be located in a bordering state (likely Turkey or Jordan)[26] and be funded by the international community. Its proponents have gone so far as to put forward a statute for such a tribunal.[27] Not all are convinced that such an ad hoc tribunal

23 Estimates vary significantly, but UN and Arab League Envoy to Syria, Staffan de Mistura, has estimated that 400,000 people have been killed during five years of civil war. See *Al Jazeera*, 'Syria Death Toll: UN Envoy Estimates 400,000 killed' (23 April 2016), accessed 9 June 2017 at www.aljazeera.com/news/2016/04/staffan-de-mistura-400000-killed-syria-civil-war-160423055735629.html.

24 In May 2015, a UN Security Council resolution that would have referred Syria to the ICC failed after it was vetoed by both Russia and China. A full draft of the resolution was first published at Kersten, Mark, 'Full Draft: UN Resolution Referring Syria to the ICC', *Justice in Conflict* (12 May 2014), accessed 9 June 2017 at justiceinconflict.org/2014/05/12/full-draft-un-resolution-referring-syria-to-the-icc/.

25 See 'US House Passes Smith Bill Urging New Syrian War Crimes Tribunal' (14 March 2016), accessed 9 June 2017 at chrissmith.house.gov/news/documentsingle.aspx?DocumentID=398771.

26 See Schaack, Beth Van, 'Alternative Jurisdictional Bases for a Hybrid Tribunal for Syria', *Just Security* (29 May 2014), accessed 9 June 2017 at www.justsecurity.org/10968/alternative-jurisdictional-bases-hybrid-tribunal-syria/.

27 See The Chautauqua Blueprint for a Statute for a Syria Extraordinary Tribunal to Prosecute Atrocity Crimes (2013), accessed 9 June 2017 at publicinternationallawandpolicygroup.org/wp-content/uploads/2014/01/Chautauqua-Blueprint-2014.pdf.

would be 'the solution most likely to provide justice' in Syria.[28] However, given the unlikelihood of an ICC referral, such an institution may yield better prospects for even a modicum of accountability to be achieved.

Much attention has also focused on the possibility of Sri Lanka setting up a tribunal to investigate and prosecute war crimes and crimes against humanity perpetrated during the civil war between Sri Lankan government forces and Tamil Tiger militants.[29] UN High Commissioner for Human Rights Zeid Ra'ad Al Hussein has pushed for a hybrid tribunal in Sri Lanka and, in a detailed report released in September 2015, observed that accountability in Sri Lanka 'will require more than a domestic mechanism'.[30] According to Rhadeena de Alwis and Niran Anketell, a hybrid tribunal for Sri Lanka is 'an idea whose time has come'.[31] Concerns remain over generating and maintaining the necessary political will in Sri Lanka for an institution that would likely have to target senior and political figures currently in positions in power, overcoming the evident reluctance of Sri Lankan officials to allow any international role in a criminal tribunal, as well as related doubts about the ability of any judicial mechanism to impartially and genuinely investigate members of the current government allegedly responsible for mass atrocities during the final stages of the civil war in 2009. Current President Maithripala Sirisena has committed Sri Lanka to a programme of transitional justice and has engaged positively with recommendations by the UN High Commissioner for Human Rights.[32] However, he has also insisted that Sri Lanka's war crimes court should be 'internal and indigenous' and that he 'will never agree to international involvement'.[33] According to Zeid, however, international presence is critical to the legitimacy of any proposed tribunal for Sri Lanka, due to '[t]he levels of mistrust in State authorities and institutions by

28 See comments by Richard Dicker, Director of the International Justice Program for Human Rights Watch, Diane Marie Amann, 'Potential for ICC role in Syria' (4 November 2013), accessed 9 June 2017 at dianemarieamann.com/2013/11/04/potential-for-icc-role-in-syria/.

29 For an excellent overview, see Van Schaack, Beth, 'More than a Domestic Mechanism: Options for Hybrid Justice in Sri Lanka', Stanford Public Law Working Paper No. 2705097 (17 December 2015).

30 See United Nations Human Rights, *Office of the High Commissioner, Zeid Urges Creation of Hybrid Special Court in Sri Lanka as UN Report Confirms Patterns of Grave Violations* (16 September 2015), accessed 9 June 2017 at www.ohchr.org/en/NewsEvents/Pages/DisplayNews.aspx?NewsID=16432#sthash.gVmt8nku.dpuf.

31 de Alwis, Rhadeena, and Niran Anketell, 'A Hybrid Court – Ideas for Sri Lanka', *South Asian Centre for Legal Studies* (2015), 1.

32 See the letter from the Ministry of Foreign Affairs of Sri Lanka to the Office of the United Nations High Commissioner for Human Rights (15 September 2015), accessed 9 June 2017 at www.ohchr.org/Documents/HRBodies/HRCouncil/OISL/ResponseSriLanka15092015.pdf.

33 Ameen, Azzam, 'Sri Lanka President Wants "Internal" War Crimes Court', *BBC* (21 January 2016), accessed 9 June 2017 at www.bbc.com/news/world-asia-35376719.

broad segments of Sri Lankan society should not be underestimated ... A purely domestic court procedure will have no chance of overcoming widespread and justifiable suspicions fuelled by decades of violations, malpractice and broken promises'.[34] It remains unclear whether the Sri Lankan government will permit any international role in its proposed tribunal – and thus whether it will be hybrid at all. However, de Alwis and Anketell believe that 'if handled with care and professionalism, [a hybrid tribunal] could help break with the past and help herald a new era of accountability and human rights protection; essential components in Sri Lanka's quest for reconciliation'.[35]

In addition to Syria and Sri Lanka, there has also been some discussion regarding the creation of ad hoc and/or hybrid tribunals to investigate and prosecute systemic violations of human rights in Israel,[36] North Korea,[37] and South Sudan.[38] Whether these situations, along with Syria and Sri Lanka, are eventually the locus of a hybrid tribunal remains to be seen. Together, however, these cases once again illustrate the remarkable re-engagement of the international community with the hybrid tribunal model of international criminal justice.

II. Limitations and opportunities – explaining the rebirth of hybrid tribunals

That there has been a resurgence in hybrid tribunals is clear. But what explains this dramatic renewal of interest in hybrid courts? This section argues that this trend is the result of a confluence of three factors: the limitations and shortcomings evident in the ICC's record to date; an increasing recognition that the ICC need not be the only avenue for international criminal justice; and the continued utility of ad hoc and hybrid tribunals to the international community.

II.1 The limitations of the International Criminal Court

Among scholars and observers of international criminal justice, the preponderant reasoning for the resurgent interest in establishing ad hoc and hybrid tribunals suggests that members of the international community are seeking alternatives to

34 See United Nations Human Rights (2015), fn.30 above.

35 Rhadeena and Anketell (2015), fn.31 above, 3.

36 See *AfricaNews*, 'Arab League Chief Calls for Special Court to try Israel' (22 April 2016), accessed 9 June 2017 at www.africanews.com/2016/04/22/arab-league-chief-calls-for-special-court-to-try-israel/.

37 See Cumming-Bruce, Nick, 'North Korea Leader Should Be Told He Could Face Trial, U.N. Official Says', *New York Times* (15 February 2016), accessed 9 June 2017 at www.nytimes.com/2016/02/16/world/asia/north-korea-leader-should-be-told-he-could-face-trial-un-official-says.html.

38 See Nichols, Michelle, 'U.S., Britain Back South Sudan War Crimes Court', *Reuters* (10 June 2016), accessed 9 June 2017 at af.reuters.com/article/topNews/idAFKCN0YW0M0.

the ICC because the Court has not or cannot lived up to expectations. As Beth Van Schaack writes,

> Originally envisioned as a standing institution that would obviate the need for new ad hoc courts, it is now clear that the ICC cannot handle all of the atrocity situations ravaging our planet. As such, there is an enduring need for the international community to create, enable, and support additional accountability mechanisms to respond to the commission of international crimes when the political will for an ICC referral is lacking, the ICC is inappropriate or foreclosed for whatever reason, or only a fraction of the abuses or perpetrators in question are before the ICC.[39]

It is often said that the ICC has suffered from an expectations gap – one partly of its own making.[40] Former ICC Judge and Second-Vice President of the Court, Hans-Peter Kaul declared in 2011 that:

> In all likelihood there will always be a tension between the high hopes and expectations put into the Court on the one side, and what the Court can actually achieve in terms of more international justice on the other. Compared with the problems and violent crises in this world, the Court will always be small and weak, more symbol, more moral authority than real might. The main responsibility to prosecute international crimes must remain with the States. If only for reasons of capacity the Court will never be able to do more than conduct a few, exemplary trials.[41]

Sergey Vasiliev cogently adds that '[t]he benefits promised by the ICC to victims ... are unprecedented ... [W]hat seems to be at stake ultimately is the very idea of international justice. The risks of leaving promises unfulfilled and frustrating

39 Van Schaack, Beth, 'International Justice Year-in-Review: Looking Backwards, Looking Forwards', *Just Security* (19 January 2016), accessed 9 June 2017 at www.justsecurity.org/28870/international-criminal-justice-2015-part-2/; see also Van Schaack, Beth, 'The Building Blocks of Hybrid Justice', Stanford Public Law Working Paper No. 2705110 (22 March 2016).

40 Dov Jacobs, for example, has written that 'there is a disconnect between people's expectations and what the ICC can achieve in affected communities, or in relation to general goals of peace and security'. See Jacobs, Dov, 'Post Conflict Justice and the ICC: some thoughts on false expectations and the illusion of staying together "for the kids"', *Spreading the Jam* (15 December 2014), accessed 9 June 2017 at dovjacobs.com/2014/12/15/post-conflict-justice-and-the-icc-some-thoughts-on-false-expectations-and-the-illusion-of-staying-together-for-the-kids/.

41 Kaul, Hans-Peter, 'The International Criminal Court – Current Challenges and Perspectives', Keynote speech given at Salzburg Law School (8 August 2011), accessed 9 June 2017 at www.icc-cpi.int/nr/rdonlyres/289b449a-347d-4360-a854-3b7d0a4b9f06/283740/010911salzburglawschool.pdf.

the hopes created with the victims are enormous'.[42] Kaul's and Vasiliev's comments point to the apparent schism between what the Court seems to promise and what it can and has been able to achieve.

In recent years, the ICC has responded to this expectations gap by partially redefining its mission and inventing the principle of 'positive complementarity', a process whereby the Court galvanizes domestic actors to conduct genuine investigations and prosecutions of international crimes. The Court's senior officials insist that the institution cannot be seen as a silver bullet for justice and that ultimate responsibility for accountability must rest with domestic authorities. ICC Chief Prosecutor Fatou Bensouda has stated that the Court cannot be seen as a 'panacea', but instead as 'the ultimate backstop: addressing the injustices that fall through the gaps when national courts can't or won't step in'.[43] When the Court does intervene and when it is unable to bring its targets into custody in The Hague, the ICC typically employs this rhetoric of positive complementarity in order to claim that it supports domestic proceedings.[44] In Libya, for example, the institution was unable to gain custody of either of the suspects when it issued arrest warrants for Abdullah al-Senussi or Saif al-Islam Gaddafi.[45] The ICC's response has been to claim it supports Libyan justice by Libyan judges and that the prosecution of Abdullah al-Senussi and Saif al-Islam Gaddafi represents a potential 'Nuremberg moment' for the country.[46]

The localization and domestication of international criminal justice as a means to fulfil the expectations of international justice has been generally supported by civil society organizations. Human Rights Watch (HRW), a long-time defender

42 Vasiliev, Sergey, 'Victim Participation Revisited: What the ICC is Learning About Itself', in Carsten Stahn (ed.), *The Law and Practice of the International Criminal Court* (Oxford: Oxford University Press, 2015).

43 See The Hague Justice Portal, *Statement of the Prosecutor of the International Criminal Court, Fatou Bensouda: 'The ICC is an Independent Court that Must be Supported'* (24 November 2015), accessed 19 June 2017 at www.haguejusticeportal.net/index.php?id=13403.

44 See Nouwen, Sara, M. H., *Complementarity in the Line of Fire – The Catalysing Effect of the International Criminal Court in Uganda and Sudan* (Cambridge: Cambridge University Press, 2013), pp.13–14.

45 Libyan leader Muammar Gaddafi was also indicted by the ICC but he was killed following his brief capture outside of Sirte in October 2011. The Gaddafi summary execution raised concerns that the Libyan opposition had committed a war crime, with former ICC Chief Prosecutor Luis Moreno-Ocampo suggesting that he would investigate the Libya leader's death. However, not only has no investigation been initiated into Gaddafi's killing, the ICC has issued no warrants of arrest for any other Libyan combatants.

46 See International Criminal Court, Office of the Prosecutor, *Statement to the United Nations Security Council on the Situation in Libya, Pursuant to UNSCR 1970 (2011)* (8 May 2013), accessed 19 June 2017 at www.icc-cpi.int/iccdocs/otp/Prosecutor-statement-to-UNSC-08-May-2013.pdf. See also, Kersten, Mark, *Justice in Conflict – The Effects of the International Criminal Court's Interventions on Ending Wars and Building Peace* (UK: Oxford University Press, 2016), pp.145–155.

and proponent of the ICC, has argued that the way to bridge the expectations gap in international criminal justice more broadly is to foster and promote domestic trials for international crimes. Tribunals have, according to HRW,

> raised expectations – among victims and policymakers alike – that perpetrators of war crimes, crimes against humanity, and genocide should be held to account in fair trials. As these expectations have developed, so too has the realization that these tribunals can only try a relatively small number of perpetrators because of jurisdictional and resource constraints. Credible national prosecutions and trials have emerged even more clearly as the logical next step to enhance the reach of justice.[47]

There is little dispute that genuine domestic proceedings, in close proximity to where victims and witnesses reside, are ideal. As Rapp observes: 'In order to have a global justice system to deal with atrocities, you need to strengthen the local judiciaries.'[48] He adds, however that 'where they are broken you can use a local court and mix in international judges and lawyers'.[49] The same original reason justifying the creation of the ICC remains true today: national judicial systems in 'candidate states' for an accountability mechanisms are often unwilling or unable to prosecute international crimes. This is true of states in the midst of, or emerging from, large-scale violent political conflicts as well as states enjoying relatively stability.

In Syria, aside from the fact that President Bashar al-Assad and his regime have been consistently implicated in war crimes and crimes against humanity, five years of brutal conflict has displaced millions, killed over a quarter-million people, and led to the siphoning off of parts of the country to Islamic State. It is evident that the country's judiciary is incapacitated and thus unable to investigate and prosecute war crimes domestically. In Kenya, a democracy that has not experienced large-scale and long-term conflict and remains largely stable, officials are simply unwilling to investigate and prosecute atrocities committed during the 2007–2008 post-election violence, likely due to the fact that it would implicate many individuals in Kenya's political class. Despite widespread hopes that such crimes would be prosecuted via the creation of an International Crimes Division, this institution has yet to be formally established and, more pertinently, Kenyan officials have openly declared that no crimes against humanity would be

47 Human Rights Watch, 'Justice for Atrocity Crimes Lessons of International Support for Trials before the State Court of Bosnia and Herzegovina' (12 March 2012), accessed 9 June 2017 at www.hrw.org/report/2012/03/12/justice-atrocity-crimes/lessons-international-support-trials-state-court-bosnia.

48 See Simons (December 2015), fn.2 above.

49 Ibid.

investigated or prosecuted domestically.[50] In short, the original conditions that led to the need for (at least partially) internationalized tribunals remains.

However, it does not follow from this analysis that all atrocity crimes must be investigated and prosecuted at the ICC. While the Court fills the gaps evident in domestic judiciaries, it too has gaps and is limited in meting international criminal justice in a number of notable respects.

While there are 124 ICC Member States, the majority of the world's population resides beyond the institution's territorial jurisdiction. Those living in areas of severe political violence including, but not limited to, South Sudan, Syria, and North Korea, all remain outside the Court's jurisdictional reach. Situations on the territories of non-Member States can only come under the ICC investigation if the United Nations Security Council refers them to the Court or if the alleged perpetrators are citizens of ICC Member States. But the record here is grim: as noted above, an attempted referral of Syria to the ICC was vetoed by permanent Security Council members China and Russia.[51] Moreover, there is no interest in referring recent violence in South Sudan to the Court[52] and a possible Security Council referral of North Korea would be vetoed by Beijing and likely also Moscow.[53]

But the Court is also limited in what it can achieve in situations where it does have jurisdiction. The ICC's relationship with the UN Security Council as well as states that self-refer situations to the ICC has enforced the ad hoc nature of the

50 See Kiplagat, Sam, 'Most PEV cases cannot be prosecuted – Tobiko', *The Star* (6 February 2014), accessed 9 June 2017 at www.the-star.co.ke/news/2014/02/06/most-pev-cases-cannot-be-prosecuted-tobiko_c892628; Maliti, Tom, 'Kenyan Prosecutor: Insufficient Evidence has Made Prosecuting Post-Election Violence Cases Difficult', *International Justice Monitor* (26 October 2012), accessed 9 June 2017 at www.ijmonitor.org/2012/10/kenyan-prosecutor-insufficient-evidence-has-made-prosecuting-post-election-violence-cases-hard/.

51 See UN News Centre, 'Russia, China block Security Council referral of Syria to International Criminal Court' (22 May 2014), accessed 9 June 2017 at www.un.org/apps/news/story.asp?NewsID=47860#.V5Z7pY7q-LM.

52 No resolution referring South Sudan to the ICC has ever been put forward by the UN Security Council. Current South Sudanese President has declared that he would 'never accept' the Court. See VOA, 'South Sudan's President Says "Never" to ICC' (23 May 2013), accessed 9 June 2017 at www.voanews.com/content/south-sudan-president-says-never-to-icc/1667226.html. An op-ed that was written by South Sudan President Salva Kiir and Vice President Riek Machar, exclaimed that South Sudan needed 'truth, not trials' even if 'it could mean that some South Sudanese guilty of crimes may be included in government, and that they may never face justice in a courtroom.' See Kiir, Salva, and Riek Machar, 'South Sudan Needs Truth, Not Trials', *New York Times* (7 June 2016), accessed 9 June 2017 at www.nytimes.com/2016/06/08/opinion/south-sudan-needs-truth-not-trials.html. Machar later denied that he had contributed to the piece.

53 It is notable that the UN General Assembly has passed a non-binding resolution calling on the situation in North Korea to be referred to the ICC. However, reports have suggested that China would veto a referral. See Charbonneau, Louis, 'China, Russia Oppose U.N. Council Meeting on North Korea' (7 December 2015), accessed 9 June 2017 at www.reuters.com/article/us-northkorea-rights-un-idUSKBN0TR01X20151208.

justice the Court metes out.[54] The ICC's record demonstrates that the institution is prone to selective justice, tending to prosecute only one side of given conflict, depending on who refers to the Court.[55] Moreover, the ICC can only prosecute those 'most responsible' of international crimes. This translates into the targeting of only a tiny fraction of perpetrators. Together, this inevitably leaves the vast majority of perpetrators, and often all of them from a particular side of a conflict, beyond the scope of an ICC investigation. These issues of selectivity are compounded by the fact that the ICC has been hampered in its ability to conduct effective investigations in conflict zones. For example, investigators from the Court only arrived in Libya after the conclusion of the 2011 civil war. Despite Darfur being referred to the ICC more than 11 years ago, no investigators from the Court have ever been able to step foot on the Sudanese territory.

These limitations are further exacerbated by the limited resources at the ICC's disposal. While the institution's 'case-load' has increased, for some observers and for the Court itself, its yearly increases in budget have not kept pace.[56] According to Elizabeth Evensong and Jonathan O'Donahue, the Court is facing a 'capacity crisis' whereby even increases in the Office of the Prosecutor's (OTP) budget still 'fall far short of the what's needed'.[57] Funding limitations, as well as limits on the institution's resources (such as workstations and courtrooms in the ICC's headquarters), have led the OTP to declare that it can only function under a 'basic size' and will only open a limited number of investigations and prosecute a limited number of cases per year.[58] The risk, however, is not only that the supply of ICC justice cannot meet its demand, but that the restricted resources at the OTP's disposal will magnify the above-described issues of selectivity by making ICC actions dependent on available resources rather than the need for even-handed and impartial accountability.[59]

54 See Kersten, Mark, 'A Fatal Attraction? The UN Security Council and the Relationship between the R2P and the ICC' (2012), accessed 9 June 2017 at www.academia.edu/2017669/A_Fatal_Attraction_The_UN_Security_Council_and_the_Relationship_between_R2P_and_the_International_Criminal_Court.

55 For an explanation of this selectivity, see Tiemessen, Alana, 'The International Criminal Court and the Politics of Prosecutions', *The International Journal of Human Rights* (2014), 18 (4)–(5), 444–61; see also Kersten, Mark, *Justice in Conflict* (2015), fn.12 above, 162–184.

56 This is the result of two factors: ICC budget increases have been modest and the UN Security Council has refused to provide funding for either the Darfur or Libya referrals.

57 Evenson, Elizabeth and Jonathan O'Donahue, 'Still Falling Short – The ICC's Capacity Crisis', *Open Democracy* (3 November 2015), accessed 9 June 2017 at www.opendemocracy.net/openglobalrights/elizabeth-evenson-jonathan-o-donohue/still-falling-short-icc-s-capacity-crisis.

58 International Criminal Court, Assembly of States Parties, *Report of the Court on the Basic Size of the Office of the Prosecutor*, ICC – ASP /14/ 21 (17 September 2015), accessed 9 June 2017 at www.legal-tools.org/uploads/tx_ltpdb/ICC-ASP-14-21-ENG.pdf.

59 See Kersten, Mark, 'Buying Justice: The Supply, Demand and Cost of ICC Justice', *Justice in Conflict* (9 July 2011), accessed 9 June 2017 at justiceinconflict.org/2011/07/09/buying-justice-the-supply-demand-and-cost-of-icc-justice/.

Finally, it is notable that the ICC has been experiencing a political backlash from a constituency that has traditionally supported the institution – African states.[60] While the strained relationship between African states and the Court is often over-exaggerated and prone to rhetorical flair, it has resulted in attempts to explore alternative avenues to ICC justice, including the creation of hybrid tribunals.

These limitations do not necessarily undermine the ICC's overall mandate or purpose. The point of this analysis is not to deride the Court. However, if a global regime of international justice is ever to be edified, it won't be – it can't be – through the ICC alone. The Court's limitations and gaps have been exposed in recent years, contributing to a greater focus on achieving accountability through alternative institutions – including hybrid tribunals. The global justice pendulum is always oscillating. It is now passing, and in some ways favouring, hybridized courts.

II.2 The ICC – not the only game in town

The evident limitations and limited reach of the ICC help to explain the (re)turn to ad hoc and hybrid tribunals. Unsurprisingly, then, there is a concomitant and growing acceptance that the ICC need not be the 'only game in town'; not all situations that demand international criminal justice must be served by the ICC. This can be seen in the attitudes of key international institutions as well as the Court itself.

Established by the UN Human Rights Council, the Independent International Commission of Inquiry on the Syrian Arab Republic was originally set up in August 2011 to investigate crimes perpetrated during the ongoing Syrian civil war to recommend appropriate remedies. In its first report, the Commission recommended that Syria ratify the Rome Statute of the ICC as well as 'introduce domestic legislation consistent with it'.[61] In subsequent reports, the Commission recommended that the UN Security Council refer the situation in Syria to the ICC.[62] Only in 2014 was a referral of Syria to the Court officially presented to the Council. However, as noted above, it was thwarted by a double veto from Russia and China. Given the improbability of the ICC gaining jurisdiction over Syria, the Inquiry's commissioners reluctantly endorsed the possibility of an ad hoc tribunal

60 See, e.g., Mills, Kurt, 'Bashir is Dividing Us': Africa and the International Criminal Court, *Human Rights Quarterly* (May 2012), 34(2), 404–47; Du Plessis, Max, Tiyanjana Maluwa and Annie O'Reilly, 'Africa and the International Criminal Court', *Chatham House* (July 2013).

61 Independent International Commission of Inquiry on the Syrian Arab Republic, *Report of the Independent International Commission of Inquiry on the Syrian Arab Republic*, A/HRC/S – 17/2/Add.1 (23 November 2011), 21.

62 See, e.g, Independent International Commission of Inquiry on the Syrian Arab Republic, *Report of the Independent International Commission of Inquiry on the Syrian Arab Republic*, A/HRC/25/65 (12 February 2014), 27.

being established for Syria. In its latest reports, the Commission recommended that the Security Council '[t]ake appropriate action by referring the situation to justice, possibly to the International Criminal Court or an ad hoc tribunal, bearing in mind that, in the context of the Syrian Arab Republic, only the Security Council is competent to refer the situation.'[63] The shift in the Commission's thinking illustrates its growing acceptance that accountability for atrocities committed in Syria is not ICC or nothing.

A similar attitude has been increasingly expressed more directly by ICC Chief Prosecutor Bensouda in response to the prospect of expanding the jurisdiction of the African Court of Justice and Human Rights (ACJHR) to include, inter alia, Rome Statute crimes. While it is unclear when, and indeed if, such a jurisdictional expansion will take place, Bensouda has not only expressed support for the ACJHR but has insisted that there is no reason to consider it as competing with the ICC: 'I don't know why what they are doing, setting up their court, should be a slap in the face for ICC. Setting up a court to try these atrocity crimes is also not against ICC principles.'[64] Bensouda's remarks seem to indicate both a growing recognition of the limits of the Court, the need for the ICC to complement other courts and tribunals, and a diminished insecurity that its raison d'être would be threatened by the creation and existence of other international institutions mandated to prosecute atrocity crimes. This is an indication of an ICC that is more mature and sees itself as complementary to regional institutions and thus *part* of the solution to end impunity for mass atrocities rather than *the* solution.

II.3 The continued utility of hybrid and ad hoc tribunals

The resurgence of hybrid and ad hoc tribunals cannot only be explained through negative arguments – i.e. as a result of what the ICC cannot achieve. There is also the positive argument that hybrid tribunals continue to be useful. In his exploration of the 'sociological legitimacy', Harry Hobbs argues that, despite their 'period of dormancy', hybrid tribunals retain certain attractive qualities:

> hybrid tribunals still hold significant promise for many in the international criminal justice field – not to mention for victims of international crimes. For countries suffering from systemic violations of international criminal law, hybrid tribunals are seen as offering the potential for a catalytic transition to

63 Independent International Commission of Inquiry on the Syrian Arab Republic, *Report of the Independent International Commission of Inquiry on the Syrian Arab Republic*, A/HRC/30/48 (13 August 2015), 23.

64 See Deutsche Welle, '13 years, 1 billion dollars, 2 convictions: Is the International Criminal Court worth it?' (27 January 2016), accessed 9 June 2017 at www.dw.com/en/13-years-1-billion-dollars-2-convictions-is-the-international-criminal-court-worth-it/a-19006069.

> normalcy based on a tripartite grounding of legitimacy, capacity building, and norm penetration.[65]

Others have also extolled the advantages and role of hybrid tribunals. Padraig McAuliffe writes that '[t]here will always be a role for a court model that can mix the expertise of the international community with the legitimacy of domestic actors and situation in the *locus delicti*'.[66] During discussions to endorse a hybrid tribunal to investigate crimes in Syria, US Congressman Chris Smith spoke of the 'significant advantages' of hybrid tribunals over the ICC, focusing on the significantly larger number of individuals that are typically prosecuted and convicted in such courts, as well as the importance of local 'ownership' in enhancing the effectiveness of hybrid tribunals.[67] Long before the recent revival of the hybrid model, Alberto Costi espoused their utility, observing that '[s]ome of the potential advantages of hybrid courts include the ability to foster broader public acceptance, build local capacity and disseminate international human rights norms. The collaboration of national and international legal personnel helps bring international law and norms to bear in ways that can be internationalized and institutionalized'. Costi concludes that 'hybrid courts represent a sincere and laudable effort to improve on past transitional justice experiences and to remedy many of the major shortcomings of purely international tribunals'.[68]

In addition to the above advantages and those resulting from the shared responsibility between domestic and international actors, it is important to recognize that hybrid courts can offer what the ICC often cannot. Hybrids can be based in the region with nationals of the country or those from the region among its staff. Hybrids can also include the involvement of non-ICC Member States such as the US, Russia, China, India etc., thus potentially increasing their 'international legitimacy'.[69] They can fill key gaps evident in the justice offered by the ICC. These include cases where: 1) there is limited political interest and will to refer situations outside of the Court's jurisdiction to the ICC (e.g. Syria, North Korea, and Sri Lanka); 2) the atrocities committed occurred outside the ICC's temporal jurisdiction (e.g. Kosovo and Chad); 3) states seek to investigate and prosecute 'excess' mid- and lower-level perpetrators who are not sufficiently

65 Hobbs, Harry, 'Hybrid Tribunals and the Composition of the Court: In Search of Sociological Legitimacy', *Chicago Journal of International Law*, 16(2) (Winter 2016), 485.

66 McAuliffe, Padraig, '*Hybrid Tribunals at Ten* – How International Criminal Justice's Golden Child became an Orphan', *Journal of International Law and International Relations, 7* (2011), 64.

67 See U.S. House Passes Smith Bill (2016), fn.25 above.

68 Costi, Alberto, 'Hybrid Tribunals as a Valid Alternative to International Tribunals for the Prosecution of International Crimes', 3rd Annual Victoria University Symposium on Human Rights (2005), 26.

69 This is, of course, a double-edged sword as major powers such as these may also try to manipulate the work of the tribunals.

senior to be targeted by the ICC (e.g. CAR); and 4) the crimes committed may not be defined under the ICC's Rome Statute (e.g. terrorism at the Special Tribunal for Lebanon).

For all these reasons, hybrid tribunals retain utility as distinct elements of the international criminal justice toolbox. As Mathias Holvoet notes: 'As it currently stands, hybrid courts will not play a secondary role but, to the contrary, will be a crucial complement to the ICC's and domestic courts' work.'[70]

III. Towards a 'network' of international criminal justice

To date, the international community has been either unwilling or unable to establish and maintain a coherent and cohesive *system* of global justice. Similar to Rapp's observations cited at the outset of this chapter, in 2009, Cesare P.R. Romano observed that there is no such 'system' because the existence of one would imply 'a level of coordination that does not exist'.[71] Instead, as Romano argues, what we can see is an 'emerging "international judicial network"'[72] – an arrangement of institutions and actors that is loosely cohesive but does not have the level of coordination, application, or predictability of a system or regime.

The creation of the ICC, itself a response to the previous, piecemeal commitment to international criminal justice, was unable to transcend the international community reluctance to engender such a system. For reasons noted above, the performance of Court strikes the observer as more ad hoc and selective than permanent and universal. While the ICC seemed poised to displace the need for ad hoc and hybrid tribunals, recent years have seen the resurgence of such institutions. However, rather than seeing domestic judiciaries, ad hoc tribunals, hybrid courts, and the ICC in opposition or in simple zero-sum terms, it would be useful to view them as elements of a growing *network* of international justice. Without embracing the potential of such a network, international criminal justice will be predisposed to oscillating fits between favouring hybrid tribunals until their promises and expectations are unmet and then favouring the ICC until the structural and political limitations of its work inspire a renewed interest in hybrid tribunals. This would exacerbate the expectations gap by creating a mirage of international criminal justice as permanent and consolidated whilst in actuality offering accountability on an ad hoc and selective basis.

Still, such a network of international criminal justice cannot be furthered simply by embracing hybrid tribunals. After all, as Rachel Kerr and Eirin Mobekk have

70 Holvoet, Mathias, 'The Continuing Relevance of Hybrid Criminal Courts in the Era of the ICC', *Lex Lata, Lex Ferenda*, Washington University School of Law (9 November 2015), accessed 9 June 2017 at law.wustl.edu/harris/lexlata/?p=801.

71 Romano, Cesare, 'Can You Hear Me Now? The Case for Extending the International Judicial Network', *Chicago Journal of International Law*, 10(1) (2009), 239.

72 Ibid.

observed, while hybrid courts 'seemed to offer all of the advantages and none of the pitfalls of international courts', 'as they have come into operation, it has become clear that they might not be the universal solution'.[73] Indeed, the pitfalls evident in the first 'batch' of such courts need to be avoided with the emerging and forthcoming series of hybrid tribunals. One way to do so would be to create a permanent hybrid tribunal.

III.1 A permanent hybrid tribunal?

One possibility to consolidate a network of international justice without having to rely solely on the ICC, on piecemeal commitments in fragile states, or on pushing unreasonable expectations on the national judiciaries of post-conflict conflict states, is to establish a permanent hybrid tribunal.[74] The notion of creating such an institution is not entirely new. Drawing on the experience of hybrid tribunals prosecuting international crimes, Erin Creegan has advocated the establishment of a permanent hybrid tribunal to prosecute the crime of terrorism, something that has also been proposed by Romania and Spain.[75] Such an institution, according to Creegan,

> could provide weaker states with international support and build capacity while giving them a role in achieving communal justice ... [A] permanent court would mitigate time and money expenditures involved in perpetually establishing new courts with similar features ... [A] single court would have economy, legitimacy, more deterrent value, consistent personnel, resources and guiding law.[76]

Such an institution would provide the critical infrastructure – the courtroom, the offices, the legal resources – for states interested in establishing a hybrid tribunal but wary of doing so on their own territory. It would be particularly helpful for those states, such as CAR and South Sudan, which continue to face widespread instability and remain politically volatile. A permanent hybrid tribunal would allow staff to work in security beyond, but not too far from, the often volatile

73 Kerr and Mobekk (2007), fn.8 above, 81.

74 This concept was first explored in an online article, upon which this analysis draws. See Kersten, Mark, 'The Case for a Permanent Hybrid Tribunal for Mass Atrocities', *Justice in Conflict* (8 January 2016), accessed 9 June 2017 at justiceinconflict.org/2016/01/08/the-case-for-a-permanent-hybrid-tribunal-for-mass-atrocities/.

75 Creegan, Erin, 'A Permanent Hybrid Court for Terrorism', *American University International Law Review*, 26(2) (2011), 237–313. See also Romanian Ministry of Foreign Affairs, 'MFA officially initiates consultations on Romania's initiative to create an International Court to combat terrorism' (16 April 2015), accessed 9 June 2017 at www.mae.ro/en/node/31628.

76 Ibid., 267–9.

political contexts in which the crimes under consideration were perpetrated. Such an institution could also be a dependable locus of much-needed expertise and cross-fertilization of experiences and knowledge between international and domestic actors. As such, it would allow governments and the international community to avoid the consistent process of having to repeatedly 'reinvent the wheel' on hybrid tribunals and thus help to avoid hybrid tribunal 'fatigue'.[77] It could also potentially be an institution capable of meting out justice closer to where victims and survivors reside. In Africa, a well-suited location for such a tribunal would be the premises of the recently closed International Criminal Tribunal for Rwanda (ICTR) in Arusha, Tanzania.[78] The ICTR now houses the UN's Mechanism for International Criminal Tribunals but its courtroom could certainly handle additional cases and staff. An additional bonus for Arusha could be its emergence as a capital of international justice to rival The Hague. Other regions could create regional permanent tribunals to locate proceedings closer to where victims and survivors reside.

Such an institution could complement, and fill in the gaps apparent in, the international criminal justice network. However, unlike the establishment of an alternative to the ICC, such as the extension of the African Court of Justice and Human Rights jurisdiction to include war crimes, crimes against humanity, and genocide, a permanent hybrid tribunal would allow for a modicum of national ownership over the judicial process.[79] Domestic counsel, judges, and legal staff could be employed. A nationally agreed-upon mix of international and domestic law could form the basis of adjudication. In brief, such an institution would allow states to outsource the location, but not responsibility or ownership, of justice to an externally located institution. If such an institution were more insulated from bouts of instability, violence, and political interference, it would also benefit international criminal justice more broadly.

Creating a permanent hybrid tribunal would not be without its own challenges. Officials would have to work out how such an institution could 'time-share' between situations and cases under investigation. The institution and its staff would be required to juggle different combinations of domestic and international law for one set of investigations and prosecutions versus another. There is also the permanent question of funding. International tribunals have always suffered from the international community's lack of political will to pay for their work through

77 Ibid., 269.

78 The ICTR officially closed on 31 December 2015. See United Nations News Centre, 'UN Tribunal on Rwandan Genocide Formally Closes – Major Role in Fight Against Impunity' (31 December 2015), accessed 9 June 2017 at www.un.org/apps/news/story.asp?NewsID=52926#.V5Zvzo7q-LM.

79 On the extension of the ACJHR and the Malabo Protocol, see Amnesty International, 'Malabo Protocol – Legal and Institutional Implications of the Merged and Expanded African Court' (2016), accessed 9 June 2017 at www.amnesty.org/en/documents/afr01/3063/2016/en/.

time. Still, these issues should not detract from thinking through and imagining means to consolidate a network of global justice and problem-solve the deficiencies of the various generations of tribunals that have emerged to date. A permanent hybrid tribunal holds out the promise of consolidating a network of international justice by addressing some of the shortcomings of previous hybrid tribunals whilst offering states with varying degrees of capacity, resources, and even domestic will, a permanent infrastructure to house ad hoc justice and accountability processes.

IV. Conclusion – ad hoc reflections on more than ad hoc resurgence of hybrid tribunals

The supply of judicial responses to mass atrocities is vastly overshadowed by the demand to address international crimes. Still in its infancy, the network of international criminal justice is not sufficiently consolidated to supply accountability regularly, impartially, and consistently to victims and survivors of mass atrocities. Dependency, initially on the ad hoc tribunals in the former Yugoslavia and Rwanda, then on the ICC and, in some instances, on hybrid tribunals, has distracted from the possibility of a broader network of global justice that does not inherently favour one tribunal-type over another but instead sees the various models as potentially commensurate to the demand for justice and complementary to each other. No single type of tribunal will or can fulfil the expectations of those victims and survivors living in situations of conflict or mass atrocity and who do not have recourse to genuine domestic justice.

In Williams' list of hybrid tribunals, cited above and published in 2014, she included six institutions: the Special Court for Sierra Leone (SCSL), the Extraordinary Chambers in the Courts of Cambodia (ECCC), the Special Panels for Serious Crimes in Timor Leste (SPSC), the International Judges and Prosecutors Program in Kosovo (IJPP, or Regulation 64 Panels), the War Crimes Chamber in the State Court of Bosnia and Herzegovina (WCC), and the Special Tribunal for Lebanon (STL).[80] Prior to 2015, the most recent hybrid court established by the international community was the STL, set up in 2009 and based in The Hague. As evidenced by the analysis above, however, members of the international community have considered or created at least that many hybrid tribunals to investigate and prosecute international crimes.[81] Together, the recent creation and possible future establishment of hybrid and ad hoc tribunals signals the return to fashion of such institutions as a response to mass atrocities and international crimes.

80 Williams (2014), fn.7 above.

81 Beth van Schaack's has a more exhaustive list than that above: the international community in 2015 considered new hybrid accountability mechanisms for a range of historical and current atrocity situations, including Syria, the Central African Republic (CAR), the Democratic Republic of Congo (DRC), Colombia, Sri Lanka, Chad, Kosovo, and even the July 2014 downing of Malaysian Air Flight 17 over rebel-controlled Ukraine.

The resurgence of hybrid tribunals described in this chapter should be welcomed. It does not represent a nefarious challenge to the international criminal justice project. It is, instead, a symptom of its limitations and gaps as well as a positive indication of its development and maturity. The resurgence of ad hoc and hybrid tribunals suggests the need to adjust expectations of what the ICC can, and has, achieved, as well as the continued belief that hybrid tribunals continue to have utility and can yield advantages over the ICC in certain instances. As Kerr and Mobekk have written, 'there is a pragmatic case for continuing to develop this type of court, based on the potential advantages.'[82] The challenge, for proponents and practitioners of international criminal law, is to ensure that the various elements of this network of global justice complement, rather than compete with, one another. As McAuliffe writes, 'hybrid courts can be deployed in all sorts of post-conflict and post-repression societies like they have in the past, either as an alternative or complement to the ICC.'[83]

International criminal justice has shown itself to be like a pendulum, always in motion and never stationary. As a project it is constantly responding and recalibrating to the gaps and limitations of various models and approaches. The current swing (back) towards hybrid tribunals may not last. Hybrid courts could fall out of fashion – as they did between 2009 and 2015. But even if that is the case, proponents of international criminal justice would do well to encourage their use in order to fill the gaps apparent in the current project of international criminal justice. Recent evidence suggests that, even if hybrids are again displaced by interest in the ICC in future years, the pendulum will continue to swing, and they will be back in fashion.

82 Kerr and Mobekk (2007), fn.8 above, 95.
83 McAuliffe (2011), fn.66 above, 64.

Index

Alphabetization is word-by-word. Locators in **bold** refer to tables and those in *italic* to figures.

For Product Safety Concerns and Information please contact our EU representative GPSR@taylorandfrancis.com
Taylor & Francis Verlag GmbH, Kaufingerstraße 24, 80331 München, Germany

www.ingramcontent.com/pod-product-compliance
Ingram Content Group UK Ltd.
Pitfield, Milton Keynes, MK11 3LW, UK
UKHW010955180926
475701UK00004B/378
* 9 7 8 0 3 6 7 2 3 2 4 0 5 *